Getting Started in

COMMODITIES

The *Getting Started In* Series

Getting Started in Online Day Trading by Kassandra Bentley

Getting Started in Asset Allocation by Bill Bresnan and Eric P. Gelb

Getting Started in Online Investing by David L. Brown and Kassandra Bentley

Getting Started in Investment Clubs by Marsha Bertrand

Getting Started in Internet Auctions by Alan Elliott

Getting Started in Commodities by George A. Fontanills

Getting Started in Stocks by Alvin D. Hall

Getting Started in Mutual Funds by Alvin D. Hall

Getting Started in Estate Planning by Kerry Hannon

Getting Started in Online Personal Finance by Brad Hill

Getting Started in REITs by Richard Imperiale

Getting Started in 401(k) Investing by Paul Katzeff

Getting Started in Internet Investing by Paul Katzeff

Getting Started in Security Analysis by Peter J. Klein

Getting Started in Global Investing by Robert P. Kreitler

Getting Started in Futures by Todd Lofton

Getting Started in Financial Information by Daniel Moreau and Tracey Longo

Getting Started in Emerging Markets by Christopher Poillon

Getting Started in Technical Analysis by Jack D. Schwager

Getting Started in Hedge Funds by Daniel A. Strachman

Getting Started in Options by Michael C. Thomsett

Getting Started in Six Sigma by Michael C. Thomsett

Getting Started in Rental Income by Michael C. Thomsett

Getting Started in Fundamental Analysis by Michael C. Thomsett

Getting Started in Swing Trading by Michael C. Thomsett

Getting Started in Real Estate Investing by Michael C. Thomsett and Jean Freestone Thomsett

Getting Started in Tax-Savvy Investing by Andrew Westham and Don Korn

Getting Started in Annuities by Gordon M. Williamson

Getting Started in Bonds by Sharon Saltzgiver Wright

Getting Started in Retirement Planning by Ronald M. Yolles and Murray Yolles

Getting Started in Online Brokers by Kristine DeForge

Getting Started in Project Management by Paula Martin and Karen Tate

Getting Started in
COMMODITIES

George A. Fontanills

John Wiley & Sons, Inc.

Published by John Wiley & Sons, Inc., Hoboken, New Jersey.
Published simultaneously in Canada.

Wiley Bicentennial Logo: Richard J. Pacifico.

For general information on our other products and services or for technical support, please contact our Customer Care Department within the United States at (800) 762-2974, outside the United States at (317) 572-3993 or fax (317) 572-4002.

Wiley also publishes its books in a variety of electronic formats. Some content that appears in print may not be available in electronic books. For more information about Wiley products, visit our web site at www.wiley.com.

Library of Congress Cataloging-in-Publication Data:

Fontanills, George.
  Getting started in commodities / George A. Fontanills ; foreword by Frederic Ruffy.
    p. cm. — (The getting started in series)
  Includes index.
  ISBN 978-0-470-08949-1 (pbk.)
  1. Commodity exchanges. I. Title.
  HG6046.F66 2007
    332.64'4—dc22   2006103095

Printed in the United States of America.

10 9 8 7 6 5 4 3 2 1

This book is dedicated to my parents, Lugui and Philip.

Without your courage to leave Cuba when I was only a one-year-old child, I could never have achieved the American dream.
You are the reason I can live each and every day knowing that greater opportunities are always ahead of me.
I love you always.

Contents

Foreword   ix

Acknowledgments   xv

About the Author   xix

Chapter 1

What Is a Commodity?   1

Chapter 2

How the Commodities Markets Work   15

Chapter 3

Commodity Trading in the Stock Market   65

Chapter 4

Commodity Trading in the Index Markets   115

Chapter 5

Fundamental Analysis of the Commodities Markets   147

Chapter 6

Technical Analysis of the Commodities Markets   163

Chapter 7

Elliott Wave Trading for Commodities   209

Chapter 8

Options Trading in the Commodities Markets   231

Chapter 9

Money Management: Staying in the Game   281

Chapter 10

Psychology 101: Winning the Mind Game   335

Chapter 11

Trading Commodity-Related Growth Stocks   369

Chapter 12

Seasonal Commodity Patterns   399

Chapter 13

Brokers and the Online Revolution   419

Chapter 14

Putting It All Together   437

Appendix   449

Glossary   467

Index   485

Foreword

Opportunities to make money in the commodities markets have never been better. Not only have the costs of trading come down, but technology has made the process a lot faster and more efficient. It's easier than ever for individuals to make profits and develop an income stream trading commodities. Meanwhile, the number of products has grown exponentially; countless opportunities exist today that simply weren't available a few years ago.

Yet, while the commodities markets offer a plethora of trading opportunities, entering the futures arena might seem daunting for the inexperienced trader. I am constantly amazed by all of the questions and misconceptions I've heard about commodity trading. How much capital do I need? How does it all work? Why should I even bother? What kind of commodities can I trade? Isn't it too complex and risky for the average investor? If I don't know what I'm doing, will I wake up one morning to find 100,000 bushels of corn in my front yard?

This is the beauty of the book you are about to read. In *Getting Started in Commodities*, George Fontanills demystifies commodities trading. The truth is that commodities are an important element of diversification that most investors don't know enough about. Since very little correlation exists between commodities prices and other financial markets, adding commodities to your portfolio—especially if you already own stocks or bonds outright or through mutual funds—can create some necessary diversification and actually lower your vulnerability to market volatility.

Although you might not realize it, you already have experience with many commodities. Gasoline is just one example. If you drive up to the gas pump and prices are $2.50 one day and then $2.60 a week later, you have personally experienced how a commodity's price can change over time. In the first few chapters, George Fontanills shows the reader how to take advantage of everyday life experiences and translates this knowledge into profit-making trading techniques.

Many books teach strategies, but can't really tell you what type of trading is right for you. In this book, strategy selection is discussed in detail, as well as the psychology required to implement them. When reading through the text, keep in mind that there are many ways to participate in the various commodities markets, each with its own unique characteristics. For example, both gold futures contracts and gold exchange-traded funds (ETFs) offer ways to participate in the price moves of this precious metal. However, these two investment vehicles have very different characteristics.

The first four chapters are designed to help the reader sort through the various types of investments available to trade commodities. Chapters 1 and 2 provide a closer look at commodity futures contracts, while Chapter 3 digs deep into the trading of commodity-related stocks. Chapter 4 discusses index markets including trading the indexes and exchange-traded funds. Bottom line, different types of investments will behave in their own unique ways. Traders need to determine which investment instruments are most suitable, given their own risk tolerance, goals, time, and capital.

One reason commodities sometimes get a bad rap is the leverage some traders misuse when trading futures contracts. Specifically, margin allows traders to control large amounts of a commodity with relatively little capital, but it is a double-edged sword. On the one hand, leverage gives traders the opportunity to generate relatively large-percentage returns on their capital. On the other hand, it also adds an element of risk because it can lead to large-percentage losses. Traders—especially inexperienced traders—are encouraged to fully understand the effects of margin on futures contracts before using it. Detailed discussions of margin are provided in later chapters of the book.

Options strategies are discussed in detail as well. Options are extremely versatile trading instruments and can provide opportunities to profit from the rise or fall in the price of a commodity, stock, or index. Some options strategies can even be used to take advantage of range-bound markets. George Fontanills is actually a recognized expert in the field of options. His expertise is highlighted in Chapter 8, "Options Trading in the Commodity Markets." New traders are generally encouraged to focus or specialize in one or two options strategies before branching out into others.

Like futures, options are sometimes viewed with skepticism. Since options are derivatives, they are sometimes considered too risky for the average investor. However, while options are often used to speculate, these instruments can be used to protect positions as well. The reader is encouraged to study the strategy reviews and risk graphs in the appendix to see how options can be used to develop a variety of different risk-reward scenarios. After all, options don't lose money; people do. The key to your success lies in continually educating yourself and using that information to make smart trading decisions.

Risk management is another key to long-term trading success. This is true not just in the commodities markets, but in any financial market. Risk management starts at the most basic level by not committing too much capital to one market or one trade. It's simple really: Don't put all of your eggs into one basket!

Experienced traders also understand what to do if a trade moves against them. Risk management involves developing effective exit strategies before even entering trades. George Fontanills recommends that, before placing a new trade, investors always ask the question "What if I'm wrong?" It is often better to cut losses early rather than simply hope the market will turn around and break even someday. While developing an exit plan and sticking to it can often be a challenge for new traders, it can prove to be the key to long-term success. Additional risk management tools—such as stop-loss orders, asset allocation, and spread trading strategies—are also explained in later chapters of the book.

When looking for trading opportunities, readers are encouraged to combine fundamental and technical analysis. Fundamental analysis is the study of a market or an investment based on factors that determine value over time. For example, the decision of the Organization of the Petroleum Exporting Countries (OPEC) to raise or lower output quotas is a fundamental factor that drives crude oil prices higher or lower. A rise in gasoline prices ahead of the busy summer driving season in the United States is a fundamental factor that affects gasoline prices. Strong demand from jewelers ahead of the holidays is a fundamental event that can drive gold prices. A drought in the Midwest can affect the fundamentals of the corn market. Chapter 5 offers a complete discussion of fundamental analysis in the commodity markets.

Technical analysis, the subject of Chapter 6, is the study of price and volume. While technical analysis is most often associated with charting, it involves a lot more than just gazing at charts. Yes, technicians use charts to view trends, history, and other data related to prices, but ultimately technical analysis seeks to understand how changes in supply and demand affect prices over time. Technical analysts seek to understand the market forces that are driving prices now, in order to predict what might happen in the future. The key considerations for technicians include price, volume, and price movement.

Most successful traders today use a combination of fundamental and technical analysis. Fundamental analysis helps traders understand the economics behind the movement in commodities prices. Technical analysis enables traders to better understand the strength of the price move, how long it might last, where it might find support or resistance, and whether a change of trend might be at hand.

In addition to fundamental and technical analysis, the tone of the market as well as trader sentiment are also important considerations. Sometimes economics seems to suggest that the commodity price should move higher, but it doesn't. When the price action is not consistent with the fundamentals, the tone of the market is not good. If so, it might be a case where investors are reacting irrationally and driving prices based on emotions such as greed and fear rather than logic. In Chapter 10, "Psychology 101: Winning the Mind Game," readers are offered some examples that can help them recognize dangerous situations where a market has been overcome by irrationality.

In Chapter 11, the reader is introduced to trading commodity-related growth stocks. A stock is a form of ownership that gives investors a piece of a company. When that company is involved in commodities, the share price tends to react to changes in commodity prices. However, not all commodity stocks are winners. It takes some time and effort to find the company that is poised to take advantage of rising commodity prices. Chapter 11 explains some of the tools and methods that George Fontanills has developed to identify winning commodity-related growth stocks.

What about timing? How do you know when to get in or out of a commodity market? Technical analysis can help. Seasonality is also important. Commodities often experience seasonal trends that are sometimes predictable. For example, natural gas prices often rise in the fall ahead of the cold winter months, as the market begins to anticipate the higher demand for heating fuel. The anticipation of cold weather causes natural gas prices to rise. Seasonal trends are an extremely powerful factor in commodity markets, and for that reason Chapter 12 is completely devoted to exploring them.

Once an opportunity is identified, whether it is based on technical analysis, seasonality, fundamental analysis, or a combination, the next step is to initiate a position. One of the more common approaches is to wait for a buy signal and then go long the commodity, futures contract, or shares. The winning strategy is to buy low and sell high. However, in *Getting Started in Commodities*, the reader is encouraged to look beyond a "long only" approach by looking for profit opportunities to trade bearish and/or sideways-moving (flat) markets. Thinking vertically—in both directions as well as horizontally—provides the trader with an infinite number of possibilities for making money in the markets.

Regardless of the approach or strategy, your broker is an important part of the trading process. Brokers are the link between investors and the financial markets. However, not all brokerage firms are the same. Some specialize in futures and/or commodities, while others specialize in stocks and funds. One of the most important decisions a new trader must make is to decide the kind of securities he or she wants to trade and which brokerage firm is best suited to accommodate this decision. It's also vital to assess the potential brokerage's commission rates, the speed of its trade executions, as well as the research and tools it can provide. No single broker is right for every investor. The right broker for you ultimately depends on your needs, goals, and objectives. A good starting point is to ask other traders, friends, or people you trust for recommendations. However, there is no real substitute for research. Chapter 13 helps the reader narrow down the list of brokerage firms to make the process easier, as well as offering information designed to explore the online trading revolution.

Readers will find that a lot of the information, techniques, and tools discussed in this book can be applied in areas outside of commodities trading. For example, after reading the book, it will become easier to see how changes in commodities prices might affect economic activity, inflation, and interest rates—including home mortgage and car loan rates. It also might help to explain why coffee prices at the grocery store are higher this month when compared to last year. Readers can use the information on technical analysis to better understand the trends in their stock or mutual fund holdings.

Hopefully, like us, you will find the information and ideas motivating and exciting. The commodities markets are both fascinating and lucrative. This dynamic world of trading can provide a lot of personal and financial rewards to those investors who put aside the myths that the commodities markets are too complex or risky to trade and who are willing to educate themselves about how it all works.

So, as Brian Tracy, one of my favorite motivational speakers once said, "Commit yourself to lifelong learning." Opportunities to learn something new occur everyday. Learning and education are the keys to a prosperous life, and they are extremely important when pursuing a career as a successful investor or trader. If you are taking the time to read this book, you are heading in the right direction. Don't let anyone or anything stop you or stand in your way. You deserve success.

Good trading.

FREDERIC RUFFY
Senior Writer and Trading Strategist
Optionetics

Acknowledgments

When I am asked to write a new book, I initially feel excited and then slowly a little apprehension creeps in. Excitement is derived from the challenge of once again putting down on paper the information I've gleaned from many years of trading. I enjoy being able to share this knowledge with a wide range of readers who are interested in learning something that will change their lives for the better. Apprehension stems from the knowledge that time pressures and creative turmoil will certainly loom in my future. I tend to experience more than my fair share of sleepless nights as my subconscious mind digs deep to find those pieces of information that the readers might find valuable. I know how important it is to create a solid trading foundation in order to make success a reality in the future. Bottom line, writing a new book is both exciting and challenging at the same time.

Fortunately, after all these years of trading (and having a worldwide company of great traders, instructors, and writers, as well as an incredible support staff), I know that even with the tightest of deadlines, we can meet our objectives. As this manuscript goes to print, I know we have produced a great book that will help a lot of people find some success in the exciting world of commodity trading. I certainly hope this book will illuminate the lightbulb that can change your life.

To those traders/writers who contributed many long hours assisting in the writing of this book—Jay Kaeppel, Meng Ng, Frederic Ruffy, Chris Tyler, and Brad Zigler—I want to thank you for your amazing inspiration and dedication to the completion of this great book. Together, we have an incredible wealth of knowledge that has helped us to achieve our objectives. Due to the ridiculously tight deadline, I didn't get a chance to tell all of you how much I appreciated your insights and contributions. This is my chance to extend to each of you my thanks and congratulations on a job well done.

To Frederic Ruffy, who has made incredible contributions to many of my projects, I have to give a special thanks. I want you to know how much I appreciate your contributions and the many hours of hard work you put into each and every book that I write. You have done a great deal to help us get the message across regarding just how much we love trading and how we sincerely want to help motivate others to become better traders.

To Kym Trippsmith, my Editor in Chief, what can I say? Thank you for your many years of hard work and incredible editing talent, which have made me look so good. It's sometimes hard to believe how many years have passed since you joined Optionetics. You've edited virtually every book and article I have written since the very beginning. I'm grateful to know that whenever a project has to be finished—no matter how tight the deadline—if you say it can be done, it will get done. I've never once had to question your outstanding ability to finish a project and make it a success. You rock!

Thanks go to Tom Gentile (Senior Vice President and Chief Options Strategist), who continually helps me to become a better trader simply by sharing his creative ideas. Being able to bounce ideas off Tom is one of my favorite pastimes. I can't even count the number of hours we have spent doing this over the past 14 years.

I've known Tony Clemendor (Chief Operations Officer) for more than 20 years, starting with those first days sitting in class at Harvard Business School. We sure have gone through a lot. I am thankful for your innovative approach to business that just keeps the company churning ahead.

I want to thank Richard Cawood (Chief Executive Officer), who has helped build Optionetics into a worldwide powerhouse in the field of education. We've gone through a lot together, and although I don't say it enough, thank you for the many years of hard work it has taken to move this company forward. It's not always easy, but we always make new advances.

And a big thanks to all our students, who challenge us to come up with new ideas to master the markets. Thanks to you, we continue to take great strides forward. Our greatest successes are the result of your achievements.

I want to thank my wonderful wife, Charlene, who motivates me each and every day to look ahead with a positive attitude. No matter what obstacles block my way, she reminds me that anything is possible.

You can't imagine how grateful I am for your loving companionship and the daily motivations that help to foster my success.

Last, I need to thank my mom and dad. Without your sacrifices, this book would never have been even a possibility. Dedicating this book to you is but a small way that I can express my love to you both and simply say thank you.

GEORGE A. FONTANILLS
Founder
Optionetics

About the Author

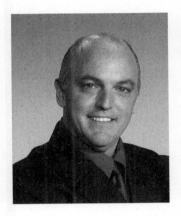

Optionetics was pioneered in the early 1990s by master trader George Fontanills. The development of this innovative trading approach is a testament to human will and perseverance. Fontanills's journey was not an easy one. Having struggled to overcome a life-threatening illness as a young man, George received his MBA from Harvard Business School and went out to conquer the world. His first business failed. Undaunted, he started a second business that never left the starting gate. Running low on money, George became a real estate investor and did quite well until the bottom fell out of the real estate market.

George's next move was to begin trading. Rather than concentrate on his losses, he began studying successful traders to see what they were doing differently. Using the analysis skills he learned at Harvard, he conducted a comprehensive investigation to determine what differentiated the winners from the losers. Risking money he made in real estate, George tested his conclusions and eventually developed a creative approach that used options to mathematically control risk every time a trade is placed, thereby consistently producing profits without the stress of unbridled losses. In 1993, he founded Optionetics to teach traders to profit using these strategies. Today, more than 250,000 people in more than 50 countries have seen Optionetics' high-profit, low-risk, low-stress trading techniques in action.

As his net worth soared, George gained a reputation as one of the world's most respected traders. As a highly regarded expert in options trading, George's trading strategies have been featured in the *Wall Street Journal, Barron's, Red Herring*, CBS MarketWatch, TheStreet.com, and other publications, and have led to numerous guest appearances on radio and television shows throughout the country.

Today, George spends much of his time concentrating on his own active stock and equity trading, while his strategic trading approach is taught through the popular Optionetics seminar series. Specializing in stock and index options, he has instructed thousands of traders in the United States and overseas.

In addition, George has five best-selling hardcover releases (some of which were cowritten with Tom Gentile): *The Options Course, Trade Options Online, The Stock Market Course, The Volatility Course,* and *The Index Trading Course* (all published by John Wiley & Sons). These definitive trading guides have added to his critical acclaim as one of the best options trading instructors in the country and around the globe.

1

What Is a Commodity?

While this book covers a multitude of issues, it is designed to answer one central question: What is a commodity? This may seem like a difficult question to some people, but it's really quite simple. If you can touch it, see it, feel it, or eat it, it's a commodity. If you are driving through Texas and you see an oil field, there's a commodity being pumped out: oil. If you are cruising through miles of wheat fields in Kansas, then you are passing an agricultural commodity: wheat. If you are vacationing in Florida, you're sure to see fields filled with orange groves; once again, you are looking at a commodity: orange juice. Even when you find yourself in a jewelry store eyeing a beautiful gold chain, you are checking out a traded commodity: gold. Commodities are all around you, but not all commodities are traded.

Smart Trader Tip

The process of trading a commodity is done typically in a trading pit located at one of the major commodity exchanges or by computerized trading, one of the predominant means to trade commodities today. A trade occurs when a *buyer* of the commodity and the *seller* of the commodity agree on a price for that commodity based upon a standardized unit for the commodity being bought or sold.

Lumber, wheat, crude oil, heating oil, natural gas, corn, copper, gold, sugar, and coffee are just a few of the commodities you may come across every day of your life. You probably just never looked at them that way. Each time you buy a pound of coffee, the price you pay is based on the commodity price established for a pound of coffee beans. But as strange as it may sound, the future price of coffee is being traded right now, and that price can have wide fluctuations today, tomorrow, and over the many months to follow.

The next time you drive up to the gas pump to inspect the price of a gallon of regular gas, keep in mind that the price you pay is directly related to how gasoline is trading as a commodity. Today's volatile world means that this price will keep changing on a daily basis; hence, as oil is traded, prices fluctuate. These prices eventually translate to a change in the price of a traded gallon of gas, which will ultimately be filtered into what you pay at the pump.

Smart Trader Tip

The prices of commodities change frequently throughout the day. You can watch prices fluctuate by observing how they change at the commodity exchanges. For example, if you want to scrutinize how gasoline prices change throughout the day, surf the Internet to the New York Mercantile Exchange website (www.NYMEX.com).

What Is a Commodity Market?

offer

an indication by an investor or trader of willingness to sell a security or commodity. The offer, or asking price, is the price at which an investor can buy the security from another investor in the market.

As we have already explored, commodities are all around us. The prices we pay each day for just about everything have been established, in most cases, by the trading of commodities at exchanges. A commodity market is a place where buyers and sellers of commodities gather to buy and sell the raw materials used in products bought and sold in the open markets. Sellers *offer* their commodities to buyers at a certain price, while buyers *bid* for a commodity until a seller agrees to a price; a trade is then established. This is the process of trading in its simplest form.

Let's take a real-world example in a market most of us are acquainted with: shopping for an automobile. Suppose you live in a small town in the middle of Texas and you would like to buy a new hybrid minivan to save money on gas and do your part to contribute less to global warming. You go to the one dealer in town who specializes in hybrids to negotiate a good deal. You want to buy the minivan for $26,000 (buyer's bid), but the dealer wants to sell it for $32,000 (seller's offer). Since there's only one dealership within a 100-mile radius, this dealer refuses to negotiate. Basically, the dealer doesn't have to compromise because there isn't any competition for many, many miles. Since you (the buyer) and the car dealer (the seller) cannot agree on a price, there is no transaction. In the trading world, this means there is no trade.

bid
an indication that an investor or trader is willing to buy a security or commodity at a specific price. The current bid price is the price at which an investor can sell the security or commodity to another investor.

So, instead, you decide to try a bigger town that hosts two hybrid dealers. Now you have three potential sellers—the original dealer in your hometown and the two new dealers—who may be a little more willing to negotiate. The competition among these dealerships means you have a little more negotiating power.

Since more dealers means better prices, you decide to drive all the way to Dallas because a bigger city will have a multitude of hybrid dealers (making it a little more difficult to decide) including Toyota, Honda, Chevrolet, Dodge, Nissan, Ford, and Saturn. Since they all want your business, the deals are not only getting better in terms of price, they are throwing in incentives. This scenario is superior thanks to the diversity of the offers from the many dealers.

But not so fast! There's another way to find the best price available: the Internet. By surfing the Net, you can look at offers from dealers all over the world. Now that's a *liquid market!* You've gone from one local dealer and no price competition to a multitude of options. This means you can adjust your bid or just leave it as is until you get the price you want. When you finally make the purchase, you have made a *trade*—that is, the buyer (you) and the seller (the dealer) have agreed to a price and terms, and now you have formally completed a trade.

Smart Trader Tip

A *liquid market* is one in which there are a large number of buyers and sellers willing to buy and sell at various price points. For a commodity trader, a liquid market is usually a better market to trade, as you will be able to get better prices since more people are willing to make a market. *Market making* is the process of bidding (as a buyer) and offering (as a seller). The more people willing to make a market, the easier it will be to find someone to take the other side of your trade.

This is exactly how the commodity markets work. There will be a *market* in which there are buyers and sellers going back and forth—bidding (as a buyer) and offering (as a seller)—until the price and terms are agreed upon. When there is an agreement on the price and terms, a trade is made. Once a trade is completed, the details of the transaction are reported to a central reporting party who is responsible for the transmission of price of the transaction around the world. In today's highly computerized environment, this process moves extremely fast. Not too long ago, traders would have been stuck waiting for tomorrow's newspaper to get a price or have to call their broker. These days, computers enable us to get this information instantaneously!

Let's now take a look at a real commodity market: oil. Crude oil is one of the most liquid and volatile commodities and is traded at the New York Mercantile Exchange (NYMEX)—the primary open outcry exchange. Traders have either purchased or leased a seat to have the right to buy and sell the specific commodity on that exchange. The term *seat* is a bit of a misnomer. It actually provides the individual with the right to stand in a small area of the trading pit and yell and scream orders to buy and sell (in this case) oil futures. What are they trading? They are trading a standardized unit of a commodity. The standardization of the contract ensures that everyone knows exactly what is being traded.

Smart Trader Tip

Open outcry is the term used to describe the process of trading whereby traders stand eye to eye and toe to toe in a trading pit and make trades by interacting with other traders who want to take the opposite side of the trade. (Just think of the trading scenes in Eddie Murphy's movie *Trading Places* and you'll get the visual picture on this one.) They signal with their hands, and when a trade is made they signal back acknowledgment and write their trades down on a card for record keeping. Today, computers do most of this work.

Using our previous auto example, if everyone was trading a hybrid minivan with exactly the same options, color, and so on, then it would be a *standardized* unit. If you were trading a silver Toyota Prius but everyone else had a different model, no trading would occur, as no one would be on the same page. Standardized units mean that everyone knows and agrees on exactly what is being traded. For example, if traders are trading light sweet crude oil, then they are actually trading 1,000 U.S. barrels of light sweet crude oil during the hours of 9 A.M. and 2:30 P.M. (eastern standard time). That's a lot of oil for one futures contract, which is why it's so important to make sure you know exactly what you're trading.

Smart Trader Tip

Over the many years that I've been teaching people how to trade, I've learned that specializing in the study of just a couple of markets is the easiest way to attain success. The trick is to avoid analyzing too many commodities at one time. So start by picking one or two favorite commodities and then investigate them very carefully. It may take a few months until you understand the specifics and rhythms of these commodities, but after a while that knowledge will guide you to the right strategies to take advantage of specific market scenarios. Start by going to the NYMEX website (www.NYMEX.com) and take a look at everything you can trade. There's a lot to be learned simply by looking at the contract specifications of each commodity. Your success depends on your ability to do your homework on any commodity you are considering trading—the more in-depth your study, the easier it is to plan your trade.

Let's get back to our traders. At the end of the day, the traders and their assistants hand over their trades to their clearinghouse. All the accounting of the buys and sells are then tallied and the next-day profit-and-loss statements are issued for the previous day's activities. This is how the trader in a pit works day in and day out. It looks like a stressful job and it is, but it's one of the most exciting jobs I can imagine.

But to quote Bob Dylan, "The times they are a changing . . ." As the world changes thanks to the rapid integration of computer and online technologies into every possible human endeavor, the information flow at home and work continues to advance as well. In the markets, the emergence of computers have given birth to a whole slew of opportunities in the exciting world of commodity trading.

What Is the Difference between a Commodity and a Futures Contract?

The answer to this question is not as precise as I would like it to be. At first look, a commodity is a physical product (wheat, oil, lumber, soybeans, etc.) that can be touched, eaten, processed, or delivered—whether it is today, tomorrow, or next year. In contrast, a futures contract is a commodity that (as was explained in the example of the oil traders at the NYMEX) is standardized in its unit of measurement (i.e., 1,000 barrels of oil) to be delivered at some future date. For example, a light sweet crude oil futures contract can be traded in all months of many years to come. So if people want to trade oil futures contracts for December 2008 or oil futures contracts for March 2009, they are able to do so, as there is a market of traders looking to buy and sell those contracts.

Why would anyone do that? Well, the market is made up of a large number of people with diverse views and many different desires. For example, in the oil industry, a big oil company might want to sell a certain portion of what it produces next year. For example, Exxon Mobil (XOM) produces countless barrels of oil. If it sees oil prices at what it considers a good level, it may sell a certain number of barrels at that price for delivery next year. This way, the company knows specifically how much it will make on those barrels of oil. This process is known as hedging and, in this example, the oil company is considered a hedger.

Who would buy that oil? Well, let's say you are Southwest Airlines (LUV). The cost to fuel your fleet of planes is a major problem, as airplanes use a massive amount of oil every day. Airlines may choose to offset any potential rise in the cost of fuel by locking in today's prices. Hence, a futures oil contract can help Southwest Airlines avoid the risk of having to pay higher oil prices if the price of oil rises in the future. For example, if the price of oil fluctuates between $60 and $90 a barrel, it would behoove Southwest Airlines to lock in the $60 price and save a huge amount of money over the next year. It's easy to see why the airline would want to hedge its fuel risk by going to the oil futures market and buying oil contracts for delivery next year that guarantee a specific price. In this example, the airline company is also a hedger. They are turning to the futures market to lock in prices and hedge themselves against an adverse price move in the oil market.

Hopefully, this process is starting to make more sense. The buyer and the seller make a trade in order to achieve an objective that makes economic sense for both of them. In the previous example:

- Exxon Mobil, the seller, wants to lock in profits for next year by selling oil in the future at today's trading price.
- Southwest Airlines, the buyer, wants to hedge its risk so it buys oil in the future at today's trading price.

Do Southwest Airlines and Exxon Mobil call each other up to discuss their deal over the phone? Of course not; they go to the oil futures market and buy and sell from traders on the floor who act as intermediaries. This is the fastest and most liquid way to achieve the objective they both want to achieve; this kind of trading happens day in and day out.

The next party in the futures market is the *speculator*. The speculator is an individual trader (like me or you) who wants to trade a futures contract and make a profit on the price fluctuations of the oil futures contract. Let's say you believe oil prices are likely to go up. As an oil futures speculator, you can buy an oil futures contract. If you are right and oil futures rise, you can profit from being right on the move up. If the price of the oil futures contract goes from $70 to $71, you would make $1,000. If you are wrong, and the price of the oil futures contract goes from $70 to $69, then you lose $1,000. There are many speculators buying and selling futures contracts who are making money trading commodities to be delivered someday in the future. Speculators are the ones who create a great deal of the liquidity that exists in the daily trading of

speculator
a trader who hopes to benefit from a directional move in the underlying instrument, attempts to anticipate price changes, and, through buying and selling futures contracts, aims to make a profit. The speculator does not use the futures market in connection with the production, processing, marketing, or handling of a product, and thus has no interest in making or taking delivery. So, while speculators attempt to bank profits from moves in the futures contract on a short-term basis, *hedgers* turn to the commodities market to protect themselves from adverse moves in prices. Taken together, the hedgers and speculators are responsible for the buying and selling in the commodities and futures markets.

hedger

an investor who uses the futures market to minimize the risk in his or her business. Hedgers may be manufacturers, portfolio managers, bankers, farmers, and so on. Hedging can help lock in existing profits and/or reduce the overall risk of loss due to fluctuating prices.

the futures market. Unlike Southwest Airlines, speculators are not interested in receiving the actual physical commodity someday in the future. They are just speculating to make profit; hence, the name.

Back to Commodities

All over the world, farmers grow and sell a vast array of agricultural products. Regardless of the product they are farming, they are all trying to make money on their crops. Wheat farmers in Kansas are trying to maximize their yield on their many acres of farmland. Coffee growers in Colombia are trying to maximize the yield on their families' coffee plantations. Sugar growers in Brazil are working hard to harvest as much sugarcane as possible from the land. Additionally, traders of agricultural products are wise to monitor weather conditions and assess how they may affect certain markets. Even your neighborhood contractors have to assess how much they can ask for a house in order to pay for all the commodities necessary to build it. They are dependent on a variety of commodities including lumber and oil—both for their roof shingles and for the cost of transporting the materials it takes to build the house.

Day in and day out, 24 hours a day, seven days a week, commodities are affecting your life in every way. In fact, it can be asserted that the consumption of commodities makes the world go 'round. Now that you are more aware of this, you might look at the world a little differently. Next time you find yourself shopping at the local grocery, you may notice that just about everything there is a commodity. They just happen to be commodities that have now been delivered (no longer futures contracts) and now are available to you as an individual shopper. The grocer is making an *offer* to purchase; so when you buy something, you have made the trade. Advancing your knowledge of how the world revolves around commodities is one of the keys to understanding how they work. It's important to open your eyes to the big picture as well as to study the details of specific markets that make it a very profitable and exciting business.

How Can a Stock Trader Use This Information for Financial Gain?

We have already established that commodities affect your everyday life. Those who study them can make a very good living as commodity speculators or as longer-term commodities investors. If you only trade stocks, you may be wondering why you should even care about commodities. Bottom line, you can also use the knowledge you gain by studying commodities to make money in the stock market.

Since global economic cycles are very much driven by commodity prices, stock investors need to pay attention to the commodity markets. Commodity prices filter themselves into the earnings of virtually every business. For example, rising oil prices can directly increase Exxon Mobil's earnings. In contrast, rising oil prices hurt the airlines (such as Southwest, American, and Delta) and the cruise lines (like Carnival and Royal Caribbean), unless they hedge their oil price risk. If lumber prices go up, it hurts the homebuilders such as KB Homes. If coffee prices go up, it hurts Starbucks but helps the producer. If cocoa prices go up, it hurts the candy makers. This kind of trickle-down progression goes on and on. In fact, most of these companies are affected by multiple commodity prices. In essence, they can be helped (or hurt) by a variety of different commodities. As a stock trader, you must recognize the importance of investigating the commodities that affect the share price of any company you are interested in trading. As the prices of these commodities fluctuate, keep an eye on them, as company earnings may be affected as well.

On a broader scale, commodity prices affect the entire economy and the stock market. Just listen closely to what they are talking about on television regarding economic catalysts (i.e., factors that can affect the overall economy). First and foremost, the talking heads and pundits on television are constantly talking about oil. If oil prices are too high, then many companies are affected and not just because of the way this affects the price of a gallon of gas. Oil and oil by-products are used in a whole host of products. In addition, if oil prices increase too much and the price of a gallon of gas rises too high, this pinches the pockets of the average consumer, and spending patterns could shift accordingly. When consumers reduce spending, every company and the economy in general are affected.

Let's go one level higher and evaluate how commodity prices affect the global economy. Once again, let's use oil as an example. Table 1.1 shows the world's top oil producers, exporters, consumers, and importers in 2004, providing clues to international production and consumption.

TABLE 1.1 Top World Oil Producers, Exporters, Consumers, and Importers, 2004 (millions of barrels per day)

Producers	Total Oil Production	Exporters	Net Oil Exports	Consumers	Total Oil Consumption	Importers	Net Oil Imports
1. Saudi Arabia	10.37	1. Saudi Arabia	8.73	1. United States	20.5	1. United States	11.8
2. Russia	9.27	2. Russia	6.67	2. China	6.5	2. Japan	5.3
3. United States	8.69	3. Norway	2.91	3. Japan	5.4	3. China	2.9
4. Iran	4.09	4. Iran	2.55	4. Germany	2.6	4. Germany	2.5
5. Mexico	3.83	5. Venezuela	2.36	5. Russia	2.6	5. South Korea	2.1
6. China	3.62	6. United Arab Emirates	2.33	6. India	2.3	6. France	2.0
7. Norway	3.18	7. Kuwait	2.20	7. Canada	2.3	7. Italy	1.7
8. Canada	3.14	8. Nigeria	2.19	8. Brazil	2.2	8. Spain	1.6
9. Venezuela	2.86	9. Mexico	1.80	9. South Korea	2.1	9. India	1.5
10. United Arab Emirates	2.76	10. Algeria	1.68	10. France	2.0	10. Taiwan	1.0
11. Kuwait	2.51	11. Iraq	1.48	11. Mexico	2.0		
12. Nigeria	2.51	12. Libya	1.34				
13. United Kingdom	2.08	13. Kazakhstan	1.06				
14. Iraq	2.03	14. Qatar	1.02				

Source: Energy Information Administration (www.eia.doe.gov/emeu/cabs/).

Much of the run-up in oil prices is attributed to recent growth in the Chinese economy. Oil prices have been driven up as the once stagnant communist economy experiences massive economic growth, driving China to thirst for more and more oil. China needs virtually every type of commodity to fuel this growth, so commodity prices will most likely be affected for many years to come. Now when you drive up to the gas station pump and look at what you are paying for that gallon of gasoline, remember that this price is closely tied to what is happening in China and other countries around the world—not to mention the volatile ramifications of looming *peak oil* declines.

As you can see, commodity prices affect everything. For astute investors or traders, understanding how commodities work, locally and globally, is essential to being able to develop an edge against competing traders and investors.

> **peak oil**
> an idea originally sparked by Shell Oil geologist M. King Hubbard back in 1956 that the world will reach a peak in the rate at which it can extract oil from the ground. Once this peak is reached, production rates will decline and will not be able to keep up with demand. When demand outpaces production, the world economy will no doubt receive a major shock. The ramifications of peak oil continue to be a hot topic of discussion, but unlike global warming, the forces underlying peak oil are generally not disputed. (See Figure 1.1.)

Summary

Commodities are everywhere; the world depends on them. Every person on this planet comes in contact with commodities every day. Since commodities affect important parts of your life, this information can be used to generate profits in the commodities and futures markets. For example, do you buy coffee? Do you notice the price changes from one day to the next? What about when you are filling your gas tank? We all feel the effects from rising and falling gasoline prices. So the first step in becoming a successful commodities trader is easy: Pay attention to what is going on around you.

This book is designed as a guide to trading success in the commodity markets. It will show you how to get started in the diverse world of commodities trading and how to make a profit using this knowledge. The book is written with the novice reader in mind and starts at a very basic level, with an explanation of the different types of investments or trading vehicles that can be used to generate profits in the commodity

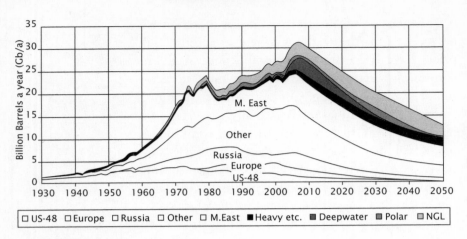

FIGURE 1.1   Peak oil timeline.
Courtesy the Association for the Study of Peak Oil & Gas.

markets. The reader is also introduced to various types of analysis tools, trading strategies, and risk management techniques. The book also explores finding the right broker, which is an extremely important part of becoming a successful trader in the commodity markets.

So get ready to learn how commodities work, how to analyze these markets and identify profitable opportunities, and how to structure trades to maximize rewards while managing risk.

Key Summary Points

1. Commodities are all around us. Lumber, oil, wheat, gold, coffee, and sugar are a few examples.

2. Not all commodities are traded in the financial markets, but many are.

3. The first step in becoming a successful trader in the commodity markets is to understand which commodities are traded and which ones are not.

4. Some of the actively traded commodities today include metals such as gold and silver, agricultural goods like wheat and coffee, energy such as oil and natural gas, as well as livestock such as cattle and pork bellies.

5. The commodities exchanges offer a central place for buyers and sellers to meet and trade the various commodities.

6. The New York Mercantile Exchange (NYMEX), the Chicago Board of Trade (CBOT), and the Chicago Mercantile Exchange (CME) are examples of active commodities exchanges.

7. Once buyers and sellers meet and agree on a price for a commodity, a trade is made.

8. For most investors, the buying and selling of commodities does not take place on the exchange but is handled by a licensed commodities broker (additional discussion in Chapter 13).

9. Many traders prefer to trade futures on commodities rather than the physical commodities themselves.

10. A futures contract is an agreement between two parties to buy or sell a commodity at a specific price sometime in the future.

11. The futures market consists of two principal players: hedgers and speculators. Hedgers, such as farmers and oil companies, turn to the futures market to lock in set prices and protect themselves from adverse moves in the market. Speculators use futures to speculate on possible moves in commodity prices.

12. While hedgers and speculators are the most active players in the futures market, commodities are all around us. Whether you are filling up the gas tank, going through the aisles at the grocery store, or buying a cup of coffee at your local Bohemian cafe, commodity prices will affect you.

13. Commodity prices have an important impact on the overall economy. Being aware of the importance of commodities not only makes you a better shopper and smarter investor, but also serves as the appropriate starting point for your journey to becoming a successful commodities trader.

2

How the Commodities Markets Work

I f you mention commodities in conversation, most people picture a trading floor packed with screaming, wildly gesturing traders. This isn't surprising. Most of us know of commodity trading only through news reports or movies punctuated with colorful pictures of the floor action from Chicago or New York. Commodity traders, by nature, are supposed to call attention to themselves by sight and sound. By doing so, they're more likely to find another trader with whom they can transact business. So what are all those people in the funny jackets actually doing?

First of all, it's important to know that floor action represents only a part of modern commodity trading. There's an ever-growing proportion of trading that takes place electronically nowadays. But let's not get ahead of ourselves. To understand how the modern commodity markets work, we first need to review a bit of history. Just how and why did commodity trading develop?

The Need for a Commodities Market

If you're a wheat farmer in southern Illinois, you can find a bevy of potential buyers for your crop in Chicago among its flour millers, cereal manufacturers, and glue factories. Naturally, Chicago's industrial consumers are interested in buying wheat at the lowest obtainable price, while you want the highest possible price for your crop.

Without a prearranged contract with a Chicago mill or factory, you must compete with other farmers simultaneously offering their product in the *cash*, or *spot*, *market*. When supplies are ample, millers and factory purchasers are likely to offer only low prices. In a year where a hard winter or spring flooding diminishes yields, however, you can command higher per-bushel prices for your crop in the spot market.

spot market
same as the cash market. It is the immediate market where a commodity or other investment can be bought or sold.

Forward Contracts

The uncertainty of spot market prices gave rise to *forward* or *to arrive contracts*, whereby buyers and sellers agree upon a price for grain to arrive at a later date. While a price is set, no cash changes hands until the commodity is actually delivered. By negotiating a price (say, in October) that anticipates a reasonable profit for you and the flour mill, you're freed from fretting over the price of wheat the following June. Cash flows can be more reliably projected as a result, helping you—and your counterparty, the mill—make better plans.

forward contract
an agreement between two parties to buy or sell a commodity at some time in the future. Similar to futures contracts, but not as easily transferred or canceled.

Forward contracts, of course, eliminate windfall profits. As an example, suppose you negotiate a contract price of $4 per bushel for June delivery of your wheat. A poor Russian harvest might later bring big buyers into the market, pushing spot prices up to the $5 to $6 range. Unfortunately, you're still obliged to deliver your crop at $4. This is good news for the mill: Its forward contract insulated it from paying an inflated price for its grain. But it's not so good for you. However, a glut of wheat could have sent prices tumbling down to $3, giving you the advantage instead of the mill.

Forward contracts are purely commercial transactions; they're too cumbersome to use effectively for *speculation* or investment purposes. First of all, each party to a contract must be in a position to make or take delivery of the underlying commodity. If you're not ready to deal in

railcars full of grain, you don't belong in the forwards market. There's no provision for turning the
contracts into cash, either. You might think the
prospect of a glut would make your forward contract valuable as spot prices decline, but unless the
mill is willing to let you transfer your obligation to
another, you're virtually stuck.

> **speculation**
> the selection of
> investments with
> higher-than-aver-
> age risk in order
> to profit from
> forecasted price
> movements.

In a forward contract, you also face the risk
that your counterparty might *default*. If the mill
goes out of business and doesn't honor its purchase
commitment, you've got to find another buyer for
your grain. When the market is awash with wheat,
you'll probably end up losing money.

> **default**
> a failure to live up
> to the terms of a
> contract or debt
> obligation.

Each party to a forward contract is on its own
when it comes to finding a counterparty. It was primarily for this reason that a group of merchants at
the Chicago Board of Trade (CBOT)—originally a marketplace for spot
grain sales—developed a centralized forwards exchange. From this, commodity futures trading, as we now know it, gradually developed.

Modern Commodity Trading

One of the key innovations wrought at the CBOT was standardization.
To attract speculators, contracts had to be transformed from customized
commercial vehicles into readily tradable investments. By standardizing
contract sizes as well as delivery grades and procedures, the CBOT created *fungible* or interchangeable instruments. Traders now know that
each wheat contract calls for the delivery of 5,000 bushels of No. 2 Red
Winter or Northern Spring grain through selected warehouses in Illinois,
Indiana, and Ohio. Delivery dates are also standardized, providing a
range of contract lengths to suit buyers' and sellers' needs. As such, all
CBOT December wheat contracts are identical in every respect except
one: the delivery price.

The *fungibility* of futures contracts allows them to be readily offset,
or closed out, before delivery. Buyers of futures who don't wish to actually take delivery at contract maturity, for instance, can simply sell their
contracts during market hours. Likewise, contract sellers can relieve
themselves of the obligation to make delivery by buying back the same

fungibility
the ability to interchange assets of identical quality. Wheat stored in a grain elevator is fungible, as it is not specifically identified regarding its ownership.

contract that was sold. Like unwinding a stock position, selling a contract previously bought, or buying a contract that had been sold, leaves the trader flat (i.e., devoid of a contract). Realizing a profit or loss is based upon the difference between the contract's purchase and sale prices. Unlike forwards, you can buy or sell commodities in the futures market whether or not you own, or need, the commodity in question. In fact, less than 4 percent of all futures contracts actually result in deliveries. The vast majority are offset prior to the delivery month.

Smart Trader Tip

When a trader has an open futures contract and closes that trade, he or she is *flat*. This means the trader has no open positions. Many short-term traders like to be flat ahead of the weekend or an important event like an economic release in order to avoid getting caught in volatile markets.

margin
a good faith deposit required to establish or maintain a commodity futures position. In the futures market, both sides of a trade—buyer and seller alike—post margin.

Another innovation that increased the attractiveness of futures as an investment was the introduction of *margin*. In the old days, forward contracts were formed with only a handshake and the promise of payment upon delivery of the commodity. When futures are traded, however, both buyers and sellers post good faith deposits. Unlike the margin used in stock trading, these deposits don't represent down payments. Instead, they are *performance bonds* that guarantee that the contracts will be honored by each side.

Futures margins are small. Speculators might be asked to put up as little as 5 percent of the total contract value to open their positions. These initial margin deposits vary by commodity and market conditions. If the commodity's price declines below its purchase price, the buyer—the long position—sees the loss deducted from his or her margin balance while the seller—the short position—is credited with a gain. This *marked to market* ensures that both parties to the contract continue to meet their financial obligations. Traders may be required to replenish their accounts when market action goes against them.

Spot Market versus Futures Contracts

A futures market, of necessity, is inextricably tied to its underlying spot market. By definition, the cash price for a commodity is its face value when available for delivery *on the spot*. The futures price for a commodity, however, reflects all the costs associated with holding it for future delivery. Take gold, for example. You can buy gold from a bullion dealer at the spot price today and walk away with your purchase. If you buy bullion through the futures market, though, you have to wait for the delivery month to get your gold. In the time you wait for delivery, your gold must be stored, it must be insured, and it must be financed.

> **marked to market**
>
> the process of repricing a commodity futures position against the current settlement price to reflect its current market value. Marking to market is done daily to determine account equity for margin purposes. Year-end marking to market, however, is required under the Internal Revenue Code to determine current tax liability. Each open Section 1256 position is *theoretically* closed out on the last business day of the year to arrive at a current gain or loss.

Let's say the price of spot gold bullion in early August is $650 per ounce. If you wanted to lock in today's price of gold for delivery in, say, September—a month from now—you shouldn't be surprised when you're asked by a dealer to pay the equivalent of $652.60 per ounce. The $2.60 per ounce premium over the spot price reflects the dealer's cost for holding your gold until September. If you want the dealer to hold your gold until December, a premium of $12.00 per ounce might be levied to cover the additional storage charges.

That's exactly how the futures market works. For any given commodity, several delivery months may be trading simultaneously, each at a different price level reflecting the carrying costs for each delivery. The near-term market for gold on the COMEX division of the New York Mercantile Exchange, for example, might look like Table 2.1.

TABLE 2.1 Near-Term Market for Gold in the COMEX Division of the NYMEX	
NYMEX—CMX Gold *(100 oz.—dollars per oz.)*	
Month	*Last*
August	650.50
September	652.60
October	655.50
December	662.00
February	669.60

Prices for different delivery months vary, reflecting the costs of storing, insuring, and financing the commodity as well as supply and demand for specific contracts. In a normal market such as this, the prices of deferred deliveries are higher than those of nearby deliveries. The spot month—in this case, August—typically trades at the lowest price.

Smart Trader Tip

The prices of commodities typically increase over time due to carrying costs such as storing, insuring, and financing the commodity.

Remember, all these contracts call for the delivery of the same quantity and quality of metal: 100 ounces of .995 fine (24-karat) gold, which currently sells in the cash market for $650.00 per ounce. The closer a contract is to expiration, and to the cash market, the smaller the carrying charges, until, at the end of a contract's delivery period, the *cash market* price and the expiring futures price converge.

cash market
another term for the spot market. It is the current price of the commodity in the open market and differs from the futures market, which is based on expectations about future prices.

This pricing phenomenon exists because of the futures markets' delivery mechanism. If the alignment of futures and cash market prices was significantly disturbed, sharp-eyed *arbitrageurs* (a.k.a. *arbs*) would likely step in to capitalize upon pricing disparities. When futures trade too far above the cash market (reflecting abnormally high carrying charges), for example, arbs could sell the overpriced futures, buy an equivalent amount of spot gold, store it, and then deliver the gold against the short futures in the delivery month. The inflated carry premium would thus be captured as a profit. The arbitrage, too, squeezes the pricing disparity away. Sales of overpriced futures exert downward price pressure in the contract market as spot metal prices are bid up by offsetting purchases.

> **arbitrageurs (arbs)**
> players who attempt to profit from price differences between two substantially equal assets. This might involve, for instance, buying a commodity on one exchange and simultaneously selling a similar commodity on another exchange in order to profit from the price differences of the two.

If futures markets don't reflect full carrying charges for some reason, arbs could step in to exploit the mispricing by doing a reverse version of this trade. The discount would be corrected when underpriced futures are purchased and spot metal is sold (the gold received at delivery against futures offsets the arbs' short cash market sales). Cash market and futures market prices are thus brought closer together as bids increase for cheap futures against the stepped-up spot market sales.

The mere fact that arbitrage could occur keeps prices from getting out of line most of the time, as futures traders don't want to be caught in the arbs' sights for overly aggressive bids or offers. Still, different delivery months can seem to move out of step within a normal or carrying charge market without attracting the wrath of arbs. A normal market reflects ample supplies across all delivery months. Not all markets appear that way; sometimes seemingly large disparities appear because of inherent differences in supply and demand for storable commodities.

For example, winter wheat is planted in late fall, remains dormant during the winter (hence its name), and is harvested in early summer. Nearby delivery months (i.e., those before the summer harvest in May or June) reflect the old crop, while more distant delivery months reflect a market with new crop supplies. A shortage in old crop months, therefore, may not be reflected in new crop months. It wouldn't be that unusual, in fact, to see new crop months trade at a relative discount to old crop months, reflecting ample quantities of new wheat. Bullish movements in old crop months, then, may not be reflected in new crop months.

Some delivery months attract more interest than others. December gold, for example, attracts more commercial interest than others, as jewelry manufacturers *hedge* their Christmastime sales. Prices in other, more thinly traded delivery months may be more volatile, allowing for more persistent price disparities.

Smart Trader Tip
Contract volumes for each delivery month are posted by the exchanges daily. Smart traders gravitate to high-volume contracts to minimize transaction costs and delays.

Inverted Markets

inverted markets

a term used to describe a situation where prices in the spot market are greater than in the futures market. Inverted markets can occur when there is strong present demand for a commodity.

Normal markets reflect normal supplies of a commodity. Shortages, however, can cause a market to invert. *Inverted markets* develop as spot or near-term supplies are hoarded. Inverted markets reflect consumer unwillingness to wait for delivery of a commodity. They want it *now*, not later.

The energy markets are particularly prone to inversion because a large amount of supply is controlled by a sometimes whimsical OPEC. As you can see by looking at Table 2.2, the prices of deferred deliveries are *lower* than those of nearby deliveries in an inverted market. The spot month—in this case, July—is priced highest (see Table 2.2).

As supplies increase, or demand wanes, an inverted market may return to normalcy. Arbitrage is more dangerous in an inverted market, as the natural brake (i.e., carrying charges that separate one delivery month from another) is absent. Inverted markets pose unique risks for certain trades known as *spreads*, which we'll look at a little later.

TABLE 2.2 NYMEX Crude Oil	
NYMEX Crude Oil *(1,000 barrels—dollars per bbl.)*	
Month	Last
July	78.84
August	78.78
September	78.70
October	78.60
November	78.50

Speculators

Futures markets greatly depend upon speculators to supply liquidity. Somebody, after all, has to take the other side of the hedging trades made by commercial users. As previously mentioned, speculators seek profits by correctly forecasting price changes. If you think, for instance, that December cocoa will rise to $1,800 per ton, you might be tempted to speculate on that expectation by purchasing futures at the current $1,600 price. You have no intention of actually taking delivery of the cocoa in December, as you just don't need 10 tons of cocoa beans. Instead, you expect to offset your futures position before the delivery period. That, in a nutshell (cocoa husk?), describes the intent of a long speculator.

Let's say cocoa's price rises to $1,820 per ton by October. You could take $2,200 in profits ($220 per ton times the 10-ton contract size) by selling your contract. If prices move southward to $1,470 per ton as December approaches, however, you may be forced to liquidate your position at a $1,300 loss ($130 times the 10-contract size) to avoid the risk of delivery. This risk will be further explained in the "Deliveries" section.

Speculators are attracted to futures because of *leverage*. The initial margin required for your cocoa trade might be only $1,700, for instance, but you're trading cocoa with a total contract value of $16,000 ($1,600 per ton × 10 tons). Your leverage is nearly 10-to-1. In other words, you're putting up only 10.6 percent of the commodity's value, but your profits and losses are the same as those of someone who had paid the full cash price for a wholesale lot of cocoa.

leverage
using small amounts of capital to control large amounts of a commodity or other asset. Margin is an example of using leverage.

By calculating your profit and loss potential in the scenarios we've described, we'll see how leverage can work for (or against) you (see Table 2.3).

The attraction of a $2,200 gain on a $1,700 investment is obvious. Notice that the underlying commodity had to move less than 14 percent to crank out a 129 percent return. Leverage, however, is a two-edged sword that can cut deeply. Losses can pile up dramatically on small moves, too (see Table 2.4).

In either case, whether you make a profit or a loss, your transactions are limited to the futures market; you never touch the actual commodity. Keep in mind that speculators avoid deliveries because of the substantial costs associated with the transfer and storage of the underlying commodities.

TABLE 2.3   Leveraged Profits

Profit /Loss Potential

	Price per Ton	Margin
	$1,600	$1,700
Bought 1 contract December cocoa		
Sold 1 contract December cocoa	$1,820	
13.8% Price gain	$220	
Contract = 10 tons	× 10	
Gross profit	$2,200	
Margin	÷ $1,700	
Return	**129.4%**	

TABLE 2.4   Leveraged Losses

Profit /Loss Potential

	Price per Ton	Margin
	$1,600	$1,700
Bought 1 contract December cocoa		
Sold 1 contract December cocoa	$1,470	
8.1% Price decline	−$130	
Contract = 10 tons	× 10	
Gross loss	$1,300	
Margin	÷ $1,700	
Return	**−76.5%**	

rollover

reinvesting money from one maturing security to another one with a more distant expiration.

What if your price expectations take a little longer than you forecast to be realized? As an example, let's say December cocoa reaches only $1,760 on the eve of the delivery period and you believe there's room for a further price advance. If you wish to maintain a long position, you'll need to execute a *rollover* of your long position to the next available delivery month. To do so, you'd sell the December contract and simultaneously buy March futures, the following contract month.

You could have just as easily speculated on a decline in cocoa's price. If you thought a drop to the $1,500 level was likely, you could sell December cocoa short at $1,600.

A short position is established by opening your futures trade with a sale instead of a purchase. How do you sell a commodity you don't already own? Remember that you're selling futures, not the actual cocoa. Futures are obligations to make or take delivery, secured by margin. A short sale is simply a wager that prices will decline before the contract's last trading day. Offsetting the short sale with a purchase before delivery precludes the need to actually deliver the commodity.

If December cocoa declines to $1,470 per ton, a $1,300 ($130 per ton × 10 tons) profit could be generated by buying back the December contract to close out your short position. This is the exact reverse of the loss in the long position described previously. Since the margin is the same for a short position as it is for a long position, you'd make (instead of lose) 76.5 percent. If you thought there was further softening in cocoa's price ahead, you could roll your short position forward by buying back December futures while simultaneously shorting March cocoa. As you can see, the possibilities are endless.

Fundamental versus Technical Analysis

Successful speculation requires a method for analyzing and forecasting price movements. There are two classic analytic approaches: fundamental analysis and technical analysis. *Fundamental analysis* focuses on the value of the asset and its true worth. For example, the fundamental analysis of a company might look at the earnings it generates, revenues, business strategy, and management. In brief, fundamental analysis seeks to identify changes in supply and demand that can then be used as justification for undertaking futures positions. A forecast of tighter supplies, for example, may be the reason for speculation with long positions. Prognostications of large overhanging supplies or weakening demand, likewise, might warrant short positions.

> **fundamental analysis**
> the study of all factors that might impact the supply and demand of a commodity. Weather is an example of a fundamental analysis tool for agricultural commodities.

technical analysis
the study of the price action of a security based on the theory that market prices display repetitive patterns that can be tracked and used to forecast future price movement; technical analysis evaluates price movement by analyzing statistics generated by market activity—such as past prices and volume—to study market performance.

option
a trading instrument that enables the buyer to purchase (call) or sell (put) the underlying market at a specific strike price until a specific expiration date.

spread
a trading strategy that involves the simultaneous purchase of a futures or options contract with the sale of another.

Technical analysis, however, is the study of past price movement in an asset or investment security. For example, technical analysis of the gold market involves looking at the price chart, volume, and other indicators that might reveal predictable price patterns. Technical analysts (a.k.a. chart readers) rely upon noneconomic data for their projections. Projections are based upon the assumption that certain patterns in price and trading volume can be recognized and are persistent. Examples of technical analysis include Elliot Wave Theory, moving average convergence/divergence (MACD), relative strength, volume, and stochastics. (Fundamental and technical analyses are discussed later, at greater length, in their own chapters.)

Options Spreads

Adopting a short or long stance in a commodity is known as an *outright* position. In an outright position, you take on the full risk of any changes in the price of the commodity. As we've seen, the inherent leverage in futures trading can translate small movements into outsized profits or losses. Speculators can moderate their risk or capitalize upon more subtle price movements by trading *options, spreads,* or *straddles* instead.

Spreads, in their simplest form, are trades in which a purchase of one futures contract is made against the sale of another in the same or a related market. Spreads are considered less risky than outright trades because the prices of the related contracts tend to move in the same general direction, providing a hedge of sorts.

In a spread, the price differential between the contracts is the subject of the speculation. For an outright trade, there's only one scenario that produces a gain for the speculator: The commodity must rise above (if long), or fall below (if short),

the entry price. There are more profitable outcomes available to the spreader, however. The long
contract rising in price, or the short contract declining, can produce a gain. The potential gain
would be even greater if both contracts moved fa-
vorably. Spreads may thus offer more attractive reward-to-risk ratios (RRRs) than outright trades
and may be, therefore, better trades for novice
speculators.

straddle
the simultaneous
purchase of a call
and put option
with the same at-
the-money strike,
expiration date,
and underlying
market.

To understand spreads, you first must know
the difference between the prefixes *intra* and *inter*. Intra means "within";
inter means "between." You'll see why this is important as we examine
the three main types of spreads:

- *Intracommodity:* This is, by far, the most common type of spread.
  As the name implies, the spread takes place within the market
  for a given commodity. It's constructed by purchasing a futures
  contract in one delivery month while selling futures in a different delivery month of the same commodity. Going long October sugar and shorting July sugar is an example of an
  intracommodity spread, also known as an interdelivery spread.

- *Intercommodity:* Taking a long position in one commodity and a
  short position in a related commodity is an example of an inter-
  commodity spread. The relationship between feeder cattle and
  live cattle, for example, can be exploited in a source/product
  spread. For example, feeder cattle are steers fattened in feedlots
  until they reach market weight. There's a futures contract on
  feeder cattle (the source) as well as the finished, or fattened, cattle
  (live cattle, the product). Some spreads may pit competing products against one another. You could, for example, buy live cattle
  futures and sell live hog futures if you think beef demand will
  outstrip that of pork in the near term. Usually, but not always,
  intercommodity spreads involve the same delivery months (e.g.,
  long December live cattle/short December live hogs). Different
  delivery months may be used, however, when there's not a match-
  up in the contracts' calendars or when specific pricing disparities
  have been pinpointed for exploitation.

- *Interexchange:* Buying May wheat on the Chicago Board of Trade
  while selling May wheat on the Minneapolis Grain Exchange is an

example of an interexchange spread. Most often, this kind of spread is used to profit from seasonal or other anticipated changes in the historic price relationship between the two types of wheat. These are also known as intermarket spreads.

To get a better idea of how a spread works, let's take a closer look at the July/October sugar trade. Let's assume you've noted that the spread (i.e., the price difference between July and October futures) doesn't seem to reflect full carrying charges. In other words, either the nearby July contract is trading too rich or the more distant October delivery is too cheap. You can exploit this mispricing by selling the overpriced futures and buying the underpriced contracts (see Table 2.5).

tick

an increment of change in the price of a security. For example, if the S&P 500 futures contract rises from 1,300.00 to 1,300.25, it has increased one tick because it moves in .25 increments and each 25-point change is one tick.

On April 3, you sell July sugar at 14.10 cents per pound and simultaneously buy October sugar at 14.15 cents per pound. In futures parlance, the spread now is *five under*. Whenever interdelivery spreads are discussed, the reference point is always the nearby contract. In this case, the nearby (July) is trading for five *ticks*, or 5/100 of a cent, under the deferred (October) delivery. Selling the nearby contract and buying the distant month, puts you in a *bear spread*. That means you expect the spread to widen and become more negative over time. Another way of putting this is to say you're *short the spread*. Notice the pattern: *short* nearby + long deferred = *short* the spread. Bear spreads are so named because nearby months typically fall faster than distant months when supplies are abundant and prices are soft.

TABLE 2.5 Bear Spread Specifics

Bearish July/October Sugar Trade

	Short 1 July Sugar	Long 1 October Sugar	(Short) Spread
April 3	14.10	14.15	−0.05
April 7	14.25	14.38	−0.13
	−0.15	**+0.23**	**+0.08**

During the life of the spread, it doesn't really matter whether sugar prices go up or down, though. As long as the price of the nearby option gets cheaper in relation to the deferred option by more than five ticks, a profit will be produced. That can happen whether sugar prices are at the 24-cent or the four-cent level.

bear spread
a type of strategy that generates profits as the price of the underlying asset falls.

Now fast-forward to April 7. July sugar is trading at $14.25. Covering your short position leaves you with a 15-tick loss. October sugar, meantime, has risen to $14.38. Selling that contract earns you a 23-tick gain. The net effect is an 8-tick profit as the result of the spread widening to 13 under.

Eight ticks translate to an $89.60 gain. Each tick is equal to $11.20 based on the contract size of 912,000 pounds per contract, which doesn't sound like much until you consider your margin investment. The exchange might have set $700 as an initial requirement for an outright position in sugar, but demanded only $210 for a spread. Thus, your bear spread made a 42.6 percent *return on margin* ($89.60 ÷ $210). Had you been outright long in the October contract instead, your gain would have been $257.60 (23 ticks), or 36.8 percent ($257.60 ÷ $700). Similarly, being outright short the July contract would have left you with a 15-tick, or 24 percent, loss.

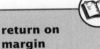

return on margin
the percentage of profit or loss based on the amount of margin used to enter the trade. If margin is $2,000 and the profit is $200, the return on margin is 10 percent.

This begs the question: Which trade has the best reward-to-risk ratio? In this case, the bear spread turns out to be the obvious winner. That may not always be the case. When more dramatic market movements occur, spread returns can seem paltry compared to those of outright trades. An outright long position in the October delivery, for example, might have earned you an 85-tick, or 136 percent, return on margin if sugar rose to the 15-cent level.

Now, if you saw the spread as too wide in April (i.e., it reflected more than normal carrying charges), you could have created a *bull spread* by purchasing the nearby (July) and selling the deferred (October) contracts. That would make you

bull spread
a type of trade that makes money when the price of the underlying security moves higher.

Smart Trader Tip
While spread margins are lower than those of outright trades, a spread may be every bit as risky as a single-contract position.

long the spread. Aside from that, this spread is deemed bullish because any perceived tightness of supply, indicative of a bull market, would tend to cause nearby deliveries to rise faster than deferred months. The pattern for your account table would then be: *long* nearby + short deferred = *long* the spread (see Table 2.6).

Here, you're wagering that the spread will narrow (become less negative) as market equilibrium is restored to reflect normal carrying charges. A 15-tick gain on the spread's long (nearby) leg, netted against a 10-tick loss on the short (deferred) leg, leaves you five ticks, or $56, in the black.

full carry
the total costs associated with holding or maintaining a securities position. It is the full cost of carry, or the carrying cost.

A bull spread is generally considered a true limited-risk trade because a deferred month's premium over the nearby is ordinarily limited to *full carry*. While occasional aberrations may pop up, they're usually short-lived in a normal market.

Carrying charges, however, aren't reflected in an inverted market. When near-term supplies are hoarded, there's no limit to the premium nearby contracts can command over deferred deliveries. Bear spreads (short the nearby, long the deferred) would be especially risky trades in inverted markets, while bull spreads could profit handsomely.

TABLE 2.6 Bull Spread Specifics

Bullish July/October Sugar Spread

	Long 1 July Sugar	Short 1 October Sugar	(Long) Spread
April 3	14.10	14.25	−0.15
April 7	14.25	14.35	−0.10
	+0.15	−0.10	+0.05

Hedging

As mentioned before, speculators provide liquidity. Futures markets need to attract speculators, so hedgers—commercial entities that use the markets to manage risk—have somebody to take the other side of their trades.

A *hedge* is really nothing more than a substitute sale or purchase used to offset the risk of a cash market position. Think of wheat farmers. When wheat is planted, and all through the growing season, they are long cash wheat. They own it. They hope that the price they obtain at harvest pays back their production costs (seed, fertilizer, fuel, irrigation, etc.) and affords them a margin of profit. Until they can actually sell their crop, perhaps seven or eight months after planting, they are exposed to the risk of wheat prices falling below their target level. To hedge against falling prices, the farmers could short wheat in the futures market now as a proxy for their harvest transaction. That will lock in today's price, subject to shifts in the relationship between prices in the local cash market and the futures market.

hedge
a position that serves to mitigate the risk associated with holding another asset or investment.

The important thing to remember is that hedgers have *two* positions in a commodity—one in the cash market and one in futures. These positions are complementary; one is long, the other short. To the extent the positions are equal in size, gains made in one market tend to offset losses in the other, insulating the hedger from much of the commodity's price *volatility*.

volatility
measure of the magnitude or speed of price moves over time.

Let's assume a farmer decides to hedge part of his winter wheat production when the cash market price is $3.70. By selling one May futures contract (5,000 bushels), he attempts to lock in the current cash price for a portion of his crop. Table 2.7 shows how his hedge might look.

If our farmer was in a position to sell wheat in February, he could fetch $3.70 per bushel in his local market. But the wheat is still in the ground and can't be harvested until May. At this point, he's worried that crop forecasts might put downward pressure on prices. Selling futures now serves as a substitute for the cash market transaction he intends to make at harvest.

TABLE 2.7   Winter Wheat Hedge Specifics

	Winter Wheat Hedge		
	Long 5,000 Bushels Cash Wheat	Short 5,000 Bushels May Wheat	(Long) Basis
February 3	3.70	3.82	−0.12
April 7	3.02	3.16	−0.14
	−0.68	**+0.66**	**−0.02**

basis

the difference between the local spot price of a deliverable commodity and the price of a futures contract—usually the nearby—for the same commodity. One commercial user's/producer's basis may vary from another's owing to variations in local spot market prices.

widened

an increase in the difference between the spot price and futures price.

The *basis*—the difference between our farmer's cash market price and that of futures—is now 12 under. Remember how we calculated spreads before? That same method is applicable to hedge transactions. The nearby (in this case, the cash market) price is 12 cents under the deferred delivery price. Similar to the spreads we diagrammed before, selling futures to hedge long cash market exposure makes you *long the basis*, meaning that you want the basis to narrow, or grow less negative, over the life of the trade.

By April, the cash price has declined 68 cents per bushel. Futures have fallen, too, but only 66 cents. As a result, the basis has actually *widened* by 2 cents per bushel. Does this mean the hedge failed? Not at all. The farmer's unhedged loss would have been 68 cents per bushel, as now he'd be obliged to accept only $3.02 in the cash market. With the hedge, he's effectively selling his production at $3.68 per bushel (the current cash market price, $3.02, together with the 66-cent gain on his futures position). That's only 2 cents worse than his original target price of $3.70 (hence, the adverse two-penny movement in his basis).

Producers of commodities, like our wheat farmer, use selling hedges to protect against a decline in the market prices of their outputs. Not surprisingly, users of commodities employ buying hedges to contain the risk of price increases in their inputs. A gold jewelry manufacturer, for example,

TABLE 2.8 Buying Hedge Profit Specifics

Buying Hedge Gold

	Short *100 Troy Ounces* *Gold*	*Long* *1 December* *Gold*	*(Short)* *Basis*
October 20	655.50	664.60	−9.10
November 23	669.80	675.10	−5.30
	−14.30	**+10.50**	**−3.80**

might use gold futures to hedge bullion purchases ahead of the peak Christmas season (see Table 2.8).

Suppose our jewelry maker forecasts a need for an additional 100 ounces of gold to meet her production quota. Having the need to buy gold in the future makes her short in the cash market now. As long as she remains short, she risks paying more than the current price of $655.50 per ounce. Buying futures, as a substitute for her anticipated cash market purchase, shields her from some or all of this risk.

Buying futures makes the manufacturer *short the basis*, meaning her ideal scenario would be to witness a widening of the difference between cash and deferred-delivery gold prices.

In October, spot gold is $9.10 per ounce under December futures. A month later, amid rising gold prices, the basis actually narrowed $3.80. Still, the jewelry manufacturer has managed to insulate herself from most of the $14.30 price increase in the spot market. With an effective purchase price of $659.30, her $10.50 gain in gold futures saved her $10,500 before commissions.

Hedging, despite its obvious benefits, isn't utilized in knee-jerk fashion by commercial users and producers. Often, when commercials decide that the cash market risk is tolerable, they elect to proceed unhedged. Hedging, remember, offsets not only cash market losses or opportunity costs, but also gains. Imagine if gold prices had fallen between October and November. Our jewelry manufacturer might have actually *lost* money as the result of hedging (see Table 2.9).

Had the jewelry maker held off hedging, she could have shaved $18.30 per ounce from the October spot price when she purchased her bullion a month later. Instead, her futures loss cost her $24.80 per ounce, pushing her effective purchase price to $662.00, well above the cash price.

TABLE 2.9   Buying Hedge Loss Specifics

Buying Hedge—Gold

	Short 100 Troy Ounces Gold	Long 1 December Gold	(Short) Basis
October 20	655.50	664.60	–9.10
November 23	637.20	639.80	–2.60
	+18.30	**–24.80**	**–6.50**

U.S. Commodity Exchanges

At present, there are eight commodity exchanges actively trading futures in the United States. Exchanges can be found in Chicago, New York, Kansas City, and Minneapolis as well as in cyberspace. Each trades a unique set of commodity contracts and establishes its own rules, subject to the oversight of the *Commodity Futures Trading Commission* (CFTC). The CFTC is a federal regulatory agency with responsibilities similar to those administered by the Securities and Exchange Commission (SEC) over stock markets. In addition, an industry self-regulatory body—the National Futures Association (NFA)—handles the registration and testing of professionals involved in the execution of futures trades (www.nfa.futures.org).

Commodity Futures Trading Commission
the CFTC is an independent government agency that regulates the commodities market. See also www.cftc.gov.

It's the Pits

Economics professors like to say that commodity exchanges are centralized marketplaces where buyers and sellers meet to foster *price discovery.* That doesn't mean that an exchange itself sets the prices of commodities; the traders using the facilities of the exchange do that.

price discovery
the process of finding the price that will match buyers and sellers.

Traditionally, U.S. futures trading is conducted by *open outcry auction* (we'll look at electronic trading later). This kind of auction is a bit different from the kind you may have attended.

First of all, there's no single auctioneer. Each trader, in effect, is an auctioneer, shouting the quantity of the commodity he or she is buying or selling, and the price he or she wants. Hand signals accompany the shouting, which ensures the trader's verbal bid or offer is understood above the din of the trading crowd. A palm facing inward signals a desire to buy; an outward-facing palm indicates selling. Fingers held vertically indicate quantity, while horizontally extended fingers convey price.

The auction itself takes place in octagonal *trading pits* or circular *rings* dotting the exchange floor. Pits are found on most exchanges, while rings are used at the New York Mercantile Exchange. Each pit or ring is designated as the exclusive floor trading location for certain commodities. Some pits or rings trade only one commodity (e.g., soybeans on the CBOT, crude oil on the NYMEX), while less active contracts may share locations.

trading pits
areas within the commodities exchanges where buy and sell orders are presented and matched.

The open outcry auction may appear chaotic, but is, in fact, a well-ordered affair governed by strict rules. In the auction, only the best (highest) bid and best (lowest) offer are allowed to emerge as the market. As previously defined, a *bid* is a price a trader is willing to spend to *buy* a commodity; the price a trader will accept to *sell* a commodity is known as an *offer*. If a trader is willing to pay the highest price offered, he or she announces this intention to the crowd, immediately silencing lower bids. Likewise, a willingness to sell at the lowest price bid, once announced in the crowd, quashes higher offers. Exchange rules prohibit a trader from bidding under another trader's bid or ask above another's offer.

It's here where the price discovery occurs. Through the auction, the commodity's current value, at least as perceived by market participants, is revealed. You might say the commodity's worth, at any given time, is somewhere between the highest current bid and the lowest current offer.

All this buying and selling is done by exchange members known as brokers and traders. *Brokers* are companies or individuals who execute orders for other exchange members, public customers, or commercial institutions. Brokers, acting as agents, receive commissions for executing trades. They have no capital risked in the trades they execute. Traders don't earn commissions. Instead, they invest their own (or their firm's) money in each trade, hoping to make a

brokers
in the trading pits, brokers are the people who bring in customer orders to traders.

locals
traders in the pits who are not members of large organizations.

profit. Traders can work for large organizations, or they can be independent *locals*.

And what about those funny-looking jackets? They're like uniforms; they help brokers and locals identify each other. The staffpersons of each member firm all wear jackets of the same color and pattern, making them more easily recognized on a busy trading floor. Independent traders usually wear trading jackets in colors or patterns of their own choosing or they may wear the jacket of their *clearing firm*, the exchange member that handles the trader's account.

clearing firm
an exchange member that is also a member of the clearinghouse. Clearing members deal directly with the clearinghouse to settle trades, deliveries, and margin. Nonclearing exchange members contract with clearing members to handle their back-office functions.

In the pits, traders dealing in certain delivery months congregate in designated segments of the pit. Traders wanting to trade December corn, for example, congregate in one "pie slice" of the octagon, while those interested in the May delivery occupy another. Brokers tend to stand at the edges of the pit so they can easily see other traders, be accessible to runners bringing them customer orders, or view flashed orders from the phone desks ringing the trading floor. Locals typically stand near the center of the pit. Exchange employees, known as *trade reporters*, occupy the "pulpit" overseeing the pit and record trade prices for dissemination to the financial wire services.

In ring trading, exchange employees known as *card clockers* occupy the center of the ring to receive reports of executed trades, while brokers and traders congregate around the periphery.

Electronic Trading

A growing number of exchanges have instituted screen-based trading of their contracts, allowing traders to bypass the pits and send buy or sell orders from their computers to the exchange's electronic marketplace. Traders gain access to the exchange's electronic marketplace through designated platforms offered by brokerages.

To avoid competition with pit trading, screen-based trading was originally limited to the after hours (i.e., outside of regular market hours). However, exchanges are now permitting the electronic and open outcry markets to trade side by side during regular trading hours.

A quick look at the appendix to this book will give you an idea of strength of this trend. A large number of contracts trade in both the pit and the electronic environments. Some contracts, in fact, trade *only* in cyberspace. Electronic trading will be discussed more fully in Chapter 13.

Exchange Ownership and Membership

Traditionally, exchange members have been exclusive owners of the exchanges, but that's now changing. Today, many exchanges are publicly traded organizations with far-flung shareholders, many who have never even set foot on a commodity trading floor. You can now buy into the profit (or loss) stream of the Chicago Mercantile Exchange and the Chicago Board of Trade simply by purchasing their shares through your stock brokerage account.

In 2002, the Chicago Mercantile Exchange (CME: NYSE), became the first U.S. futures exchange to go public. The Chicago Board of Trade (BOT: NYSE), followed suit in 2005. TheIntercontinentalExchange, Inc. (ICE), which operates an electronic global futures market for trading of energy products, went public in late 2005. Other futures marketplaces, such as the New York Mercantile Exchange, are now considering public offerings as well.

Shareholders, however, aren't entitled to trade on the exchange unless they are also members. To become a member, an individual must meet strict exchange criteria with respect to credit standing, financial responsibility, and character, as well as demonstrating knowledge of exchange rules and trading practices.

A membership, or *seat,* must also be purchased from another member through a bid-offer market administered by the exchanges. The value of a seat, like that of a commodity, is subject to the forces of supply and demand. As of mid-2006, seat prices at the two major Chicago exchanges hovered at the $450,000 level, about midway between their 20-year highs and lows.

To ensure brokers and traders don't dodge their financial obligations by hiding behind a corporate veil, exchange membership is open only to individuals. To comply with this rule, large brokerages and trading organizations such as Merrill Lynch and Timber Hill appoint certain employees as *nominees* to their seats and indemnify them against outsized losses.

Clearinghouses

At the time a trade is made, a financial obligation is created between the contract buyer and the seller. Remember that sellers undertake the obligation to *make* delivery of the commodity while buyers promise to *take* delivery. Trading is largely anonymous, so neither side likely knows the identity of the counterparty. How, then, can market participants be sure the other side will actually make good on their delivery promise? More important, when the long side wants to sell, does he have to track down the short and get him to buy back his contract?

The answer to both of these questions is no. Each exchange has an associated *clearinghouse* to ensure the financial integrity of its markets and facilitate the settlement of trades. At the end of each business day, the clearinghouse steps in to break the link between the contract parties, interposing itself as the buyer to every seller and the seller to every buyer. By doing so, market participants now look to the clearinghouse for performance on their contracts. With that in mind, there's really no need to be concerned about the counterparty's identity. Ultimately, it's the clearinghouse, and the clearinghouse has substantial assets and borrowing power to meet its obligations.

To get the clearinghouse performance guarantee, trades take place on the books of a clearing firm—a member of the clearinghouse. Not all exchange members are members of the clearinghouse. Locals, for example, aren't typically clearing members. Instead, they contract with other firms to clear their trades.

To become a member of the clearinghouse, a substantial capital commitment is required, as each clearing firm is obliged to post a guarantee deposit, which may be tapped to cover defaults.

Margin

The clearinghouse also handles the flow of margin that secures each contract according to exchange rules. Exchanges set two margin plateaus for each commodity. The initial margin requirement is the cash needed to open a position—short or long. *Maintenance*, or *variation*, *margin* is the equity required to keep a position open.

For example, when October crude oil was trading at $77 per barrel, the New York Mercantile Exchange set the initial margin requirement for near-term delivery months of crude oil futures at $4,725. Since a contract calls for the delivery of 1,000 barrels, initial margin represents 6.1 percent

of the total contract value [$4,725 ÷ ($77 × 1,000)].
Keep in mind that the exchange sets *minimum* margin levels. Brokerages may impose greater—but
never smaller—requirements on their customers.

Let's say two speculators—one *bullish* and one
bearish—elect to take opposite positions in October
crude oil at $77. Both maintain accounts at broker-
ages that allow them to trade on exchange minimum
margins. Both would be required to put up the
$4,725 performance bond to open their positions.

**maintenance
margin**

the minimum
amount of money
that a trader must
maintain in his or
her account in
order to continue
to hold a trade in a
given commodity.

Smart Trader Tip

Opening an Account

One of the first steps in trading futures is finding a broker and opening a
futures account. Once a firm is selected, the customer must complete a
new account form that will ask questions pertaining to the individual's
net worth, trading history, and other pertinent financial information.
Most brokers will require that the new customer have a certain net worth
and experience. Once the account is approved for trading, the customer
then deposits funds and can begin buying and selling futures contracts.

Our traders would likely be aware that the exchange also set $3,500
as the maintenance requirement for their contracts. That means that up
to $1,225 ($4,725 − $3,500) in losses could be sustained before a main-
tenance *call* is issued. This translates into a price change of $1.22 per bar-
rel ($1,225 ÷ 1,000 barrels). Any price movement in excess of $1.22 per
barrel will put one of them (assuming there are no other positions or cash
in account) into margin call territory. Let's see what happens if October
crude rises to $78.36 (see Table 2.10).

TABLE 2.10 Crude Rises to $78.36		
October Crude Rises to $78.36		
	Long at $77	Short at $77
Initial margin deposit	$4,725	$4,725
Price rises to $78.36	+$1,360	−$1,360
Equity	$6,085	$3,365
Maintenance requirement	$3,500	$3,500
Call	0	$1,360

A price rise creates additional equity in the long account, while depleting the equity of the short account. Equity in excess of the account's initial requirements can be withdrawn in cash or used to meet the requirements of additional positions. Here, the long can withdraw as much as $1,360 ($6,085 equity – $4,725 initial requirement). The short's equity, however, has dipped below the maintenance level, requiring the short trader to restore it to the *initial* requirement ($4,725). Notice how the gains of one trader are subsidized by the losses of another. This is why futures trading is sometimes referred to as a *zero-sum game*. Add the gains to the losses and you end up with a sum of zero (before commission costs, of course).

zero-sum game

a game where the winnings from one player are equal to the losses of another. The futures market is considered a zero-sum game because profits from one player are losses to another.

In the commodities markets, there's no uniform rule dictating margin levels as there is the securities market. Exchanges set margins at will, often raising or lowering requirements to encourage or discourage speculation (i.e., liquidity) as needed. Margins will generally be raised when price volatility increases; they're lowered as volatility contracts. Margin requirements, too, may be set higher in spot month contracts to discourage weak hands from holding positions into the delivery period.

Keep in mind that changes in margin requirements are most often retroactive: The new levels may apply not only to positions entered after the effective date of the change, but also to existing positions. Thus, there's a possibility of receiving a variation call even if the market isn't moving against you.

To get a better idea of margin flows, let's follow our long crude oil trader through his first few days as a futures customer.

First, he opens his futures trading account with a *futures commission merchant* (FCM), a commodities brokerage (alternatively, he can open an account with an *introducing broker*, a limited-service firm that contracts with an FCM to carry its customers' accounts). He deposits $6,000 in cash (see Table 2.11).

TABLE 2.11 Futures Customer Account

Long Crude Trader's Futures Performance

Date	Activity	Credit/ Debit	Equity	Margin Requirement	Cash Available
July 30	Deposit: $6,000	$6,000	$6,000	0	$6,000
July 31	Buy 1 Oct crude @ 77.00			IM $4,725/ MM $3,500	
	Oct crude settles @ 76.85	−150	5,850	"	1,125
August 1	Oct crude settles @ 77.66	810	6,660	"	1,935
August 2	Oct crude settles @ 78.35	690	7,350	"	2,625
August 3	Oct crude settles @ 79.60	1,250	8,600	"	3,875
August 4	Withdrawal: $2,000	−2,000	6,600	"	1,875
	Oct crude settles @ 77.23	−2,370	4,230	"	−495
August 7	Oct crude settles @ 76.04	−1,190	3,040	"	−1,685
	Maintenance call: $1,685			"	
August 8	Deposit: $1,685	1,685	4,725	"	0
	Oct crude settles @ 77.22	1,180	5,905	"	1,180
August 9	Sell 1 Oct crude @ 77.72	500	6,405	0	6,405
	Commissions/fees	−25	6,380	0	6,380

On July 31, our trader buys an October crude oil contract at $77 per barrel, meeting the $4,725 initial margin (IM) requirement account with his account equity. At the close, his account is marked to market for a $150 loss in equity based upon the $76.85 settlement price for October crude. His $5,850 equity is still well above the $3,500 maintenance margin (MM) requirement. In fact, his equity still exceeds the initial margin requirement, leaving him the option to withdraw up to $1,125 or open additional futures positions with initial requirements up to $1,125.

After three days of favorable market action, our trader decides to take some money off the table. He withdraws $2,000 on August 4. Unfortunately, the market weakens to $77.23 on that very day. With the market action and the withdrawal, his equity declines to $4,230, which is still

round-trip commission

the total commission costs associated with buying or opening a position and also selling and closing that same position. Normally, futures brokerage commissions are charged on a round-trip basis when a position is closed, either through a purchase, a sale, or a delivery. Commissions on futures options, however, are typically not charged on a round-trip basis; you pay a commission when you enter as well as when you exit the market.

above his maintenance requirement. After the weekend, crude oil continues to sell off. The August 7 settlement price of 76.04 puts the trader's equity below the maintenance level, resulting in a call to restore the account to the initial level. After the call is met with a cash deposit, our trader decides to look for the exits. He liquidates his position on August 9 and pays his *round-trip commission* on the way out.

So how did our trader do? To figure that out, just net out the total cash credits and debits. He originally deposited $6,000 and later had to meet a maintenance call of $1,685. That makes $7,685 in total cash he's contributed. The $2,000 he withdrew would be a debit, as would be his ending equity of $6,380 if he wanted to close his account now. Total potential debits, then, are $8,380. Netting that against his credits, he's made $695 for return on margin of 14.7 percent.

Mind you, our trader started out rather thinly capitalized. He wouldn't have been able to withstand much adverse market movement early with only $6,000 supporting his crude oil position. Conservative money management rules usually call for capitalizing each position at three to five times their margin requirements.

Traders don't have to leave their margin money idle. Treasury bills can be used to meet initial margin requirements, though maintenance calls must be answered with cash.

Smart Trader Tip

A futures commission merchant (FCM) offers more services to traders than an introducing broker (IB). An IB is essentially a marketing organization that must contract with an FCM to transact customer business. An IB cannot directly hold customer cash or securities.

Orders

When placing a futures order, either orally or electronically, you must convey five elements:

1. *Action:* Designate whether you're buying or selling.

2. *Quantity:* Typically, you'll specify the number of contracts to be bought or sold. There's an exception for grains and soybeans, however. Orders for these commodities are denominated in thousands of bushels. If you wanted to buy two corn contracts sized at 5,000 bushels each, your order would specify "10" for 10,000 bushels.

3. *Delivery month:* Each delivery month is its own market, with its own bid-ask spread. A sale of July orange juice will *not* offset a long position in November juice, for instance. You must close out a position with an offsetting transaction with the *same* delivery month; otherwise, you'll create a new spread.

4. *Commodity:* Exactitude here is important, because a commodity may trade on more than one exchange or be offered in different contract sizes. Contracts for 100 troy ounces of gold, for example, trade on the New York Mercantile Exchange (its COMEX division) and the Chicago Board of Trade. Additionally, mini gold contracts (sized at 33.2 troy ounces) are offered on the Board's Mid-America division. To minimize confusion, each commodity is designated by a unique *ticker symbol.* New York's gold contracts are GC, while the mini contracts on the Mid-Am are YG. Commodity tickers also include letter designations for the delivery month. The exchange, for example, would disseminate a quote for December COMEX gold, as GCZ, with the "Z" signifying December. You can find commodity tickers and month codes in the appendix of this book.

5. *Time, price, or execution contingency:* If you only want your order executed with a specific time period or price level, you must note that on your order. We'll look at the various types of contingencies shortly.

With the foregoing in mind, then, an order to buy three contracts of May soybeans at $6.02 per bushel or better would sound like this if placed orally: "Buy 15 May beans at 602." A written or electronic version of the order would appear as "Buy 15 SBK 6020."

Price punctuation is usually missing in futures orders, so space can be conserved on quote boards and streaming tickers. The *tick sizes*—the smallest price variations allowed in trading or quoting commodities—are understood by market participants. Soybeans and the grains, for example, are quoted in dollars and cents per bushel, but the minimum tick is an eighth of a cent. The extra zero shown in the electronic soybean order above signifies "zero eighths." Similarly, a ticker quote from the bean pit of 6022 would mean $6.02 1/4 or $6.02 2/8 per bushel. The numerator is always expressed as an even number in grain and oilseed quotes.

Types of Orders

There is a myriad of order types used in the commodities markets, with each exchange setting its own rules regarding order acceptability. Orders executable on the Chicago Mercantile Exchange may be prohibited on the Chicago Board of Trade; wise traders check with their brokerages to see if a contemplated order is acceptable before the trade is attempted. The most common types of orders include:

- *Day versus good 'til canceled orders:* All orders received by a broker or an execution system will be considered good for the day unless there is another time parameter designated. A *day order* may be executed only on the day it is entered. If it's not executed by the close of the market, it expires. The aforementioned soybean order is an example of a day order. An order marked "good 'til canceled" (GTC) can be held open for execution at a later date if it can't be executed on the day it is entered. As its name implies, a GTC order is good until executed, until it is canceled by its originator, or until the underlying contract expires, whichever occurs first. GTC orders are sometimes referred to as *open orders*.
- *Market orders:* Market orders call for execution "at the market," or the best available price upon receipt by the floor broker (or electronic mart). Market orders have priority over all others and are used when certainty of execution is more important than price. Keep in mind, however, that a market order may not be executable if the market is offered *limit down* or bid *limit up*.

Exchange rules impose daily *price limits* on some commodities, allowing a future's price to fluctuate only so much from the previous trading day's *settlement price*. The imbalance found in a market *locked* at the daily limit impedes order executions. An oral order without a specified price (for example, "Buy 15 May beans") is considered a market order, but nowadays most order entry systems require a specific designation, such as "market" or "at the market," to be attached to an order if immediate execution is desired.

market orders
buying or selling securities at the price given at the time the order reached the market.

- *Limit orders:* If price, rather than certainty of execution, is paramount to traders, they are more likely to use limit orders than market orders. Limit orders may be executed only at the specified price or better. For that reason, there's no assurance that a limit order can ever be executed.

settlement price
the official price at the end of the trading day that is based on a range of closing prices for a specific contract. It is used to determine margin requirements.

  — The order to buy May beans at $6.02 is a limit order. Hence, execution is acceptable only if May soybeans can be purchased at $6.02 or less (a lower price is better for a buy, right?). Unless and until the contract can be bought at that price, the or-

limit orders
orders to buy or sell investments at a specific price.

  der rests. This is also a day order; if we can't get our beans within our limit today, we'll have to place a new order for the next trading day if we still want to buy.

  — Buy limits are placed *below* the market. If our order to buy at $6.02 is unexecuted, it's because May beans are offered above our limit. Sell limits, likewise, are placed *above* the current market and call for execution at or above the limit price.

  — Traders may occasionally place limit orders when the market is currently trading at or through their limit price. If this is the case, the order should be flagged "or better" as a signal to the floor broker that the order, which might look suspiciously like a stop, is, in fact, a limit order.

- *Stop orders:* Stops, like limits, are resting orders; the market must move to trigger their execution. Stops, however, are placed on the side of the market opposite that of limits. A sell stop, for example, is placed *below* the current market. Once the commodity is offered at the stop, or a trade takes place at or through the stop, the order is executed at the market. Notice the difference here: A sell limit can be executed only at the limit price or better, but a sell stop can be executed at *any* price once the stop is touched. A sell stop would sound/look like this: "Sell 3 October crude oil at 76 stop GTC" or "Sell 3 CLV 7600 stop GTC."

  — Buy stops are placed *above* the current market and are triggered when a bid is made or a trade takes place at or through the stop price.

    stop loss

    a risk management tool used to limit the losses from an open position. For example, a trader might place a stop loss 5 percent below the current price of a long position in order to limit the losses to only 5 percent.

    — Stops are often called *stop-loss* orders because they're used to limit losses or to protect open trade gains in the event of a market reversal. You could use the preceding stop order, for example, to protect the gains made in your long crude oil position. Thus, you'd be using the order to exit the market.

    — Stops can be used to enter the market as well. Let's say you noticed $76.10 was a support area that had been tested before in the October oil market. You reason that once support is broken, October crude could sink to the $72 level. You're willing to short oil only if the market takes out support, so you place the order above to enter the market.

- *Stop-limit orders:* Stop limits, as the name indicates, have the features of two different orders. A stop price acts as a trigger: Once the market touches the stop price, the order is activated. Unlike a straight stop, which becomes a market order when set off, a stop limit becomes a limit order, executable only at the limit price or better. If you wanted to sell short October crude once support was breached, but were willing to sell only at $75.90 or better (higher), your order might look like this: "Sell 3 October crude oil at 76 stop, 75.90 limit GTC" or "Sell 3 CLV 7600 stop, 7590 limit GTC." The stop and limit prices could be the same. You could have placed your order as "Sell 3 October crude oil at 76 stop limit GTC" or "Sell 3 CLV 7600 stop limit GTC." By doing so, you'd accept an execution only at or above $76. Naturally, this limits the likelihood of an execution.

- *Market-if-touched orders:* An MIT order rests on the same side of the market as a limit order, but once the specified price is touched, it becomes a market order. Accordingly, the likelihood of an execution for an MIT order is greater than that of a limit order at the same price. A picture might help clarify where all the resting orders alight (see Table 2.12).

Remember, limit and stop-limit orders can be executed at the limit price or better; stops and MITs are executable as market orders once triggered, so they can be filled at any price.

- *Spread (or roll) orders:* Spreads, as we've seen, are multicontract trades. Let's go back to the bear spread in sugar to see how a trader would actually enter opening and closing transactions. Remember our motivation for trading the spread? We didn't think the market reflected full carrying charges. When we looked at the market on April 3, the spread between the July and October deliveries was only 5 ticks. Ordinarily, the spread is 10 ticks. A bear spread entails holding a short position in the near-term (July) delivery while owning the deferred (October) contract. Despite the fact that two contracts were traded on April 3, we entered only *one* trade ticket. The ticket references the two contracts and requests execution in terms of the *spread* price, not the prices of the individual contracts. When placing a spread trade orally, the spread is quoted in terms of the *buy* side (this is a throwback to the way futures order tickets are printed; the buy side is on the right and, therefore, read first). For our bear spread, we'd place a telephone order like this: "Buy 1 October, sell 1 July sugar at 5 over" or "Buy 1 October/sell 1 July sugar +5."

TABLE 2.12 Resting Order Landscape

	Sell limit	Buy stop	Sell MIT	
		Buy stop-limit		
Market price	————	**Market price**	————	**Market price**
	Buy limit	Sell stop	Buy MIT	
		Sell stop-limit		

We're not so concerned about the actual execution prices of the two contracts in a spread. All we really care about is the spread between the July and the October prices. We'd like a fill at whatever prices are obtainable that makes October sugar five points (or less) above the July delivery. That's right, this is a *limit* order. Buying October sugar at 15.20 cents while selling July at 15.16 cents is just as good as buying October at 13.01 cents and selling July for 12.97 cents. Buying the spread at three under would be even better.

When it's time to unwind—to close out—the spread, we'd again use a single ticket and quote, as always, the buy side first. We might, for example, relay the following order to our broker on April 7:

— "Buy 1 July, sell 1 October sugar at 13 under" or

— "Buy 1 July/sell 1 October sugar –13"

This, like the order used to enter the spread, is a limit order, executable anytime the discount July is offered under October is 13 ticks or more.

Deliveries

Ever heard someone's misadventure in the futures market resulting in 40,000 pounds of frozen bacon being dumped on his front lawn? In actuality, deliveries don't happen that way. The clearinghouse is the conduit through which all deliveries contracted through futures are settled, and most of it involves the movement of paper, not actual railcars of goods. Deliveries are a rare occurrence in the futures markets, but a delivery mechanism must exist to keep the futures market aligned with the spot market.

Each exchange has its own specific rules regarding deliveries, and they can vary from one commodity to another, but there are elements with respect to deliveries common to all markets. First is a basic calendar of key dates. They're called delivery months because that's when deliveries can occur. Shorts—potential sellers of the commodity—typically control the delivery process, so longs who hold open positions into the delivery month take on the risk that they may be tapped to accept, and pay for, the underlying commodity.

Each delivery month has a *last trading day*, the date after which the contract ceases to exist. You can't do any trading in the contract after this date. That said, if you're long past the last trading day, you can't avoid a delivery. Usually, but not always, the last trading day will be a date in the contract's delivery month. In the case of gold, the last trading day for the August delivery is, indeed, near the end of August.

Shorts, however, can tender *delivery notices* through the clearinghouse just ahead of *first notice day*. For gold, that's actually the second-to-last business day of *July*. On first notice day, the clearinghouse can start assigning delivery notices, in turn, to outstanding longs. Actual deliveries can commence the day after, on *first delivery day*. For August gold, that means the first business day of August.

Smart Trader Tip

Delivery notices are randomly assigned by the clearinghouse to clearing members carrying long positions. The FCM, in turn, doles out notices to long customers by any equitable basis of its choosing, such as random assignment, allocation to the oldest net long, or the like. You typically won't know when you're likely to receive a delivery notice if you're long into the delivery period.

In summary, this means you don't want to be long going into the delivery month unless you're willing to actually take a delivery. And what if you do get stuck with a delivery notice? Some exchanges may permit longs to retender delivery notices to the clearinghouse in limited circumstances. When a delivery notice is retendered, the long takes offsetting short positions in the spot contract in an amount equivalent to the size of the commodity covered by the delivery notice. Accordingly, retendering cannot be done after last trading day in the spot contract.

If you can't retender, the clearinghouse will deliver a warehouse receipt or other paper evidence of ownership and your account will be debited for the contract price, adjusted for any premiums or discounts for permitted variations from the contract grade. No goods will be deposited on your front lawn.

Volume and Open Interest

Prices are the natural highlight of reports from the futures exchanges. Everybody wants to know the price of oil or gold. Reports, however, include more than just price. Accompanying *volume* and *open interest* figures are important liquidity indicators.

volume

the amount of trading activity associated with a specific investment or market. Stock volume is measured in shares. Futures and options volume is based on number of contracts.

Volume is simply the total number of contracts that changed hands over a certain period of time. If you bought a futures contract today, you'd add one contract to today's volume. A sale of your contract later in the day would add yet other contract to volume. Volume numbers give a sense of the market's activity and liquidity at any given time and can be tracked to better understand market trends.

Open interest figures add more perspective on a market's liquidity. Open interest refers to the number of futures contracts that remain outstanding. Put another way, open interest reflects the total of contracts that haven't yet been closed out by offset or delivery. Open interest increases by one contract whenever a new long meets a new short. Conversely, open interest declines by one contract when an existing long sells to an existing short. If a new buyer purchases a contract from an existing long or if a new seller sells to existing short, open interest remains unchanged (see Table 2.13).

open interest

the number of options or futures contracts that have been opened and not yet closed out. Open interest gives a good indication of the contract's liquidity.

TABLE 2.13 Open Interest Mechanics			
	Existing Long	*No Position*	*Existing Short*
New long buys from	Unchanged	Increase	Increase
Existing long sells to	Unchanged	Unchanged	Decrease
New short sells to	Increase	Increase	Unchanged
Existing short buys from	Decrease	Unchanged	Unchanged

TriVan Truck Body

Travis Siebol
Repair / Paint Manager

1385 West Smith Rd.
Ferndale, WA 98248

Phone Number: (360) 380-0773
Toll-free: (866) 874-8261
Fax Number: (360) 312-1398
email: travis@trivan.net

Open interest figures, together with volume data, can help traders pinpoint the most liquid contract months in which to trade. Volume and open interest are reported for each contract month of each commodity. Some contracts exhibit substantial volume and open interest, while others appear nearly dormant. Traders gravitate to the more liquid contracts because they're more likely to encounter narrower spreads between bids and offers in an active market.

Popular Commodity Contracts

Listed here are summaries of key contracts traded on each exchange. Commodity futures contracts are typically sized to represent one railcar of each commodity—a quantity mirroring a wholesale lot. The appendix to this book contains a more complete list of commodity (nonfinancial) futures.

Chicago Board of Trade (CBOT)

141 West Jackson Boulevard
Chicago, IL 60604
Phone: (312) 435-3500
Web site: www.cbot.com

The CBOT is generally regarded as the country's (and, debatably, the world's) oldest organized futures exchange. From its founding in 1848 as a grain cash market, the CBOT has played a pivotal role in developing modern futures trading. Forward contracts began trading shortly before the Civil War. By the war's end, formal rules governing margins and delivery procedures were in place. The CBOT began publishing futures prices in 1877, and, in 1883, the first clearing organization was established to guarantee the performance on CBOT contracts.

Principal Commodities

Commodity	Contract size
Corn	5,000 bushels
Wheat	5,000 bushels
Soybeans	5,000 bushels
Soybean oil	60,000 pounds
Soybean meal	100 tons

Corn: Corn is the largest crop in the United States, in terms of both value and acres planted. Corn is used primarily as livestock feed. Other uses include alcohol (ethanol) additives for gasoline, adhesives, corn oil for cooking and margarine, sweeteners, cereals, packaged/processed foodstuffs, and fresh produce. Corn prices reflect the highly seasonal nature of a summer crop. Supplies are generally tight in the spring when planting takes place, so prices tend to peak in March and April, followed by a decline during the summer growing months. A spike may occur in August or early September as final yield estimates are adjusted. Seasonal lows are typically reached in late September/October when harvest supplies weigh on the market.

Wheat: The single largest use for wheat is the making of flour, but it's also used in brewing and distilling, and the manufacture of oil, gluten, livestock feed, hay, newsprint, and other products. U.S. wheat is primarily the spring and winter wheat varieties, with winter wheat accounting for nearly three-fourths of total domestic production. Winter wheat is typically planted in late fall, remains dormant during the winter, and is harvested early the following summer. Wheat futures traded at the CBOT mirror the market for the soft red winter (SRW) variety. SRW is grown in a wide swath of the country from central Texas, to the Great Lakes and east to the Atlantic. SRW flour is used to make cakes, cookies, snack foods, crackers, and pastries. The Kansas City Board of Trade's wheat contract is a proxy for hard red winter wheat (see "Kansas City Board of Trade").

- Spring wheat varieties are planted in the spring and harvested in the fall. Hard red spring wheat futures trades on the Minneapolis Grain Exchange (see "Minneapolis Grain Exchange").

- CBOT wheat has two prominent seasonal tendencies: One is a strong tendency to decline, beginning in January/February, through the spring as harvest approaches. The other is a rise from harvest lows—usually in June or July—into October/November.

Soybeans: Now the third largest crop—behind corn and wheat—produced in the United States, soybeans are used to produce a wide variety of food products. Their key value lies in their high protein content (about 40 percent), making them an excellent meat and dairy substitute. Whole soybeans are used in snacks and other prepared products, as well as in the manufacture of soy flour, protein concentrates, soy milk and baby formula, tofu, soy sauce, and meat alternatives such a soy burgers and breakfast sausage. Soybeans are usually planted in May or June and are harvested in autumn. Seasonally, soybean futures tend to rise from early spring through the summer planting season. July and August are usually bearish for bean futures.

Soybean meal: Soybean meal is produced through the processing and separation of soybeans into oil and meal components. Soybean meal typically accounts for a third of the weight of raw soybeans. The bulk of soybean meal is used as animal feed, though some goes into the production of soy flour and isolated soy protein. Seasonally, meal prices follow those of beans, most typically rising in the spring and peaking in early summer.

Soybean oil: About a fifth of a soybean's weight can be extracted as oil. Soybean oil is used to produce cooking and salad oils, shortening, and margarine. It's also used to produce inedible products such as paints, varnish, resins, and plastics. Oil prices mimic the seasonal pattern of beans and meal for the most part, typically rising through spring and topping out in summer. Conventional market wisdom holds that crushing one bushel, or 60 pounds, of soybeans produces 11 pounds of oil and 44 pounds of meal. Converting the bean and product contracts into a common denominator (say, dollars per bushel) we can determine the *gross processing margin*, otherwise known as the *soybean crush*. Converting the oil price is easy: Just multiply the oil price (quoted in dollars per pound) by 11—the number of pounds of oil yielded by the average bushel of soybeans. You'll have to multiply the soy meal price by .022 (44 pounds per bushel divided by 2,000—the number of pounds in a short ton) to arrive at a dollar-bushel equivalent. Add the two results and subtract the cost of soybeans and—*voilà*—you have the gross margin. As an example, suppose we see:

> **gross processing margin**
>
> also known as crush, this is the amount of oil and/or meal that can be produced from soybeans.

> November soybeans at $6.07 per bushel.
> December soybean oil at $0.2692 per pound.
> December soybean meal at $172.70 per ton.
> GPM = [($0.2692 × 11) + ($172.70 × .022) − $6.07]
>   = $0.6796 per bushel
>   [(Oil Yield + Meal Yield) − Bean Cost]

The GPM tends to widen when the price of meal and oil are strong relative to soybeans. This could occur in the face of supply disruptions or an increase in demand. Processors then would have a strong incentive to buy raw soybeans and boost the output of the oil and meal products, which will, in turn, bring the GPM in line with its long-term equilibrium.

Speculators, too, can capitalize on shifts in the margin through spread trades. Buy the source (beans) and sell the products (oil and meal) when you expect the GPM to widen. The reverse—selling the products and buying beans—should be undertaken in the expectation of narrowing margins. The spread is undertaken on a 1:1:1 contract ratio.

Chicago Mercantile Exchange (CME)

20 South Wacker Drive
Chicago, IL 60606
Phone: (312) 930-1000
Web site: www.cme.com

Founded as the Chicago Butter and Egg Board in 1898, the market became the CME in 1919. In 1961, with the introduction of pork belly futures, the CME became the first exchange to trade contracts for storable meat. Another CME first came three years later when the first futures contract on a nonstorable commodity—live cattle—was launched.

Principal Commodities

Commodity	*Contract size*
Feeder cattle	50,000 pounds
Live cattle	40,000 pounds
Frozen pork bellies	40,000 pounds
Lean hogs	40,000 pounds
Random-length lumber	110,000 board feet

Feeder cattle: Feeder cattle are 650- to 849-pound steers placed in feedlots for fattening. Feeder prices are influenced by factors that affect both the feed grain and fed (live) cattle markets. In general, feeder cattle prices tend to rise most strongly from May through early August. Summer volatility ends typically with peak prices being reached in October. Prices stabilize at lower levels in the fall.

Live cattle: Live cattle are fed steers weighing about 1,200 pounds, finished to yield USDA Choice or Select cuts. Live cattle prices, like those for feeders, see their greatest strength in the first half of the year, reaching a seasonal peak in May before stabilizing in early summer.

Pork bellies: Pork bellies are nothing more than bacon in storage. Prices are influenced by the supply and demand for hogs, other pork products, and competing meats. Pork bellies exhibit two significant seasonal trends: Prices tend to decline from May through mid-June, and then rise dramatically through July and August.

Lumber: Lumber futures call for the delivery of structural two-by-fours. Not surprisingly, prices are influenced heavily by building demand. Seasonal peaks are usually reached in February, ahead of a decline lasting through mid-May. After bottoming in fall, prices usually turn bullish through year's end.

Ethanol: The demand for ethanol (grain alcohol) has soared with its increasing use as a fuel additive and replacement. In the United States, ethanol is made primarily from corn. Brazil's feedstock is sugarcane. Ethanol futures don't have a lengthy trading history, so long-term seasonal patterns haven't yet been established. Ethanol prices are significantly influenced by corn supply factors and roughly parallel movements in the unleaded gasoline market. The recent call to increase the use of ethanol to decrease our dependence on foreign oil could have a profound effect on this market.

New York Board of Trade (NYBOT)

World Financial Center
One North End Avenue
New York, NY 10282
Phone: (800) 433-4348
Web site: www.nybot.com

The NYBOT was created in 1998 as the Coffee, Sugar and Cocoa Exchange and the New York Cotton Exchange entered into a multistage merger agreement. By June 2004, the merger was completed, making the NYBOT the nation's primary marketplace for *softs*, or soft commodities (see the following).

Principal Commodities

Commodity	Contract size
Cocoa	10 metric tons
Coffee "C"	37,500 pounds
Frozen concentrated orange juice	15,000 pounds
Sugar #11	112,000 pounds
Cotton #2	50,000 pounds

Cocoa: Ivory Coast, Ghana, Nigeria, and Cameroon account for nearly two-thirds of the world's production of cocoa. Ivory Coast alone produces more than 40 percent. Brazil, too, is a significant source, but disease has recently curtailed production. Seasonal tendencies in cocoa are not very strong. Still, cocoa tends to peak in March, followed by slackening demand through June. Prices tend to rise most dramatically after the seasonal low through July.

Coffee: Coffee is second in value only to crude oil as a cash commodity. The most widely produced coffee variety is Arabica, accounting for 70 percent of world production. Arabica grows in high altitudes, with Brazil and Colombia being the single largest producers. Brazil's frost season runs from May through early August. In anticipation of frost-induced tightness, the price of coffee is firm in February and rises through May. This seasonal tendency may be tempered by supplies from competing producers such as Mexico. Another bullish trend usually develops during the winter when coffee consumption tends to rise.

Orange juice: Since frozen concentrated orange juice was developed in 1945, oranges have become the main fruit crop in the United States. Still, the world's largest producer is Brazil, followed by Florida, the U.S. primary supplier. Seasonality in orange juice prices is most often influenced by harvest, production, and demand factors. While freezes rarely factor into the supply equation, cold snaps in the growing regions can force prices upward. The most significant seasonal tendency is a general price decline from November to January.

Sugar: Sugar is produced in more than 100 countries around the world. About 25 percent is processed from sugar beets and the remainder from sugarcane. Brazil, a cane sugar producer, is the world's largest exporter. Production in the United States is evenly divided between beet sugar and cane sugar. Sugar prices tend to peak in November, following seasonal lows in September as northern hemisphere demand rises. Declines in the August–to–early September time frame usually set up the rally.

Cotton: Cotton is the United States' fifth largest cash crop and a principal agricultural export. The U.S. Cotton Belt stretches from northern Florida, up to North Carolina and westward to California. Within the Belt, planting season can stretch from February to early June. Prices tend to rise over this period, then ease over the long growing season. Lows are generally reached by October. Dry weather is required for harvest, so unexpected precipitation can lower yields and impact prices.

New York Mercantile Exchange (NYMEX)

World Financial Center
One North End Avenue
New York, NY 10282
Phone: (212) 299-2000
Web site: www.nymex.com

Founded as the Butter and Cheese Exchange of New York in 1872, NYMEX adopted its current name in 1882. It has since become best known for energy trading. In 1994, NYMEX merged with the Commodity Exchange, Inc.—the nation's primary marketplace for metals futures. COMEX now operates as a subsidiary division of NYMEX.

Principal Commodities

Commodity	Contract size
Light sweet crude oil	1,000 barrels
Heating oil	42,000 U.S. gallons
Unleaded gasoline	42,000 U.S. gallons
Gold	100 troy ounces
Silver	5,000 troy ounces
Copper	25,000 pounds
Platinum	50 troy ounces

Crude oil: Crude oil is the first-stage product of oil drilling. Crude oil is designated by grades of viscosity and sulfur content. Light sweet crude—the grade that serves as the basis of the NYMEX contract—is a preferred refinery feedstock because of its low sulfur content and high yield of end products such as gasoline, diesel fuel, heating oil, and jet fuel. Crude oil prices tend to rise during the summer driving season (June to September) and decline thereafter to a seasonal bottom in early December.

Heating oil: Second only to gasoline, heating oil is the single largest end product of oil refining. Heating oil accounts for a quarter of the yield from a barrel of crude oil. Common knowledge holds that a $1 increase in the price of crude oil translates into a 2.5-cent-per-gallon rise in heating oil, so heating oil prices are highly correlated with those of crude. Nonetheless, heating oil prices also respond quickly to supply and demand shifts due to weather or refinery shutdowns.

Gasoline: More than half of each barrel of crude oil refined in the United States is processed into gasoline, making this fuel the most significant distillate. Though highly correlated with crude oil prices, gasoline prices tend to be more volatile. The most dramatic price increases tend to occur in the March-to-April time frame, with another bull run typically seen in the summer drive season. Like soybean processors, refiners also try to maximize their profit margins by monitoring the price of crude oil in relation to the value of distillate products, namely heating and gasoline. The *crack spread*—named for the cracking towers in which the crude is separated under heat and pressure into various derivatives—represents the gross profit derived from refining. A classic crack spread can be simulated by comparing the value of three crude oil contracts to that of two unleaded gasoline contracts and one heating oil contract. This reflects a yield of two barrels of gasoline and one barrel of heating oil for every three barrels of crude oil refined. Keep in mind that there are 42 U.S. gallons in a barrel of oil, so oil contracts are actually the same size as gasoline and heating oil futures. All you need to do is multiply the distillate prices by 42 to determine their barrel-equivalent levels.

October crude oil at $75.17 per barrel.
October gasoline at $2.0857 per gallon.
October heating oil at $2.0808 per gallon.
Crack spread (gross refining margin)

Product Yield ($2.0857 × 42 gallons × 2)	
+ ($2.0808 × 42 gallons × 1)	262.59
Less Crude Oil Cost ($75.17 × 3)	− 225.51
Margin	$ 37.08
	÷ 3
Per Barrel	$ 12.36

At these prices, the refining margin is approximately 16 percent ($12.36 ÷ $75.17).

Gold: Valued for its rarity, beauty, and near-indestructibility, gold has served as a store of value for millennia. Aside from being employed as bullion and coinage, gold is used in jewelry, electronics, and dentistry. South Africa is the world's largest-producing nation, followed by Australia and the United States. Gold generally exhibits bullishness from August through early October, as jewelry manufacturing demand steps up in anticipation of the coming Christmas season.

Silver: Along with gold, silver has been used as money for centuries. In fact, this white metal has even more industrial applications than gold. Photographic materials are the greatest consumers of silver, followed by electronics, brazing alloys and solders, batteries, jewelry, tableware, and mirrors. Mexico, Peru, Australia, China, and the United States are the world's primary suppliers. Silver exhibits its greatest seasonal strength from November through mid-February. Prices tend to decline thereafter through midsummer.

Copper: Copper, because of its conductivity, corrosion resistance, and malleability, has diverse industrial uses. Electrical applications account for about three-quarters of total copper demand, with the building construction being the single largest market. Not surprisingly, copper demand is strongly correlated with general economic growth factors and, in particular, with the strength of the building industry. Chile tops the list of world copper producers. The United States, Indonesia, and Australia are secondary suppliers. A seasonal uptick in copper prices is usual during summer, most particularly in July.

Platinum: Platinum is one of the world's rarest metals, more scarce than gold. Like gold, platinum does not tarnish, so it is highly valued in the jewelry industry. In fact, the jewelry industry is the single largest consumer of platinum, accounting for more than half of total demand. Automobile catalytic converters use another fifth of platinum production, with the balance going for use in the production of electronic equipment, fertilizers, explosives, and other automotive components. South Africa is the largest supplier of platinum, followed by Russia, Canada, and the United States. Seasonality is weak in the platinum market, though prices normally rise most briskly in February.

Kansas City Board of Trade (KCBOT)

4800 Main Street, Suite 303
Kansas City, MO 64112
Phone: (816) 753-7500
Web site: www.kcbot.com

KCBT was founded in 1856. Formally chartered in 1869, KCBOT commenced trading futures in 1876.

Principal Commodity

Commodity	Contract size
Wheat	5,000 bushels

Kansas City Board of Trade's wheat contract is based on hard red winter wheat (HRW). Used primarily in the manufacture of flour for bread making, HRW accounts for nearly half of domestic production. HRW is grown predominantly in Kansas, Nebraska, Oklahoma, and the Texas panhandle.

Minneapolis Grain Exchange (MGE)

400 South 4th Street
Minneapolis, MN 55415
Phone: (800) 827-4746
Web site: www.mgex.com

Established in 1881 as the Minneapolis Chamber of Commerce, MGE launched its first futures contract in 1883. In 1947, the market-place formally became known as the MGE.

Principal Commodity

Commodity	Contract size
Wheat	5,000 bushels

Hard red spring wheat (HRS) is the basis for contracts traded at the MGE. Grown in the Northern Plains states of Montana, Wyoming, the Dakotas, and Idaho, HRS is milled primarily for hearth breads, bagels, and blending with HRW wheat for bread and bun production.

CBOE Futures Exchange (CFE)

400 South LaSalle Street
Chicago, IL 60605
Phone: (877) 843-2263
Web site: cfe.cboe.com

Launched in March 2004, CFE is a wholly owned subsidiary of the Chicago Board Options Exchange (CBOE), one of the primary market-places for stock and index option trading. CBOE itself was created by members of the CBOT in 1973 as the world's first exchange dedicated to the trading of equity options.

Principal Commodity

Commodity	Contract size
Gas at the Pump	10,000 U.S. gallons

CFE trades half-a-dozen gas-at-the-pump futures that track prices of regular-grade gasoline sold at retail gasoline outlets throughout the United States. One contract is based on the nationwide weighted average price. Additional contracts reflect the retail price of gasoline in five geographic regions: the East Coast, the Midwest, the Gulf Coast, the Rocky Mountains, and the West Coast.

CFE's contracts differ from the gasoline futures traded on the NYMEX in several ways. First, CFE contracts are about one-quarter the size of NYMEX's standard futures. The Chicago contracts, too, reflect retail prices, where NYMEX futures are based upon wholesale lots. Finally, CFE contracts are *cash-settled*, meaning there is no opportunity for physical delivery. At expiration, outstanding contracts result in an exchange of cash based upon the final settlement price.

HedgeStreet

P.O. Box 5861
San Mateo, CA 94402
Web site: www.hedgestreet.com

Principal Commodities

Commodities	Contract size
Gasoline	$100
Crude oil	$100
Silver	$100
Gold	$100

Launched in 2004, HedgeStreet is a nontraditional exchange offering cash-settled *binaries* and *capped futures*. Binaries—actually a type of *option*—are "yes" and "no" positions built around a proposition such as "Will retail gasoline prices exceed $3.05 per gallon by July 15?" Traders

binaries

a type of options
contract with
a "yes" or "no"
feature. Bullish
traders choose
yes. Bearish
traders
choose no.

**capped
futures**

a type of futures
contract that is
limited in price by
a ceiling on the
upside and a floor
on the downside.

adopting the "yes" position buy the contract, while those believing "no" would sell. Binaries offer fixed payouts of either $0 or $10 ($0 or $100) at expiration, depending upon the contract size.

Capped futures offer wagers on a price range for a particular commodity, bound by a ceiling (or cap) on the upside and a floor on the downside. For example, a capped future based upon the proposition "Gold $650-670 (July 22)" offers variable payouts between $0 and $100, depending on incremental movements in the price of gold by the July 22 expiration.

Buyers make $5 for every $1 increase in gold above $650, up to $670—making $100 the maximum possible gain if gold trades at or above $670. For sellers, the reverse is true. Sellers make $5 for each $1 *decrease* in gold below $370, down to $350, with the $100 maximum gain earned if gold sells for $350 or less.

HedgeStreet is unique in that it is an all-electronic market designed for retail investors. No brokers are involved in HedgeStreet dealings, at least as far as retail investors see. All transactions are conducted through the HedgeStreet web site. Traders, in fact, become members of the HedgeStreet exchange when they open their trading accounts.

Summary

Actively traded commodity futures contracts include precious and industrial metals, energy products, grains, oilseeds, livestock, and soft commodities such as cocoa, coffee, sugar, orange juice, and cotton. The spot or cash market refers to the market for the immediate sale or purchase of these commodities. Futures represent contracts between two parties to sell or purchase a specific commodity by a specific date in the future.

The futures market has developed into an efficient way for producers and users of commodities to hedge price risk. Farmers, oil companies, and airlines are examples of entities that sometimes use futures to hedge against changes in commodity prices. Speculators enter the futures market to make profits from possible moves in commodity prices. Therefore, the futures market consists of two main players: hedgers and speculators.

Chances are, if you are reading this book, you are not a hedger but an investor interested in making profits or diversifying your portfolio by using commodities. If so, chances are that you will not be actively buying the commodity itself, but using other investments that move with commodity prices, including options, stocks, and futures contracts. This chapter was designed to provide you with a solid introduction into the futures market, which can be used in conjunction with the remainder of this book to develop and apply strategies using commodities futures.

Key Summary Points

1. Commodities and futures markets serve an important purpose—they bring buyers and sellers together in one location.
2. Through the years, the markets have developed into an efficient way for producers and users of commodities to hedge price risk.
3. Hedgers often use futures to protect positions.
4. A hedger will have two positions in a commodity—one in the cash market and one in the futures.
5. Basis is the difference between the price on the spot or cash market and the price in the futures market.
6. Speculators use futures in an effort to earn profits by correctly forecasting price movements.
7. Speculators add liquidity to the market.
8. Buying futures obligates a trader to take delivery of a specific amount and quality of a commodity within a specified period, unless the contract is sold before the delivery period.
9. A seller of a futures contract undertakes the obligation to deliver the commodity unless the contract is subsequently repurchased.
10. Futures transactions are secured by good faith deposits known as margin.
11. A margin deposit represents a small portion of a commodity's actual value, so futures gains and losses are highly leveraged.
12. Futures are traded on centralized exchanges either by open outcry auction or by electronic price matching.
13. Clearinghouses ensure the financial integrity of the markets, facilitate the settlement of trades, and handle delivery.

14. Delivery occurs when a futures contract is exercised and the ownership of the commodity is transferred from one party to the next.

15. Most traders avoid delivery.

16. Volume represents the number of contracts traded over a period of time.

17. Open interest is the number of contracts outstanding and helps reflect the contract's liquidity.

18. Actively traded commodity futures contracts include precious and industrial metals, energy products, grains, oilseeds, livestock, and "soft" commodities such as cocoa, coffee, sugar, orange juice, and cotton.

Commodity Trading in the Stock Market

Ask a stockbroker about the dos and don'ts of commodity futures trading and you're likely to get a laundry list that includes a lot more. The inherent risk of leverage will undoubtedly be highlighted as well as the volatility of commodity prices. It's a safe bet the broker will end up asking why you'd want to trade commodity futures when you could invest in commodity stocks instead.

But are commodity futures really all that risky? Wharton finance professor, Gary Gorton, and finance professor at the Yale School of Management, K. Geert Rouwenhorst teamed up to research this very issue. Their findings indicate that commodities aren't *that* risky. Their paper, entitled, "Facts and Fantasies about Commodity Futures," examined the risks and returns of commodity futures, stocks, and bonds over nearly five decades. To measure risk, the researchers built an index from data maintained by the *Commodity Research Bureau*, which has tracked futures contract prices since 1959. The index covered more than three dozen domestic and foreign commodity contracts—from aluminum to zinc— traded between July 1959 and December 2004. As each contract expired, a new one was acquired to maintain continuity. Holdings were rebalanced

Commodity Research Bureau
established in 1934, the CRB is a provider of market information for commodities and futures prices.

standard deviation

a statistical measure that tracks scattering from the mean.

every month to maintain an equal investment in each commodity. The Yale futures index actually displayed *less* risk than stocks in the 45-year span examined. Commodities exhibited a *standard deviation* of only 12.10 percent compared to 14.85 percent for the Standard & Poor's 500 stock index. A bigger standard deviation means an investment is more volatile, with wider swings up and down.

But can commodity producers' stocks actually substitute for futures themselves? The Wharton/Yale study attempted to match publicly traded companies engaged in the production of commodities with futures on the underlying products. Of the 17 historical matches found, the cumulative performance of futures significantly exceeded the cumulative returns of their corresponding equities. The *correlation* between commodity prices and those of commodity stocks was fairly low—lower, in fact, than the correlation to the S&P 500. That said, it seems that commodity company stocks act more like other stocks than futures, making them a rather poor substitute for commodity investments.

correlation

a statistical measure of how two investments move in relation to one another. Correlation ranges between −1 and +1. Positive correlation denotes that the investment vehicles move in the same direction, while negative correlation characterizes an inverse relationship. A correlation of zero indicates that movements are completely random.

Still, people invest in commodity stocks hoping to derive some of the benefits that commodities offer. To the degree that the revenues of commodity producers tend to increase in inflationary periods, some producers' stocks, in fact, do exhibit bullishness. Increasing demand for oil from China and India, for instance, puts sustained pressure on crude prices and also has benefited holders of oil refiner stocks. A falling U.S. dollar, too, can lead to increases in commodity prices and commodity stocks. Jim Rogers, former hedge fund manager, professor, and author of the book *Hot Commodities*, looks for a bull run in commodity prices extending into the next decade, singling out sugar in particular for outsized gains.

If you can't trade futures, commodity stocks may be your next best bet. Still, you must pick the *right* stock to derive the full benefit of a commodity price trend. Some companies are low-cost producers; others are less efficient. The Wharton/Yale researchers found nearly 300 publicly traded natural gas producers to match up to natural gas futures. In a market like that, you're left to ask, "Which one of these is the *best* proxy for natural gas itself?" (The Wharton/Yale study dispensed with that question by including *all* companies in its index.) It's a challenge for most investors to find the right company because they must deal with management concerns, competitive market issues, and a myriad of other matters that have nothing to do with the price of the actual commodities.

Commodity pricing tends to be pretty straightforward. It boils down to supply and demand. If there's too much natural gas around, prices are likely to go down; when supplies are scarce, prices rise.

Another complication arises when you consider that that there may not be a direct match between a commodity and a publicly traded producer. For example, there are no pure plays for beef production in the stock market. You can't buy a feedlot operator's stock on the open market.

You have to decide how much "purity" you want in your stock selection as well. Norsk Hydro ASA, for example, can be classified as an aluminum producer, although it's better known for its oil, gas, and hydropower business. Platinum is another example. There are no platinum pure plays traded in the U.S. equities market, though stocks based on platinum's sister metal, palladium, can be found.

To help you pinpoint commodity stock plays, major commodity producers are listed here, ranked by market value. Only those stocks traded in the United States, on the New York Stock Exchange, the American Stock Exchange, or the NASDAQ marketplace, are shown. The tables are pretty straightforward, but some terms may require definition. (All figures are current as of August 2006 and may be subject to change.)

- *American Depository Receipts (ADRs) and American Depository Shares (ADSs):* A certificate issued by a U.S. bank representing a certain number of a foreign company's shares. ADRs and ADSs are traded in U.S. dollars on American exchanges just like a domestic stock, negating the need for currency conversion or a foreign brokerage account.

- *Market capitalization:* A measure of a company's total value, calculated by multiplying the number of outstanding shares by the current market price of one share. At most, the five largest public companies producing a given commodity are shown. Some commodity categories may have fewer publicly traded producers.

- *Average volume:* An indication of a company's liquidity, this is the average number of shares traded daily over the past quarter.

- *Price-earnings ratio:* Found by dividing a company's stock price by its annual earnings per share, a P/E ratio expresses the value of a company in terms of its ability to generate profits. In general, a high P/E suggests that investors are expecting higher earnings growth in the future compared to companies with lower P/Es. The P/E ratio is sometimes referred to as the "multiple" because it shows how much investors are willing to pay per dollar of earnings. For example, a company trading at a multiple of 18 offers investors the opportunity to buy one dollar of current earnings for each $18 of share price. Value-minded investors prefer to own shares of companies with low multiples.

- *Dividend yield:* Some, but not all, companies pay out part of their earnings to their shareholders in the form of cash dividends. Calculated by dividing the annual dividend by a stock's current price, the dividend yield shows how much a company pays in dividends each year relative to its share value. Dividends are a cushion: The dividend yield represents the return on investment for a stock if no capital gains were earned through price appreciation.

Metals

Several producers of precious and industrial metals are publicly traded. Your ability to find the right stock in large part depends upon *transparency*—the degree to which a company accurately discloses vital data. Some companies are simply more forthcoming about their *production costs* and metal reserves than others.

production costs
the outlays associated with producing goods or services.

To be a successful mining stock investor, you first must make a distinction between those companies already producing metal profitably and those still in the exploration stage. Not surprisingly, producers are safer bets; exploration companies are far more speculative.

Smart Trader Tips

Mining is a capital-intensive business, so companies with lots of money in the bank or access to financing from large investment banks are more conservative plays, especially for novice investors.

Size *does* matter for mining stocks. Small producers have trouble convincing lenders or equity investors to finance operations. Buying into these, therefore, can be highly speculative—generally speaking, the larger the potential resource, the better. With gold mines, experts suggest looking for outfits with proven reserves of 2 to 3 million ounces and more. With silver, 100 million ounces is the threshold. For copper, a million tons in an open-pit mine is a smallish operation; a billion tons is huge. Care should be taken when looking at reserves. Sometimes reports are made in *long tons* rather than *short tons*. A long ton is 2,200 pounds; a short ton is 2,000 pounds.

Even with large resources, a mining company must still get the metal out of the ground at a reasonable cost. If deposits are too deep under the surface or of very low grade, recovery costs can run too high, making mining economically unsound. A near-surface gold deposit of 1 or 2 grams—1 gram is about .032 ounce—per ton in an open-pit environment might justify mining, but underground, or shaft, mines are another matter. Costs for underground mines are invariably higher. The depth, the continuity, and the width of the ore vein come into play, as well as other factors. Generally, underground mines must seek high-grade ore deposits across wide zones to make them competitive with open-pit operations. Environmental cleanup in either case can be costly.

Production costs figure highly in the mining stock selection process. Companies with high production costs are inherently more risky since low metal prices can make them unprofitable. A mine producing gold at $350 per ounce doesn't make much when gold trades at $375, but at $450, mining profits soar. Companies operating at high costs—within $100 of gold's market price, for instance—are generally shunned by all but the most aggressive investors. Also, some gold mining companies hedge their exposures to changes in gold prices. Others do not. Those companies that do not hedge tend to have more volatility as share prices react to daily moves in spot gold prices.

Earnings per share (EPS), a critical measure followed by most stock investors, can be a muddle where mines are concerned because of a multitude of noncash charges and accounting complexities associated with metal production.

earnings per share (EPS)
the amount of profits generated for each of the company's shares outstanding.

Smart Trader Tip

Looking solely at a company's income statement, where earnings per share (EPS) are found, can be deceiving. Noncash charges such as depreciation and depletion allowances are included in a company's bottom-line numbers. Cash flow is calculated by adding back these noncash charges to net income after taxes, thus backing out everything but the *real* cost of doing business.

cash flow
the amount of net cash generated by an investment or business during a specific period of time. Or the money received by a business minus the money that is paid out.

Cash flow is a much more clear-cut measure. Cash flow represents a company's ability to throw off cash. Attention, in particular, should be paid to *operating* cash flows, which reflect the cash generated by actual mining. The greater and more consistent the cash flow, the better. You can gauge the relative bargain a stock represents by noting its *price–cash flow (P/CF) ratio,* which is found by dividing a company's stock price by its cash flow per share; the lower the ratio, the better the bargain.

Costs are another benchmark for mining stocks. If you can reduce costs to a per-ounce or per-pound basis, you can put one mining company against another in a direct comparison. A buck invested in an outfit that gets you $25 of metal in the ground is a better deal than a company with very similar fundamentals and reserves offering only $15 in resources. Again, your ability to make such comparisons depends on the forthrightness of the mining companies to accurately divulge their production costs and reserves.

There are obvious differences between precious and industrial metal mining operations. Gold is the polar opposite of an industrial metal like copper. The demand for gold is almost entirely financial or jewelry-related; very little gold is actually consumed. Copper, on the other hand, is used primarily in construction applications, either in plumbing or electrical systems. Silver has a foot in both worlds; some is bought for consumption, some held for financial protection or profit.

Silver, gold, and copper often are linked at the source, though. Most silver mines, in fact, are primarily operations looking for other metals (i.e., lead, zinc, copper, or gold). Silver is a by-product of these operations. In fact, 70 to 80 percent of all silver is produced as a by-product of copper, lead, and zinc mining. Because the by-product element is so large in the supply of new silver, production doesn't respond much to price. This makes the few mines that do produce primarily silver extremely risky. Over the past two decades—with silver being dug out by copper, lead, and zinc miners regardless of how low the price went—most pure silver mines consistently lost money. None were especially profitable.

Aluminum is produced primarily from bauxite, an ore containing aluminum oxide. Alumina, an intermediate product, is first extracted from the bauxite, and then oxygen is removed from the alumina by an electrolytic process. This usually requires large amounts of electric power. Aluminum manufacturing is a highly cyclical and capital-intensive industry. Economic slowdowns influence the demand for aluminum; user industries like infrastructure, transportation, consumer durables, and housing are affected.

Cost efficiency plays a critical role in the industry, especially control over raw material expense. Raw material and power typically constitute more than half of a producer's total operating expenses. An integrated operation (i.e., a firm with a captive mining capacity) is better able to protect its input costs. Captive power facilities can also keep a check on costs.

Palladium, a platinum group metal, is generally little known to investors. Palladium, like platinum, is much less abundant than gold. And like platinum, palladium can be used in catalytic converters to reduce emissions from internal combustion engines. Palladium is mostly a by-product of nickel mining. At present, Russia controls around three-quarters of the world's nickel supply. Through its state-owned monopoly, Russia can easily put a squeeze on palladium supplies.

Gold

See Table 3.1.

- *Anglo American plc:* The market value leader among gold producers is Anglo American plc (AAUK), a London-based company that owns worldwide stakes in gold, platinum, diamond, and ferrous and base metal mines, as well as coal operations.

AAUK's price–cash flow (P/CF) ratio last stood at 11.2 (www .angloamerican.co.uk).

- *Barrick Gold Corporation:* Toronto-based Barrick (ABX) has operations in North and South America, Africa, and Australia with 88.6 million ounces of total proven and probable gold and mineral reserves. ABX's P/CF was clocked at 19.8 in 2006 (www.barrick.com).

- *Newmont Mining Corporation:* With 93.2 million ounces of proven and probable gold reserves, Denver's Newmont Mining Corporation (NEM) has operations stretching from North and South America to Asia, Africa, and New Zealand. NEM carried an 18.7 cash flow multiple at press time (www.newmont.com).

- *AngloGold Ashanti Ltd.:* AngloGold Ashanti (AU), producing 6 million ounces annually, has operations on four continents. Its major stakeholder—with a 42 percent interest—is Anglo American plc. The company's P/CF ratio was a whopping 113.2 in 2006 (www.anglogoldashanti.com).

- *GoldCorp Inc.:* With proven and probable reserves exceeding 25 million ounces, Vancouver's GoldCorp (GG) concentrates its mining operations in the Americas and in Australia. GG's cash flow multiple of 20.0 makes it one of the more expensive producers (www.goldcorp.com).

TABLE 3.1   Gold Producers

Company	Symbol	Market Capitalization	Average Volume	Price-Earnings Ratio	Dividend Yield
Anglo American plc ADR	AAUK	$71.3 billion	1.4 million	47.0	4.2%
Barrick Gold Corporation	ABX	$28.5 billion	4.5 million	23.3	0.7%
Newmont Mining Corporation	NEM	$23.6 billion	6.6 million	42.4	0.8%
AngloGold Ashanti Ltd. ADR	AU	$13.8 billion	1.4 million	(negative)	1.3%
GoldCorp Inc.	GG	$12.7 billion	6.7 million	25.8	0.6%

Silver

See Table 3.2.

- *Silver Wheaton Corp.:* A separately traded subsidiary of Gold-Corp, Vancouver-based Silver Wheaton (SLW) purchases silver from mines in Mexico, Sweden, and Peru. The company's 36.8 price–cash flow ratio is middling for top silver producers (www.silverwheaton.com).

- *Pan American Silver Corporation:* Peru and Mexico are the principal mining sites for Pan American Silver Corporation (PAAS). The Vancouver company also has operations in Argentina and Bolivia. Total production currently stands at 14 million ounces. The company's P/CF ratio is 25.78 (www.panamericansilver.com).

- *Silver Standard Resources Inc.:* An exploration company, Silver Standard (SSRI) has five principal property interests in Argentina, Australia, Mexico, and the United States. Smaller interests in Peru, Chile, and Canada round out the portfolio of this Vancouver company. SSRI's speculative posture is reflected in its 135.1 cash flow multiple (www.silver-standard.com).

- *Apex Silver Mines Limited:* Based in the Cayman Islands, Apex Silver Mines (SIL) claims its principal project in Bolivia has total proven and probable ore reserves totaling 231 million tonnes. SIL has additional interests in Peru, Argentina, and Mexico. SIL's cash flow multiple is –5.5 (www.apexsilver.com).

TABLE 3.2 Silver Producers

Company	Symbol	Market Capitalization	Average Volume	Price-Earnings Ratio	Dividend Yield
Silver Wheaton Corp.	SLW	$2.3 billion	1.4 million	39.1	–
Pan American Silver Corporation	PAAS	$1.6 billion	1.4 million	(negative)	–
Silver Standard Resources Inc.	SSRI	$1.3 billion	765 thousand	131.1	–
Apex Silver Mines Limited	SIL	$1.0 billion	641 thousand	(negative)	–
Hecla Mining Company	HL	$732.3 million	1.7 million	23.3	–

- *Hecla Mining Company:* Cranking out 6 million ounces of silver annually, Hecla Mining (HL) is the sole American company in the top five. The company, based in Coeur d'Alene, Idaho, holds interests in Venezuelan, Mexican, and U.S. operations. HL's 11.5 cash flow multiple makes it one of the cheapest silver producers (www.hecla-mining.com).

Copper

See Table 3.3.

- *Phelps Dodge Corporation:* The Phelps Dodge (PD) Mining Company division produces copper out of five U.S. sites and three South American operations. Operations include open-pit and underground mining, as well as other extraction methods. The Phoenix-based company has a 10.4 P/CF ratio (www.phelps dodge.com). Note: Phelps Dodge is currently being acquired by Freeport-McMoRan Copper & Gold.

- *Inco Limited:* Headquartered in Toronto, the principal mining and processing operations of Inco (N) are located in Canada and Indonesia. Primarily noted for nickel production, Inco produced 277 million pounds of refined copper and related products in 2005. Inco's 12.2 P/CF ratio offers a modest value play (www.inco.com).

- *Southern Copper Corporation:* Another Phoenix-based company, Southern Copper (PCU) is a subsidiary of Americas Mining Corporation. Mining and exploration operations are located in Peru and Mexico; additional exploration activities are conducted in Chile. Production totaled 1,521 billion pounds of copper in 2005. The company's 6.8 P/CF ratio makes it the cheapest stock in the top five (www.southernperu.com).

- *Freeport-McMoRan Copper & Gold Inc.:* Freeport-McMoRan (FCX), based in New Orleans, operates mining operations in Indonesia. The company claims to be the lowest-cost copper producer in the world, after taking into account credits for related gold and silver production. FCX's efficiency is reflected in its 7.2 cash flow multiple (www.fcx.com).

TABLE 3.3 Copper Producers

Company	Symbol	Market Capitalization	Average Volume	Price-Earnings Ratio	Dividend Yield
Phelps Dodge Corporation	PD	$18.6 billion	7.4 million	14.3	0.9%
Inco Limited	N	$15.4 billion	2.5 million	25.2	0.6%
Southern Copper Corporation	PCU	$13.5 billion	1.7 million	8.2	8.9%
Freeport-McMoRan Copper & Gold Inc.	FCX	$10.7 billion	5.2 million	9.5	2.3%
Ivanhoe Mines Ltd.	IVN	$2.1 billion	711 thousand	(negative)	–

- *Ivanhoe Mines Ltd.:* Ivanhoe Mines (IVN) is an exploration- and development-phase company with copper operations in southern Mongolia, Myanmar (Burma), and Australia. A –24.1 P/CF ratio bespeaks the company's status as a development enterprise (www. ivanhoe-mines.com).

Aluminum

See Table 3.4.

- *Alcoa Inc.:* New York–based Alcoa Inc. (AA) produces primary aluminum and fabricated products for use in aircraft, automobiles, commercial transportation, packaging, consumer products, building and construction, and industrial applications. Sales of aluminum and alumina (an intermediate product) account for three-quarters of AA's revenues. Activities are based in Australia, Brazil, China, Iceland, Jamaica, Russia, and Trinidad, and the U.S. AA's cash flow multiple is 8.0 (www.alcoa.com).

- *Alcan Inc.:* Alcan Inc. (AL), based in Montreal, engages primarily in bauxite mining and alumina refining activities in the United States, Europe, and Asia Pacific, as well as finished product manufacturing. AL's recent purchase of French aluminum maker Pechiney gave the company its European foothold. AL boasts a rather modest 10.4 P/CF ratio (www.alcan.com).

TABLE 3.4   Aluminum Producers

Company	Symbol	Market Capitalization	Average Volume	Price-Earnings Ratio	Dividend Yield
Alcoa Inc.	AA	$24.9 billion	6.5 million	13.5	2.1%
Alcan Inc.	AL	$17.5 billion	2.3 million	28.1	1.7%
Aluminum Corporation of China ADS	ACH	$7.3 billion	101 thousand	8.1	4.0%
Kaiser Aluminum	KALU	$800.1 million	27 thousand	(negative)	–
Maxxam Inc.	MXM	$161.4 million	3 thousand	(negative)	–

- *Aluminum Corporation of China:* Based in Beijing, the primary market for Aluminum Corporation of China (ACH) is the People's Republic of China and Hong Kong. ACH engages in the production and sale of alumina, primary aluminum, and bauxite mining. A P/CF ratio of 6.3 makes ACH one of the world's cheapest aluminum producers (www.chalco.com.cn).

- *Kaiser Aluminum:* A producer of aluminum ingots and fabricated aluminum products used in automotive, aerospace, and general engineering applications, Kaiser Aluminum (KALU) is based in Southern California. KALU also owns a large stake in a Welsh aluminum smelter. KALU's negative 3.0 cash flow multiple reflects its recent emergence from Chapter 11 bankruptcy (www.kaiseral.com).

- *Maxxam Inc.:* Houston's Maxxam Inc. (MXM), through it subsidiaries, has grown into a diversified firm engaged in exploiting old growth forests for lumber products, real estate investments, and pari-mutuel racing. MXM's involvement in the aluminum business comes through its 62 percent stake in Kaiser Aluminum. MXM boasts a 4.0 P/CF ratio.

Palladium

See Table 3.5.

- *Stillwater Mining Company:* A subsidiary of Norimet Limited, Stillwater Mining Company (SWC) refines palladium, platinum, and associated minerals from its Billings, Montana, base. The company claims 2.5 million ounces in proven reserves of palladium plus platinum. SWC carries a 12.7 cash flow multiple (www.stillwater mining.com).

TABLE 3.5 Palladium Producers					
Company	Symbol	Market Capitalization	Average Volume	Price-Earnings Ratio	Dividend Yield
Stillwater Mining Company	SWC	$907.4 million	718 thousand	(negative)	–
North American Palladium	PAL	$388.2 million	213 thousand	(negative)	–

- *North American Palladium Ltd.:* Headquartered in Toronto, North American Palladium (PAL) mines platinum group metals as well as other metals. PAL's principal property is an open-pit operation that produces platinum, gold, copper, and nickel as by-products. The speculative nature of PAL's operations is reflected in its –14.0 P/CF ratio (www.napalladium.com).

Energy

When oil prices soar, energy stocks generally move higher. At the same time, the rest of the stock market, concerned about the inflationary impact of expensive oil, tends to sell off. Thus, holding energy stocks is often thought of as a buffer against stock market losses when near-term oil supplies tighten.

Down cycles, however, punctuate every market. Some pundits warn that energy stocks may eventually end up like tech stocks in the last decade: driven skyward by irrational exuberance, ultimately fated for a hard landing. Certainly, the lower-than-market P/E ratios of energy stocks reflect an expectation of below-average growth in the energy sector in the future. The market is simply not valuing these companies as if they're likely to achieve the same level of growth they've enjoyed in the past. With that in mind, investors in energy stocks are wise to look for financially solid stocks paying decent dividends to help mute future share price swings.

Petroleum products can be broadly classified as kerosene, diesel, gasoline, naphtha, aviation fuel, and liquefied petroleum gas (LPG). As the name itself implies, crude is refined into various usage-based products or distillates. Without going into much complexity, the three broad classifications are heavy distillates such as heating oil, middle distillates like diesel and aviation fuel, and the light distillates such as LPG and gasoline. Margins are higher for the middle and light distillates.

The energy sector is inextricably linked to economic growth. When growth gains momentum, demand for petroleum products especially tends to increase, as petroleum is a primary source of energy. In terms of *elasticity,* demand for petroleum products is relatively inelastic relative to price changes, meaning that price hikes don't generally curb demand. However, increases in electrical power capacity, growth in tourism, and better agricultural sector performance tend to have a positive impact on petroleum companies, as these user segments rely heavily on petroleum products.

elasticity

the degree to which consumers respond to price changes in a commodity. A measure of elasticity can be taken by dividing the percentage change in demand by the percentage change in price. A quotient over 1 indicates relatively high elasticity; inelastic demand is indicated by a quotient under 1.

Oil refining is a very capital-intensive industry, so barriers to entry are high. New players have a hard time stealing market share from established operations. A refiner with a diverse product mix is better able to manage revenues by altering distillate output to match market demand; hence, the larger the refining capacity, the better.

Integrated operations combining exploration, refining, and distribution generally have an advantage over stand-alone refiners, as stand-alones must rely on external distribution networks to market their products.

Alternate fuel sources, such as natural gas, have the potential to adversely affect demand for refined distillates. Over the next decade, in fact, projections call for natural gas demand to grow faster than the demand for oil. Within 20 years, energy experts see natural gas commanding one-third of total energy demand. Most of the world's natural gas is now supplied by pipeline, but demand for liquefied natural gas (LNG), which can be transported by ship, is steadily rising. Many oil companies are diversifying into the business of producing and distributing natural gas.

Propane is produced as a by-product of natural gas processing and petroleum refining. Used primarily for home heating and as an alternative fuel for vehicles, most propane is domestically produced. Only a tenth of U.S. propane supplies are imports, coming via pipeline and railcar from Canada or by sea from West Africa, the Middle East, South America, and Western Europe.

Oil

See Table 3.6.

- *Total S.A.:* A French producer with proven reserves of 11.6 billion barrels of oil and gas equivalent, Total S.A. (TOT) has interests in 27 refineries and operates in 130 countries. Total engages in all aspects of the petroleum industry, including upstream (exploration), midstream (refining), and downstream (distribution and sales) operations. The company sells for an 8.0 cash flow multiple (www.total.com).

- *BP plc:* Based in London, BP plc (BP) is a producer of crude oil and natural gas and is also an oil refiner as well as a marketer of petrochemicals, natural gas, and natural gas liquids. BP operates the Trans-Alaska Pipeline and has interests in the Americas, Europe, Africa, the Middle East, and Asia. BP claims proven reserves of 18.3 billion barrels of oil and gas equivalent. BP's P/CF ratio was last measured at 7.7 (www.bp.com).

- *PetroChina Company Limited:* The oil- and gas-producing properties held by PetroChina Company (PTR) are located in the People's Republic of China, with proven reserves of approximately 11.5 billion barrels of crude oil and 48.1 trillion cubic feet of gas. PTR operates 25 refineries and 18,000 retail service stations. PTR is headquartered in Beijing, China. Its 9.0 cash flow multiple makes it the priciest integrated oil marketer in the top five (www.petrochina.com.cn).

- *ConocoPhillips Company:* Houston-based ConocoPhillips (COP) operates worldwide, producing and marketing crude oil, natural gas, and natural gas liquids as well as exploiting oil sands in Canada and the United States. COP claims proven reserves of 9.4 billion barrels of oil and gas equivalent. A 5.5 P/CF makes COP the cheapest of the big five integrated oil and gas firms (www.conocophillips.com).

- *Eni S.p.A.:* An Italian firm with proven reserves of 6.8 billion barrels of oil and gas equivalent, Eni (E) produces oil and gas through its interests in Africa, the Indian subcontinent, Australia, and the Gulf of Mexico. Eni also owns electricity generation stations in Italy with installed capacity of 4.5 gigawatts. Eni's 6.8 cash flow multiple places it near the cheap end of the top refiners (www.eni.it).

TABLE 3.6   Oil Refiners

Company	Symbol	Market Capitalization	Average Volume	Price-Earnings Ratio	Dividend Yield
Total S.A.	TOT	$334.1 billion	1.6 million	20.2	3.0%
BP plc	BP	$232.5 billion	3.6 million	11.9	3.4%
Petrochina Company Limited ADS	PTR	$208.4 billion	645 thousand	12.0	3.7%
ConocoPhillips Company	COP	$110.4 billion	9.2 million	6.2	2.2%
Eni S.p.A. ADR	E	$4.6 billion	392 thousand	6.4	4.2%

Natural Gas

See Table 3.7.

- *Exxon Mobil Corporation:* Exxon Mobil Corporation (XOM) operates in 200 countries and territories from its Texas base. XOM's natural gas division boasts of being the world's largest nongovernment marketer of natural gas, though Royal Dutch Shell (see following) asserts a competing claim for LNG. In any event, XOM sells 175 billion cubic meters of gas annually in addition to natural gas liquids. XOM's cash flow multiple stands at 8.4 currently (www.exxonmobil.com).

- *Royal Dutch Shell Class A:* Royal Dutch Shell (RDSA), through its Gas and Power segment, liquefies and transports natural gas from its base in the Netherlands. Exploration, development, and pipeline operations in North America and other countries round out RDSA's portfolio. RDSA claims proven reserves of 3.7 billion barrels of oil and gas equivalent and earns a 6.4 P/CF ratio (www.shell.com).

- *Chevron Corporation:* California's Chevron Corporation (CVX) oil-equivalent reserves are claimed to total 9 billion barrels. CVX's largest natural gas resources are in the United States, the Gulf of Mexico, Australia, and western Africa. Outside the United States, the majority of CVX's natural gas sales occur in southeast Asia, Europe, Australia, and Latin America. At 6.4, CVX's cash flow multiple is the same as Royal Dutch Shell's (www.chevron.com).

TABLE 3.7 Natural Gas Producers					
Company	Symbol	Market Capitalization	Average Volume	Price-Earnings Ratio	Dividend Yield
Exxon Mobil Corporation	XOM	$415.6 billion	22.0 million	10.9	1.9%
Royal Dutch Shell Class A	RDSA	$134.3 billion	1.1 million	9.4	3.0%
Chevron Corporation	CVX	$146.1 billion	9.5 million	9.2	3.1%
Petroleo Brasileiro S.A.	PBR	$101.2 billion	3.1 million	0.0	1.1%
Statoil ASA ADS	STO	$60.9 billion	633 thousand	10.3	1.7%

- *Petroleo Brasileiro S.A.:* From its headquarters in Rio de Janeiro, Petroleo Brasileiro (PBR) supplies oil, liquefied natural gas, and natural gas to the Brazilian and offshore markets. PBR also trades and transports natural gas within Brazil, as well as investing in natural gas transportation companies and natural gas distributors. The company's majority stakeholder is the Brazilian federal government. PBR claims a 7.5 P/CF ratio (www.petrobras.com.br).

- *Statoil ASA:* The proven reserves of Statoil ASA (STO) consist of 1.8 billion barrels of oil and 404 billion cubic meters of natural gas. STO explores, develops, and produces gas in the Norwegian continental shelf and in fields located in Africa, central Asia, western Europe, South America, and the People's Republic of China. STO is headquartered in Stavanger, Norway, and has a 7.3 cash flow multiple (www.statoil.com).

Propane

See Table 3.8.

- *Enterprise Products Partners L.P.:* Based in Houston, Enterprise Products Partners (EPD) was formed as a limited partnership and midstream company in the natural gas and natural gas liquids market. The company's NGL Pipelines & Services segment includes its natural gas processing business and propane production as well as related marketing activities. EPD owns 23 natural gas processing plants in Texas, Louisiana, Mississippi, and New Mexico as well as 13,000 miles of pipeline. EPD is valued at an 11.9 P/CF ratio (www.epplp.com).

- *Dynegy Inc.:* Houston's Dynegy Inc. (DYN) is primarily a producer and seller of electricity generated by burning coal, natural gas, and oil. Dynegy is a player in the propane market by virtue of its gas supply and transportation contracts and trading positions. DYN's cash flow multiple stands at 7.7 (www.dynegy.com).

- *Rosetta Resources Inc.:* Another Houston firm, Rosetta Resources (ROSE) owns oil and natural gas properties with proven reserves equivalent to 2.5 million barrels of oil and 344 billion cubic feet of gas. ROSE owns interests in the Sacramento Basin of California, south Texas, the Gulf of Mexico, and the Rocky Mountains. ROSE's 15.2 cash flow multiple makes it relatively pricey (www.rosettaresources.com).

- *Transportadora Gas:* Transportadora de Gas del Sur S.A. (TGS), based in Buenos Aires, transports natural gas to residential, commercial, industrial, and electric power generation customers throughout Argentina. The company operates a nearly 5,000-mile pipeline system and also processes natural gas liquids at a complex located near Bahía Blanca. Treatment and gas compression are rendered at two plants in the company's production fields. A 4.7 P/CF ratio makes TGS the cheapest producer in the category (www.tgs.com.ar).

TABLE 3.8   Propane Producers

Company	Symbol	Market Capitalization	Average Volume	Price-Earnings Ratio	Dividend Yield
Enterprise Products Partners L.P.	EPD	$11.2 billion	488 thousand	25.6	6.7%
Dynegy Inc.	DYN	$2.9 billion	4.0 million	23.7	–
Rosetta Resources Inc.	ROSE	$879.8 million	165 thousand	24.9	–
Transportadora Gas ADS	TGS	$802.4 million	28 thousand	9.2	–
Linn Energy, LLC	LINE	$668.0 million	92 thousand	(negative)	3.0%

- *Linn Energy, LLC:* Linn Energy, LLC (LINE) has 193.2 billion cubic feet of proven gas reserves in its Appalachian Basis properties. LINE is headquartered in Pittsburgh, Pennsylvania, and is the category's most expensive producer, valued at a 19.7 cash flow multiple (www.linnenergy.com).

Lumber

See Table 3.9.

To say the lumber industry depends upon economic growth is to grossly understate the case. Construction, especially new home building, is the lifeblood of the forest products business. Due to the competitive nature of the market, margins can be thin, so economies of scale and efficiency are decisive advantages for any producer. Bottom line, energy costs are the single greatest expense factor for market participants.

In addition, a rise in "green" thinking over the years has led to wood product companies being subject to increasingly stringent environmental laws and regulations concerning air emissions, water discharges, and waste handling and disposal. These improvements can significantly impact their bottom lines at a time when timber products face increasing competition from nonwood substitute products.

- *Weyerhaeuser Company:* Based in Federal Way, Washington, Weyerhaeuser (WY) grows and harvests timber, manufactures forest products, and develops real estate in the United States and Canada. WY manages 38 million acres of commercial forestland and operates in 19 countries in the Americas, Australasia, and Europe. WY's P/CF ratio is 13.6 (www.weyerhaeuser.com).
- *Rayonier Inc.:* Rayonier Inc. (RYN) manages forestland, sells standing timber and logs to third-party manufacturers, and manufactures dimension lumber for residential and industrial construction use. RYN owns, leases, or manages 2.5 million acres of timberland and real estate in the United States, New Zealand, and Australia. RYN is headquartered in Jacksonville, Florida. With a 9.0 cash flow multiple, RYN has a definite value tilt (www.rayonier.com).

TABLE 3.9 Lumber Producers

Company	Symbol	Market Capitalization	Average Volume	Price-Earnings Ratio	Dividend Yield
Weyerhaeuser Company	WY	$14.9 billion	1.6 million	(negative)	4.1%
Rayonier Inc.	RYN	$3.1 billion	514 million	15.9	4.7%
Louisiana-Pacific Corporation	LPX	$2.0 billion	1.7 million	5.2	3.1%
Universal Forest Products, Inc.	UFPI	$931.6 million	221 thousand	12.2	0.2%
Massisa S.A. ADS	MYS	$915.4 million	26 thousand	80.7	0.8%

- *Louisiana-Pacific Corporation:* Nashville-based Louisiana Pacific Corporation (LPX) supplies retail home centers, manufactured housing producers, distributors, and wholesalers in the Americas, Asia, and Europe through its 29 manufacturing facilities. Most of these operations are located in North America; one is in Chile. LPX's P/CF ratio of 3.8 makes it decidedly cheap (www.lpcorp.com).

- *Universal Forest Products, Inc.:* Universal Forest Products (UFPI) is a Michigan company that supplies lumber, composite wood, plastic, and other building products through its operations in the United States, Canada, and Mexico. UFPI's construction lumber customers are primarily do-it-yourself and retail outlets and site-built home constructors as well as the manufactured housing and industrial segments. UFPI also sells engineered wood products including roof trusses, wall panels, and floor systems. UFPI is valued at a 7.90 P/CF ratio (www.ufpi.com).

- *Massisa S.A.:* Chile-based Massisa (MYS) produces sawn lumber and pulp products for the construction and furniture markets in the Americas, Europe, and Asia. MYS, headquartered in Santiago, also produces moldings and solid wood doors. With an 11.8 cash flow multiple, MYS is a middling value (www.massisa.com).

Sugar

See Table 3.10.

Refined sugar comes from two sources, sugar beets and sugarcane. Cane sugar accounts for the majority of the world's supply. The largest cane producers are Brazil, India, and Cuba, while beet growing is heaviest in Europe, Asia, and Australia.

As a producer, the United States is unique. It's the only country growing both sugarcane and sugar beets. Domestic cane is grown mostly in Hawaii, Louisiana, and Florida, while sugar beets are grown in California and Minnesota.

Sugar demand is somewhat elastic: There's a direct relationship between worldwide sugar demand and per capita income. The increasing availability of alternative sweeteners such as NutraSweet and corn syrup, however, tends to curtail demand.

Energy costs are the single largest expense in the sugar refining process. Investments in modern equipment and captive or passive sources can add to a refiner's bottom line when energy prices rise.

- *Imperial Sugar Company:* Headquartered in Texas, Imperial Sugar (IPSU) supplies refined sugar to grocery stores, food manufacturers, and food service distributors throughout the United States under its Imperial, Dixie Crystals, Holly, and Wholesome Sweeteners brands. Cane operations are based in Georgia and Louisiana. IPSU's P/CF ratio is 11.1 (www.imperialsugar.com).

TABLE 3.10 Sugar Producers					
Company	Symbol	Market Capitalization	Average Volume	Price-Earnings Ratio	Dividend Yield
Imperial Sugar Company	IPSU	$327.1 million	169 thousand	22.8	0.9%

Soybean Products

See Table 3.11.

Soybean meal and soybean oil are the by-products of soybean processing. The bulk of the soybean crop is sold to processors, known as crushers, who now use chemical extraction methods to produce soybean meal and soybean oil. On average, a bushel of beans yields 48 pounds of meal and 11 pounds of oil.

Soybean meal is the more valuable processed product, accounting for 50 to 75 percent of soybeans' value. Soy meal is primarily a livestock feed. This is a very elastic market, which means that one feed can be rather easily substituted for another. Soy meal competes with fish meal, rapeseed meal, and corn as a feed, so the pricing of these competing products can greatly impact soy meal consumption.

Demand for soybean oil comes mostly from the food industry. Soy oil accounts for two-thirds of all fats consumed in the United States. It is used in margarine, bakery shortening, salad oils, and cooking oils. The edible oil market is also quite elastic, owing to the myriad of products, from animal fats and other oilseeds that can be substituted for soy oil. Palm oil is a principal competitor. Income levels and consumer preferences also influence soy oil consumption to a lesser degree. Demand for soy oil as a feedstock for biodiesel fuels, however, is diversifying the processors' market.

Soybean costs are the largest expenses born by processors, but risk management—timing bean purchases and hedging—can substantially improve a processor's margins.

- *Archer Daniels Midland:* The oilseed processing segment of Archer Daniels Midland (ADM) breaks down soybeans and other commodities into oils and meals for the food and feed industries. Partially refined oil is marketed for use in chemicals, paints, and other industrial products. Soy protein products and natural-source vitamin E antioxidants are marketed to the dietary supplement and food industry, while soy protein meat substitutes are shipped to food manufacturers. ADM is valued at a 15.6 cash flow multiple and is headquartered in Decatur, Illinois (www.admworld.com).

		Market	Average	Price-Earnings	Dividend
Company	Symbol	Capitalization	Volume	Ratio	Yield
Archer Daniels Midland	ADM	$27.2 billion	4.5 million	22.8	1.0%
Bunge Limited	BG	$6.1 billion	1.0 million	16.0	1.2%

TABLE 3.11 Soybean Producers

- *Bunge Limited:* New York–based Bunge (BG) is an integrated agribusiness and food company. Its agribusiness division purchases, processes, stores, and sells grains and oilseeds, marketing to oilseed processors, feed manufacturers, millers, and edible oil processing companies, as well as to livestock, poultry, and aquaculture producers. BG's food products division markets edible oil products and milling products, such as soy-fortified corn meal and corn-soy blend. This division sells to food processors, food service companies, retail outlets, and government agencies. BG's P/CF ratio is 8.8 (www.bunge.com).

Cotton

See Table 3.12.

Cotton is grown in more than 75 countries throughout the world. The two largest producers of cotton are the People's Republic of China and the United States. Other large producers include Russia and India. China tends to consume most of its supply domestically to feed its burgeoning textile industry. India, however, is expected to step up cotton exports as a means to generate hard currency, which will foster growth in its blossoming manufacturing and high-tech sectors.

Most cotton production is destined for use in the manufacture of clothing. Additional demand comes from industries making household goods such as linen, drapery, and carpeting. Given cotton's primary use in clothing, demand is quite elastic, greatly influenced by consumers' tastes for competing fibers such as polyester and rayon.

TABLE 3.12 Cotton Producers					
Company	Symbol	Market Capitalization	Average Volume	Price-Earnings Ratio	Dividend Yield
Delta and Pine Land Company	DLP	$1.4 billion	521 thousand	33.9	1.5%

- *Delta and Pine Land Company:* Mississippi's Delta and Pine Land Company (DLP) breeds, produces, and markets proprietary varieties of cotton planting seed worldwide. DLP also develops and markets soybean planting seed in the United States. DLP farms 5,500 acres worldwide for research purposes and sells its products through distributors and direct in-country operations. Wholly owned operations are located in South Africa, Costa Rica, Australia, and Turkey. DLP's 27.6 cash flow multiple makes it rather pricey stock (www.deltaandpine.com).

The Value of Commodity Stocks

value plays
investments based on specific valuation considerations such as book value or net assets.

intrinsic value
the true value of a company or investment based upon factors such as net assets, dividends, earnings, and management quality, and the firm's competitive advantages and brand name.

The weighted average price-earnings and cash flow multiples of the commodity stocks we've examined make them appear to be *value plays*. Benchmarked against the average price-earnings and price–cash flow ratios of the Standard & Poor's 500 Index over the years 2003 to 2005, commodity stocks seem cheap (see Table 3.13).

Warren Buffett, one of the world's savviest investors, is a value hunter. Value investors look for companies with strong fundamentals—typically measured in terms of earnings, dividends, or cash flow—that are selling at bargains compared to their *intrinsic value*.

Intrinsic value should be easily determined— if you're a number cruncher like Warren Buffett— for the stocks of resource-dependent companies like metals and oil producers. If you know how much of the resource the company has left in the ground, the time period over which it's likely to be

TABLE 3.13 S&P 500 versus Commodity Stocks			
	Price-Earnings Ratio	Price–Cash Flow Ratio	Dividend Yield
S&P 500	20.3	12.2	1.7%
Commodity stocks	14.0	9.3	2.7%

Source: Standard & Poor's, August 2006.

recovered, and the price that can be commanded when it's sold, you can determine the company's worth. Unfortunately, many investors don't have the time or inclination to wrestle with such data. Worse still, many resource companies don't publish enough information to make this analysis practical.

Commodities are, by their nature, cyclical. The Wharton/Yale study, in fact, highlighted the *countertrend* of commodities: In expansionary times, when paper assets such as noncommodity stocks and bonds do well, commodity returns tend to be negative; in periods of recession, commodities are ascendant. For this reason, many advisors recommend that their clients hold commodities, in some form or another, as a recession hedge and portfolio diversifier.

countertrend
a move in the opposite direction during a significant advance or decline in the price of an investment.

Still, the Wharton/Yale researchers found that there were a number of commodities that perform well in the early part of a recession, but not as well near the end of an economic downturn. In particular, petroleum products, industrial metals, and foods exhibit this characteristic.

For value-minded investors, the cyclicality of commodity stocks ought to make them most attractive when the prices of their underlying products are low and the prospects for their elevation seem bleak. The contrarian nature of bargain hunters attracts them to assets that are temporarily unattractive to other investors. For them, the time to buy them is when everybody else is selling. That, oddly enough, should put value investors on the hunt to buy commodity stocks when their earnings and cash flow multiples are *high*. Selling is done when the multiples turn lower.

Commodity stocks, like commodity futures themselves, can become the objects of irrational exuberance. Warren Buffett himself decried the headlong run-up in commodity prices at a recent Berkshire Hathaway shareholders meeting. "It's like most trends," he cautioned. "At the beginning, it's driven by fundamentals, and then speculation takes over. As the old saying goes, 'What the wise man does in the beginning, fools do in the end.'"

Mutual Funds

mutual funds

a type of investment where investors pool their money and then shares are issued to represent fractional ownership in the pool.

Analyzing individual stocks is a daunting task for many investors. Luckily, specialized *mutual funds* are available that provide exposure to a mix of commodity stocks selected by a professional money manager. Buying commodity funds frees you from investing your time in the financial reports of mining companies or oil refiners. You can leave the work of deciding what to buy and sell—and when—to others with the resources to make sense of the minutiae.

When you buy shares of a commodity mutual fund, you're actually buying the stock of a company whose sole asset is a portfolio of securities. Your ownership stake in a company entitles you to a pro rata share of the profits and income derived from the portfolio.

dividends

the company profits that are paid out to shareholders.

A mutual fund is obliged to distribute nearly all of the income it receives from portfolio securities to its shareholders. You earn income from your mutual fund investment as your share of *dividends* from the stocks held in the portfolio is passed through.

If the fund's manager decides to sell portfolio securities that have appreciated, the fund realizes a capital gain, which may be either distributed in cash to you or reinvested in new securities for the portfolio. As the value of the portfolio's holdings fluctuates, the fund's share price—reflecting the total of cash and securities—moves up and down accordingly. A profit or a loss, therefore, can be sustained when you sell your fund shares.

Smart Trader Tip
Current data on mutual funds can be found through a number of sources including Morningstar (www.morningstar.com) and SmartMoney (www.smartmoney.com).

The Good (and Not-So-Good) News

A fund can solve the problem of finding the *right* commodity stock. As we'll see, some funds can hold hundreds of stocks. Odds are better that a fund will end up with the right stock than you if you're left to buy individual equities. The investments required for most mutual funds are small, so your capital can be spread out over a much larger base. Strangely, that's also a drawback, as funds have holdings in many different companies; the high returns earned by some securities can be diluted by the middling performances or losses of others in the portfolio.

The professional management of the portfolio won't come without a cost, either. All funds pass along their operating costs to shareholders. The largest ongoing cost is the fees paid to the fund's managers. Managers get their cuts whether or not the fund makes any money. Management fees and other ancillary costs are reflected in a fund's *expense ratio*, which is expressed as an annual charge against the fund's asset value. The average expense ratio for the *actively managed* commodity funds shown here are well above 1 percent per year.

expense ratio
the amount of assets needed to pay annual operating costs and management fees of a mutual fund.

When a fund is actively managed, the investment advisor selects securities to buy and sell according to his or her proprietary method in an effort to beat the market. In every case, a manager's benchmark is an index, representing a passive investment in the market. Investors have long debated whether professional money managers' costs are justified by the results of their stock picking. Many argue that investments in low-cost index funds are better bargains. (We'll examine index-based investments in another chapter.)

There's a tax consequence of successful active management, too. Whenever a portfolio manager sells appreciated stock from a portfolio, a capital gains tax liability is created. That tax liability is passed through to you, as a fund shareholder, even if the gain itself isn't distributed. Funds with a high turnover, therefore, aren't very tax-efficient since they can subject you to a boatload of levies that eat into your returns. Simply put, managers don't consider your personal tax situation when they run a portfolio.

Expenses can also eat into your returns. Management fees typically represent the biggest chunk of a fund's expense ratio. These are usually charged on a sliding scale between 0.5 percent and 1.0 percent, depending upon the fund's asset base. While this sounds like a small charge, consider this: The average size of a precious metal mutual fund is $664 million. At a .05 percent average fee level, managers earn $3.3 million—a rather substantial chunk of change.

Administrative costs are also included in the expense ratio. These include charges for record keeping, postage, and shareholder servicing. Some funds minimize these costs, while others spend freely. Ongoing charges, known as *12b-1 fees*, may also be built into the expense ratio. This expense represents a trailing commission paid to brokerage firms for servicing your investment as well as advertising and promotional costs.

There are also one-time costs known as *loads* that are not built into the expense ratio but must also be considered. Loads are nothing more than commissions that compensate brokers for selling a fund. Loads can be charged in a number of ways. A fund may offer a variety of different *share classes*, typically designated by letters, giving investors a choice in the manner in which the broker is compensated.

front-end load

a type of mutual fund that charges a fee or commission when the money is initially invested.

Funds can be loaded at the *front end*, meaning you pay the fee when you purchase the fund's shares. These are most often referred to as "A" class shares. If, for example, you invest $1,000 in a fund with a 4 percent *front-end load*, $40 of your initial investment goes to pay for the sales charge, and $960 is actually invested in the fund.

back-end load

a deferred sales charge, normally assessed when a fund investor redeems his or her shares.

Back-end loads (or deferred sales charges) are a bit more complicated. With a back-end-loaded fund, you pay a sales charge only if you liquidate your fund shares within a certain time frame. These shares—often referred to as "B" shares—do not impose a sales charge at the time of purchase, so unlike A-class purchases, all of your capital is immediately invested. But your expenses, as measured by the expense ratio, may be higher than that of A-class shares. As an example, a 5 percent back-end load may decrease to 0 percent in the sixth year of your holding period, meaning your load would be 5 percent if you sell in the first year, 4 percent in the second year, and so on.

Class B shares often convert into A-class shares when the sales charge is extinguished, lowering their expense ratio. When they convert, they will begin to charge the same asset-based sales fee as the Class A shares.

C-class shares may also be offered by a fund. C shares usually do not impose a front-end sales charge, so all of your capital is immediately invested. However, Class C shares typically levy a higher expense ratio than Class A shares, and generally do not convert; their expense ratios remain comparatively high over time.

Not all funds impose loads. Some, known as *no-load funds*, sell their shares directly to investors without sales charges. Despite the assertions of some financial advisors, there's little evidence showing a correlation between loads and performance. You don't get better performance out of load funds. In fact, when all fees and loads are taken into account, the average load fund performs worse than a no-load fund.

> **no-load fund**
> a type of mutual fund that doesn't charge a fee or commission to buy or sell shares.

Mutual funds are *open-ended* investments, meaning the fund continuously creates and redeems its shares. Mutual fund shares aren't traded on an exchange. When you buy mutual fund shares, you're purchasing newly issued shares from the fund itself, not from a selling shareholder. This is true even if your order is routed through a broker. Likewise, when you sell your fund shares, you'll be selling them to—*redeeming*, in fund parlance—the fund. The fund is your constant source of liquidity.

Redemptions of mutual fund shares take place at *net asset value* (NAV), which is determined at the end of the trading day, after the market closes. At that time, the value of each share holding is fixed, the total cash horde is tallied, and a pro rata deduction for ongoing expenses is taken. That figure, divided by the number of fund shares outstanding, is the fund's NAV. No-load funds are purchased at NAV, while the initial purchases of load funds take place at NAV plus the appropriate sales charge.

> **net asset value (NAV)**
> the value of an investment based on total assets minus liabilities divided by the number of shares. It's the amount shareholders should receive when redeeming mutual fund shares.

The good news about this pricing scheme is that there's no bid-ask spread (if you ignore the sales load) as there is with an exchange-traded security. The bad news is that you won't know at what price you're likely to buy or redeem your fund shares when you place your order. The once-a-day pricing character of most mutual funds means the value quoted to you will be the last NAV, which may be that of the previous trading day.

Smart Trader Tip

Many mutual funds require minimum initial investments of $500 or more. The minimum may be waived if you sign up for an automatic investment program (AIP). AIPs typically require at least $50 to be invested each month by electronic debits from your checking account. Regularly investing a fixed dollar amount in this manner is known as *dollar-cost averaging* (DCA). Over time, you'll end up buying more shares when prices are low and fewer shares when prices are high.

Another problem with commodity mutual funds is that there just aren't enough of them. Or rather, there aren't enough *categories*. As we've seen, it's hard to match up publicly traded companies to every commodity category. For that reason, only two commodity sectors are populated with enough players to warrant mutual funds: natural resources (i.e., energy and forest products mostly) and precious metals.

Natural Resource Mutual Funds

Natural resource mutual funds invest their assets in companies that recover or distribute oil, gas, coal, timber, and metals. Some funds, however, are a bit loose with the definition of a natural resource investment. In the eyes of some managers, hardware merchandisers belong in this category.

Natural resource funds can be narrowly focused or broad-based. Some fund families, such as Fidelity, offer portfolios targeted to specific commodity sectors, such as the Fidelity Select Natural Gas Fund (FS-NGX) or the Fidelity Select Paper and Forest Products Fund (FSPFX). Other funds take in more than one group of commodity stocks. The Ivy Global Natural Resources Fund (IGNAX), for example, is pretty much evenly split between energy stocks and the shares of industrial materials companies.

You'll need to look under the hood of fund candidates to ensure you'll get the exposure you desire. Even funds advertised as selective (e.g., energy funds) may have more modest commitments to energy stocks than you'd like. Fidelity Select Energy (FSENX) invests 88 percent of its portfolio in energy stocks, for instance, while the Guinness Atkinson Global Energy Fund (GAGEX) invests in nothing *but* energy issues.

Table 3.14 lists natural resource funds that were open to new investors at press time. Each mutual fund has a unique symbol, which appears in the first column. A handful—the seven load funds—are sold only through brokerages; the rest can be purchased directly from the fund companies. For simplicity's sake, only one share class—either the A shares or the load-waived shares—are shown for those funds with multiple shares classes. Key characteristics of each fund can be readily compared in the chart, including:

- *Minimum investment:* Table 3.14 shows the minimum initial purchase requirement for an individual nonretirement account. A fund may allow lower buy-ins for individual retirement accounts (IRAs) or systematic investment plans.

- *Front loads:* As discussed, a load represents the sales charge deducted from an investment, most of which is paid to the selling broker. The majority of the funds listed are no-load funds.

- *Expense ratio:* Ongoing annual costs for the funds listed average 1.27 percent of the funds' assets. There's considerable variation here. The Van Eck Global Hard Assets Fund (GHACX) tops the list with a 1.56 percent expense ratio. At the low end is ING's Global Resources S (IGRSX) at 0.90 percent.

- *Holdings:* Some portfolios hold hundreds of stocks; others have only a few dozen. Not surprisingly, the global funds tend to have the largest number of holdings, since they're free to own companies domiciled outside the United States.

- *Energy stocks:* On average, 80 percent of the stocks held by the natural resource funds listed are energy stocks. Clearly, some funds are purer energy plays than others.

- *Average P/E:* The average price-earnings multiple of stocks held in each fund is listed. Figures range from a high of 25.9 (Fidelity Select Energy Service—FSESX) to a low of 12.4 (Guinness Atkinson Global Energy—GAGEX).

- *Yield:* Figures in this column represent the 12-month income stream derived from the portfolio pass-through of dividends. Figures are expressed as a percentage of the funds' NAVs.

TABLE 3.14 Natural Resource Mutual Funds

Symbol	Name	Minimum Invest ($)	Front Load (%)	Expense Ratio (%)	Holdings	Energy Stocks (%)	Average P/E	Yield (%)	Annual Return (%)	Net Assets ($mm)
FSENX	Fidelity Sel En	2,500		0.94	88	88.4	14.5	0.16	37.0	2,872
IGNAX	Ivy Global NR	500	5.75	1.40	110	45.5	18.2		34.0	2,682
FSESX	Fidelity Sel En Sv	2,500		0.94	58	96.9	25.9		32.6	1,889
FSNGX	Fidelity Sel N Gas	2,500		0.95	71	95.0	17.2		35.7	1,447
FNARX	Fidelity Sel NR	2,500		0.99	157	72.1	15.2	0.14	33.9	1,238
ICENX	ICON Energy	1,000		1.21	69	94.6	18.9	0.22	37.4	974
FSTEX	AIM Energy	1,000		1.18	43	98.0	15.9		38.1	608
IGRSX	ING Glob Res			0.90	75	71.5	15.6	0.17	29.7	516
EBERX	Putnam Glob NR	500	5.25	1.22	61	76.9	12.5	0.08	31.5	466
GHAAX	Van Eck Glob HA	1,000	5.75	1.56	105	52.7	17.4		38.1	355
BACAX	BlackRock Gl Res	500	5.75	1.34	74	87.6	17.6			291
FSDPX	Fidelity Sel In Mt	2,500		1.05	55	15.9	18.0	0.62	21.4	227
GAGEX	Guinness Atk GE	5,000		1.45	40	99.9	12.4			95
MAGRX	Merrill Lynch NR	1,000		0.91	121	89.4	16.9		34.6	70
GGNAX	Gartmore Gl NR	2,000	5.75	1.47	100	79.8	14.1			26
FSPFX	Fidelity Sel P&FP	2,500		1.25	41		20.7	2.21	4.6	21
DNLAX	Dreyfus Prem NR	1,000	5.75	1.51	77	88.7	15.7	1.28		17
GAAEX	Guiness Atk Alt E	5,000								13
Average				**1.18**	**79**	**77.9**	**16.8**	**0.55**	**31.3**	**728**

Source: Morningstar as of August 2006.

- *Three-year annualized return:* Annualized returns reflect the compounded gains or losses over the three-year period from 2003 to 2005. Also known as *average annual returns*, these figures describe the return earned, on average, each year rather than a cumulative return. Annualized returns take into account the reinvestment of dividends and capital gains as well as the change in a fund's NAV. Keep in mind that this figure is a *hypothetical* rate of return that, if attained each year, would have produced the same cumulative return if performance had been constant over the entire three-year period. There could be considerable variance in returns year by year over the period.

- *Total net assets:* The sum of each fund's portfolio value, plus cash on hand and adjusted for current expenses, is shown in millions of dollars. Fund sizes run from $2.9 billion (Fidelity Select Energy—FSENX) down to $13 million (Guinness Atkinson Alternative Energy—GAAEX).

Precious Metals Mutual Funds

Nearly two dozen gold or precious metals mutual funds are open to new investment by individual investors. Some have rather steep buy-ins (Rydex Precious Metals—RYPMX), in particular), while others can be acquired for an initial investment of only $1,000. Expenses for the metals funds run higher—an average of 1.42 percent annually—than for the natural resource funds shown previously. Average P/Es are nearly double those of the natural resource funds as well (see Table 3.15).

Contact information for the top no-load funds in the commodity sectors are listed as follows. Additional information on load funds can be obtained through your stock brokerage firm. Don't be surprised, however, if your broker can't give you more information on the smaller load funds. Only a broker with an active *dealer agreement* in force with a mutual fund can market its shares.

dealer agreement

a contract between a brokerage firm and a mutual fund company that allows the brokerage to offer the company's shares and allows for the sharing of sales loads and other fees.

Vanguard
P.O. Box 2600 V26
Valley Forge, PA 19482
Phone: (800) 997-2798
Web site: www.vanguard.com

TABLE 3.15 Precious Metals Mutual Funds

Symbol	Name	Minimum Invest ($)	Front Load (%)	Expense Ratio (%)	Holdings	Average P/E	Yield (%)	Annual Return (%)	Net Assets ($mm)
VGPMX	Vanguard Pr Mtl	10,000		0.40	39	20.1	0.88	37.4	3,324
FSAGX	Fidelity Sel Gold	2,500		0.97	110	31.2	0.05	21.8	1,491
BGEIX	Am Cen Glo Gold	2,500		0.67	83	42.5	0.26	22.9	1018
UNWPX	US Glo Inv W Pr	5,000		1.48	258		2.25	46.0	972
FKRCX	Franklin Gld & Pr	1,000	5.75	0.96	73	29.0	0.51	28.1	884
SGGDX	First Eagle Gold	2,500	5.00	1.29	100	40.9	2.05	22.0	856
TGLDX	Tocqueville Gold	1,000		1.59	83			26.1	818
OPGSX	Oppenheimer Gld	1,000	5.75	1.26	46	27.2		31.8	614
USAGX	USAA Pr Mtl	3,000		1.23	61	38.0		31.2	605
EKWAX	Evergreen Pr Mtl	1,000	5.75	1.30	77	39.1	0.57	33.2	409

GOLDX	GAMCO Gold	1,000		1.50	64	38.8	0.44	25.1	402
INIVX	Van Eck Intl Gld	1,000	5.75	1.71	71	34.9	0.12	29.8	393
USERX	US Glo Inv Gld	5,000		1.97	79	8.3	0.75	39.4	225
SGDAX	DWS Gld & Pr I	1,000	5.75	1.62	54	26.1	1.26	25.1	191
RYPMX	Rydex Pr Mtl	25,000		1.24	27	23.5		16.6	169
FGLDX	AIM Gld & Pr Mtl	1,000		1.44	34	31.5		26.2	149
MIDSX	Midas	1,000		2.44	51	20.7	2.21	33.9	131
LEXMX	ING Pr Mtl	1,000	5.75	1.56	51		0.14	22.9	128
OCMGX	OCM Gold	1,000	4.50	2.24	82	30.3	0.30	23.1	109
INPMX	RiverSource Pr M	2,000	5.75	1.46	53	28.1		24.6	92
SGLDX	DWS AARP Gld	1,000		1.40	58	47.4	1.43	34.8	33
Average				**1.42**	**72**	**31.6**	**0.79**	**28.7**	**620**

Source: Morningstar as of August 2006.

Fidelity Investments
82 Devonshire Street
Boston, MA 02109
Phone: (800) 544-9797
Web site: www.fidelity.com

American Century Investments
4500 Main Street
Kansas City, MO 64111
Phone: (800) 345-2021
Web site: www.americancentury.com

Rydex Investments
9601 Blackwell Road, Suite 500
Rockville, MD 20850
Phone: (800) 820-0888
Web site: www.rydexfunds.com

Closed-End Funds

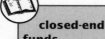

closed-end funds
a type of mutual fund with a fixed number of shares outstanding.

Actively managed commodity exposure can also be obtained through a handful of *closed-end funds*. A closed-end fund (CEF), like a mutual fund, is a collective investment. Investors buy shares of a CEF company to gain a pro rata share of the gains and income produced by the company's sole asset—a portfolio of securities. Unlike an open-end fund company, though, the shares of a CEF are finite: Once they're sold in an initial offering, there are no more shares to be purchased from the fund company. Investors wishing to obtain CEF shares have to buy them from existing shareholders. For this reason, CEF shares are exchange-traded. CEFs can be traded through a stock account just like any equity security. As such, stock brokerage commissions are levied for each transaction.

CEF shares, however, shouldn't be confused with exchange-traded index funds (ETFs). Since CEFs are subject to the tug and pull of supply and demand on the open market, CEFs may trade for a price above (a *premium*) or below (a *discount*) their net asset value. A fund with a $10 NAV, for example, offered at $11 per share would be selling for a 10 percent premium. A $9 market price reflects a 10 percent discount. Premiums emerge when funds become popular (demand outstrips supply at the current price). Discounts are, by far, the most prevalent condition, however. That said, it's possible (though maybe not probable) that an incremental gain can be earned if a fund purchased at a discount subsequently moves to a premium, provided the NAV doesn't decline.

CEF managers don't have to worry about rejiggering their portfolios to accommodate the cash needs of their shareholders. When mutual fund customers buy shares, they throw cash at the manager, who in turn must find suitable investments for the new money. It may not be a particularly opportune time to buy securities, so the new cash can actually be a drag on performance. Redemptions, too, can force a mutual fund manager to liquidate securities in a portfolio to raise cash. Since CEF shares are traded in the *secondary market*, there are no portfolio consequences.

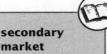

secondary market
the market where investors buy and sell existing securities.

CEFs may tend to be more volatile than mutual funds, owing to the widening or narrowing of discounts and premiums (see Table 3.16).

			TABLE 3.16	Closed-End Funds			
Sym	Name	Expense Ratio (%)	Premium/ Discount (%)	Market Yield (%)	Average Daily Volume	12-Month Market Return (%)	Net Assets ($mm)
KYN	Kayne Anderson MLP	4.37	−1.2	6.46	69,334	1.0	1,000
PEO	Petroleum & Resources	0.59	−10.9	1.78	37,028	18.2	849
KYE	Kayne Anderson Energy	1.81	−7.4	1.78	79,661	−3.0	821
CEF	Central Fund of Canada	0.51	9.4	0.11	489,958	67.1	778
BGR	BlackRock Global Energy & Resources	1.02	−12.9	5.51	84,821	16.2	684
GCS	DWS Global Commodities	1.00	−14.5	0.98	78,220	22.3	452
MGU	Macquarie Global Infrastructure	3.48	−20.0	6.60	56,008	−2.0	417
GGN	Gabelli Global Gold Natural Resources	0.47	−1.64	8.46	60,073	22.7	415
Average		**1.66**	**−7.4**	**3.96**	**119,388**	**17.8**	**677**

Source: Thomson, Closed End Fund Association, August 2006.

Additional information on closed-end funds can be found through:

- *Closed-End Fund Association:* The Closed-End Fund Association (CEFA) is the national trade association for the closed-end fund industry. CEFA is made up of nearly two dozen fund management firms throughout the United States. CEFA's web site offers a variety of educational materials related to closed-end funds.

  100 NW Englewood Road, Suite 130
  Kansas City, MO 64118
  Phone: (816) 413-8900
  Web site: www.cefa.com

- *Kayne Anderson Capital Advisors:* Advisors for Kayne Anderson MLP (KYN) and Kayne Anderson Energy (KYE) funds.

  1800 Avenue of the Stars, Second Floor
  Los Angeles, CA 90067
  Phone: (800) 231-7414
  Web site: www.kaynecapital.com

- *Adams Express Company:* Petroleum & Resources Fund advisor.

  7 St. Paul Street, Suite 1140
  Baltimore, MD 21202
  Phone: (800) 638-2479
  Web site: www.adamsexpress.com

- *Central Group Alberta Ltd.:* Manager of the Central Fund of Canada (CEF).

  Hallmark Estates
  1323 15th Avenue SW, Suite 805
  Calgary, AB T3C 0X8
  Phone: (403) 228-5861
  Web site: www.centralfund.com

- *BlackRock Advisors Inc.:* Advisor for the BlackRock Global Energy & Resources Fund (BGR).

  40 East 52nd Street
  New York, NY 10022
  Phone: (800) 882-0052
  Web site: www.blackrock.com

- *DWS Scudder (Deutsche Bank):* Manages DWS Global Commodities Fund (GCS).

  345 Park Avenue, 15th Floor
  New York, NY 10154
  Phone: (800) 349-4281
  Web site: www.dws-scudder.com

- *Macquarie Fund Advisors:* Advisory firm for Macquarie Global Infrastructure Fund (MGU).

  125 West 55th Street
  New York, NY 10019
  Phone: (800) 910-1434.
  Web site: www.macquarie.com

- *Gabelli Funds:* Investment advisor for Gabelli Global Gold and Natural Resources & Income Trust (GGN).

  One Corporate Center
  Rye, NY 10580
  Phone: (800) 336-6983
  Web site: www.gabelli.com

Commodity-Backed Open-End Funds

A recent innovation allows investors to take ownership of precious metals and oil in bite-size bits that can easily fit into their stock brokerage accounts. These instruments are referred to as exchange-traded open-end funds.

Originally designed solely as index products, the world of *exchange-traded funds* (ETFs) has been expanded to incorporate direct investments in commodities. ETFs, as their name signifies, are collective portfolios whose shares trade through the facilities of a stock exchange. But unlike CEFs, ETFs constantly issue and redeem their shares just like mutual funds. The difference between ETFs and mutual funds is the *size* in which fund share lots can be created or redeemed. Only large institutional investors interact

exchange-traded fund (ETF)

an ETF is a pooled investment with shares listed for trading on the major stock exchanges.

creation unit

a large block of exchange-traded fund shares that is redeemed by a large institutional investor and made available for trading.

redemption unit

a large block of exchange-traded fund shares that is redeemed by a large institutional investor and no longer available for trading.

specialist

an exchange member that acts as the exclusive market maker for a stock or an ETF. Specialists hold inventories of shares from which they deal, continuously put up bid and offer prices, and manage the limit order book. Specialists are charged with maintaining a fair and orderly market and use their inventories to balance surges in supply and demand.

with the ETF portfolio to exchange large blocks (25,000- to 100,000-share lots). Those trades are not cash-based, though. When an institutional firm—a large investment firm or a market maker—wants to create a share block (or *creation unit*) of an ETF, it makes an *in-kind* exchange of the portfolio's components. If the portfolio is made up of stocks, shares are delivered; if it's a gold ETF, bullion is swapped. In the reverse, an institution can demand redemption by delivering a block of ETF shares (a *redemption unit*) to the fund and get gold (or stock) in exchange.

An institutional investor may hold the shares it receives from the fund or sell some or all of them into the secondary—or exchange—market, where they are priced and traded throughout the day.

This is how bite-size trades are made possible for smaller investors. Simply put, if you're not coming to the fund with a block trade, you have to find your liquidity on the floor of the stock exchange by trading your ETF shares either with another small investor in a brokered transaction or with the institutional market maker (most often known as a *specialist*). In other words, you buy and sell ETF shares without interacting with the fund itself, in the same way CEF shares are bought and sold.

Like CEFs, ETFs can be bought and sold in lot sizes as small as one share and are subject to regular brokerage commissions. And like many stocks, ETFs are marginable and can also be sold short, meaning they can be bought or sold using 2:1 leverage. Short selling permits an investor to use borrowed shares to wager on a *decline* in an ETF's price.

There's a big difference in the way market forces work on CEF and ETF shares, though. Since ETF shares can be readily created and redeemed, an arbitrage is possible if ETF prices stray from the value of the underlying assets. Put another way, significant premiums and discounts aren't allowed to exist in the ETF market because institutional firms would exploit mispricings and, by dint of their actions, return prices to equilibrium.

For example, gold ETF shares offered at the equivalent of $650 per ounce would be considered rich if bullion was trading at $640. An institutional firm (an *authorized participant*, or AP) might be motivated to buy gold in the open market, exchange the bullion for creation units of the ETF, then sell those shares in the open market for a profit. Open market purchases of bullion would bid the metal's price up, while sales of the new share supply would put downward pressure on the ETF's price, arbitraging the premium away.

If the ETF share price is significantly *lower* than the value of portfolio assets, an AP might buy ETF shares in the open market, redeem them for bullion, then sell the gold for a profit. When the AP buys creation unit–sized blocks of ETF shares in the open market, this raises its market price; when the AP later sells the bullion, the new supply lowers its price, which narrows the gap between the ETF share price and the price of the underlying gold.

> **authorized participant**
> an investment firm that is recognized by an ETF sponsor as capable of creating and redeeming fund shares through the delivery of portfolio components (stocks or commodities). An ETF specialist (see preceding discussion) is an example.

The provision for arbitrage differentiates ETFs from CEFs. A CEF is very much like an ETF in that its shares represent a portfolio of assets tradable like a stock, but differs because there's no provision for continuous exchange of shares for portfolio assets. That's why CEF share prices so frequently deviate from their NAVs.

One thing that CEFs and ETFs have in common, though, is tax efficiency, at least when compared to open-end mutual funds. Remember that mutual funds offer continuous creation and redemption of shares to any and all investors. Thus, a wave of redemption requests could force a fund to sell portfolio securities to raise the cash needed to buy and retire the shares. In the process, the fund may have to sell appreciated securities and realize *capital gains*. The gain—or rather, the resulting tax liability—is distributed to the remaining shareholders.

> **capital gains**
> the profit from selling a security at a higher price.

Both CEFs and ETFs, by their nature, minimize portfolio transactions with investors. In the case of CEFs, there's virtually no interaction between investors and the portfolio: All buying and selling of fund shares is done in the secondary market. For ETFs, direct portfolio interaction is limited to APs who swap portfolio assets in kind. In-kind transactions are deemed to be a form of barter by the tax authorities, not subject to capital gains. That's not to say that there are no capital gains tax consequences for holding ETF shares; there are. It's just that capital gains tax liabilities are minimized compared to those with an open-end mutual fund.

There is, as yet, only a small handful of commodity ETFs available. With the rapid growth in the number of players in the ETF space and the demands of the marketplace, this number will, in all likelihood, increase over time. ETFs are especially attractive to investors wanting pure commodity exposure because, as passive investments, their expense ratios are very low.

Also, because they're marginable, ETFs allow investors more flexibility than conventional index funds. In a margin transaction, borrowing leverages an investor's purchases. For example, an investor can buy 100 ETF shares offered at $100 for $10,000 in cash. In a margin account, however, an investor can buy those same 100 shares by putting up as little as $5,000. The $5,000 deposit is a down payment toward the stock's purchase price. The balance of the purchase price is provided by the brokerage firm in the form of a loan collateralized by the ETF shares acquired. Using margin, investors can leverage their gains—or losses—twofold.

Of course, like any loan, margin debt must be repaid, though there's no specific due date. Typically, the loan is paid off when the shares are ultimately sold, so interest accrues during the life of the loan. This increases the investor's indebtedness to the broker. Unfortunately, adverse market action in combination with increasing indebtedness can lead to maintenance calls. Maintenance levels at most range from 25 percent to 35 percent of market value for long positions.

Smart Trader Tip

Traders can buy or sell in one of two types of accounts: cash or margin. A cash account requires payment in full for any securities that are bought or sold. Margin accounts allow for partial payments of investment securities. Margin works differently in the securities and commodities markets. Margin represents a performance bond, not a loan, in futures trading. In a stock trade, margin money is borrowed from a broker to buy shares. Stock buyers can borrow only half the cost of their stock in a margin transaction; the leverage in futures is much higher.

TABLE 3.17 Investor's Account

	Market Value	–	Debt	=	Equity
Deposit cash					$5,000
Borrow $5,000			$5,000		
Buy 100 @ $100	$10,000				
Initial position	**$10,000**	**–**	**$5,000**	**=**	**$5,000**

Consider the investor's account shown in Table 3.17 as an example. Our investor equity starts out at 50 percent of the ETF's market value. Let's say over time, the value of the ETF increases to $120 per share. In that time, $70 of margin interest has accrued.

Market Value	–	*Debt*	=	*Equity*
$12,000		$5,070		$6,930

If ETF shares were sold now, a portion of the liquidation value would be used to retire the outstanding debt, leaving the investor with $6,930. That's a net gain of $1,930, or 39 percent, on her initial $5,000 capital commitment. The ETF, remember, appreciated only 20 percent in value.

But what if her ETF shares had declined instead? Suppose the ETF shares fell to $75:

Market Value	–	*Debt*	=	*Equity*
$7,500		$5,070		$2,430

Now our investor's equity is only 32 percent of the ETF market value. If the house maintenance requirement is 35 percent, she'll have to restore her account's equity to the maintenance level (not the initial level, as with commodity futures) by depositing cash or marginable securities with a loan value of at least $195:

Current market value of margined securities	$7,500
35% maintenance requirement	× 35%
Required equity	$2,625
Current equity	–$2,430
Maintenance call	$ 195

ETFs can also be sold short in a margin account. Like a margined purchase, a short sale also entails borrowing, but this time *shares* (not cash) are lent by the broker. Borrowed shares are sold by the investor (hence, the term *short sale*) under a promise to repay the stock loan at a later date. Since the shares have been sold from the investor's account, the only way she can get them back is to repurchase them in the open market. Her resulting gain or loss will be based upon the difference between the short sale price and the price she pays later to buy back the ETF shares.

Short selling is a strategy used by investors who believe share prices will fall in the near future. A 50 percent initial margin requirement must be met for short sales, just as for margined purchases. Here's how an investor's account might look if he or she shorted 100 ETF shares at $10:

	Credit	−	*Market Value*	=	*Equity*
Deposit cash	$ 5,000				
Sell 100 @ $10	$10,000		$10,000		
Initial position	$15,000	−	$10,000	=	$5,000

In a short sale, the market value of the shares is a liability rather than an asset. The investor's account is credited with a margin deposit *and* the proceeds of the short sale. The amount of the proceeds remains static, but the size of the liability fluctuates with the market. Notice how the investor's equity starts out at 50 percent of the ETF's market value.

There's no direct accounting for the broker's loan of ETF shares here, since this ledger reflects only cash-based transactions. No interest will be charged for the stock loan, either.

Should the ETF price decline—say, to $75 per share—our investor's account would look like this:

Credit	−	*Market Value*	=	*Equity*
$15,000		$7,500		$7,500

If she wanted to close out her position, she'd place an order to buy 100 ETF shares, thus acquiring the shares necessary to retire her loan, and leaving with a profit of $2,500, or 50 percent. Her credit balance provides the cash needed to make the purchase, eliminating the market value liability. Her ending credit balance would be $7,500, reflecting her initial $5,000 deposit together with her $2,500 profit.

A rise in the price of the ETF spells potentially bad news for our short seller. If, for example, the ETF soared to $120 per share, the account would require an infusion to restore equity to the required amount:

Credit	–	*Market Value*	=	*Equity*
$15,000	–	$12,000	=	$3,000

Equity is now only 25 percent of market value. If the maintenance requirement is 35 percent, an equity infusion of $1,200 ($12,000 × .35 = $4,200; $4,200 – $3,000 = $1,200) is required. Cash deposits increase the amounts shown in both the credit balance and the equity columns.

Precious Metals ETFs

Precious metals ETFs are not funds per se but *grantor trusts* whose sole asset is bullion and, occasionally, cash. Each ETF shareholder has an undivided interest in the trust's assets. Since bullion ordinarily does not earn income, the trust's operating expenses are financed by sales of bullion held in the trust. As a result, the amount of bullion represented by each share is gradually reduced over time.

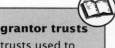

grantor trusts
trusts used to hold assets or investment securities on behalf of investors.

This creates a tax complication for ETF shareholders. The trusts are not subject to federal income tax. Instead, like mutual funds, income and gains derived from the underlying assets flow through to shareholders, meaning they'll have to report capital gains or losses on their pro rata share of the bullion sales used to pay fund expenses. Then they must adjust the *cost basis* of their ETF shares to reflect the now-smaller asset base. These calculations may require the intervention of a tax professional.

The tax bite for precious metals ETFs can be stiff, too. Gains on precious metals investments, including gold and silver ETFs, are taxed at the collectibles rate under the Internal Revenue Code. For collectibles, the maximum long-term capital gains tax rate is 28 percent; gains on noncollectible assets held for more than a year are taxed at a top rate of only 15 percent. Short-term gains—levied on any asset held for a year or less—are taxed at the investor's ordinary income rate, which could be as high as 35 percent.

Gold ETFs

- *streetTRACKS Gold Shares (GLD):* The first U.S. commodity–backed ETF to come to market, GLD is the largest fund in the category. GLD's trust holds 12.6 million ounces in bullion at the London vault of HSBC Bank USA. GLD tracks the London gold afternoon price fixing. Each GLD share initially represented one-tenth ounce (0.100 oz.) of gold when the fund was launched in November 2004, but by press time the asset backing had shrunk to 0.0993 ounce because of bullion sales. GLD is sponsored by State Street Global Advisors.

- *iShares COMEX Gold Trust (IAU):* Barclays Global Investors offers a gold-backed ETF virtually identical to GLD. IAU is pegged to the settlement of the COMEX (New York Mercantile Exchange) spot gold contract and backed by 1.4 million ounces of metal held by the Bank of Nova Scotia on behalf of the trustee. IAU was launched in January 2005, with share prices set to reflect one-tenth ounce (0.100 oz.) of gold. With bullion sales, IAU shares are now backed by 0.0994 ounces of metal.

Silver

- *iShares Silver Trust (SLV):* Another Barclays Global Investors trust is backed by 97.9 million ounces of silver bullion held in the London vault of JPMorgan Chase Bank. Designed to track the

London afternoon silver fix, SLV was launched in April 2006, with each share initially representing 10 ounces of bullion. SLV shares are now backed by 9.98 ounces of silver.

Oil ETF

A unique ETF tracks the price movements of light sweet crude oil. The United States Oil Fund (USO) is actually a commodity pool—operated as a limited partnership—that invests in crude oil futures. The general partner is California-based Victoria Bay Asset Management, LLC, a subsidiary of Wainwright Holdings Inc. The fund is treated as a limited partnership for tax purposes.

- *United States Oil Fund (USO):* Units of USO were priced at its April 2006 launch to match the per-barrel cost of West Texas Intermediate (light sweet) crude oil traded in the New York Mercantile Exchange's front-month contract. The fund holds collateral for some 5,885 crude oil futures contracts in Treasury securities yielding 4.59 percent per annum. Management fees presently stand at 0.50 percent of assets, but will drop to 0.20 percent when the fund's asset base rises to $1 billion. The fund's custodian is Brown Brothers Harriman & Co. (see Table 3.18).

TABLE 3.18 Commodity-Backed Open-End ETFs

Symbol	Name	Expense Ratio (%)	Premium/ Discount (%)	Average Daily Volume	12-Month Market Return (%)	Net Assets ($mm)
GLD	streetTRACKS Gold Shares	0.40	0.0	6,489,570	46.9	7,784
IAU	iShares COMEX Gold Trust	0.40	0.2	198,235	46.9	846
SLV	iShares Silver Trust	0.50	0.3	421,339		1,226
USO	United States Oil Fund	0.50		557,312		447
Average		**0.45**	**0.2**	**1,915,364**	**46.9**	**2,576**

Additional information on commodity ETFs can be found at:

streetTracks Gold Shares (GLD)
One Lincoln Street
Boston, MA 02111
Phone: (866) 320-4053
Web site: www.streettracksgoldshares.com

iShares COMEX Gold Trust (IAU) and iShares Silver Trust (SLV)
One Freedom Valley Drive
Oaks, PA 19456
Phone: (800) 474-2737
Web sites: www.ishares.com

United States Oil Fund (USO)
1625 Broadway, Suite 2200
Denver, CO 80202
Phone: (800) 920-0259
Web site: www.unitedstatesoilfund.com

Summary

There is more than one way to participate in the commodity markets. You don't need to buy bushels of corn or barrels of crude oil. One way to be part of it is by trading futures on commodities. The mechanics of futures trading were covered in Chapter 2.

In this chapter, we took a look at commodity-related stocks, mutual funds, and exchange-traded funds. For instance, buying shares of Exxon Mobil (XOM) gives investors exposure to crude oil prices. Newmont Mining (NEM) shares move in a direction similar to that of gold. Weyerhaeuser (WY) is a play on lumber. In addition to individual stocks, there are also a variety of mutual funds and ETFs that can give investors exposure to commodities markets. Several were discussed in this chapter.

So, for those investors looking for ways to participate in the moves in commodities, but who are not interested in futures, stocks and funds offer another option. As always, those investors should take a closer look at each company before committing any capital. Some of the factors to consider, such as earnings, dividend yields, commissions, and fees, were discussed in detail in this chapter.

Key Summary Points

1. Commodities tend to perform well over time and can add an important element of diversification to almost everyone's portfolio.

2. One way to get exposure to commodities is with shares of companies involved in those markets.

3. Exxon Mobil, Newmont Mining, and International Paper are examples of companies with businesses that are sensitive to changes in commodity prices.

4. When buying shares, investors should consider each company's fundamentals including dividends, earnings, price-earnings ratios, and market capitalization.

5. Mutual funds offer another way to participate in the commodity markets.

6. A mutual fund is a large pool of money that issues shares to investors. The pool is used to buy different assets. In some cases, the mutual fund will hold shares of commodity-related stocks. For example, Fidelity Investments offers several natural resource funds.

7. Not all mutual funds are the same, however, and investors should consider several factors before investing in one, including the expense ratio, the load, and the specific assets held in the fund.

8. Some exchange-traded funds (ETFs), such as the United States Oil Fund (USO) and the streetTracks Gold Fund (GLD), hold the actual commodity.

9. Investors can buy and sell shares of ETFs through their brokers in the same manner as when buying or selling shares of stock.

Chapter

4

Commodity Trading in the Index Markets

All investors—whether they're trading in stocks, bonds, or commodities—constantly strive to beat the market. For stock investors, the market is typically represented by the Standard and Poor's 500 Index; for domestic bond investors, it's likely to be the Lehman Brothers Aggregate Bond Index. For a long time, commodity investors have had the *Commodity Research Bureau (CRB) index* as a benchmark against which their investment prowess could be measured.

> **Commodity Research Bureau (CRB) index**
> first calculated in 1957, the index is used to track the price changes in a basket of futures and commodities prices.

Traders engage in *active management* when they attempt to produce investment returns better than a target market benchmark. By researching individual stocks, bonds, or futures, active players hope their programs of buying and selling provide incremental returns above that of the market.

There are other investors, however, who believe that attempts to outdo the market are futile. These investors try not to beat the market return, but merely to replicate it. They do so by adopting a passive style of

passive management

an investing strategy that attempts to mirror, rather than outperform, a market index. Despite the strategy's name, a commodity index portfolio manager must still buy and sell futures at times. Indexes may be reconstituted or rebalanced at times, requiring adjustments within the portfolio.

index investing

a strategy that involves mimicking the performance of an index rather than making buying and selling decisions.

portfolio management. *Passive management* entails buying and holding all, or at least a large representative sample, of the securities or commodities in a target index.

The Case for Indexing

Index investing is predicated upon the notion that investing is a zero-sum game and that investors, as a group, can only hope to earn the market return (less expenses) over a given period of time. If one investor happens to earn an above-average return through luck or skill, another must be left with a below-average return. Index investors hope only to earn the average return.

Even though index-based investments serve up only average returns, they've been able to outdo actively managed investments over the long run because passive investment is comparatively cheap. By eliminating research costs and keeping brokerage commissions at a minimum level, passive investments shouldn't have large chunks taken out of their returns.

Index-based investments can also minimize taxes. Since indexing means essentially buying and holding the commodities making up the index, these investments typically don't generate as many taxable capital gains as actively managed investments. Remember, appreciation isn't taxed until it's realized through a closing transaction.

Commodities as an Asset Class

Commodity futures have traditionally been considered too risky for most investors. Recently, though, as the strength of paper assets such as stocks and bonds has waned and commodity prices have rallied, financial advisors have looked again at the counter-cyclicality of commodities as a portfolio-balancing mechanism. We've seen the compelling demonstration of the ability of commodities to offset stock market risk in the Yale/Wharton study discussed in Chapter 3. Yet another demonstration of commodities' different drumbeat can be seen in Table 4.1.

By allocating a portion of a portfolio to commodities, many advisors now acknowledge, investors may be more likely to obtain their ultimate investment objectives—especially in an inflationary environment. At the same time, a slug of commodities can actually lower overall *portfolio volatility.*

If inflation is restrained, a portfolio's commodity allocation may lag behind other asset classes, but that underperformance, as illustrated, may very well be overcome by returns garnered from noncommodity assets.

portfolio volatility
the variability in the return or price performance of an investment portfolio.

That said, how should investors buy commodities? Finding the right combination of contracts in such diverse markets as gold, crude oil, sugar, and cattle is daunting enough for futures market professionals; it can seem virtually impossible to neophyte investors. Taking a different tack (i.e., buying a single commodity) may actually increase portfolio risk rather than provide the sought-after diversification benefit. That's where commodity index–based investments come in. Just as an investment tracking the Standard & Poor's 500 Index gives an investor exposure to the broad market of large-capitalization U.S. stocks in one swipe, a commodity index investment serves as a prebuilt proxy for a portfolio of many different futures contracts.

TABLE 4.1 Historic Stock and Commodity Price Cycles

Period	U.S. Stock Market Composite	Producer Price Index (All Commodities)
1898–1920	61%	228%
1920–1929	196%	–38%
1929–1951*	–12%	–58%
1951–1965	256%	6%
1965–1981	49%	204%
1981–2001	828%	37%

Includes distortions from years of the Great Depression.
Source: Legg Mason, U.S. Department of Commerce, U.S. Census, Standard & Poor's, National Bureau of Economic Research.

Broad-Based Commodity Indexes

benchmarks
a gauge or barometer for the performance of an investment or investment portfolio.

The Wall Street Journal estimated that there were $50 billion invested in commodity index–linked products in 2005, a rather small fraction of the total amount invested in commodities by noncommercial entities. Analysts, however, expect this total to rise in the future as institutional investors, in particular, migrate assets to this strategy.

There are a number of *benchmarks* that underlie commodity index vehicles, including:

- Commodity Research Bureau (CRB) indexes
- Goldman Sachs Commodity Index (GSCI)
- Dow Jones–AIG (DJ-AIG) indexes
- Rogers International Commodity Index (RICI)
- Deutsche Bank Liquid Commodity Index (DBLCI)

CRB, first calculated in 1957, is the oldest commodity index. GSCI was launched in 1992, while DJ-AIG and RICI were developed in 1998 and 1999, respectively. DBLCI debuted in 2003.

All of these indexes measure the total return of a fully funded futures portfolio (meaning the full contract value is deposited in Treasury security collateral), including the changes in the price of the contracts, the yield on the collateral, and the return earned—positive or negative—from rolling positions forward. These are long-only indexes; there is no short-selling. Put another way, these benchmarks represent a buy-and-hold investment strategy.

production-weighted
a type of index-weighting methodology whereby each commodity's weight is based on the amount of capital required to hold that asset.

Most of the indexes are *production-weighted*, meaning that each commodity's weight is based on the amount of capital dedicated to holding that asset, very much like market capitalization assigns weights to the components of a stock index. Some index providers, feeling that the economic significance of storable commodities is underestimated by a strict reliance on production numbers, use liquidity data as a balancing factor.

As a result of their differing constructions, each index has its own bias. Over time, however, they tend to be highly correlated, meaning they trend together, even though their returns vary. A 100 percent correlation reflects perfect lockstep movements of the indexes; a correlation of 0 percent denotes indexes whose movements bear no similarity to one another. Collectively, these five indexes share a high correlation, as illustrated in Table 4.2.

TABLE 4.2   Historic Commodity Index Correlations, 1991–2004

	CRB	GSCI	DJ-AIG	RICI	DBLCI
CRB	100%				
GSCI	65%	100%			
DJ-AIG	82%	89%	100%		
RICI	72%	92%	90%	100%	
DBLCI	59%	92%	85%	96%	100%
Average	**70%**	**91%**	**88%**	**96%**	

Source: Cole Asset Management.

Commodity Research Bureau Index

The CRB index has undergone nine major revisions since it was launched. The index, as of the last revision in 1995, now encompasses 17 commodity futures prices. Reuters, the international news agency, became the index's rights owner in 2001. In partnership with Jefferies Financial Group, a revamp was announced in 2005.

The new Reuters/Jeffries CRB (RJCRB) index is a bit broader, with 19 commodity contracts, each assigned to one of four tiers, with variable weightings. Petroleum products make up one tier, weighted at 33 percent. The remaining tiers are determined by liquidity: Highly liquid commodities make up 42 percent, liquid contracts constitute 20 percent, and so-called diversifying commodities make up 5 percent. By sector, the new benchmark is made up of 21 percent soft commodities including orange juice, sugar, coffee, cocoa, and cotton; metals, 20 percent; grains, 13 percent; and livestock, 7 percent. The balance, 39 percent, is made up of energy—a combination of petroleum products and natural gas. The new index rebalances monthly.

Continuous Commodity Index

the original CRB index, before it was modified in 2005, is now known as the CCI.

The old CRB index, in contrast, was equal-weighted and rebalanced semiannually. It was not retired, however. It's still around and is now calculated as the *Continuous Commodity Index* (CCI). The historic track record for the CRB index in Table 4.2 belongs to the CCI. Notice the comparatively weak correlation of the old CRB to the newer indexes.

Softs are the heftiest sector in the CCI, constituting 29 percent of the benchmark's weight. Metals make up 24 percent, grains and energy carry a weight of 18 percent each, and livestock comes in at 12 percent. Both the RJCRB index and the CCI are underlying assets for futures and options traded on the New York Board of Trade.

Goldman Sachs Commodity Index

The GSCI is now considered to be the most heavily followed commodity index. It's a 24-commodity production-weighted benchmark that is rebalanced annually. The component mix is also adjusted for liquidity and investability.

Currently, the GSCI is heavily weighted in energy products. Two-thirds (67 percent) of the index's weight is given over to petroleum products and natural gas. Grains make up 12 percent, metals 10 percent, livestock 7 percent, and softs 4 percent.

Since GSCI weights are based on world production, changes can be quite dramatic. Energy sector weights, for example, have varied between 44 percent and 73 percent of the index. This can make the benchmark seem volatile when compared to other broad-based commodity indexes.

Futures and options based on the GSCI trade on the Chicago Mercantile Exchange. A mutual fund, the Oppenheimer Real Asset Fund (QRAAX), is also based upon GSCI. Additionally, half of DWS-Scudder's Commodity Securities Fund (SKSRX) is invested in *derivatives* linked to the GSCI benchmark, the other half in shares of companies in commodity-related industries. More recently, an open-end exchange-traded fund, the iShares GSCI Commodity-Indexed Trust (GSG), was launched to track the benchmark.

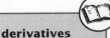

derivatives
investment securities that have values derived from the prices of other investments. Options and futures are examples of derivative securities.

Dow Jones–AIG Commodity Index

The DJ-AIG currently is made up of 19 commodities weighted primarily for trading volume and secondarily on the basis of global production. The index is rebalanced annually according to rules that specify floors and caps for each component. Index rules specify that no single commodity can constitute more than 15 percent or less than 2 percent of the index and no single sector can represent more than 33 percent of the benchmark's weight. These rules tend to dampen index volatility. By sectors, energy now carries the most weight in the DJ-AIG at 33 percent, followed by metals at 26 percent, grains at 21 percent, livestock at 11 percent, and softs at 9 percent.

Futures on the DJ-AIG are listed for trading on the Chicago Board of Trade. PIMCO's CommodityRealReturn Strategy Fund (PCRAX) is an open-end mutual fund that tracks the performance of the Dow Jones AIG Commodity Total Return Index. Credit Suisse's Commodity Return Strategy Fund (CRSAX) also tracks the DJ-AIG. A TRAKR (Total Return Asset Contract)—a small-sized, unlevered futures contract based upon the DJ-AIG index—trades on the Chicago Mercantile Exchange.

Rogers International Commodity Index

Launched in 1998, the Rogers International Commodity Index, or RICI, is the broadest and most international of the indexes. It's also the busiest; RICI is rebalanced monthly, a distinction that some experts claim produces higher returns. RICI consists of 35 commodities, including commodities not traded on U.S. futures exchanges such as adzuki beans, silk, rubber, and wool.

Weights are based on an assessment of each commodity's relative importance to international commerce. Energy consitutes 44 percent of the index; grains and metals each account for 21 percent; softs make up 8 percent; meats, 3 percent; and exotics, 3 percent.

A limited partnership, the Rogers International Raw Materials Fund, is based on RICI but is now closed to new investors. ABN-Amro also underwrote structured notes, due in 2010, based upon an agricultural subindex of RICI. A RICI-based TRAKR trades on the Chicago Mercantile Exchange.

Deutsche Bank Liquid Commodity Index

The DBLCI consists of only six commodities, all of which are purported to be the most liquid in their respective sectors. Deutsche Bank claims this narrow swath reduces transaction (i.e., roll and rebalancing) costs. Movements within each sector, it's said, are so highly correlated that the apparent diversity loss is negligible. Energy makes up 55 percent of the DBLCI; metals and grains account for the remaining 45 percent. The index includes no exposure to livestock or softs.

Energy positions (crude oil and heating oil) are rebalanced monthly, while positions in the other four contracts (aluminum, gold, corn, and wheat) are rebalanced annually. This dual rebalancing policy is thought to maximize the return (or minimize the cost) of the roll. An open-end exchange-traded fund, the DB Commodity Index Tracking Fund (DBC), is based upon DBLCI (see Table 4.3).

Smart Trader Tip

There are five different ways to invest in commodity indexes: conventional index futures, index mutual funds, exchange-traded funds, exchange-traded notes, and TRAKRs

TABLE 4.3	Commodity Index Constituents			
	CRB (CCI)	*GSCI*	*DJ-AIG*	*RICI*	*DBLCI*

Metals					
Gold	5.88%	2.12%	5.98%	3.00%	10.00%
Silver	5.88%	0.23%	2.00%	2.00%	
Platinum	5.88%			1.80%	
Palladium				0.30%	
Copper	5.88%	2.42%	5.89%	4.00%	
Aluminum		3.31%	7.06%	4.00%	12.50%
Nickel		0.93%	2.61%	1.00%	
Zinc		0.57%	2.69%	2.00%	
Tin				1.00%	
Lead		0.31%		2.00%	
Metals Total	**23.52%**	**9.89%**	**26.23%**	**21.10%**	**22.50%**

Energy					
Brent Crude Oil		11.75%			
WTI Crude Oil	5.88%	25.79%	12.81%	35.00%	35.00%
Heating Oil	5.88%	7.14%	3.85%	3.00%	20.00%
Unleaded Gasoline/RBOC		7.90%	4.00%	3.00%	
GasOil		3.83%			
Natural Gas	5.88%	10.29%	12.28%	3.00%	
Energy Total	**17.64%**	**66.70%**	**32.94%**	**44.00%**	**55.00%**

Livestock					
Feeder Cattle		0.90%			
Live Cattle	5.88%	3.74%	6.15%	2.00%	
Lean Hogs	5.88%	2.39%	4.39%	1.00%	
Livestock Total	**11.76%**	**7.03%**	**10.54%**	**3.00%**	**0.00%**

Grains and Oilseeds					
Corn	5.88%	4.11%	5.94%	4.00%	11.25%
Wheat	5.88%	5.28%	4.87%	7.00%	11.25%
Oats				0.50%	
Rice				2.00%	

(continued)

TABLE 4.3   (continued)

	CRB (CCI)	GSCI	DJ-AIG	RICI	DBLCI
Grains and Oilseeds (continued)					
Soybeans	5.88%	3.01%	7.60%	3.00%	
Soybean meal				0.15%	
Soybean oil			2.67%	2.00%	
Canola				0.67%	
Barley					
Adzuki bean				1.00%	
Grains and Oilseeds Total	**17.64%**	**12.40%**	**21.08%**	**20.32%**	**22.50%**
Softs					
Cocoa	5.88%	0.30%		1.00%	
Coffee	5.88%	0.68%	3.02%	2.00%	
Sugar	5.88%	1.26%	2.93%	1.00%	
Orange juice	5.88%			0.66%	
Cotton	5.88%	1.74%	3.23%	3.00%	
Softs Total	**29.40%**	**3.98%**	**9.18%**	**7.66%**	**0.00%**
Exotics					
Lumber				1.00%	
Rubber				1.00%	
Wool				1.00%	
Silk				0.15%	
Exotics Total	**0.00%**	**0.00%**	**0.00%**	**3.15%**	**0.00%**

Source: Cole Asset Management.

Index Performance

Reflecting their varying construction styles, the returns generated by each index can vary substantially. There can be considerable variance, too, in the risk presented by each index, at least as measured by their price volatility. Using a history of actual and backfilled data covering more than a decade, we can get a sense of the trade-off between reward and risk operating within each commodity index. An annualized standard deviation of returns measures the volatility of each index. Other things remaining the same, a lower standard deviation represents a lower risk than a higher standard deviation.

In Table 4.4, compound annual returns are put up against the standard deviations for each benchmark in order to derive reward-to-risk ratios.

We can see that the more the components that make up an index, the lower its standard deviation. More diversity, or a greater number of different types of commodities, lowers an index's standard deviation as well. For example, the DBLCI is heavily weighted toward energy, with oil (crude and heating) accounting for 55 percent of the value of the index. It has the least amount of diversity and the highest standard deviation.

Reflected by its .72 reward-to-risk ratio, RICI provides more return for a given amount of risk than the other four benchmarks, in large part because of its broad diversification. GSCI's production-based weighting scheme, however, seems to create asset concentrations that increase volatility substantially.

TABLE 4.4 Risk and Return Characteristics, 1991–2004

	Annual Return	Standard Deviation	Reward-to-Risk
CRB	3.30%	8.34%	0.40
GSCI	5.66%	18.06%	0.31
DJ-AIG	6.98%	11.82%	0.59
RICI	10.10%	14.04%	0.72
DBLCI	10.09%	18.49%	0.55

Source: Cole Asset Management.

Components of Return

rolling

the selling of futures contracts in the portfolio as they approach their expiration month and the buying of the same contracts in a deferred month.

The returns generated by a commodity index come from three sources. First, there's the return earned from the day-to-day price variations in the component futures contracts. This return, of course, can be positive or negative. Then there's the profit or loss realized from *rolling* futures positions forward. Each index has different rules dictating how the roll is conducted. For example, GSCI rules dictate that 20 percent of a soon-to-expire position be rolled on each business day within a specified five-day window; CRB index rules specify a four-day rollover schedule. Some commodities, such as those in the energy sector, have liquid futures that expire each month. Accordingly, these commodities can be rolled forward monthly. Other commodities, such as agriculturals, offer only a few contracts each year that trade with sufficient liquidity to warrant investment. Since these futures expire less frequently, rolls are more irregular.

contango

when longer-term contracts carry higher values than short-term contracts. This is normal.

Most futures markets are usually in *contango*, reflecting a normal market where deferred contract months are priced higher than nearby months. As a futures expiration month approaches, the nearby contracts tend to fall to converge with the spot market price. This depreciation can cut into gains or magnify losses when it comes time to roll long positions forward.

backwardation

when the deferred-month prices on a futures contract are lower than those of the nearby months.

However, energy futures are usually in *backwardation*, meaning that deferred-month prices are lower than those of the nearbys. Accordingly, as futures converge to the cash price, the deferred months' price *increases*. This price bias—now a boon, rather than a drag—can also be captured through the rolling process.

A third source of returns comes from the collateral deposited to fully margin the index's futures positions. Typically, institutions use short-term

Treasury securities—most often *T-bills*—in lieu of cash for futures margin deposits. That way, their money doesn't remain idle while it's held to secure their positions.

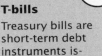

T-bills
Treasury bills are short-term debt instruments issued by the U.S. government.

Despite the powerful rise in energy and metals prices recently, the principal source of gain in the commodity indexes has been the roll return. This is largely because most indexes are so heavily weighted in energy products.

Deutsche Bank, for example, estimates that the crude oil component of its commodity index earned a compound annual return of 20 percent over the past 15 years, even though the spot return was barely 6 percent (remember, index methodology assumes fully paid, or unleveraged, commodities positions). DBLCI also realized a 5 percent return on its collateral. The biggest component of its gain came from the roll: a return of 9 percent.

Broad-Based Index Futures

Conventional commodity index futures, and their associated options, are very thinly traded on the futures exchanges. In large part, this is due to the wide array of customizable over-the-counter commodity index derivatives that are available to institutional users through large investment banks and trading houses. Smaller retail investors, too, tend to shy away from the contracts because of their large sizes. More investor-friendly vehicles offering index exposure are available elsewhere.

The futures exchanges, while keeping the index products listed, seem to be doing little to support or promote the use of these contracts.

- *CRB futures:* Two floor-traded versions, both optionable, are listed on the New York Board of Trade. The Reuters/Jeffries CRB contract is sized at $200 times the index. The larger Continuous Commodity Index version is priced at $500 times the index.

Total Return contract
a type of futures contract that accounts for three sources of return—futures, rolling of contracts, and collateral return.

Excess Return contract
known as CERF, expiring in 2011, it is a nonoptionable futures contract that is smaller than the Total Return contract.

- *GSCI futures:* The Chicago Mercantile Exchange offers two versions of GSCI futures. The *Total Return* edition follows the conventional indexing strategy discussed previously: three sources of return—futures, roll, and collateral interest. The *Excess Return contract* uses only two; it ignores the collateral return. GSCI Total Return contracts are sized at $250 times the index and trade in the pit as well as on the CME's Globex electronic platform. Options are available. There's a single GSCI Excess Return contract, known as a CERF, expiring in March 2011, that's nonoptionable. At $100 times the index, this contract is smaller than the Total Return futures.

- *DJ-AIG futures:* Traded solely on the Chicago Board of Trade's e-cbot electronic platform, the contract size is $100 times the index price. There are no options available.

Narrow-Based Index Futures

The Minneapolis Grain Exchange has listed a complex of five single-commodity indexes, all of which are optionable. Each is sized like conventional grain and oilseed contracts at 5,000 bushels, but with a 1/4-cent minimum tick. All trade electronically through the e-cbot platform and are cash-settled.

- *National Corn Index futures:* Based upon a benchmark calculated daily by Data Transmission Network (DTN), National Corn Index futures track the cash market more closely than conventional CBOT contracts, which are based upon delivery to selected terminal grain elevators.

- *National Soybean Index futures:* These futures track another DTN index and offer benefits similar to those of National Corn Index futures.
- *Hard Red Spring Wheat Index futures:* Indexing provides a more stable basis, which should be a boon for hedgers in a broad swath of localities.
- *Hard Red Winter Wheat Index futures:* See preceding entry.
- *Soft Red Winter Wheat Index futures:* See preceding entry.

Taxes on Futures

Futures on both individual commodity futures and index futures are subject to Section 1256 of the Internal Revenue Code. Gains on Section 1256 contracts are taxed as if 60 percent of the profits are long-term gains and the other 40 percent of the gains are short-term. This scheme creates a blended tax rate of 23 percent, regardless of holding period. Tax rates on other commodity index products (mutual funds, ETFs, etc.) are holding period–based. Gains on short-term holds are taxed at ordinary income rates, which can be as high as 35 percent, while long-term gains are taxed at either 5 percent or 15 percent, based on the taxpayer's nominal tax bracket.

The downside to Section 1256 treatment is that all contracts are *marked to market* at the end of each year. Taxes are due as if each contract was liquidated on December 31, so profits cannot be deferred.

marked to market
the process of repricing a commodity futures position against the current settlement price to reflect its current market value. Marking to market is done daily to determine account equity for margin purposes. Year-end marking to market, however, is required under the Internal Revenue Code to determine current tax liability. Each open Section 1256 position is *theoretically* closed out on the last business day of the year to arrive at a current gain or loss.

Smart Trader Tip

Buying and selling investment securities has tax implications. When you trade successfully over a period of time, you will pay taxes on those profits. In order to minimize the impact, it makes sense to consult a tax professional before engaging in active trading of stocks, futures, mutual funds, or any other type of investment security.

Commodity Index Mutual Funds

Debuting in 1997, Oppenheimer's Real Asset Fund (QRAAX) was the first retail mutual fund linked to a commodity index. PIMCO, one of the best-known names in bond investing, joined the fray in 2002 when it launched its CommodityRealReturn Strategy Fund (PCRAX). A number of index funds have been launched since, some broad-based, others focused upon narrow sectors of the commodity spectrum such as energy or precious metals.

Historically, broad-based commodity funds used commodity *swaps* rather than futures, to gain exposure to the target index. A swap is an over-the-counter agreement between an investment bank and an institutional investor that calls for one party to make payments to the other at a specified rate. Meanwhile the counterparty makes payments based on the total return of the underlying index.

A recent IRS ruling, however, is forcing funds that have relied upon swaps to rejigger their portfolios. Income from commodity swaps, it seems, doesn't meet the IRS test for "qualifying income" because the underlying instruments are not deemed to be securities. As a result, a mutual fund that continues to use commodity swaps for more than 10 percent of its gross income stands to lose its status as a registered investment company. That would make the taxes on portfolio income and capital gains due at the fund, rather than the shareholder, level.

structured notes

debt instruments issued by investment banks whose returns are tied to the performance of an index.

In response, funds are now turning to *structured notes* to deliver commodity returns. Structured notes are debt instruments issued by investment banks whose returns are tied to the performance of an index. Structured properly, these over-the-counter deals can qualify as securities under the Internal Revenue Code. Structured notes are pricier than swaps and less readily available, however, so this asset shift may reduce fund returns and limit the capacity of some portfolios to take in new money.

Whether a broad-based fund uses swaps or some other derivative to gain exposure to a commodity index, the bulk of its assets are likely to be held in money market instruments or short-term notes. Derivatives are leveraged, so only a small amount of capital is needed to support the positions. The balance can be held in repurchase agreements and T-bills.

While a fund's commodity exposure may be indexed, active management of the portfolio's assets may still take place. Money market collateral may be traded in an effort to generate index-plus returns for the fund (see Table 4.5).

Symbol	Name	Front Load (%)	Expense Ratio (%)	Holdings	Average P/E	Yield (%)	Annual Return (%)	Net Assets ($mm)
TABLE 4.5 Commodity Index Mutual Funds, Broad-Based and Narrow-Based								
PCRAX	PIMCO Commodity RealReturn	5.50	1.24	157		16.36	17.3	2,339
QRAAX	Oppenheimer Real Asset	5.75	1.32	265		0.90	17.3	1,118
CRSAX	Credit Suisse Commodity Return	3.00	0.95	72		2.55		228
SKNRX	DWS Commodity Securities	5.75	1.50	86	13.7	0.17		174
DXCLX	Direxion Commodity Bul 2X		1.75	8				1
ENPIX	ProFunds UltraSector Oil & Gas		1.43	94	11.9		43.7	183
OEPIX	ProFunds UltraSector Oil Equipment		1.65	92				
BMPIX	ProFunds UltraSector Basic Materials		1.58	81			23.2	
PMPIX	ProFunds UltraSector Precious Metals		1.44	13			26.8	
SNPIX	ProFunds Short Oil & Gas		1.50	92				
SPPIX	ProFunds Short Precious Metals		1.50	13				
Average			**1.44**	**88**	**12.8**	**5.00**	**25.7**	**674**

- *PIMCO CommodityRealReturn Strategy (PCRAX):* PIMCO's fund tracks the DJ-AIG benchmark. The firm relies upon its bond market expertise to manage its collateral in a mix of inflation-indexed (Treasury Inflation-Protected Securities, or TIPS) and other fixed-income securities. As a result, the fund is an enhanced index portfolio, though there's no guarantee that an incremental return can be earned in excess of the fund's target (www.allianzin-vestors.com).

- *Oppenheimer Real Asset (QRAAX):* Oppenheimer's Real Asset Fund mirrors, to one degree or another, GSCI. The fund's self-avowed goal is to maintain a correlation of at least 90 percent to the index. About a third of the fund's assets are "3X" GSCI structured notes, meaning the notes offer threefold leverage. In other words, the fund gets full exposure to GSCI by putting up only one-third of its assets. The fund makes bets on individual commodities, too, so a substantial portion of the portfolio may be held directly in futures or futures options at any given time. Oppenheimer also actively manages its collateral as a short-term bond portfolio, largely made up of U.S. government and agency debt (www.oppeneheimerfunds.com).

- *Credit Suisse Commodity Return Strategy (CRSAX):* Yet another portfolio seeking to replicate the performance of the DJ-AIG benchmark, this portfolio is a combination of commodity-linked derivatives and fixed-income securities. Unlike the PIMCO fund, however, the CSRAX fund eschews TIPS in favor of nonindexed collateral (www.credit-suisse.com/us/en).

- *DWS Commodity Securities (SKNRX):* A portion of this fund is given over to GSCI futures. The fund's benchmark is actually a blend of indexes. Half of the blend is GSCI. The other half is evenly split between the MSCI World Materials Index, which tracks global raw material equities, and the MSCI World Energy Index, which measures the performance of world-wide energy stocks. SKNRX avoids commodity-linked swaps (www.dwsscudder.com).

- *Direxion Commodity Bull 2X (DXCLX):* Managed by the firm previously known as Potomac Fund Management, DXCLX attempts to produce 200 percent of the daily price performance of the Morgan Stanley Commodity Related Index, an equal-dollar-weighted index of 20 commodity stocks. The largest portion of the fund's portfolio is devoted to over-the-counter derivatives on its benchmark, but substantial assets are also invested in exchange-traded open-end commodity funds, or ETFs (www.direxionfunds.com).

Several leveraged and inverse funds based upon narrow sector indexes are offered by ProFunds (www.profunds.com):

- *ProFunds UltraSector Oil & Gas (ENPIX):* This portfolio seeks returns corresponding to 150 percent of the daily performance of the Dow Jones U.S. Oil & Gas Index.
- *ProFunds UltraSector Oil Equipment, Services & Distribution (OEPIX):* The Dow Jones U.S. Oil Equipment, Services & Distribution Index is the target for this fund. The fund's objective is to generate returns equal to 150 percent of the benchmark's daily performance.
- *ProFunds UltraSector Basic Materials (BNPIX):* The bogey for BMPIX is 150 percent of the Dow Jones U.S. Basic Materials Index's daily returns.
- *ProFunds UltraSector Precious Metals (PMPIX):* The Dow Jones U.S. Precious Metals Index is this fund's benchmark; its target is 150 percent of the benchmark's daily returns.
- *ProFunds Short Oil & Gas (SNPIX):* There's no attempt to leverage the returns of the benchmark Dow Jones U.S. Oil & Gas Index in this fund. Its objective, instead, is to provide an *inverse* return equal to 100 percent of the index's daily performance. If, for example, the Dow index falls 5 percent in a given day, SNPIX investors would expect to see their shares *rise* 5 percent.
- *ProFunds Short Precious Metals (SPPIX):* Like SNPIX, this fund shoots for a 100 percent inverse return of its benchmark's—the Dow Jones U.S. Precious Metals Index—daily performance.

Smart Trader Tip

ProFunds UltraSector and Short funds are stock portfolios. Unlike their broad-based index cousins, there are no commodity futures held in these funds.

Exchange-Traded Index Funds (ETFs)

Exchange-traded commodity funds were introduced in the previous chapter. Some are closed-ended, meaning the number of fund shares is finite, giving rise to large value premiums and discounts. Others are open-ended portfolios that continuously create and redeem their shares.

The vast majority of exchange-traded open-end portfolios actually track indexes, including some commodity-related benchmarks. Mechanically, these index ETFs are similar to traditional mutual funds, but there are some vital differences that warrant further explanation.

Mutual fund transactions are cash-based. To create mutual fund shares, you give the fund cash; the fund then issues new shares to you and invests the cash in the fund portfolio. When it comes time for you to sell your mutual fund shares, you deliver your shares back to the fund company and receive cash in return. Your fund share is retired. Thus, the supply of open-end fund shares is open-ended; new fund shares are created as old ones are reabsorbed.

Sometimes, the fund manager must sell portfolio securities to meet the cash demand of fund redeemers. That forces the fund manager into the market and can create a tax consequence for the shareholders remaining in the fund. If portfolio securities are sold at a profit, a capital gains tax liability is created. As a mutual fund is a *pass-through* investment vehicle, the tax bite is passed through to shareholders.

In the ETF world, share creation and redemption are done only by large investors or institutions in block-size creation/redemption units (usually chunks of 50,000 shares). Share creation requires the deposit of the ETF portfolio's underlying asset, plus some balancing cash, in return for a specific number of ETF shares. If the ETF portfolio is based on a stock index, shares are delivered in quantities approximating their weight in the index, as specified by the fund sponsor. If the underlying asset is precious metal or futures, the appropriate amount of bullion or commodity contracts is transferred.

Similarly, ETF share blocks can be redeemed in return for portfolio assets. The institutional investor delivers the ETF shares to the fund and receives the appropriate amount of portfolio assets—in other words, stocks, bullion, or futures—in exchange.

These *in-kind* portfolio transactions are considered a form of barter, making them exempt from capital gains tax treatment. This process accounts for the tax efficiency of ETFs. All ETF shareholders derive benefits from this, not just the institutional creators and redeemers.

Mutual Fund Purchase/Sale Model

Figure 4.1 depicts the interaction of mutual fund investors when they buy or redeem shares. Notice that they interact directly with the fund portfolio. Most ETF shareholders, however, never deal with their funds when entering or exiting positions. For these investors, counterparties are found through the facilities of an exchange, in the form of either contrary-minded investors represented by brokers or specialists/market makers dealing from inventory (see Figure 4.2).

in-kind exchange
certain transactions are deemed nontaxable under the Internal Revenue Code. An in-kind or like-kind exchange is the most common. In an ETF redemption or creation, ETF shares are exchanged for stock or futures. Each side of the exchange deals investment assets of the same value to the other (any balancing cash is deemed incidental and isn't recognized as income to the recipient).

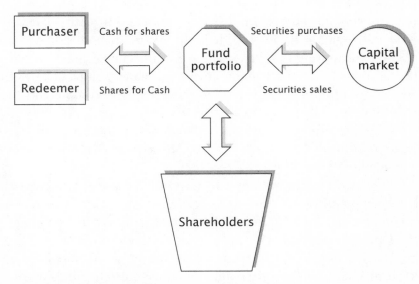

FIGURE 4.1 Mutual fund purchase/sale model.
Source: Brad Zigler.

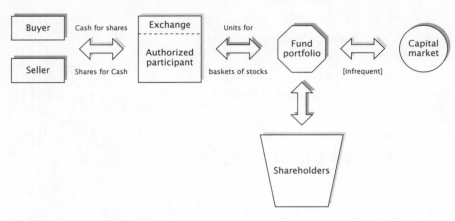

FIGURE 4.2 ETF purchase/sale model.
Source: Brad Zigler.

The prospect of arbitrage keeps ETF share prices in line with their net asset values. If an ETF begins to trade significantly above or below its portfolio value, authorized participants—those large institutional brokerages and trading houses permitted to interact directly with the portfolio—may pounce on the mispricing. By purchasing or selling the ETF stock basket and creating or redeeming the opposite position in ETF shares, arbitrageurs capture the discrepancies as profit. Arbs flatten out the price difference as the cheap side is bid up and the rich side sold off.

Also contributing to ETFs' relative tax efficiency is their passive investment style. Index fund management generates comparatively little turnover. Index fund managers tend to trade portfolio components (outside of normal rolls) only when the underlying index composition changes. Active managers, in contrast, constantly trade in and out of portfolio positions in their effort to beat the market. Turnover increases the tax liability of capital gains.

ETF expense ratios are markedly lower than those of actively traded and index mutual funds: The difference in average fund expenses between commodity index mutual funds and exchange-traded portfolios is nearly 1 percent per year. The majority of commodity-related ETFs are relatively new, so they're still flying under the radar of most fund analysts. Firms such as Morningstar will rate funds only when they've earned a three-year track record. Still, some of the older ETFs have amassed impressive reward-to-risk ratios (see Table 4.6).

TABLE 4.6 Commodity Index ETFs

Sym	Name	Expense Ratio (%)	Annual Return (%)	Standard Deviation (%)	Reward/ Risk	Yield (%)	P/E	Holdings	Net Assets ($mm)
DBC	DB Commodity Index Track	0.75							608
GSG	iShares GSCI Commodity Idx	0.75							35
XLE	SPDR Select Energy	0.26	33.4	20.2	1.65	1.10	15.5	29	4,560
IGE	iShares GS Natural Resources	0.50	34.3	18.9	1.81	0.98	13.5	130	1,453
IYE	iShares DJ US Energy	0.60	35.7	19.3	1.85	0.94	11.2	68	1,009
XLB	SPDR Select Materials	0.26	13.8	15.5	0.89	2.43	15.2	30	908
IXC	iShares SP Global Energy	0.65	33.3	18.4	1.81	1.00	11.3	63	753
IYM	iShares DJ Basic Materials	0.60	13.8	16.1	0.86	1.90	15.6	82	484
PXJ	PowerShares Dyn Oil & Gas	0.60					17.2	30	347
VDE	Vanguard Energy	0.26				1.08	11.6	149	347
GDX	Market Vectors Gold Miners	0.50						45	188
PXE	PowerShares Dyn Energy	0.60					11.8	30	127
VAW	Vanguard Materials	0.26				1.56	17.6	119	93
IEO	iShares DJ US Oil & Gas	0.48					10.7	59	34
XME	SPDR Metals & Mining	0.35						27	27
XOP	SPDR Oil & Gas Expl & Pro	0.35						35	20
XES	SPDR Oil & Gas Equip & Svc	0.35						27	14
OIH	Oil Services HOLDR						28.7	18	
Average		**0.48**	**27.4**	**18.07**	**1.48**	**1.37**	**15.0**	**59**	**647**

Broad-Based ETFs

- *iShares Commodity-Indexed Trust (GSG):* This ETF tracks GSCI by investing in GSCI Excess Return futures (CERFs) traded on the Chicago Mercantile Exchange. CERFs are used in lieu of the GSCI Total Return contracts to permit the portfolio runners to optimally manage the collateral (remember, the excess return version of GSCI comprises the futures return and the roll return, not the return on collateral). Collateral is either T-bills or T-notes (www.ishares.com).

- *DB Commodity Index Tracking Fund (DBC):* DBLCI is the benchmark tracked by this portfolio. DBC holds futures positions in the six commodities constituting the index and invests the collateral in short-term bonds (www.dbfunds.db.com).

Narrow-Based ETFs

iShares

- *Goldman Sachs Natural Resources (IGE):* This ETF tracks a modified cap-weighted roster of energy companies, timber firms, producers of pulp and paper, plantation owners, and companies engaged in the extraction of minerals.

- *Dow Jones U.S. Energy (IYE):* IYE attempts to replicate the returns generated by the Dow Jones U.S. Energy Index, which is made up of oil and gas producers as well as firms in the oil equipment, oil services, and distribution businesses. U.S. firms from all capitalization tiers—large-, mid-, and small-cap—are included.

- *S&P Global Energy (IXC):* Standard & Poor's Global Energy Sector Index is the benchmark mirrored by this ETF. Instead of full replication, the fund invests in a representative sample of the index components. Constituent companies include oil exploration and production firms, oil refiners, and oil equipment/services outfits.

Smart Trader Tip
Just as the mutual funds illustrated earlier, there are broad-based and narrow-based commodity ETFs. Broad-based ETFs own futures, while narrow-based ETFs comprise stocks. In addition to shares, many of these sector ETFs also have listed options contracts.

- *Dow Jones U.S. Basic Materials (IYM):* Companies in the mining and industrial metals, chemical, and forestry or paper sector populate the index tracked by this ETF.

- *Dow Jones U.S. Oil & Gas (IEO):* The index tracked by this ETF is a subset of the Dow Jones U.S. Energy Index. The subset comprises oil and gas producers, but excludes firms engaged in the oil equipment, service, and distribution business.

S&P Depositary Receipts (SPDRs)

- *Select SPDR Energy (XLE):* XLE is one of nine Select Sector SPDR Funds that, when aggregated, represent all of the companies in the Standard & Poor's 500 Index. The S&P 500 subset tracked by XLE comprises companies in the oil, gas, energy equipment, and services business (www.spdrindex.com).

- *Select SPDR Materials (XLB):* This ETF mirrors the aggregate performance of S&P 500 components engaged in the production of construction materials, containers and packaging, chemicals, forest and paper products, as well as mining companies. S&P 500 companies are, by definition, large caps.

- *streetTRACKS SPDR Metals & Mining (XME):* XME attempts to replicate the performance of the S&P Metals and Mining Select Industry Index, an equal-weighted subset of the S&P Total Market Index, a broad-based index covering all capitalization tiers (www.ssgafunds.com).

- *streetTRACKS SPDR Oil & Gas Exploration & Production (XOP):* The S&P Oil & Gas Exploration & Production Select Industry Index is the target for this ETF.

- *streetTRACKS SPDR Oil & Gas Equipment & Services (XES):* The bogey for XES is the S&P Oil & Gas Equipment & Services Select Industry Index.

PowerShares

- *PowerShares Oil & Gas Services (PXJ):* This portfolio mirrors the Oil & Gas Services Intellidex, a proprietary smart index that (each quarter) sorts out 30 stocks with the greatest appreciation potential based on their fundamentals, valuation, timeliness, and risk. Intellidexes are equal-dollar-weighted (www.powershares.com).

- *PowerShares Energy Exploration & Production (PXE):* The Energy Exploration & Production Intellidex is the target for this ETF.

Gold Miners

- *Market Vectors Gold Miners (GDX):* Stocks making up the AMEX Gold Miners Index are the underlying assets of this ETF. The index tracks companies primarily engaged in gold and silver mining, capitalized at $100 million or more (www.vaneck.com).

Vanguard ETFs

- *Vanguard Energy (VDE):* Vanguard's ETF follows the performance of the MSCI U.S. Investable Market Energy Index, through full replication of the index. The index includes stock in the energy sector from all capitalization tiers (www.vanguard.com).
- *Vanguard Materials (VAW):* The MSCI U.S. Investable Market Materials Index is mirrored by VAW. Companies in the metals and mining, chemical, construction materials, and paper/forest products business are included in the index.

HOLDRs

Holding company depositary receipts (HOLDRs) may look like ETFs, but they really aren't funds at all. HOLDRs shares are undivided interests in grantor trusts that hold stocks representative of a particular industry or sector. In this structure, investors receive direct voting and dividend rights to the portfolio stocks. HOLDRs investors, in fact, receive proxy materials for all the issues in the underlying basket. In contrast, ETF shareholders receive their fund's proxies, but not those of the securities in the underlying portfolio.

In another contrast to ETFs, HOLDRs purchases and sales must be done in round lots of 100 HOLDRs. There is no minimum round lot requirement imposed on ETF transactions. Trades of only one ETF share are possible, though probably not economical.

Yet another distinction: HOLDRs can also be redeemed by retail investors. Presentation of as little as 100 HOLDRs entitles an investor to take delivery of a pro rata share of securities in the portfolio. Remember that ETFs redeem shares only in large block trades negotiated with approved participants.

The securities that make up a HOLDRs portfolio are more or less static. Since there's no index to follow, there's no management of the basket. Only corporate events, like mergers, acquisitions, liquidations, or spin-offs, cause the roster to change. This can cause the component weights to change substantially over time.

Further, portfolio diversification can be compromised if component stocks are acquired by other companies; they won't be replaced in the HOLDRs basket. HOLDRs always start out as rosters of 20 stocks, but the number of components can shrink over time. For example, the Oil Services HOLDR (OIH) is now made up of only 18 issues.

When stocks are spun off from HOLDRs constituents, the spun-off issue can wind up as an orphan in an owner's brokerage account if the stock isn't in the HOLDRs sector.

HOLDRs investors pay no management fees, but a small annual custody fee—8 cents per HOLDR—is levied against cash dividends and distributions. If no dividends or cash distributions are paid on any of the portfolio stocks, the custody fee is waived.

Exchange-Traded Notes (ETNs)

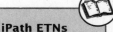

Recently, exchange-traded notes debuted to add another wrinkle to the world of commodity index investing. These securities, dubbed *iPath ETNs*, trade like ETFs but are actually debt instruments tied to one of three commodity indexes.

iPath ETNs
debt instruments tied to one of the commodity indexes that trade on the exchanges just like exchange-traded funds.

Launched in 2006 by Barclays Bank plc, the iPath GSCI Total Return Index (GSP) and iPath Dow Jones–AIG Commodity Total Return Index (DJP) track the performance of the broad commodity market, while the iPath Goldman Sachs Crude Oil Total Return Index (OIL) follows a single commodity.

ETNs, like ETFs, are designed to provide low-cost exposure to commodities. ETNs are marginable, just like ETFs, allowing investors to go long or short as they please.

There are, however, several significant differences between ETFs and ETNs. Each structure has a distinct set of advantages and disadvantages.

The iPath ETNs are 30-year senior debt securities issued by Barclays that promise to pay investors the index return, less the annual

tracking risk

the risk that an index-tracking security like an exchange-traded fund will not move in the same manner as the index it is supposed to mimic, hence, the divergence between the return of a portfolio and that of the benchmark it attempts to track.

credit risk

the risk of loss one assumes under a financial contract that a borrower or a counterparty to a derivatives contract may default or fail to perform its obligations.

expense ratio of 0.75 percent. That said, the ETN investor takes on a different kind of risk than that shouldered by the ETF investor. An ETF is only as good as its ability to track its target index faithfully. *Tracking risk*, though generally small, is borne by investors who are dependent upon fund sponsors to minimize the error. Ideally, an ETF tracking error should reflect only the fund's operating expenses, meaning the fund managers are able to match the performance of the underlying index perfectly (remember, an index is a *theoretic* portfolio, devoid of transaction and maintenance costs). Some ETF managers are better at this game than others.

ETNs offer a guarantee against tracking error—subject, of course, to the expense ratio. For that, ETN investors assume *credit risk*—the risk that the issuer won't honor its payback promises. Essentially, it's a bet that Barclays will remain solvent for the length of the investor's holding period.

ETNs could prove to be more tax-efficient than commodity ETFs. Commodity ETFs are organized as commodity pools that hold futures contracts. They continually roll positions forward, subjecting their shareholders to Section 1256 tax treatment: Sixty percent of any futures gain is considered long term and 40 percent is deemed short term. Contracts, too, are marked to market at year's end, so tax settlement takes place annually. Additionally, interest and gains from the collateral underlying the futures contracts are subject to taxation.

ETNs should, according to Barclays, be taxed as prepaid contracts mirroring an index, not an interest in an actual portfolio. Investors, then, should pay taxes only if they recognize a gain when they sell the ETN or when the note matures. There are no interim distributions expected. This advantage isn't a certainty yet because the Internal Revenue Service hasn't rendered a definitive ruling.

iPath ETNs

- *iPath GSCI Total Return (GSP):* Launched in June 2006, these notes track the conventional GSCI index. In contrast, the iShares ETF is benchmarked to the GSCI Excess Return Index, augmented with the return generated by active management of the collateral portfolio (www.ipathetn.com).
- *iPath Dow Jones–AIG Total Return (DJP):* Floated alongside GSP, this ETN has proved to be the most popular, in large part because DJP doesn't have to compete against a cannibalizing ETF.
- *iPath Goldman Sachs Crude Oil Total (OIL):* Kicked off in August 2006, this ETN is based upon a subindex of the GSCI Total Return Index. The index currently tracks light sweet (West Texas Intermediate) crude oil futures contracts traded on the New York Mercantile Exchange.

TRAKRs

A unique type of futures contract allows small investors to wager on the commodities market without the need of a futures account or the leveraged risk of a margin account.

TRAKRs (Total Return Assets Contracts) were developed by Merrill Lynch to provide small investors with market exposure to a diverse assortment of assets, including commodities. All TRAKRs are cash-settled total return index contracts and trade electronically on the Chicago Mercantile Exchanges' Globex platform.

Unlike traditional futures contracts, the buying and selling of TRAKRs doesn't require a futures account. TRAKRs can be traded inside a regular securities account, though brokerage firm representatives must first *notice-register* with the National Futures Association if they're not already registered to trade futures.

> **TRAKRs**
> Total Return Asset Contracts are a type of futures contract that allows small investors to wager on a diverse set of investments, including commodities, without a futures account.

No margin is required for retail TRAKRs purchases; investors can buy TRAKRs by simply posting a 100 percent performance bond. With the entire cash value of the contract paid up front, there are no variation margin calls looming over the heads of TRAKRs buyers. (Short TRAKRs positions *can* be undertaken, but they're margined at 50 percent, just like stock short sales.)

Most important, though, TRAKRs are small. TRAKRs start out at a nominal value of $25, less offering expenses, so they're very stock-like. Similar to an ETF, a single TRAKR can be purchased (though commission costs may make such a move financially impractical). Contracts are valued at $1 times the underlying index, which makes the minimum price fluctuation of 0.01 index points equal to 1 cent per contract.

TRAKRs offer a unique tax benefit. TRAKRs profits aren't taxed like normal futures. Instead, they're subject to taxation much like stocks, except they qualify for long-term capital gains treatment after a holding period of only six months rather one year.

TRAKRs are long-term contracts, too, so there's no roll needed to follow a buy-and-hold strategy. Most TRAKRs are now launched with expirations stretching out nearly five years.

- *Gold TRAKRs:* Expiring in December 2006, Gold TRAKRS are designed to simulate the return on bullion's spot price together with the metal's one-month lease rate. Once the most active contract in the TRAKRs' repertoire, the contract has lost ground to broader-based TRAKRs since its debut in 2002.

- *PIMCO CommodityRealReturn TRAKRs:* These contracts provide exposure to the excess return version of DJ-AIG enhanced by an index of separate accounts actively managed by PIMCO. PCT is set to expire in June 2011.

- *Rogers International Commodity TRAKRs:* Maturing in October 2010, RCI offers total return exposure to the Rogers International Commodity Index. RCI is regularly the most active commodity TRAKR traded.

One problem with TRAKRs is their relative obscurity. Brokerage firms without access to the Globex platform may not be able to provide quotes, much less transact TRAKRs business. More information on TRAKRs can be found online at www.trakrs.com or from the Chicago Mercantile Exchange.

Summary

While many investors try to outperform the market, a strong case can be made for passive investing as well. One passive approach is known as index-based investing, which is a strategy that tries to match the performance of a specific benchmark or index rather than outperform it. For example, some commodities investors measure their success or failure against the performance of the CRB index. Others, however, do not try to beat the index but choose to mimic it. Over the years, passive index-based strategies often do better than actively managed approaches.

Indexes can be used in a variety of other ways as well. They serve as benchmarks that can be used to view the broader trends within the commodities markets. Options are listed on many indexes and exchange-traded funds. These options provide additional tools for participating in price moves in the commodities markets. Commodity index mutual funds and exchange-traded funds are also tools that make it possible to gain exposure to and profit from price moves in a commodity index.

In this chapter, we explored specific examples of these tools and discussed advantages and disadvantages of each. For example, shares of mutual funds that track commodity indexes have become popular vehicles for investors. Shares of mutual funds can be purchased and can offer exposure to a variety of markets, including commodities. However, the funds sometimes impose annual expenses and are not always tax-efficient. Therefore, investors should consider other opportunities as well, including possibly trading futures, options, stocks, or exchange-traded funds. But, how do we know when to buy into these investments and when to sell? Our attention turns to that topic next, as we discuss ways to analyze the options market in Chapter 5.

Key Summary Points

1. The goal for many investors is to beat the market or outperform a benchmark or index.

2. Many commodity traders measure their success or failure against the Commodity Research Bureau index, which tracks the price moves in a basket of different commodities.

3. Passive investing is an approach that attempts to match the performance of a benchmark or index rather than trying to outperform, or beat, the market.

4. Index-based investing is a type of passive investment strategy. Actively managed portfolios, conversely, try to outperform market benchmarks.

5. The costs of active management can be substantially higher than an index approach, requiring portfolio runners to crank out higher returns just to break even.

6. While the returns from index-based investing will be only average, they tend to outperform most actively managed investment strategies over the long term.

7. To the extent an index represents the whole commodity market, using an index-based investment takes out the risk of a portfolio manager picking the wrong mix of futures or commodity-related stocks.

8. Historically, commodities are negatively correlated to stocks. When stocks rise, commodities prices usually fall, and vice versa.

9. Commodities are a portfolio-diversifying asset class that can actually reduce overall risk.

10. There are several ways to gain exposure to commodities using an index-based strategy including mutual funds, futures, and exchange-traded funds.

11. Investors should consider the advantages and disadvantages of each type of investment before committing any capital. Considerations include the expenses, tax implications, and risk associated with each investment.

Chapter

5

Fundamental Analysis of the Commodities Markets

The primary goal of a commodity trader is to accurately forecast price movements. Forecasts can be made using either fundamental or technical analysis and, in some cases, a combination of the two. *Technical analysis* relies on market data (i.e., price patterns and volume) to predict trends. In contrast, *fundamental analysis* focuses on the market environment—in particular, how supply and demand affect a particular commodity—to sense bullish or bearish trends. In a market economy, the interaction of supply and demand determines a commodity's price.

Supply

Supply represents the sum total of current commodity production together with stockpiles carried over from previous production cycles. The supply of wheat, for example, consists of the current crop,

> **technical analysis**
> the study of the price action of a security based on the theory that market prices display repetitive patterns that can be tracked and used to forecast future price movement. Technical analysis evaluates price movement by analyzing statistics generated by market activity—such as past prices and volume—to study market performance.

147

fundamental analysis

the study of all factors that might impact the supply and demand of a commodity. Weather is an example of a fundamental analysis tool for agricultural commodities.

supply

the amount of a good or commodity that is available in the market.

plus stores in grain elevators from previous harvests. From the perspective of wheat farmers, supply represents the quantities they're willing to sell over a range of prices at any given time. All things being equal, farmers are likely to grow wheat as long as its selling price remains greater than its production cost. The total supply of wheat, then, is the aggregate of each farmer's contribution to the market. To an economist, supply is represented graphically by an upward—or positive—price slope (see Figure 5.1).

Notice in Figure 5.1 how the supply, or quantity, increases along with wheat's price. This chart shows the farmer's incentive to bring more wheat to market: rising prices. As long as prices increase, the farmer will be motivated to increase production, and therefore, supply. Of course, there are other factors that can affect the wheat supply as well. Weather is an important factor, but its effect usually doesn't carry over from one crop year to the next. Technology, though, can have a long-term impact; successful technologies reduce production costs and, through their applications, increase output. That's additive to supply.

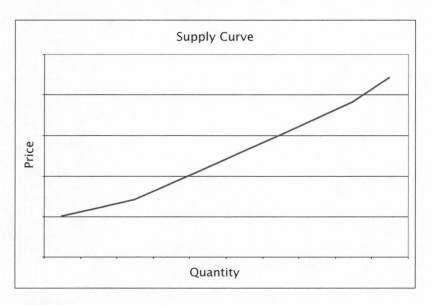

FIGURE 5.1 Supply curve.

The price of inputs, such as fertilizer and energy, can be additive or subtractive. When these costs rise, farmers have to sharpen their pencils to refigure their profit margins in light of current market conditions. These costs have the potential to turn the return on their crops into a loss; at other times, market prices may provide a comfortable cushion.

The prices of commodities competing for land use may induce farmers to curtail wheat production. Barley, for example, can be grown in the same areas as wheat. The market dynamics of the barley market may make it a more attractive crop than wheat at times. In addition, support programs, such as *government subsidies,* can induce farmers to increase production of specific products.

government subsidies
financial aid from the U.S. government.

Riding the supply curve upward, higher prices should translate into greater profits for farmers. Those profits, in turn, provide the capital needed to further increase production, which ultimately increases the supply of wheat. The now-increased supply should satisfy the existing demand. Price increases can't be sustained, however, unless this additional supply is met with new demand. Prices can be raised only if consumers show a willingness—and an ability—to pay up. Lower prices are a signal of overproduction.

Demand

There's often confusion between the terms describing the forces at work counterbalancing supply. *Consumption* represents the amount of a commodity used in a given period and is determined by price. *Demand* is the amount of a commodity that is used *at a particular price level.*

demand
the amount of a good or commodity currently used.

Along with supply, demand determines price. Consumption is *dependent* upon price. An increase in demand means that more of the commodity will be consumed at a particular price. Demand is a function of consumer behavior reflecting how much the market is willing to purchase at various prices. Demand's relationship to quantity is the reverse of supply's. Graphically, the relationship is negative: The higher the price, the lower the quantity demanded. Note in Figure 5.2 how the demand curve slopes downward as the quantity increases.

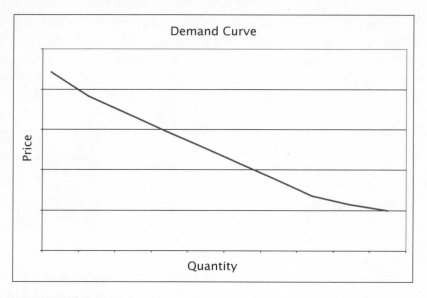

FIGURE 5.2   Demand curve.

Demand, like supply, can be influenced by other factors as well. In the case of wheat, the demand for end products such as bread, pastries, and glue is particularly influential. Higher prices ought to produce higher profits, making capital available for the expansion of production. Of course, there will be a reason to expand production only for those commodities consumers actually *want*.

When consumers aren't willing—or lack the ability—to buy at the current price, farmers have to lower prices. This ultimately results in lower profits—or, worse, losses. Losses, naturally, are a production disincentive. Production of wheat may decline, all else being equal, in the face of weak demand. More and more, farmers may turn to producing more profitable crops on their land.

Demand for a commodity is often described in terms of its *elasticity*. If demand is elastic, a change in a commodity's price produces a significant effect on demand. Elasticity is determined largely by the availability of substitutes for a commodity and the percentage of total income allocated

elasticity

the degree to which consumers respond to price changes in a commodity. A measure of elasticity can be taken by dividing the percentage change in demand by the percentage change in price. A quotient over 1 indicates relatively high elasticity; inelastic demand is indicated by a quotient under 1.

to its acquisition. The demand for soybean meal, for example, is quite elastic, since it's principally used as livestock feed. Fish meal or other products can readily replace it. Expensive commodities are more likely to be replaced if suitable alternatives are available.

Generally, the demand curves for most commodities reflect some degree of inelasticity. Change in a commodity's price isn't usually a catalyst for big shifts in demand. This lends volatility to commodity prices, especially in times of shortage.

Equilibrium

Supply and demand interact to determine a commodity's price at any given point in time. Whenever buyers and sellers agree upon a price, the bargain takes place at the *equilibrium price* (see Figure 5.3).

> **equilibrium price**
> a price level where supply meets demand. Buyers and sellers agree on price.

When the forces of supply and demand are balanced—in equilibrium—the supply and demand curves intersect. Here, buyers and sellers are willing to swap the quantity Q_1 at price P_1. At any price below P_1, the quantity demanded

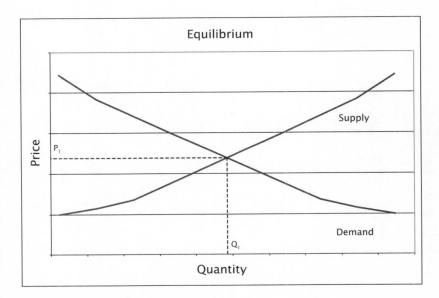

FIGURE 5.3 Equilibrium price.

exceeds the quantity supplied. Put another way, there's a shortage of supply at those prices. If prices fell below P_1, consumers would increasingly clamor for the commodity while producers would demand more compensation to bring additional product to market. Prices would rise until supply and demand were again in equilibrium.

Alternatively, at prices above P_1, the market is in surplus: there's too much supply for the current demand. Producers would have to lower prices to unload excess supply, which would, in turn, induce consumers to increase their purchases. Prices will fall until supply and demand are again in balance.

Hence, when demand or supply changes, the equilibrium price changes. For example, a bumper crop of wheat increases the available supply, but without an increase in demand, a lower equilibrium price will be found along the demand curve. Drought, however, can reduce production, but if demand remains constant, and wheat stocks on hand remain level or are reduced, a higher equilibrium price will be sought by the market.

Changes in consumer preferences can have a more long-lasting effect than weather. The market's desire for lighter foods can dramatically affect the demand for certain varieties of wheat, for example. That impact can be felt for more than one growing season. The technology that increases production output can have a depressive effect on price if demand isn't accelerating at a pace to absorb the increased supply.

The market effects we've examined apply to many, but not *all*, commodities. Wheat is a storable commodity; live cattle and hogs, however, are not. The supply curve for finished livestock looks decidedly different. In fact, there may be no curve at all; since there is virtually a *fixed supply*, it can be represented by a vertical line (see Figure 5.4).

fixed supply
a cap or limit on the amount of goods or products made available.

The supply of cattle or hogs in a given production cycle is relatively independent of market prices. Low prices won't reduce the supply, since producers have little choice but to bring animals to market once they've attained slaughter weight. High prices have little impact on supply, either, since breeding decisions have to be made a year in advance: New supply simply can't come to market any sooner.

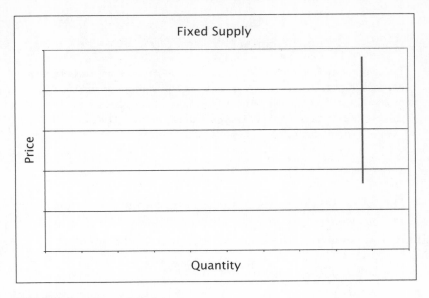

FIGURE 5.4 Fixed supply.

Sources of Fundamental Data

Armed with the proper data, economists, analysts, and traders can gauge the supply and demand pressures at work on commodities. Some sophisticated market participants build econometric models to extrapolate price trends, while others not so statistically inclined are consumers of these reports and projections.

Fundamental data can be found in diverse locales ranging from government agencies to private consulting firms. One of the oldest sources of data is the Commodity Research Bureau, which publishes the *CRB Commodity Yearbook*. The *Yearbook* provides information on more than 100 commodities including seasonal patterns and historical data. At $300 a pop, the *Yearbook* isn't cheap, but it could well pay for itself for the breadth of information it contains.

> ### Smart Trader Tip
>
> The Commodity Research Bureau (CRB) annually publishes the *Commodity Yearbook*. It provides historical data and seasonal patterns for 100 commodities. Although the book is expensive, it contains a breadth of valuable information. *The CRB Encyclopedia of Commodity and Financial Prices* is a more compact annual publication along the same lines.

The CRB also publishes a more compact annual, *The CRB Encyclopedia of Commodity and Financial Prices*, complete with long-term charts and historical analyses, for about half the price of the *Yearbook*.

Commodity Research Bureau
330 South Wells Street, Suite 612
Chicago, IL 60606
Phone: (800) 621-5271
Web site: www.crbtrader.com

For free fundamental data on specific commodities, the following resources can be consulted.

Metals

The U.S. Geological Survey, an agency within the U.S. Department of the Interior, compiles extensive data on metals such as aluminum, copper, gold, platinum, palladium, and silver.

U.S. Department of the Interior
U.S. Geological Survey
Minerals Information
988 National Center
Reston, VA 20192
Phone: (888) 275-8747
Web site: http://minerals.er.usgs.gov/minerals

Additional statistics on domestic gold and silver mining, including state-by-state production, can be obtained from the National Mining Association.

National Mining Association
101 Constitution Avenue NW, Suite 500 East
Washington, DC 20001
Phone: (202) 463-2600
Web site: www.nma.org

Data on aluminum including primary production, new orders, industry shipments, end-use estimates, and inventories is available through the Aluminum Association.

Aluminum Association
1525 Wilson Boulevard, Suite 600
Arlington, VA 22209
Phone: (703) 358-2960
Web site: www.aluminum.org

Current and historic copper supply and consumption data can be found through the Copper Development Association.

Copper Development Association
260 Madison Avenue, 16th Floor
New York, NY 10016
Phone: (212) 251-7200
Web site: www.copper.org

Energy

The U.S. Department of Energy's Energy Information Administration produces forecasts and analyses of the petroleum and natural gas markets plus a vast array of historical price data.

U.S. Department of Energy
Energy Information Administration
1000 Independence Avenue SW
Washington, DC 20585
Phone: (202) 586-8800
Web site: www.eia.doe.gov

Grains, Oilseeds, and Livestock

The U.S. Department of Agriculture (USDA) provides fundamental information on crops and livestock.

> U.S. Department of Agriculture
> 1400 Independence Avenue SW
> Washington, DC 20250
> Web site: www.usda.gov

Global supply and demand information is compiled by the USDA's Foreign Agricultural Service. The USDA also provides monthly estimates of supply and demand for grains, soybeans and products, cotton, sugar, and livestock products by e-mail though its World Agricultural Outlook Board.

Interim crop reports covering domestic production are issued weekly during the growing season by USDA's National Agricultural Statistics Service. Monthly reports on livestock are also issued by this service.

Corn

The National Corn Growers Association provides extensive production and consumption data as information on ethanol.

> National Corn Growers Association
> 632 Cepi Drive
> Chesterfield, MO 63005
> Phone: (636) 733-9004
> Web site: www.ncga.com

Wheat

The National Wheat Growers Association has an extensive reference library with self-generated reports and links to other data.

> National Association of Wheat Growers
> 415 Second Street NE
> Washington, DC 20002
> Phone: (202) 547-7800
> Web site: www.wheatworld.org

Soybeans

Educational material and market data on soybeans and biodiesel can be obtained through the United Soybean Board.

United Soybean Board
16640 Chesterfield Grove Road, Suite 130
Chesterfield, MO 63005
Phone: (800) 989-8721
Web site: www.unitedsoybean.org

Live Cattle, Feeder Cattle

The National Cattlemen's Beef Association supplies free information on beef supplies and demand.

National Cattlemen's Beef Association
9110 East Nichols Avenue, Suite 300
Centennial, CO 80112
Phone: (303) 694-0305
Web site: www.beef.org

Live Hogs, Pork Bellies

Market information and research on the pork complex is supplied by the National Pork Producers Council.

National Pork Producers Council
122 C Street NW, Suite 875
Washington, DC. 20001
Phone: (202) 347-3600
Web site: www.nppc.org

Softs

Soft commodities include cocoa, sugar, coffee, orange juice, and cotton and make up the heftiest sector in the Continuous Commodity Index (CCI), constituting 29 percent of the benchmark's weight.

Cocoa

The International Cocoa Organization is a repository for worldwide production and consumption data.

> International Cocoa Organization
> Commonwealth House
> 1-19 New Oxford Street
> London WC1A 1NU
> United Kingdom
> Phone: 44-(0)20-7400-5050
> Web site: www.icco.org

Sugar

The International Sugar Organization is the sugar industry's analogue to the International Cocoa Organization. Unfortunately, ISO charges substantially for its statistical reports. The USDA's Economic Research Service publishes free reports on the sugar market, though.

> U.S. Department of Agriculture
> 1400 Independence Avenue SW
> Washington, DC 20250
> Web site: www.usda.gov

Coffee

Another international organization, the International Coffee Organization, acts as a clearinghouse for worldwide production data and trends.

> International Coffee Organization
> 22 Berners Street
> London W1T 3DD
> United Kingdom
> Phone: 44-(0)20-7612-0600
> Web site: www.ico.org

Orange Juice

The USDA provides regular reports on orange juice.

U.S. Department of Agriculture
1400 Independence Avenue SW
Washington, DC 20250
Web site: www.usda.gov

Cotton

The cotton industry trade group, Cotton Incorporated, compiles statistics and data on the demand and production of cotton.

Cotton Incorporated
6399 Weston Parkway
Cary, NC 27513
Phone: (919) 678-2220
Web site: www.cottoninc.com

Lumber

The American Forest and Paper Products Association is the trade organization for the lumber industry. AFPPA can supply market data and reports on lumber supplies and uptake.

American Forest and Paper Association
1111 19th Street NW, Suite 800
Washington, DC 20036
Phone: (800) 878-8878
Web site: www.afandpa.org

Summary

If you're inclined enough to pore overproduction reports or consumption data, fundamental analysis can provide a perspective you can't get from merely looking at a price chart. A technical view of the market tells a trader *what* is going on, but not *why*. Fundamental analysis can explain the market's underpinnings and lend depth to the technical view. A break in a rising market may signal an overbought condition or could be attributed to a news item that doesn't alter bullish fundamentals. It's hard for a technician to know which condition exists. If you know the fundamentals of the market, you're more likely to be able to discern whether the break represents a buying opportunity in an intact bull market or whether the market trend is reversing. Of course, there's no guarantee that your fundamental data has been correctly evaluated or that your subsequent judgment will be correct, but any tipping of the odds in your favor is a benefit.

Being firmly grounded in the fundamentals of a market may also increase your confidence in a trade. You may stay with a winning trade longer if you have a feel for the market, allowing you to shake off discordant technical signals. In short, understanding the fundamentals can give you greater confidence or conviction when trading the often volatile commodities markets. That, in turn, can help you stay the course even when the markets get a bit choppy or rough.

Key Summary Points

1. Fundamental analysis of commodities focuses on the market environment and the factors that cause changes in supply and demand.

2. The supply of a commodity is the current production plus the stockpiles from previous production cycles.

3. The amount of supply in the market can depend on numerous factors including the price of the commodity, weather, and technological improvements.

4. Demand for a commodity is how much is currently being used at a particular price level.

5. Consumption is dependent on price but is not the same as demand.

6. Demand, along with supply, determines price.

7. If demand is elastic, changes in price will significantly affect it.

8. The availability of substitutes affects elasticity.

9. When buyers and sellers agree to make a transaction, that price is known as the equilibrium price. At the equilibrium price, supply and demand are balanced.

10. Changes in supply and demand cause changes in the equilibrium price.

11. A good source of information for historical prices and seasonal patterns is the *Commodity Yearbook* published by the Commodity Research Bureau.

Chapter 6

Technical Analysis of the Commodity Markets

A s discussed in the previous chapter, fundamental analysis involves the analysis of all factors that might impact the supply and demand associated with a given commodity. If there are ideal growing conditions in Colombia for coffee beans, then there would likely be an expectation of an abundant supply of coffee beans. As a result, one might rightly expect coffee futures prices to fall. Likewise, a hurricane in Florida that wipes out much of the orange crop or a drought in the Midwest that devastates the soybean crop would result in higher prices for those commodities, as traders anticipate a steep reduction in the supply of those physical commodities.

In a nutshell, fundamental analysis deals with the supply and demand factors that can cause changes to the commodity price. In contrast, *technical analysis* pays virtually no attention to the supply and demand for a given commodity. Instead, technical analysis deals with the market performance of the price of the commodity. So while fundamental analysis attempts to capture the big

> **technical analysis**
> the study of the price action of a security based on the theory that market prices display repetitive patterns that can be tracked and used to forecast future price movement. Technical analysis evaluates price movement by analyzing statistics generated by market activity—such as past prices and volume—to study market performance.

picture in terms of the factors that influence the price of a given commodity, technical analysis is used in an attempt to time the market and predict the next price move. The ultimate goal of technical analysis includes any or all of the following:

- To identify the current price trend for a given commodity.
- To identify a future price trend for a given commodity.
- To identify turning points in the price trend for a given commodity.

Each of these goals has essentially the same objective, that being to determine the optimal time to enter and/or exit a given trade in a given commodity.

Focusing on price movement using technical analysis, rather than on supply and demand factors using fundamental analysis, can be extremely important to a commodity trader due to the leverage involved in futures trading. While it can obviously be extremely useful to get the fundamental picture right, changes in fundamentals can take a long time to play out. In the meantime, commodity prices fluctuate on a daily basis. Since few traders have unlimited trading capital, most traders must protect their trading capital if the price of a given commodity moves against them.

Is it possible for a trader to get the fundamental picture exactly correct and still lose money? You bet it is. Consider a trader who enters a long position in soybeans based on the assessment that fundamental factors will cause a reduction in the supply of soybeans and that prices will ultimately move higher as a result. And let's assume that in the end this trader's opinion proves to be correct. Due to an extended period of hot weather in the Midwest, much of the soybean crop is lost, thus resulting in lower supplies and higher soybean prices. Unfortunately for the trader in this example, let's also assume that along the way soybean prices suffered a sharp, steep decline before ultimately rising to much higher levels. At some point, the open loss on this trade may exceed a tolerable limit. This tolerable limit may be some amount that the trader personally sets arbitrarily, based on his or her own account size and/or personal risk tolerance. Or perhaps a loss limit is imposed by the brokerage firm, also know as a *margin call*. As we explained in earlier chapters, a margin call is a notice from your brokerage firm to place more money into your account once it falls below a certain acceptable minimum amount based on

margin call
a brokerage firm's request for additional funds in a customer's trading account.

the trades that you presently have open. If the arbitrary stop-loss level is reached, or if the trader receives a margin call and cannot, or does not want to, enter more money into his account, the trade must be exited at a loss. At that point, the fact that soybean prices may subsequently rise is of no consequence because the trader is out of the trade.

While you can reenter the position later if your trading funds allow, the point of this discussion is that it is possible to be exactly right about the fundamental outlook for a given market, yet still lose money. This can be an extremely frustrating experience and can often cause traders to second-guess themselves the next time around, which leads to an entirely different set of problems. This is where technical analysis enters in.

Technical analysis enables traders to identify the likely direction of price movements over a given time frame for a given commodity. The ultimate goal is to enter a position at a time when the market is about to move in the desired direction without experiencing any setbacks that might compel traders to exit their positions prematurely. One of the underlying assumptions regarding the use of technical analysis is that all of the information that influences the price of a given commodity is already reflected in the price of that commodity. Or to put it another way, the markets are thought to discount changes in fundamentals either as they happen or in advance of those actual changes.

For example, if the *Farmer's Almanac* is predicting an exceptionally dry planting season for the grains, it is quite possible that grain prices will begin rising during the spring months, far in advance of the actual adverse weather conditions. Traders relying solely on fundamental information would not begin to participate in this rise until after it becomes clear that growing conditions are being adversely affected. However, traders relying on technical analysis have the opportunity to get on board much earlier, as they may react to the initial rise in prices as the beginning of a new uptrend unfolds.

Types of Indicators: Leading, Turning Point, and Lagging

Technical analysis is the study of price patterns using charts and indicators. In terms of indicators, traders often use three distinct types. A leading indicator is one that is designed to anticipate price moves before they happen. For example, a leading indicator might turn up and give a buy signal before the price of the commodity moves higher. A turning point indicator is designed to anticipate reversals or warn that prices will soon reverse directions. Lagging indicators often turn after the commodity prices, but can be used to gauge the strength or weakness of a trend. Let's take a closer look at these three types of indicators.

Leading Indicators

leading indicators

tools, data, or gauges that provide signals regarding future changes in the economy or security prices.

signal

an alert to enter or exit a position.

Leading indicators, as the name implies, attempt to identify impending changes in the trend of the price for a given commodity market. While the hope of finding some indicator that will consistently predict the future is considered by many to be the holy grail of trading, in reality this type of analysis must be done in conjunction with some real-world common sense. In other words, it is one thing to get an indication from some market indicator that the trend will be changing in the not too distant future. This type of information can obviously be extremely useful if correct. Nevertheless, an intelligent trader would not want to bet the farm solely on some prediction about the future. What many successful traders do is use leading indicators as an early warning *signal* to alert them to a potential impending change in price trend. By being alert to this potential change in trend, a trader may be able to enter a position in the direction of the new trend much earlier—and thus much more profitably—than if he or she waited for the trend-following indicators to confirm that a new trend has, in fact, developed.

Turning Point Indicators

Turning point indicators are intended to identify fairly closely when a given market trend is changing from one direction to another. Obviously, a turning point indicator that is accurate can be worth its weight in gold. The more closely the indicator comes to identifying an exact top or bottom in market prices, the sooner the user of that indicator can enter a position in the direction of the new trend. This action enables traders to maximize their profitability by allowing them to get in early on the new trend. The danger with many turning point indicators is that the process of attempting to pick tops and bottoms is fraught with peril. One danger is that these indicators sometimes generate signals that turn out to be early. To put it more bluntly, a market might be falling sharply, the indicator generates a buy signal, the trader enters a long position, but unfortunately, the market continues to decline in price. This creates two problems. First, and most obvious, the position quickly begins to generate a loss. Second, and potentially more dangerous, traders who have developed a great deal of confidence in a particular turning point indicator may feel a compulsion to give the market a little more room to turn around before cutting their losses. This can lead to larger-than-expected losses. So while turning point indicators can be tremendously useful, you must make sure to maintain your discipline if a particular signal does not work out the way you expect it to.

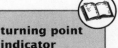

turning point indicator

an economic or financial variable that signals changes in economic activity or price changes in financial assets. For example, a turning point economic indicator might signal a bottom in economic activity and a potential rebound.

Lagging Indicators

Lagging indicators are most often referred to as *trend-following* indicators. They are referred to this way because they do not generate signals until after a change in price trend has already taken place and some evidence has occurred to suggest that a new trend is now in place. On the face of it, trend-following indicators sound like the least useful of the three types of indicators mentioned. However, in reality, it is likely that more money has been made using trend-following methods than with leading or turning point indicators. It's simply difficult to accurately predict the future (as with leading indicators) on a consistent basis. Likewise, since market prices fluctuate widely, it is extremely difficult to consistently pick important price tops and bottoms

lagging indicators

economic or financial variables that tend to follow economic activity or price moves in financial assets. A lagging economic indicator, for example, will reach a peak after a peak in economic activity.

with great accuracy (as with turning point indicators). Conversely, it is often not all that difficult to objectively identify a trend that is currently in place. The concern, of course, is whether that trend will continue. And this concern is what causes some traders to eschew trend-following methods. Still, history has shown that trading in the direction of the current trend typically affords traders the greatest likelihood of achieving long-term success.

Classic Technical Analysis Tools

Technical analysts have many tools at their disposal. While many use sophisticated computer software programs to develop advanced indicators, simple charts, trendlines, and other classic tools often work the best. Let's look at a few examples.

Moving Averages

moving average

a measure of the average price for a given commodity over the past *x* number of days, typically used to define a market's trend.

One of the most common forms of technical analysis is the use of *moving averages*. What is a moving average? In its most simplistic form, a moving average is simply a measure of the average price for a given commodity over the past *x* number of days, with *x* being a variable set by each individual trader, given his or her own preferences. As I will discuss momentarily, there are several different ways that a moving average can be calculated. The two most popular methods are referred to as the simple moving average and the exponential moving average.

Regardless of the method that a trader chooses to use to calculate a moving average, the end goal is to construct an indicator that will help identify the current trend of the market in question. When selecting a moving average to use, there are several factors to consider. Some traders prefer to use a shorter-term moving average in order to focus on the most recent market activity. Other traders prefer to use a longer-term moving average in an effort to identify the longer-term trend of the market in question. Furthermore, still other traders utilize a method known as a *moving average crossover* to identify market trends. A moving average crossover occurs when one moving average crosses from below to above (or from above to below) another moving average. Oftentimes traders will use these types of crossovers to designate a change in trend.

Simple Moving Averages

To calculate a simple moving average, or any moving average, you must first decide on the length of the moving average you want to follow—be it 2 days, 10 days, 100 days, or whatever. The closing prices for a specific market for that number of previous trading days is then added together and divided by the number of days considered. For example, if you wanted to know the 10-day moving average for May soybeans, you would simply add up the closing price for the July soybean contract over the past 10 days and then divide the sum by 10. Likewise, if you wanted to know the 200-day moving average for May soybeans, you would simply add up the closing price for the July soybean contract over the past 200 days and divide the sum by 200. This process is referred to as a *simple moving average*. Figure 6.1 displays soybeans with a 10-day simple moving average and Figure 6.2 displays soybeans with a 200-day simple moving average.

simple moving average
the arithmetic mean or average of a series of prices over a period of time.

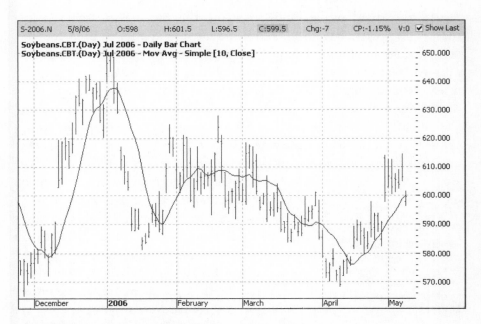

FIGURE 6.1 Soybeans with 10-day moving average.
Source: ProfitSource.

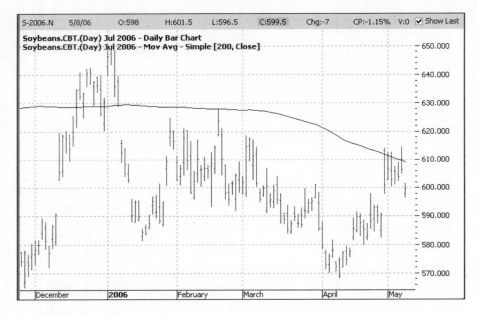

| S-2006.N | 5/8/06 | O:598 | H:601.5 | L:596.5 | C:599.5 | Chg:-7 | CP:-1.15% | V:0 | ✓ Show Last |

Soybeans.CBT.(Day) Jul 2006 - Daily Bar Chart
Soybeans.CBT.(Day) Jul 2006 - Mov Avg - Simple [200, Close]

FIGURE 6.2   Soybeans with 200-day moving average.
Source: ProfitSource.

As you can see in Figure 6.1, a trader looking at this chart might interpret the trend to be bullish because the moving average is rising sharply and prices have been above the moving average as of late. However, a trader looking at Figure 6.2 would likely interpret the trend to be negative because the 200-day moving average is trending lower and prices have invariably been holding below that moving average for a number of months.

Figure 6.3 displays both moving averages on the same chart. You can see several points in time when the two moving averages crossed over one another. This type of action is referred to as a moving average

whipsaws
short-term trading signals without any follow-through. Instead, prices bounce higher and lower without developing a trend.

crossover. The typical interpretation of a moving average crossover is that the trend is considered to be bullish when the shorter-term moving average is above the longer-term moving average and bearish when the shorter-term moving average is below the longer-term moving average. While this obviously will not always be the case, many traders prefer using moving average crossovers to simply compare the latest price to a single moving average in order to reduce the number of *whipsaws* that can occur.

In other words, a commodity trading in a narrow range may bounce above and below a given moving average repeatedly, thus generating a number of trending indications that do not ultimately follow through. At the same time, two moving averages are more likely to cross over much less often. The downside to using a moving average crossover is that when a strong new trend does arrive, a moving average crossover may be slower in reacting to the new trend than a simple price versus moving average approach.

FIGURE 6.3 Soybeans with 10-day and 200-day moving average.

Source: ProfitSource.

Exponential Moving Averages

exponential moving average (EMA)

a type of moving average that gives greater weight to the latest data. Some traders prefer exponential moving averages over simple moving averages because they offer more reliable information regarding the most recent trends or prices.

An *exponential moving average* (EMA) is very similar in nature to a simple moving average. The primary difference is in the method of calculation and the smoothness of the resulting average. A simple moving average simply drops a day of data and adds a new day of data to the sum each day. For example, if you are using a 20-day moving average, then on the twenty-first day, the first day's closing price is dropped from the sum of daily closing prices and the closing price of the twenty-first day is added. In the case of extreme daily price movements, this can cause the moving average to occasionally move in a herky-jerky fashion. An EMA attempts to generate a smoother average.

An EMA is calculated using the following formula:

Today's EMA = (Previous Day's EMA × Multiplier #1)
+ (Today's Closing Price × Multiplier #2)

Variable A = # days used for the exponential moving average

Multiplier #2 = 2/(Variable A + 1)

Multiplier #1 = (1 − Multiplier #2)

Now let's look at how these formulas would work for a trader who wanted to use a 25-day exponential moving average (see Figure 6.4).

Variable A = 25 days

Multiplier 2 = 2/(25 + 1), or 0.0769

Multiplier 1 = (1− 0.0769), or 0.9231

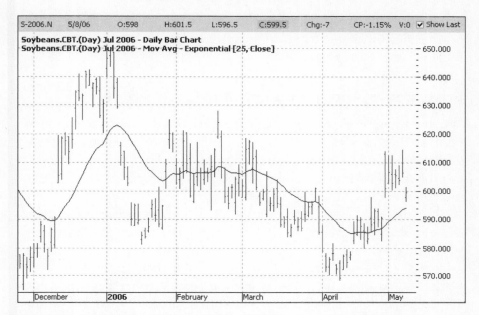

| S-2006.N | 5/8/06 | O:598 | H:601.5 | L:596.5 | C:599.5 | Chg:-7 | CP:-1.15% | V:0 | ☑ Show Last |

FIGURE 6.4　Soybeans with 25-day exponential moving average.
Source: ProfitSource.

So now let's assume that July soybeans closed yesterday at 603 and that yesterday's 25-day EMA was 598. Now let's say that today soybeans lost 2 cents and closed at 601. Let's look at how today's 25-day exponential moving average would be updated:

$$\text{Today's EMA} = (\text{Previous Day's EMA} \times \text{Multiplier \#1}) + (\text{Today's Closing Price} \times \text{Multiplier \#2})$$

$$\text{Today's 25-Day EMA} = (598 \times 0.9231) + (601 \times 0.0769) = 598.23$$

Moving Average Trading Applications

Computing moving averages is relatively straightforward and, with the use of computers, is really quite easy. However, plotting the averages is not enough. In order to trade profitably with moving averages or any other indicator, strategists must develop a system or a method for identifying reliable trading signals.

Price Moves Above or Below Moving Average

Whatever length of moving average traders choose to use and whatever method they choose to calculate the moving average, there are several ways to commonly interpret the action of moving averages and the action of the market in question around that moving average or a set of moving averages.

In the early days, many traders used moving averages as a stand-alone tool to determine when to enter and exit trades. For example, a trader might do some testing and determine that the optimum moving average for trading coffee is 25 days. So from then on, anytime coffee futures closed above their 25-day moving average, the trader would enter a long position. Likewise, anytime coffee futures closed below their 25-day moving average, the trader would reverse from a long position to a short position. At times, most notably when a market was trending strongly, a trader could generate very profitable results using this simple approach.

However, as trading has evolved and technology has gotten more sophisticated, the game has changed somewhat. Since so many more people are now following any given commodity market—thanks to the advent of computerized trading, which allows traders to track more information than ever before—the commodity markets typically do not trend as much as they used to. There tends to be more corrections, pauses, and pullbacks than in the past, even during strong trends. Therefore, traders relying solely on a single moving average to generate all of their trades are likely to experience many short-term movements, or whipsaws.

Whipsaws occur when a market closes above and then below a moving average in very short order, thus causing traders to continually reverse positions, all the while chalking up a series of losses. While each individual loss may be small, the sum can eventually run into a lot of money. There is also the psychological wear and tear that traders experience during a string of losing trades. As a result of these factors, fewer traders rely solely on moving averages to generate entry and exit signals in the commodity markets.

In today's more sophisticated markets, traders will typically use moving averages as a *filter* to help identify the current trend of the market they are analyzing. The most simple and common interpretation includes the following generalizations:

filter
a device or program that separates data or information in accordance with set criteria.

- If the price of the commodity is presently above a given moving average, the trend is considered bullish.
- If the price of the commodity is presently below a given moving average, the trend is considered bearish.

This does not necessarily imply that a long or short position will always be held. Many trading systems have been developed that incorporate moving averages in an effort to trade in the direction of the major trend of the market in question. While some traders attempt to use moving averages in a mechanical way, it's important to remember that not every cross of a given moving average necessarily generates a *tradable signal*. Likewise, there are no magic moving average numbers that always work best with all markets. As a result, many successful traders use moving averages simply as a tool to filter, or try to identify, the current trend of the market. For example, one useful application among successful traders is to take only long trades if the commodity is above the moving average of choice and to take only short trades if the commodity is below the moving average of choice. In other words, a trader may use a moving average or combination of moving averages to determine the current trend of the market, then utilize another indicator to generate actual trading signals only in the direction of that trend. While there are pros and cons to any technique, the advantage to this approach is that it can greatly reduce the number of whipsaws that a trader must endure and also can allow a trader to focus on trades that have the highest probability of generating a profit.

Figure 6.5 shows soybean oil crossing several times above and below its 20-day moving average. While in this example, buying every upside cross and selling short at every downside cross might well have proven profitable, this won't always be the case. Therefore, some traders might use the moving average as a filter and consider taking long trades (triggered or confirmed by another indicator) only when bean oil is trading above its 20-day moving average and taking short trades only when bean oil is trading below its 20-day moving average.

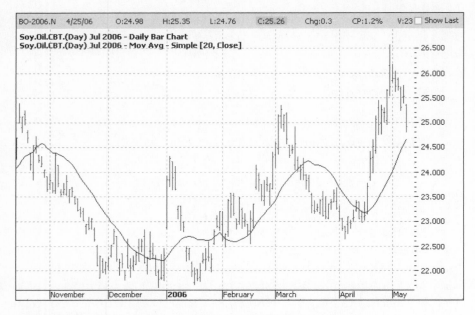

FIGURE 6.5 Soybean oil with 20-day simple moving average.
Source: ProfitSource.

Moving Average Crossovers

Figure 6.6 shows the same soybean oil price data, but this time 20-day and 55-day exponential moving averages are applied rather than just one single moving average. In theory, a trader might use this information in a systematic way, entering a long position when the 20-day average rises above the 55-day average and/or, reversing a short position when the 20-day average drops below the 55-day average. Whether that approach might be profitable can be determined only by actually testing the idea against previous data. And even if the method proved to be profitable in the past, there is no guarantee that it will be profitable in the future.

Smart Trader Tip

Moving averages are among the most basic indicators, but they are not all the same. One important factor to consider is the number of days used to compute the moving average and the investor's trading time frame. For example, day traders and other short-term players are not likely to rely on 50- or 200-day moving averages for entering trades. Instead, they might use 9- or 16-day averages.

| BO-2006.N | 3/7/06 | O:25.17 | H:25.2 | L:24.57 | C:24.67 | Chg:-0.48 | CP:-1.91% | V:32 ☐ Show Last |

FIGURE 6.6   Soybean oil with 25-day simple moving average and 55-day simple moving average.
Source: ProfitSource.

Another useful interpretation might be to consider taking long trades only when the 20-day average is above the 55-day average and placing short trades only when the 20-day average is below the 55-day average. Since moving average crossovers typically occur less frequently than crossovers of price above and below a given moving average, this can reduce the number of false signals generated.

Moving Average as Support or Resistance

Oftentimes a given moving average acts as a support or resistance level for a given market. In other words, as prices approach a given moving average from above (i.e., as prices fall toward a particular moving average), often the decline will pause when the moving average is hit. Likewise, as prices approach a given moving average from below (i.e., as they rise toward the moving average), often the advance will pause when prices reach the moving average.

As an example of this phenomenon, Figure 6.7 displays gold prices with a 50-day exponential moving average overlaid. Note that on at least four or five occasions the price of gold pulled back and touched the

| GC-2006.M | 2/14/06 | O:546.3 | H:555.5 | L:542.7 | C:553.7 | Chg:6.8 | CP:1.24% | V:31 ☐ Show Last |

FIGURE 6.7 Gold with simple 50-day exponential moving average.
Source: ProfitSource.

50-day exponential moving average—in several cases, temporarily break-ing down to trade below the moving average. In each case, however, the market reversed back to the upside.

Many traders look for opportunities to buy into a pullback or sell short into a rally. Looking for a market to bounce off of and reverse back away from a moving average often provides traders with this very opportunity.

If you are an active trader, another useful approach can be to iden-tify a market that is trending strongly and then look for that market to pull back to a shorter-term moving average. Very often this can give you the opportunity to enter new trades in the direction of the overall trend, thus allowing you to multiply your profits.

In Figure 6.8, you can see that gold trended strongly higher be-tween November and May and was especially bullish during January and April. The bar chart displays gold prices along with the 8-day simple moving average. Note how many times during these strong rallies the 8-day average was touched and then followed by a reversal back to the up-side. A trader who had used these touches of the moving average as buying opportunities could have generated a number of profitable trades.

Many novice traders begin by using moving averages in a mechani-cal way to generate automated buy and sell signals. While this can be a profitable approach when a market is trending strongly either up or

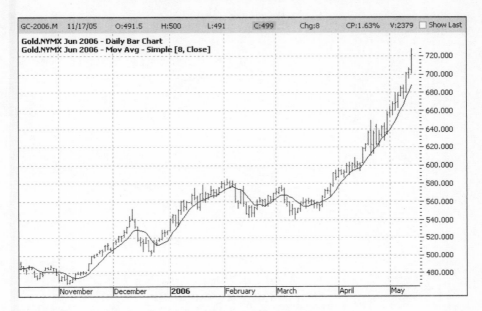

| GC-2006.M | 11/17/05 | O:491.5 | H:500 | L:491 | C:499 | Chg:8 | CP:1.63% | V:2379 | ☐ Show Last |

FIGURE 6.8 Gold with 8-day simple moving average.
Source: ProfitSource.

down, it can also lead to long periods of little or no new profits as a market experiences a trendless period. What I hope you learn from the preceding examples is that there are ways to use moving averages that do not involve having to act on every cross above or below a given moving average. Using a single simple or exponential moving average, or a moving average crossover, to designate the overall trend as bullish or bearish is a simple but powerful technique that allows traders to focus on only the best opportunities (i.e., long trades in an uptrend and short trades in a downtrend). Likewise, using moving average as support or resistance can allow traders to enter into low-risk trades just before a market powers back in the direction of the major trend. Remember, thinking differently than the average trader is one of the keys to long-term success as a trader.

Moving Average Convergence/Divergence (MACD) Indicator

The *moving average convergence/divergence (MACD) indicator* was developed by Gerald Appel and is one of the most popular and commonly used technical indicators. While the MACD indicator is typically considered a trend-following tool, many traders like to employ this versatile indicator because it incorporates momentum into its formula and can thus, at

moving average convergence/ divergence (MACD) indicator

an indicator developed by Gerald Appel and calculated using three separate exponential moving averages. Typically used to track market trend, it can also be used to identify market turning points.

times, generate signals in advance of actual turning points in a given market.

The MACD is calculated in several steps. First, two separate exponential moving averages of varying lengths are calculated using the formula described in the earlier discussion about moving averages. Then, for each trading day the difference between these two exponential moving averages is recorded. Last, a third exponential moving average can be calculated that uses the daily differences between the first two averages. This may sound like a mouthful and would, in fact, require a fair amount of work to actually calculate each day by hand. The good news is that virtually any charting package will instantly display the MACD indicator on a bar chart for any given commodity.

The typical default settings for the MACD indicator are 13, 26, and 9. What this means is that a 13-day and a 26-day exponential moving average are calculated each day. Then the daily difference between these two averages is smoothed using a 9-day exponential moving average. Figure 6.9 displays a graph of crude oil futures with

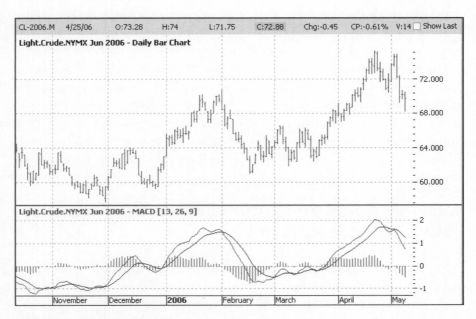

FIGURE 6.9 Crude oil with MACD indicator.

Source: ProfitSource.

the 13/26/9 MACD overlaid at the bottom of the graph.

As you can see in Figure 6.9, the indicator calculates two lines. The first line represents the difference between the 13-day and the 26-day exponential moving averages. The second line is the 9-day moving average of the first line. The graph also displays a *histogram* that plots the raw difference between the two values. This histogram is designed to help traders identify at a glance whether the MACD trend is presently up or down.

histogram
a method of plotting data at the bottom of charts that appears as a graph similar to a frequency distribution chart in statistics.

MACD Trading Applications

Traders typically use the MACD indicator in one of two ways: either as a trend filter or as an actual mechanism for signaling trade entries and exits.

MACD as a Trend Filter

As explained in the discussion of moving averages, successful traders will often trade only in the direction of the major trend of the market. Simple and/or exponential moving averages offer one way to accomplish this task. The MACD, because it is also calculated based on moving averages derived from price movement, can also be used very effectively in this role. And because the MACD indicator contains some elements of data *smoothing*, it can often be more reliable than a simple moving average that drops an old day of data from its calculation each trading day. Figure 6.10 displays a graph of live hogs with both the MACD indicator and a 20-day simple moving average overlaid.

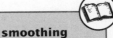

smoothing
a mathematical technique that removes excess data unevenness.

As you can see, at any given point in time, live hogs will trade above or below the 20-day moving average. Likewise, at any point in time, the MACD histogram may be positive or negative. Many savvy traders gain advantage by focusing only on trading the long side when both the price trend and the MACD trend are bullish (i.e., only long trades will be taken when live hogs are trading above the moving average and the MACD histogram is positive). On the flip side, it also makes sense to focus only on trading the short side of the market during those times when both the price trend and the MACD trend are bearish (i.e., only short trades will be taken when live hogs are trading below the moving average and the MACD histogram is negative).

FIGURE 6.10   Live hogs with MACD indicator.
Source: ProfitSource.

Another important consideration is what to do whenever there is a conflict between two trend-identifying indicators. For example, at times live hogs may be trading above the moving average but the MACD histogram will be negative, or live hogs may be trading below the moving average but the MACD histogram will be positive. During these times when the indicators are not in agreement, an alert trader may choose to avoid that market and seek another opportunity in a different commodity where the trend indicators do line up on the same side—whether bullish or bearish.

MACD as a Signal Generator

By design, the MACD indicator measures momentum in the marketplace as well as trend. As a result, traders looking to get a jump on a new trend will often consider using crosses above or below zero by the MACD histogram as actual buy and sell signals. Figure 6.11 displays a graph of sugar futures with buy and sell signals generated by the MACD indicator highlighted on the price chart. Up arrows indicate buy signals and down arrows indicate sell signals. While it is generally not recommended that traders base their trading decisions entirely on just one indicator, the signals displayed in Figure 6.11 do give you an idea of the potential usefulness of objectively derived trading signals.

FIGURE 6.11 Sugar with MACD indicator.
Source: ProfitSource.

As with many trend indicators, buy and sell signals will occasionally capture major trending moves, thus resulting in potentially big profits. However, these big trending moves will occasionally be countered by whipsaws. As discussed earlier, this is a situation where a signal is given in one direction and the market then quickly reverses in the opposite direction, resulting in a new signal occurring in short order. Traders who engage in this type of trading must be prepared to act quickly and without hesitation when whipsaws occur.

Smart Trader Tip

The MACD is most useful as a trend-filtering indicator. If you choose to use it to generate buy and sell signals, you might consider using another indicator as confirmation.

Stochastics

The *stochastic* indicator was developed by George Lane and has a number of potential uses for the active commodity trader. As with many technical indicators, different traders may use stochastics in different ways. Some will

stochastics

an oscillator used to indicate overbought and oversold conditions for a security.

use this indicator as a trend-following tool and others will use it as a means for identifying turning points in a given market. This indicator considers where the current price of a given commodity is in relation to its corresponding range of high and low prices during a given window. The typical default value assigned to the stochastic indicator is 14. Using this 14-day default, you can attempt to determine where the current price is in relation to the 14-day high and 14-day low. Then this value, which is calculated daily, is smoothed several times to establish a useful indicator. As you will see shortly, this value can be varied greatly, with the effect of generating some very interesting and, at times, useful information.

%K

the primary indicator value used to create or compute stochastics. %K is based on the high, low, and closing values of a commodity.

The stochastic indicator generates two indicator values: *%K* and *%D*. %K is the primary indicator generated from the calculations. %D is derived by smoothing a %K reading over the previous several trading days. As a result, in the finished product, %K will rise and follow and %D will trail %K. In Figure 6.12, %K is depicted by the solid line in the "Stochastic" window at the bottom of the graph. %D is represented by the dashed line. Notice that as %K rises, %D follows below. Eventually %K tops out and declines, thus crossing below %D. As %K declines, %D follows %K to lower ground until %K ultimately moves back above %D. There are a number of ways to utilize this information to trade.

%D

a secondary indicator used in computing stochastics. %D is computed by smoothing %K over a set period.

Stochastics Trading Applications

The majority of commodity traders use stochastics as an overbought/oversold indicator. In other words, when the %K value reaches a low level, these traders begin looking for a crossover of %K back above %D to generate a buy signal or an upside reversal in trend. Likewise, when the %K value reaches a high level, these traders begin looking for a crossover of %K back below %D in order to generate a buy signal or a reversal in trend.

Figure 6.12 displays a bar chart for corn futures with the standard 14-day stochastic %K and %D plotted below it. In this example, turning points in the stochastic indicator while in overbought or oversold territory typically coincided quite closely with turning points in price and resulted in some very useful trading signals. Useful buy signals occurred in December,

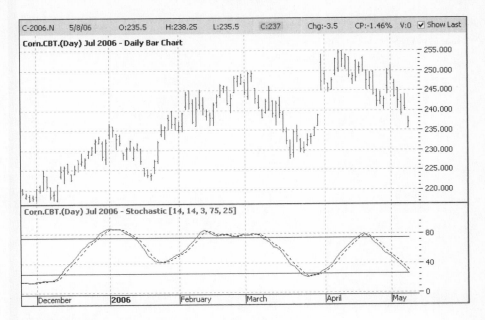

| C-2006.N | 5/8/06 | O:235.5 | H:238.25 | L:235.5 | C:237 | Chg:-3.5 | CP:-1.46% | V:0 | ☑ Show Last |

FIGURE 6.12 Corn with 14-day stochastics.

Source: ProfitSource.

January, and March. Likewise, peaks in the value of the stochastic indicator in December, February, and April preceded declines in the price of corn. Still, it is important to remember that while the turning points identified in this chart generated useful information, this is not always the case.

One danger to be aware of regarding the use of stochastics arises when a market makes an extended price movement, either up or down. When a market embarks on a major, extended advance, the stochastic indicator can reach overbought or oversold territory very quickly and, more important, can remain there for an extended period of time. In Figure 6.13, you can see that copper futures broke out to a new high in March and that stochastics reached overbought levels around the same time. Despite the fact that this market was supposedly overbought according to the stochastic indicator, the market continued to move sharply higher. In addition, in mid-April the stochastic indicator began to roll over (i.e., the %K value dropped below the %D value). However, unlike the corn example in Figure 6.12, this rollover in the stochastic %K and %D values did not produce a good trading signal. In fact, the price advance actually accelerated to the upside during this time frame. Therefore, while stochastics can be extremely useful at times, traders who use this indicator must be aware that not every cross of %K over %D will generate a useful trading signal.

Many successful traders learn to customize indicators to suit their own preferences, rather than relying on the standard interpretation. One

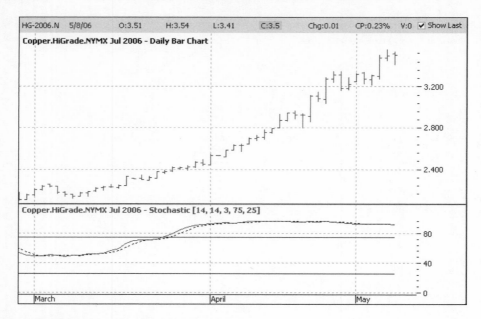

FIGURE 6.13 Copper with 14-day stochastics.
Source: ProfitSource.

way to customize the stochastics indicator is to go to an extremely short-term interpretation or an extremely long-term interpretation. Consider the examples that appear in Figures 6.14 and 6.15. Figure 6.14 displays a bar chart of live cattle with the stochastic indicator set to very short-term variable values. As one might expect, this method stays in tune with the very short-term gyrations of the market and will reach peaks and troughs much more quickly. Figure 6.15 displays a bar chart of live cattle with the stochastic indicator set to very long-term variable values. In this chart, the stochastic indicator is bullish during the initial major advance, then rolls over and stays negative as live cattle top out and then decline. A potential bottom is suggested when %K once again rises back above %D.

Alert traders can find uses for both types of information. Others might consider combining the two. For example, a trader might consider taking long trades when the long-term version of the stochastic indicator is bullish (i.e., %K is greater than %D) and the short-term version of stochastics is oversold. This configuration can afford a trader the opportunity to buy during dips within a longer-term uptrend.

Each interpretation of the stochastics indicator, whether used with standard values typically employed throughout the industry or some custom setting that best reflects one's own trading time frame, can have a place in any trader's toolbox.

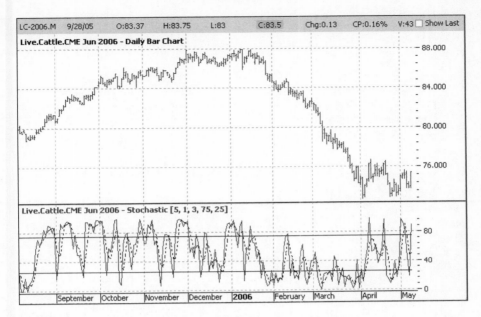

FIGURE 6.14 Live cattle with short-term stochastics.

Source: ProfitSource.

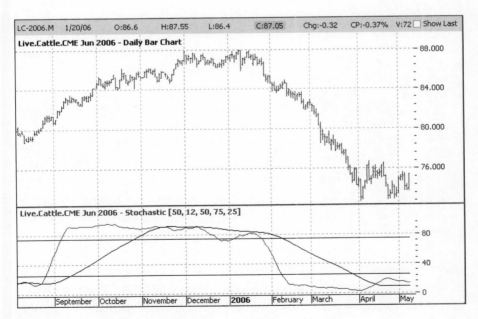

FIGURE 6.15 Live cattle with long-term stochastics.

Source: ProfitSource.

Smart Trader Tip

Experiment with the stochastic indicator. Try it as a trend-following indicator, as a turning-point indicator, and as an overbought/oversold indicator. You may want to also experiment with much longer and shorter day windows than the standard 14-day that most people use as a default.

Relative Strength Index (RSI)

an oscillator calculated by using daily price changes over a specified day window, typically used to identify overbought or oversold situations, with high readings suggesting an overbought market and low readings an oversold market.

countertrend indicator

if an indicator declines to a low level, it signals oversold conditions, and traders look to buy. When it reaches a high level, the market is overbought, and traders look to sell.

Relative Strength Index (RSI)

The *Relative Strength Index* (RSI), developed by Welles Wilder, was originally designed to identify overbought and oversold situations in the market. Like the stochastics indicator, RSI is one of the first basic indicators that many commodity traders become familiar with. Also, like the stochastic indicator, the typical default value for the RSI indicator is 14 days. While the RSI is typically used as a *countertrend indicator,* as with many other indicators, different traders may use it in a variety of ways. Some will use short-term indicator values, others will use long-term values, and still others will simply use the typical default value. In addition, some traders will interpret the RSI on a trend-following basis rather than as an overbought/oversold indicator.

The RSI value for a given market is calculated by summing up separately all of the advancing days and the declining days over the past *x* number of days. So, if a trader used the typical default of 14 days, she would look at the last 14 days of trading data and add up all of the advances for any days on which the price for that market closed higher. In addition, she would add up a separate total by summing up all of the declines for any days on which the price for that market closed lower. The RSI value is then arrived at by dividing the sum total of all advances by the sum total of all declines and then multiplying the result by 100. The calculation may sound complicated; however, any trader using software to analyze markets need not worry about the inner calculations of a given indicator. A computer will handle that. The trader's more important task lies in determining how to interpret the results and how to trade more profitably.

RSI Trading Applications

The majority of commodity traders use the RSI as an overbought/oversold indicator. In other words, when the RSI reaches a low level, these traders begin looking for a reversal in the market back to the upside. Likewise when the RSI reaches a high level, these traders begin looking for a reversal in the market back to the downside.

Figure 6.16 displays a bar chart of corn futures with a 14-day RSI overlaid. The classic interpretation of RSI states that when the 14-day RSI reaches 70 or higher, the market is overbought and may be due to decline. Conversely, when the 14-day RSI reaches 30 or lower, the market is oversold and may be due to bounce higher. Figure 6.16 displays examples of this classic interpretation. The RSI for corn fell below 30 in November; these oversold readings preceded an advance to higher prices in December. During that December advance, the RSI touched the overbought level of 70. Shortly thereafter, corn witnessed a short-term decline in price.

As with most indicators, there are alternative ways to interpret the data, rather than relying solely on the typical analysis done by the majority of traders. The RSI fits into this category. In addition to the classic interpretation shown in Figure 6.16, the RSI can be used as a trend filter and as a shorter-term trading tool.

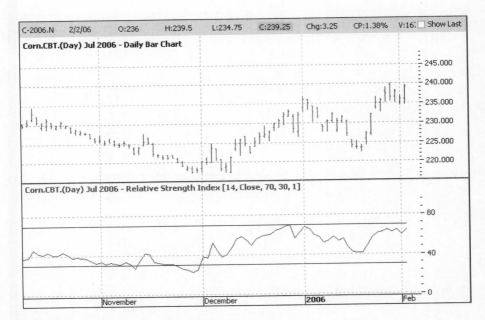

FIGURE 6.16 Corn with 14-day RSI.
Source: ProfitSource.

RSI as a Trend Filter

The usefulness of identifying the current trend and focusing on the direction of that trend has already been discussed. While the majority of traders use the RSI as a countertrend indicator, it can be used as a trend filter. Typically, a longer-term value of, say, 25 days will be used in order to attempt to minimize the number of *whipsaw signals* that may be generated. A trader might assume that as long as the RSI is above the neutral level of 50, the trend is up. On the flip side, when the RSI is below the neutral level of 50, then the trader will assume that the trend is down. Figure 6.17 displays a bar chart of cotton futures with the 25-day RSI indicator overlaid.

whipsaw signals

signals that lead to an entry into a position and are followed by an abrupt move in the opposite direction. Whipsaw signals can occur frequently in choppy markets and will cause traders to enter trades, only to exit them for a loss shortly thereafter.

As you can see in Figure 6.17, the RSI was typically above 50 while cotton was trending higher in January and February. Likewise, the RSI was typically below 50 while cotton was trending lower in March, April, and into May. Consider how useful it might have been to have traded cotton only from the long side during January and February and only from the short side during March through May.

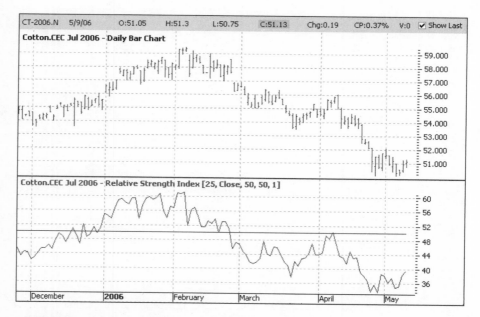

FIGURE 6.17   Cotton using 25-day RSI as a trend filter.
Source: ProfitSource.

RSI as a Short-Term Indicator

While the typical default value for the RSI is 14, many active commodity traders have learned to use a much shorter-term version of this useful indicator to help identify good short-term buying and selling opportunities. Figure 6.18 displays the same price chart for cotton as the one that appeared in Figure 6.17. What is different, however, is that the RSI default value has been changed from 25 days to 3 days. As you can see, and as one would expect, the short-term version of the RSI in Figure 6.18 fluctuates much more actively than the long-term version in Figure 6.17.

Once again, the important thing to note is that not every move above 70 or below 30 by the RSI will automatically generate a profitable trading signal. However, consider what might happen if you used a longer-term version of the RSI (as in Figure 6.17) to identify the overall trend of a given market, and then used a shorter-term version of the RSI (as in Figure 6.18) to generate trading signals in line with the overall trend. For example, if the 25-day RSI is above 50, thus suggesting an uptrend, you might consider buying when the 3-day RSI drops into oversold territory. This is an example of buying on a dip within an existing uptrend. On the short side, if the 25-day RSI is below 50, thus suggesting a downtrend, you might consider selling short when the 3-day RSI rises

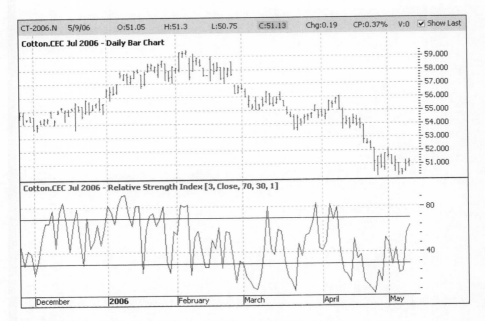

FIGURE 6.18 Cotton using 3-day RSI as a trend filter.
Source: ProfitSource.

into overbought territory. This is an example of selling short within an existing downtrend. In Figure 6.18, these methods would have generated several good short-term buy signals in January and February and several outstanding sell short signals in March and April.

This example is one more illustration of the potential usefulness of combining two or more indicators and of the flexibility available to traders who are willing to look at traditional indicators in nontraditional ways.

Smart Trader Tip

Like stochastics, the Relative Strength Index (RSI) is quite useful when longer- or short-term day windows are employed. A 25-day window makes a good trend-confirming indicator. A 3- to 6-day window can be extremely useful as a short-term overbought/oversold tool.

Average Directional Index (ADX)

The *Average Directional Index*, or ADX, was also developed by Welles Wilder and is fairly unique among market indicators. What makes the

Average Directional Index (ADX)

a chart indicator designed to help traders measure trend intensity. Readings below 20 indicate a weak trend, while readings above 40 indicate a very strong trend.

oscillator

technical indicator used to identify overbought and oversold price regions.

basic ADX indicator unique is that by itself, it does not generate any buy or sell trading signals. The purpose of the ADX is simply to measure the strength of the current major trend. Determining whether the market is trending or not trending (moving sideways) is useful information, because certain indicators give more useful results depending on the market doing one or the other. The ADX indicator is an *oscillator* that fluctuates between 0 and 100. Even though the scale is from 0 to 100, readings above 60 are relatively rare. Low readings, below 20, typically indicate a weak trend; high readings, above 40, indicate a strong trend. The indicator does not grade the trend as bullish or bearish, but merely assesses the strength of the current trend. A reading above 40 can indicate a strong downtrend as well as a strong uptrend.

The ADX can also be used to identify potential changes in a market from trending to nontrending. When the ADX begins to strengthen from below 20 and/or moves above 20, it is a sign that the trading range is ending and a trend could be developing. Wilder originally utilized a default value of 25 days when he began using the ADX. Nevertheless, today the typical default value used for the ADX indicator is 14 days.

Smart Trader Tip

Oscillators work well in identifying overbought and oversold conditions, but can also give early buy or sell signals in strong trending markets. There is an adage among traders that goes, "An overbought market can stay overbought." So, during a powerful advance, an oscillator might give a sell signal too early. Instead, these indicators work better in range-bound or sideways markets.

ADX Trading Applications

The theory behind the ADX is that the higher the ADX value, the stronger the present trend. Likewise, a low value for the ADX suggests the lack of a meaningful trend. Many traders use the ADX as a filter for deciding whether to trade a given market and/or to determine which market to trade when faced with a choice between one or more trading opportunities. In theory, a trader using a trend-following approach should benefit from trading those markets that are trending most strongly. Many commodity traders utilize a trend-following approach whereby they attempt to identify the current trend of a given market and then attempt to ride that trend as long as possible. As a result, many traders utilize the ADX in an effort to identify those markets that are presently exhibiting the strongest trends. In other words, a commodity with a high ADX value is considered to be trending more strongly than a commodity with a low ADX value. As a result, a trader may find it advantageous to focus on trading the market with the high ADX value.

There are no hard-and-fast rules regarding what constitutes a high value versus a low value for the ADX. Typically, traders who use the ADX as a filter look for an ADX value of at least 25 using a 14-day window. Some traders use a higher cutoff of, say, 30 and others consider anything over 30. Finally, still other traders look to see which markets presently have the highest ADX values and focus on trading those markets, regardless of the actual raw level for the ADX.

Figures 6.19 and 6.20 display two different markets with the 14-day ADX value overlaid. In Figure 6.19, you can see the cocoa market chopping around fairly trendlessly. In the period displayed, the ADX value never rose above 20. So any trader using a cutoff value of at least 20 would have completely avoided this choppy, trendless state of affairs.

In Figure 6.20, you can see the copper market break out to a new high and then accelerate to the upside. After dropping below 20 in mid-March, the ADX value then rose back above 20 and then 30 in a matter of about 12 trading days. By about the end of April, the ADX value had reached the extremely high level of 60 before leveling off. Oftentimes a market that moves sharply in one direction spooks traders, and they are hesitant to climb aboard for fear that they have missed the move. No one wants to buy the top. A sharply rising ADX value that has not already reached extreme levels of, say, 50 or 60 is typically a positive indication that a strong, enduring trend is taking place.

Smart Trader Tip

The ADX is a great tool for deciding which markets to trade when you have more opportunities than you can realistically trade at one time. Particularly if you are using a trend-following approach, focus on those markets that are exhibiting the strongest trends. That being said, once the ADX exceeds 50, be aware that the current trend is getting long in the tooth and profit taking may soon be in order.

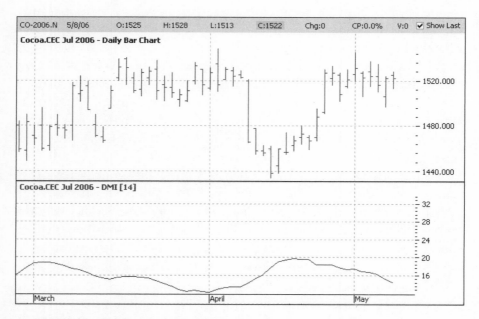

FIGURE 6.19 Cocoa with 14-day ADX.
Source: ProfitSource.

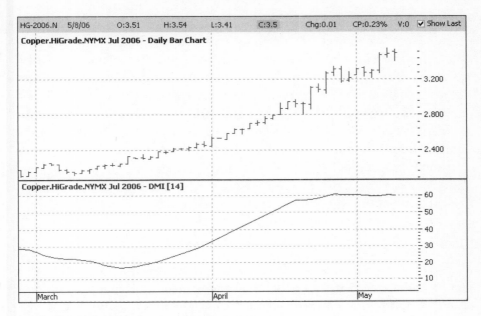

| HG-2006.N | 5/8/06 | O:3.51 | H:3.54 | L:3.41 | C:3.5 | Chg:0.01 | CP:0.23% | V:0 | ☑ Show Last |

Copper.HiGrade.NYMX Jul 2006 - Daily Bar Chart

Copper.HiGrade.NYMX Jul 2006 - DMI [14]

FIGURE 6.20 Copper with 14-day ADX.

Source: ProfitSource.

Bollinger Bands

Bollinger bands are named after their creator, John Bollinger. Bollinger first came to fame as a stock market analyst in the 1980s and has since gone on to become a widely respected analyst and investment advisor. The theory behind Bollinger bands is that regardless of the fluctuations in price that any market experiences, ultimately prices have a tendency to *regress to the mean*. This simply implies that a market will typically move only so far in one direction before reversing course, even if only temporarily. Thus, an alert trader who can identify when prices have moved too far in one direction can often identify such movements as good trading opportunities.

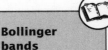

Bollinger bands

an indicator developed by John Bollinger to measure volatility and overbought/oversold markets by drawing standard deviation bands above and below an *x*-day moving average.

Bollinger bands are calculated using two variables. The first variable is the number of days in a simple moving average; the second is a multiplication factor. The typical default value for the moving average day window is 20 days. So if a value of 20 is used, then at the close of each trading day the 20-day simple moving average of the market in question is calculated. The second variable is a multiplier, or multiplication factor. The typical default value for Bollinger bands is 2.0. The *standard deviation* of the daily change in closing prices over the past *x* days (*x* is the moving average day window just discussed) is calculated. Standard deviation is a mathematical formula that measures volatility and shows how the price of a given commodity is spread around its true value. This value is then multiplied by the multiplication factor and then added to and subtracted from the simple moving average to generate an upper Bollinger band and a lower Bollinger band. The bands will expand and contract as the price action of an issue becomes volatile (expansion) or becomes bound into a tight trading pattern (contraction).

Bollinger Bands Trading Applications

The typical use of Bollinger bands is as a *countertrend indicator*. In other words, most traders will look for a buying opportunity or an opportunity to cover a short position once the lower Bollinger band is penetrated. Likewise, they will look for opportunities to sell short or exit a long position if the upper Bollinger band is penetrated. Figure 6.21 displays a bar chart of soybean prices with Bollinger bands (using the default of 20 and 2) overlaid.

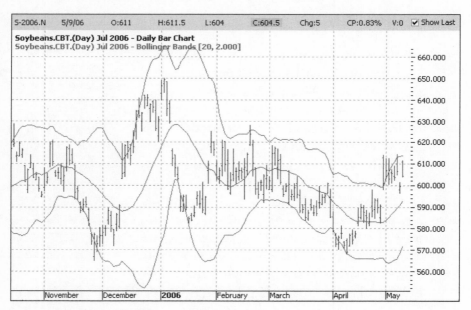

FIGURE 6.21   Soybeans with Bollinger bands.
Source: ProfitSource.

One important thing to note is that not every touch of the upper or lower Bollinger bands will result in a useful trading signal. Much like the situation when using stochastics and the RSI, traders need to be aware that a market may touch the upper Bollinger band and keep right on going to much higher levels before ultimately pulling back to touch the moving average. As a result, traders will often look for some type of market reversal to begin to unfold before acting on a touch of the upper or lower Bollinger band.

In addition to identifying relative price levels and volatility, Bollinger bands can be combined with price action and other indicators to generate signals and foreshadow significant moves. For example, a *double bottom buy* signal is given when prices penetrate the lower band and remain above the lower band after a subsequent low forms. Either low can be higher or lower than the other. The important thing is that the second low remains above the lower band. The bullish setup is confirmed when the price moves above the middle band, or the simple moving average.

double bottom buy

a type of chart pattern where a security reaches a low price, rallies up, drops to retest the previous low, and then reverses again to begin a major move higher.

Figure 6.22 provides an example of a double bottom buy signal. Gold penetrated the lower band in mid-February. It then retested that support level and briefly touched the lower band again in early March (see arrow). The subsequent *breakout* above the middle band provided the bullish confirmation. Gold subsequently embarked on a multimonth advance.

Sharp price changes can occur after the bands have tightened and volatility is low. For example, the chart in Figure 6.23 shows how Bollinger bands do not give any hint as to the future direction of prices. Direction must be determined using other indicators and aspects of technical analysis. Many commodities go through periods of high volatility followed by periods of low volatility. Using Bollinger bands, these periods can be easily identified with a visual assessment. Tight bands indicate low volatility and wide bands indicate high volatility. Volatility can be important for options players because options prices will be cheaper when volatility is low.

In Figure 6.24, you can find several examples of the bands tightening before a big move in live cattle. In August, November, and January, the bands tightened. In each case, a meaningful move followed shortly thereafter.

FIGURE 6.22 Gold with Bollinger bands.

Source: ProfitSource.

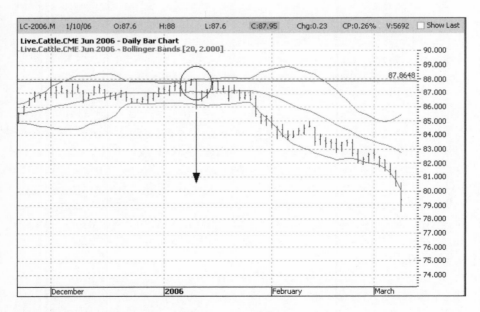

FIGURE 6.23 Live cattle with Bollinger bands.

Source: ProfitSource.

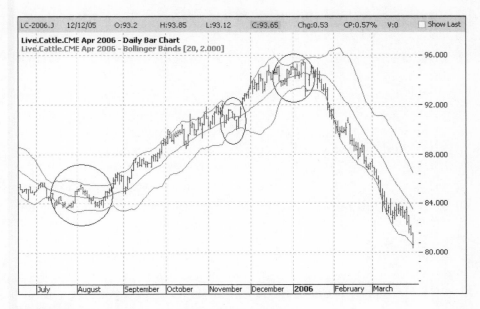

| LC-2006.J | 12/12/05 | O:93.2 | H:93.85 | L:93.12 | C:93.65 | Chg:0.53 | CP:0.57% | V:0 | ☐ Show Last |

Live.Cattle.CME Apr 2006 - Daily Bar Chart
Live.Cattle.CME Apr 2006 - Bollinger Bands [20, 2.000]

FIGURE 6.24 Live cattle with Bollinger bands.
Source: ProfitSource.

Smart Trader Tip

Don't assume that every tag of a Bollinger band generates a valid and useful trading signal. Upper and lower Bollinger bands are measures of relative value, not automatic reversal points. Look to buy on tags of the lower band if the overall trend is up; look to sell short on tags of the upper band if the overall trend is down.

Support and Resistance Trading

One of the risks of investing in the stock market is the risk that a company you own will go out of business, thus resulting in the price of the stock declining to zero. The price of a physical commodity, however, will never go to zero. Ultimately, the price of a physical commodity will fluctuate based upon the supply and demand for that commodity. If supply is low and demand is high, you will invariably see prices rise. If a true shortage occurs, prices can rise to absurdly high levels, at least temporarily. Likewise, if supply is overly abundant—for example, if planting and growing conditions are perfect for wheat—then the price of wheat will drop significantly. Still, no matter how abundant the supply and how low the demand, the price of that physical commodity will never fall to zero. Farmers are not going to give away their wheat for no charge. Orange growers in Florida are never going to give away all of their oranges.

On the flip side of things, buyers of physical commodities will attempt to lock in a price for their supplies by purchasing futures in advance of an anticipated shortage. If a company needs copper to manufacture its product, and the company expects that a shortage may soon develop, it will attempt to buy as much copper at present prices as it can. Given that it will continue to need more in the future and that it may not have room to store all it may need for future use, the company may buy futures contracts to lock in today's price up to some date in the future.

support

a price area where a security has a history of finding buyers and moving higher.

resistance

a price area where a security has a history of meeting selling pressure and moving lower.

The upshot of all of this is that there are limits to how much or how little the users of a physical commodity will pay to buy the commodity in question. As a result, it is quite common to see commodities establish *support* and *resistance* levels. A support level is a price or range of prices where declines in price tend to stop. A resistance level is a price or range of prices where advances in price tend to stop. For example, it is not uncommon for a market to fall to a particular price level and then bounce back up to higher ground. As that advance ends and prices head back down in the direction of the initial low, traders consider that previous low price to be a *support* level and will watch to see if prices can break through that support level to the downside, or whether that support level will hold and create a second low. Likewise, a market may advance to a particular price level and then fall back to lower ground. As that decline ends and prices reverse back to the upside in the direction of the initial high, traders consider that previous high to be a *resistance* level and will watch to see if prices can break through that resistance level to the upside, or whether that resistance level will hold and create a second high.

The classic interpretation regarding support and resistance is that the more times a market bounces off a given support or resistance level, the stronger that support or resistance becomes, the more likely it will hold, and prices will reverse the other way in a sustainable trend. Another point of view holds that when a meaningful support or resistance level is broken—either by an upside breakout above resistance or by a downside breakout below support—then it is more likely for that move to continue.

Figure 6.25 displays a bar chart for soybean oil along with two classic examples of support and resistance in action. First let's look at the support level that formed at 21.85 between November and January. Bean oil touched 21.78 near the end of November. Then in December this market touched this price three more times. After the third touch in the last week of December, bean oil immediately shot 2.50 points (or $1,500 per contract) higher in just a matter of days. That sharp advance failed to follow through. Nine trading days after the advance topped out, bean oil was once again back down at its support level for another test. An alert trader might have paid close attention to the action of bean oil at this time. After three days of testing support, bean oil once again reversed to the upside and went on a 3.30-point rally (or $1,980 per contract) that lasted more than a month and a half. An alert trader who had been following this test of support might have bought bean oil after it reversed once again off the 21.85 level and could have entered into a very profitable long trade.

Looking again at Figure 6.25, notice that the previously described rally ran out of steam as soon as it hit the resistance level first established in September and October of the previous year. In the first few days of March, bean oil finally reached the resistance level established earlier; the advance stopped in its tracks and almost immediately headed to lower

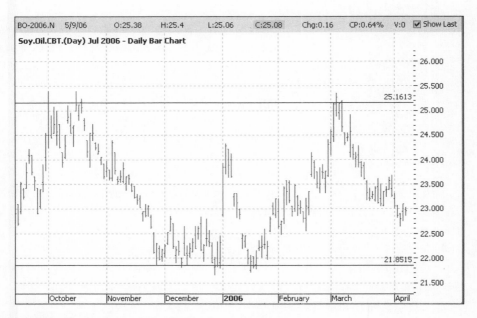

FIGURE 6.25 Soybean oil with support and resistance.
Source: ProfitSource.

ground. Once again, an alert trader who had been paying attention might have taken advantage of this opportunity to trade the short side of the bean oil market.

Trading Off of Support and Resistance

reversal

a change in the underlying trend of an investment.

head fake

a false breakout or reversal that is followed by a move in the previous direction.

breakout

a move above a resistance level or below support. A breakout accompanied by heavy volume is generally an indication that a market is ready to make a significant move higher or lower.

Not every test of a support or resistance level will fail; thus, it is important to consider the various possibilities once a support or resistance level is approached. In general terms, there are three basic possibilities. We will call them the *reversal*, the *head fake*, and the *breakout*. We already saw two examples of a reversal in the bean oil chart that appeared in Figure 6.25. During a reversal, the market runs headlong into a support or resistance level and almost immediately halts its progress. You may get one or two closing prices beyond the level in question, but overall the market goes nowhere before turning back in the other direction. Please also remember that the more times that a market bumps up against a given support or resistance level, the stronger that level tends to be at containing any breakouts.

The *breakout pattern* involves just exactly what the name implies. A market approaches an obvious support or resistance level and without much hesitation, if any, breaks through that previously significant price level to new high ground (if breaking resistance) or new low ground (if breaking support). Figure 6.26 shows a situation where gold established a resistance level at $584.84 in early February, then pulled back over $40 an ounce. Near the end of March, gold was once again nearing this resistance level. As you can clearly see in the graph, during the last few days of March, the price of gold blew through that resistance level and did not look back before surging to sharply higher levels.

The breakout scenario is the one most traders hope for, since it can oftentimes lead to quick profits. Typically, if a meaningful support or resistance level is pierced, that market will accelerate in the direction of the trend.

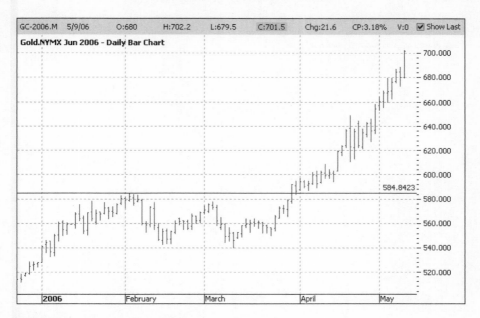

| GC-2006.M | 5/9/06 | O:680 | H:702.2 | L:679.5 | C:701.5 | Chg:21.6 | CP:3.18% | V:0 | ☑ Show Last |

Gold.NYMX Jun 2006 - Daily Bar Chart

584.8423

FIGURE 6.26 Gold breaking out to the upside.
Source: ProfitSource.

The *head fake* is the pattern that causes support and resistance traders the most headaches. If a market reaches a support or resistance level and immediately reverses, it can be a fairly straightforward move to climb on board in the direction of the reversal. When a market cleanly breaks out beyond support or resistance, here, too, it is a pretty simple notion to jump on board and ride the trend. The most frustrating scenario, however, is when a market breaks out long and far enough to convince you to enter in the direction of the prevailing trend, only to witness an unexpected reversal a few days later.

Figure 6.27 displays this scenario as it occurred in soybean meal. As you can see in the chart, bean meal made a bottom in November at around 175. After a strong rally and a subsequent decline, bean meal once again tested the 175 level in March. Finally, in April bean meal appeared to break out to the downside. It is likely that many support and resistance traders jumped on the short side of this market at that time. And they were thus frustrated when bean meal began to play with their minds. In short succession, bean meal moved back above the 175 level, then fell back, then rebounded again.

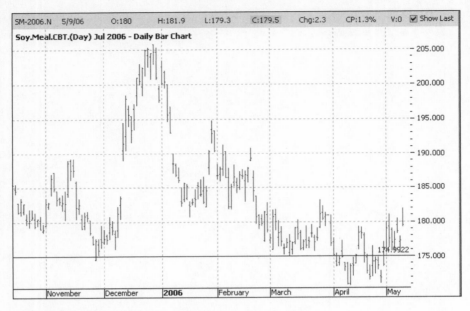

FIGURE 6.27   Soybean meal and false breakout.
Source: ProfitSource.

So the trick in trading off of support and resistance is to be aware of the possible outcomes—reversal, breakout, head fake—as the test unfolds and attempt to determine as early as possible which scenario is likely taking place. Traders often look for some confirmation or lack thereof to try to ascertain whether a given support or resistance level is likely to hold or be broken. Typically, traders will look for a *divergence* between the action of the price of the market itself and an indicator or set of indicators designed to measure momentum in the market.

> **divergence**
> when the move to a new high (or new low) in a market or security is not accompanied by a new high (or new low) in a technical indicator such as the Relative Strength Index (RSI).

Figure 6.28 zeroes in on the November through January test of support for bean oil that appeared in Figure 6.27. At the bottom of the graph are two indicators: RSI and momentum (or rate of change). As you can see in the RSI graph, each time bean oil tested the November support level, the RSI had advanced to slightly higher ground. This is an example of a positive, or *bullish, divergence* between price and indicator. In other words, the RSI is hinting that a reversal in trend may be imminent by

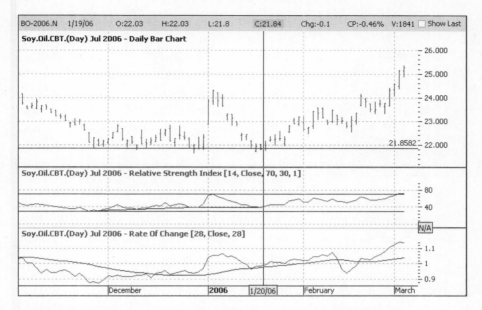

FIGURE 6.28 Soybean oil with support and bullish divergences.
Source: ProfitSource.

virtue of the fact that it is moving higher, despite the fact that prices are moving sideways to slightly lower. A *bearish divergence* occurs when the price of the underlying security hits new highs, but the indicators do not confirm that move by also moving to new highs.

The other indicator at the bottom of Figure 6.28 is referred to as the *momentum indicator*. It measures the rate of change of closing prices for the market in question over the number of days set as the default. In this case the default is 28 days. In addition, a 28-day simple moving average of the daily momentum readings itself is also plotted, and the daily momentum value fluctuates above and below this moving average. The theory is that as long as the daily momentum value is above its moving average, then momentum is increasing in the market. Conversely, if the daily momentum value is below its moving average, then momentum is decreasing in the market. As you can see in

bullish divergence

occurs when an indicator starts moving to higher ground while price is declining or moving sideways.

bearish divergence

occurs when an indicator starts moving to lower ground while price is rising or moving sideways.

momentum indicator

an indicator that uses price and volume for predicting the strength or weakness of a current market.

the chart, on that day in January, as bean oil makes its final low during its test of support, the momentum indicator is well off its low established in November and the daily value is above the 28-day moving average of momentum. This combination of factors—a repeating test of an obvious support level, a divergence between price and RSI, and momentum on the rise—will often presage a very low-risk buying opportunity for the trader willing to do the work required to track these important factors.

Traders who are prone to questioning themselves or getting frustrated when things don't go as they had expected can suffer losses in this type of situation. The key in this case, as in most cases in commodity trading, is proper money management. Never underestimate the power of risk management!

Smart Trader Tip

Pay careful attention to markets trading near significant support or resistance levels. The likely outcomes are a quick reversal, a breakout, or a false breakout and then a reversal. Confirming indicators such as RSI and rate of change can offer clues to the likely outcome. If price is headed in one direction and the indicators are headed in another, look for a failure to break through support or resistance.

Summary

Technical analysis offers traders the ability to profit in various commodity futures via the analysis of price movements. As you have seen in this section, there are many different types of technical tools available. Some indicators are designed to predict when a change in a price trend is imminent. Others attempt to generate a signal that coincides with a change in price trend. Still others are designed to identify a new trend only after it has been established.

The trick for most traders is to sift through the various indicators available and to find the most effective ones that they are most comfortable using. This can be a time-consuming process but is well worth the effort when you consider the profits that can be reaped from a successful commodity trading campaign. You should also remember to look at standard indicators in unique ways. Often it pays to do something just a little bit differently than the crowd.

This chapter introduced you to several classic indicators—moving averages, stochastic, relative strength, and so on; however, it also detailed a few ways to use some of these indicators in a nonclassic manner. This information should provide an excellent jumping-off point for you to expand your own imagination by studying a variety of technical analysis techniques.

Key Summary Points

1. Unlike fundamental analysis, which focuses on supply and demand factors for a given commodity, technical analysis focuses on the price performance of the commodity itself.

2. The primary goals of technical analysis can be any or all of the following:
   - To identify the current price trend for a given commodity.
   - To identify a future price trend for a given commodity.
   - To identify turning points in the price trend for a given commodity.

3. The ultimate goal is to enter a position at a time when the market is about to move in the desired direction without experiencing any setbacks that might compel the trader to exit his or her position prematurely.

4. There are three types of technical analysis tools: leading indicators, turning point indicators, and lagging or trend-following indicators.

5. Moving averages are one of the most widely used trend-following technical tools. Traders can use different time frames and different calculation methods depending upon their own preferences.

6. The MACD is a versatile indicator that can be used as a trend-following tool as well as a method for identifying turning points in market momentum. The MACD can also be used to identify bullish divergences, that is, situations where price continues higher while the MACD works lower, thus signaling impending weakness; or bearish divergences, that is, situations where price falls lower while the MACD works higher.

7. Stochastics offers traders another versatile tool that can be used in several different ways. A stochastic using a longer-term window can be used to help identify the underlying market trend. Shorter-term windows can be used to identify overbought or oversold situations as well as market turning points.

8. The Relative Strength Index (RSI) is typically used as an overbought/oversold indicator. The typical default value is 14 days; however, shorter windows tend to offer more useful overbought/oversold information. The index can range from 0 to 100. High readings suggest an overbought market, while low readings suggest an oversold market.

9. The ADX is designed to identify markets that are trending strongly and can be especially useful in determining which market or markets to trade at any given point in time.

10. Bollinger bands allow traders to take advantage of the fact that prices typically will revert to the mean; hence, once a market moves too far in one direction, a reversal is likely to take place. Bollinger bands offer a way to objectively identify when prices have moved too far in one direction. In addition, Bollinger Bands can give indications regarding whether the commodity is experiencing a period of high or low volatility.

11. Support and resistance levels can be extremely useful to commodity traders. Commodities are hard goods that users buy and sell actively as a part of their business. As a result, it is common for price levels to be established where users of a given commodity will consider the commodity to be cheap or expensive. Buying near meaningful support levels and/or selling short near meaningful resistance levels can offer traders low-risk opportunities.

Elliott Wave Trading for Commodities

Introduction

Most successful traders have one thing in common: They find an edge or a few edges and keep trading them—be it an edge in money management, asset allocation, technical analysis, or a combination of these. In this chapter, a couple of advanced technical analysis methods will be discussed in great depth.

Basic technical analysis consists of price pattern recognition and repetition for an underlying asset over time. With the advancements of computer processing and its affordability to the average person, highly complex and advanced technical analysis is now readily available to retail traders. However, technical analysis studies are often lagging in time or correct only after an event has occurred. *Elliott Wave analysis* constitutes one of the very few technical tools that can be predictive in nature and provide traders with a decisive edge when used with other, simpler indicators.

> **Elliott Wave Analysis**
> named after Ralph Nelson Elliott, this form of technical analysis is based on the premise that markets can be predicted by observing and identifying repetitive patterns or waves. The three major aspects of wave analysis are pattern, time, and ratio.

Dow Jones Industrial Average (DJIA)

an average made up of 30 blue-chip stocks; 28 that trade daily on the New York Stock Exchange, and 2 stocks that trade on the NASDAQ.

Ralph N. Elliott recognized that the price patterns of the *Dow Jones Industrial Average* (DJIA) were repetitive up to the mid-1940s. Through his research, he constructed principles that forecasted precisely the stock market advance in the decades beyond 1929, when most investors thought the Dow had already peaked.

In 1995, Elliott's work resurfaced and spread like wildfire when Robert R. Prechter predicted a huge market crash as inevitable during the Internet bubble era of the stock market. However, the crash did not come until a few years later. What most people do not know is that prior to Prechter's market doom prediction, he set an all-time record in a real-time monitored options trading account during a four-month contest period in the 1984 United States Trading Championship—a stunning 444 percent return. Prechter attributed this feat to his use of the Elliott Wave principles on intraday charts.

The Wave Principles

Elliott believed that the stock market is driven by mass human psychology of demand and supply. He also pointed out that a bullish market unfolds in patterns of five waves up and three waves down to form a complete cycle of eight waves (see Figure 7.1).

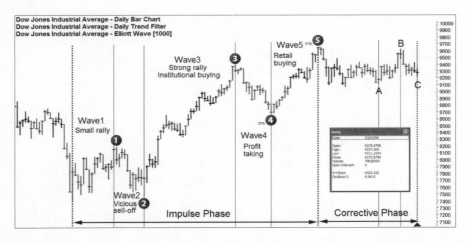

FIGURE 7.1 Daily bar chart 8/3/98 to 3/3/99, eight-wave bull cycle.
Source: ProfitSource.

The eight-wave Dow bullish cycle illustrated in Figure 7.1 is broken down into five impulsive waves during which the main trend plays out and three corrective waves after the main trend is over or is pausing. The five impulsive waves can be broken down into the following:

Wave 1: A small rally starts off a new trend, usually after a major bear or nontrending market.

Wave 2: A vicious sell-off occurs, as the small rally in Wave 1 is seen as nothing more than a correction from an oversold condition.

Wave 3: A strong rally gets going after the sell-off from Wave 2 did not go below the low of the previous bearish trend. The rally gets stronger as the price breaks above the Wave 1 high. This stage is usually triggered by institutions.

Wave 4: Institutions take profits after the buying stops.

Wave 5: Retail investors join the buying and see the Wave 4 decline as an opportunity to get in.

The three corrective waves after the main moves happen are usually nontrending or put the trend into a sideways action. Simply labeled as Waves A, B, and C, these waves often bounce between the support and the resistance levels established by the Wave 5 high and the Wave 4 low.

Smart Trader Tip

After the ABC corrective waves complete, a new trend will begin, usually triggered by the break above the Wave 5 high or the Wave 4 low. On the one hand, price action above the former will lead into another bullish cycle or extend the existing bullish cycle. On the other hand, price action breaking below the Wave 4 low will create a countertrend or a new bear cycle.

The ABC corrective can sometimes be relabeled as new Waves 1, 2, and 3 on the countertrend after Wave C breaks below (or above) Wave 4 of the previous trend. In Figure 7.2, the wave count is 12345-ABC. As soon as the support level established by the Wave 4 low gets broken, the wave count is relabeled as 12345-12345 (see Figure 7.3). In this case, the eight-wave bullish cycle develops into a new bear cycle.

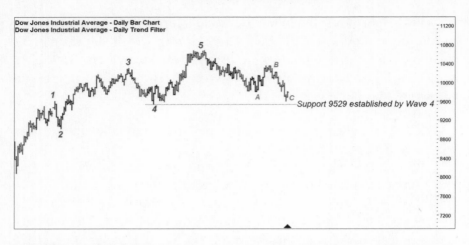

FIGURE 7.2 DJIA—daily bar chart 9/19/01 to 6/5/02, eight-wave bull cycle.
Source: ProfitSource.

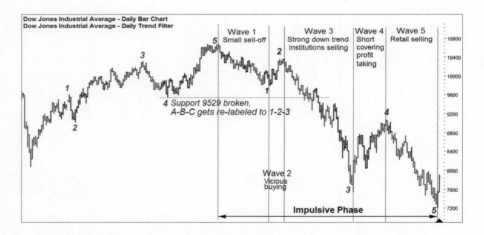

FIGURE 7.3 DJIA—daily bar chart 9/19/01 to 10/11/02, ABC waves developed into a new bear cycle after the Wave 4 support level was broken.
Source: ProfitSource.

Similar to the bull cycle, the five-wave bear cycle in Figure 7.3 can be divided into the following:

Wave 1: A small sell-off starts as the major bull trend ends.
Wave 2: Vicious buying occurs, as the small sell-off in Wave 1 is seen as nothing more than a correction from an overbought condition.

Wave 3: Strong selling gets going after the buying from Wave 2 did not go above the high of the previous bull trend. The selling gets stronger as the price breaks below the Wave 1 low. This stage is usually triggered by institutions.

Wave 4: A short covering profit is taken by the institutions after the selling stops.

Wave 5: Retail investors join the selling, as they see the Wave 4 decline as an opportunity to get out.

The question is: How can a trader know when each of these waves begins and ends in order to profit from them? Until the entire rally or decline has been completed, it is very difficult to identify the stage or label the wave counts. However, there are some rules and guidelines that govern the length of each wave in terms of both price and time. The length of each wave is related to those of all the others; Elliott based their relationships on Fibonacci ratios.

Fibonacci Ratios

Leonardo Fibonacci was an Italian mathematician who was born around the year 1170. According to most historians, Fibonacci discovered what are now called *Fibonacci numbers* after studying the Great Pyramid of Giza in Egypt. Fibonacci numbers are a number sequence generated whereby each successive number is the sum of the previous two numbers: 1, 1, 2, 3, 5, 8, 13, 21, 34, 55, 89, 144, and so on to infinity. A Fibonacci ratio is the ratio of any number in the sequence to the one adjacent to it. After the first few numbers in the sequence, the ratio of any number to the next higher number is 0.618 to 1, and the ratio of any number to the next lower number is 1.618 to 1. In addition, 0.618 is the inverse of 1.618, and vice versa. Also, the ratios of alternate numbers are 0.382 and 2.618, which are also the inverse of one another. These ratios occur naturally in most beings and are pleasing to the eye. Examples are the proportions of the human body, the arrangement of seed curves on a sunflower, the golden spiral that mollusk shells

Fibonacci numbers

Leonardo Fibonacci discovered certain sequences of numbers whereby each successive number is the sum of the previous two. For example: 1-1-2-3-5-8-13-21-34-55-89-144, and so on. Similar ratios are believed to exist in financial markets.

follow, and the curves of some animals' horns. At first it may not seem obvious that Fibonacci ratios occur all around us, but take a look at a picture frame or a door or any object whose proportions are pleasing to the eye. If you measure the ratio between the lengths and the widths, you will be surprised! It is likely to be 0.382, 0.618, 1.0, 1.618, or 2.618.

In ancient times, the Egyptians and Greeks used these ratios when they tried to express nature in some ordered mathematical form. Consequently, much ancient architecture was built using these ratios to be both functional and aesthetically pleasing.

Elliott made observations and theorized that the Dow movements also followed Fibonacci ratios. The most common ratios, or multiples, used are the following:

- 1, 1.618, 2.618, 4.236, and 6.85 (multiples for wave extensions)
- 0.14, 0.236, 0.382, 0.50, and 0.618 (ratios for wave retracements)

retracements
a move counter to the prevailing trend. Technical analysts consider 33 percent, 50 percent, and 61.8 percent retracements to be significant.

Wave 2

Wave 2 = either 50 percent of Wave 1 or 61.8 percent of Wave 1. See Figure 7.4.

- 73 percent of the time, Wave 2 *retraced* between 50 and 61.8 percent of Wave 1.

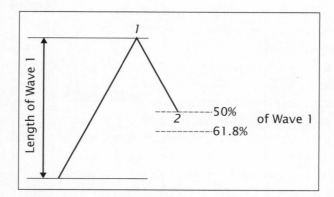

FIGURE 7.4 Wave 2 retracements.
Source: Advanced GET User's Guide.

Wave 3

Wave 3 = either 1.618 × Wave 1 or 2.618 × Wave 1 or 4.236 × Wave 1. The multiples for Wave 3 are usually 1.618 and 2.618. If Wave 3 is extended, then 2.618 and 4.236 are more frequent. See Figure 7.5.

- 2 percent of the time, Wave 3 extends less than Wave 1.
- 15 percent of the time, Wave 3 extends between 1 and 1.618 × Wave 1.
- 45 percent of the time, Wave 3 extends between 1.618 and 1.75 × Wave 1.
- 30 percent of the time, Wave 3 extends between 1.75 and 2.618 × Wave 1.
- 8 percent of the time, Wave 3 extends greater than 2.618 × Wave 1.

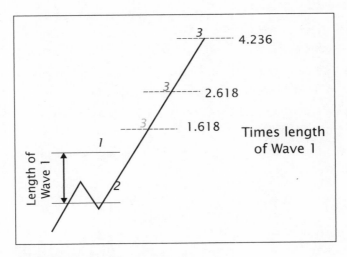

FIGURE 7.5 Wave 3 extensions.
Source: Advanced GET User's Guide.

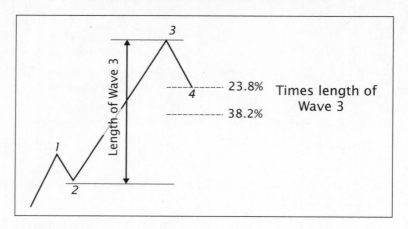

FIGURE 7.6   Wave 4 retracements.
Source: Advanced GET User's Guide.

Wave 4

Wave 4 = either 24 percent of Wave 3 or 38 percent of Wave 3 or 50 percent of Wave 3. See Figure 7.6.

- 15 percent of the time, Wave 4 retraced between 23.8 and 30 percent of Wave 3.

- 60 percent of the time, Wave 4 retraced between 30 and 50 percent of Wave 3.

- 15 percent of the time, Wave 4 retraced between 50 and 61.8 percent of Wave 3.

- 10 percent of the time, Wave 4 retraced greater than 61.8 percent of Wave 3.

Wave 5

Wave 5 has two variations. If Wave 3 is greater than 1.618 × Wave 1 or extended, then Wave 5 = Wave 1 or 1.618 × Wave 1 or 2.618 × Wave 1. See Figure 7.7.

- If Wave 3 is less than 1.618 × Wave 1, the ratio of Wave 5 will be based on the entire length from Wave 1 to the top of Wave 3; that is, Wave 5 = 0.618 × entire length or 1.0 × entire length or 1.618 × entire length. See Figure 7.8.

- Wave 5 usually lies within 61.8 percent to 100 percent of the entire length.

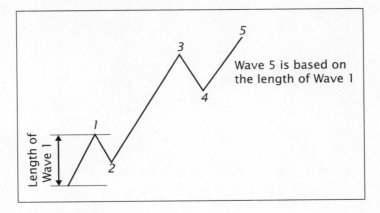

FIGURE 7.7 Wave 5 extensions.
Source: Advanced GET User's Guide.

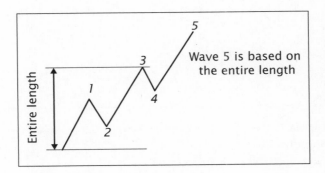

FIGURE 7.8 Wave 5 extensions.
Source: Advanced GET User's Guide.

Fibonacci Time Ratios

Fibonacci ratios apply in wave relationships not only in terms of price but also in terms of time. Their application to time is an attempt to predict when a trend might change in direction in the future. The two most common ratios are 1.618 and 2.618 on the time interval between two significant highs or lows; they are used to look for a potential change in trend at a time period in the extended future. See Figures 7.9, 7.10, and 7.11.

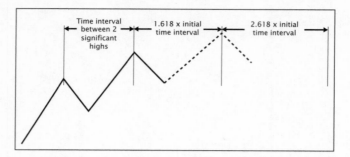

FIGURE 7.9   Fibonacci time extensions between two significant highs.

Source: Advanced GET User's Guide.

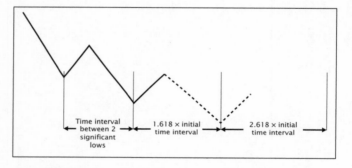

FIGURE 7.10   Fibonacci time extensions between two significant lows.

Source: Advanced GET User's Guide.

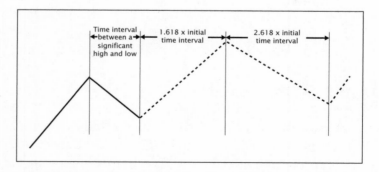

FIGURE 7.11   Fibonacci time extensions between a significant high and low.

Source: Advanced GET User's Guide.

Elliott Wave Trades

The Elliott Wave Theory works well in the commodities market, too. In some instances, it actually works better with commodities because some of them tend to trend directionally very strongly. There are four types of trades that have a high probability of success: the Wave 4 buy, the Wave 4 sell, the Wave 5 buy, and the Wave 5 sell trades.

The Wave 4 trades have a higher probability of success compared to the Wave 5 trades because the former are trades following the direction of the overall trend. Wave 4 trades are attempts to capture the Wave 5 move once small profit taking or short covering has been completed by the large institutions and the overall trend resumes.

The Wave 5 trades go against the overall prevailing trend when the trend ends. Wave 5 trades offer a larger reward-to-risk ratio (RRR) compared to Wave 4 trades. In essence, Wave 5 trades are attempts to get onto a new trend, which would be spurred by the institutions, resulting in Wave 3. Wave 3s are always larger and stronger moves compared to Wave 5s.

Trading with the Trend

Wave 4 Buy

Over the past few years, gold has continued to make higher highs and higher lows. It is very tempting to jump on the bandwagon and employ the buy-and-hold strategy. The buy-and-hold strategy begs the questions: When do I get in and when do I get out? The larger risk is that commodities can sometimes end their trend abruptly for less-informed investors, causing serious damage to trading capital. Applying the Elliott Wave Theory can put traders in a better position to pick spots to buy gold after a retracement has completed and the overall bullish trend resumes. However, using the Elliott Wave Theory alone may not necessarily make a Wave 4 buy trade successful. A few more technical indicators and studies were added in Figure 7.12 to increase the probability of success on a potential Wave 4 buy trade setup.

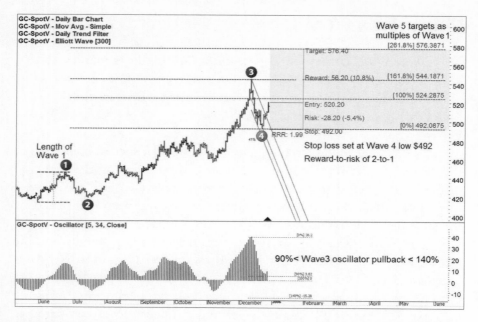

FIGURE 7.12 Wave 4 buy trade setup on gold futures on 12/28/2005.
Source: ProfitSource.

momentum

an indicator that alerts traders to overbought or oversold conditions using a formula that considers closing prices over a number of days. Momentum will oscillate above and below zero. When it falls to low levels, it indicates that the stock or index is oversold and due to bounce higher. However, when it rises to the high end of its range, the stock is overbought and likely to move lower.

The following technical indicators are added:

- The (5, 34) oscillator measures the *momentum* of the move. The oscillator calculates the difference between the 34-day moving average and the 5-day moving average. The numbers 5 and 34 were chosen because they are both Fibonacci numbers. Also, based on statistical research, their difference best represents the price momentum. In a Wave 4 buy trade setup, the Wave 3 oscillator needs to retrace or pullback by at least 90 percent, but not more than 140 percent. This is to ensure that the retracement is not too much for the overall trend to resume.

- The linear regression trend channel (three parallel down-sloping lines) envelopes the immediate price movement of Wave 4. In Figure 7.12, we are looking for Wave 4 to end and the uptrend to resume. A break above the upper trend channel might signify the end of Wave 4. Here, two price bars have broken above the Wave 4 trend channel.

- A stop-loss level is set at the Wave 4 pivot low of $492 in case the rally fails. Like any trading system, nothing is 100 percent.
- Wave 5 price targets are measured in the Wave 1 multiples to establish a profitable exit. Here, multiples of 1.0, 1.618, and 2.618 of Wave 1 are being used, since Wave 3 has extended above 1.618 × Wave 1.
- Finally, a reward-to-risk ratio is measured based on the entry price high on 12/28/2005 at $520.20, stop loss at $492, and price target at $576.40 (2.618 × Wave 1). The reward-to-risk ratio (RRR) is 2.0, which is acceptable for a Wave 4 buy setup. The RRR will increase dramatically if a limited-risk, bullish option strategy was used instead of buying the gold futures outright.

Figure 7.13 shows the gold futures price movement. Gold futures reached the projected price of $576.40 in just over a month after the entry date. Three days later, the gold price dropped, which marked the end of Wave 5 and the overall bullish trend. Gold then entered a consolidation phase.

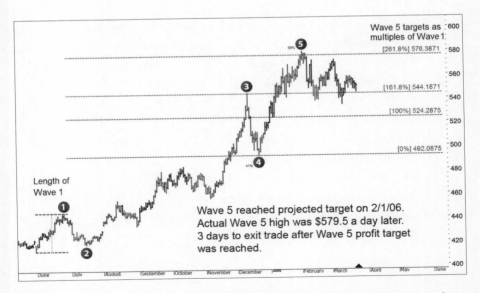

FIGURE 7.13 Gold futures reached the projected Wave 5 price target of $576.40 on 2/1/06, just over a month after the entry date.

Source: ProfitSource.

Smart Trader Tip

Computing the reward-to-risk ratio (RRR) before taking a trade makes a lot of sense. The RRR is defined as the amount of capital at risk compared to the potential profit from a trade. For example, when the amount of capital at risk is $1,000 and the potential profit is $2,000, the RRR is 2.00. Generally, trades with extremely high RRRs are long shots and will have a lower probability of success. Traders must therefore find a balance between RRR and probability of achieving profits.

Wave 4 Sell

Similar to the Wave 4 buy setup, the Wave 4 sell setup requires the overall trend to be bearish instead of bullish. Figure 7.14 shows a Wave 4 sell trade setup on the five-year Treasury futures. The additional technical indicators would have to meet the same criteria mentioned previously. More specifically:

- The (5, 34) oscillator retracement is about 110 percent in this case, well within the 90 to 140 percent retracement levels. Wave 4 in itself was 42 percent of Wave 3, just 4 percentage points above the ideal of 38 percent.

- The linear regression trend channel (three parallel up-sloping lines) envelopes the immediate price movement of Wave 4. In Figure 7.14, we are looking for Wave 4 to end and the downtrend to resume. A break that is below the lower trend channel might signify the end of Wave 4. Here, two price bars have broken below the Wave 4 trend channel.

- A stop-loss level is set at the Wave 4 pivot low of $105.45 in case the continued sell-off fails. Like any trading system, nothing is 100 percent.

- Wave 5 price targets are measured in multiples of the entire downtrend length of 0.618 and 1.0, since Wave 3 did not extend. Wave 3 was exactly $1.618 \times$ Wave 1.

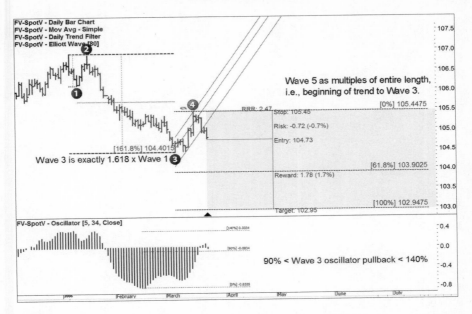

FIGURE 7.14 Five-year Treasury futures Wave 4 sell trade setup on 3/23/06.
Source: ProfitSource.

Finally, an RRR is measured based on the entry price low on 3/23/2006 at $104.73, stop loss at $105.45, and price target at $102.95 (1.0 × entire length). The RRR is about 2.5, which is good for a Wave 4 sell setup. The RRR is about 1-to-1 if the target used for Wave 5 was $103.90 (0.618 × entire length) instead. Not exactly tempting, but it can be improved with option spreads.

The five-year Treasury futures reached the projected price of $103.90 (0.618 × entire length) in three weeks from the date of entry. It took an additional nine weeks to extend to the second price target of $102.95 (1.0 × entire length). A lot of *consolidation* happened around the $103.90 area. Sometimes price movement can get stuck in a Fibonacci level, in this case the 0.618 × entire length. See Figure 7.15.

consolidation
a pause that allows participants in a market to reevaluate the market and sets the stage for the next price move.

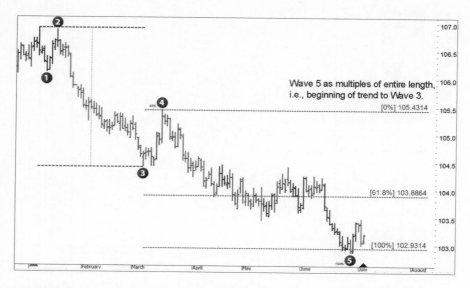

FIGURE 7.15 Five-year Treasury futures Wave 5 reached 0.618 × entire length on 4/13/06, three weeks after entry. It reached the 1.0 × entire length on 6/23/06, just over two months afterward.
Source: ProfitSource.

Trend Reversal Trades

Trend reversal trades are positions that are structured in an attempt to profit when the trend has ended and is in the process of changing its direction. Two types of trend reversal trades are (1) buying after a bearish phase has completed and (2) selling after a bullish trend has ended. The former is known as Wave 5 buy and the latter is known as Wave 5 sell.

Wave 5 Buy

After a 12345 wave sequence gets completed, the trend tends to consolidate, then reverses. Although this is rare, sometimes the trend will reverse straight after the end of Wave 5. It happens more frequently in commodities than with individual stocks. Figure 7.16 shows the overall downtrend of crude light reversing on 12/27/2005 after a Wave 5 down move ended. As trend reversal trades are less likely to work out, it is important to wait for confirmations. There are important technical indicators to check for a trend reversal confirmation. They include:

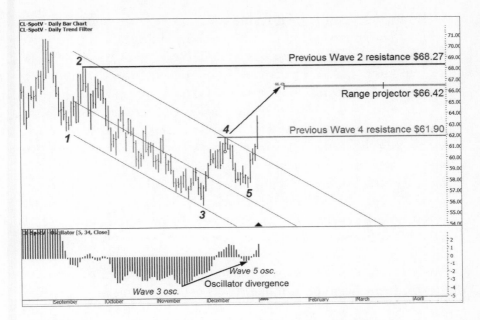

FIGURE 7.16 Crude light futures completed uptrend 12345 wave sequence on 12/27/2005. Trend reversal Wave 5 buy trade trigger occurred on 01/03/06.

Source: ProfitSource.

- Oscillator divergence: The (5, 34) oscillator measures the momentum of the preceding trend. Here, the Wave 5 oscillator is smaller in magnitude than the Wave 3 oscillator, indicating that the overall trend has ended. Divergence simply means that although the price continues to fall lower, the Wave 5 oscillator magnitude is getting smaller.
- A price bar must break out of the overall trend channel (three down-sloping parallel gray lines) and close above it. In Figure 7.16, the first price bar that closed above the overall trend channel occurred on 1/2/2006.
- A second price bar broke above the trend channel and, more important, it went over the previous Wave 4 resistance level of $61.90 the very next day. Most Elliott texts say the price always retraces to the previous Wave 4 in a trend reversal. In this case, the Wave 4 resistance was taken out and a new uptrend was definitely on its way.

Always measure the RRR before entering the trade—not necessarily a technical confirmation, but as a risk assessor. In this case, the buy entry point was the second breakout bar on 01/03/2006, with a high at $63.80 and a stop loss at the same price bar low of $60.81. Normally the Wave 4 resistance that is now the support would be used, but since the price bar low is lower, the low was used as the trade stop. The price target for the rally at the next resistance of $68.27 was established by the Wave 2 high. Using these RRR numbers (1.5-to-1) is not so great because the confirmations that were used delayed the buy entry. The probability of this trade being successful, however, has improved greatly. A fine balance exists between RRR and the probability of success. The software (ProfitSource) that was used to analyze this trade showed a lower resistance level, at $66.42, based on statistical data. This price—$66.42—would be used as a profit scaling-out point. It is always wise to take some money off the table and reduce risk when a trade works out. Scaling out of positions in one-third increments is a popular money management technique.

Figure 7.17 shows how the trend reversal buy trade worked out. Crude light reached the lower resistance level (using statistical data)

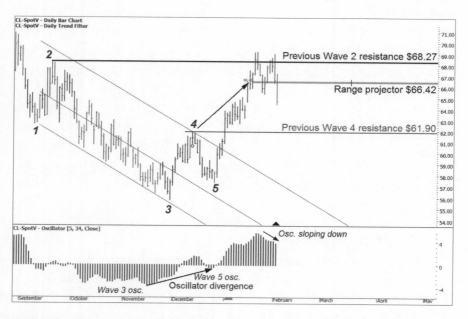

FIGURE 7.17   Crude light futures trend reversal Wave 5 buy reached the statistical projected price target of $66.42 on 01/17/06 (two weeks) and the previous Wave 2 resistance of $68.27 three days later.
Source: ProfitSource.

of $66.42 in two weeks after the trade was initiated. Three days later, it increased to the previous Wave 2 resistance level of $68.27. The actual high during this rally was $69.20.

Anyone trading without predetermined profit exit points should pay careful attention to the (5, 34) oscillator. As soon as the oscillator starts sloping down, be ready to exit the bullish trade entirely.

Smart Trader Tip

Scaling out of a position refers to taking some profits as a trade moves in your favor. For example, if the strategist has a $1,000 profit in a trade that consists of two contracts, she might take $500 off the table by selling one of those contracts and then letting the other position ride.

Wave 5 Sell

The Wave 5 sell setup looks for a completed 12345 uptrend wave sequence. After soybeans had a long bull run for nearly a year, a Wave 5 sell trade setup emerged on 05/12/04. A sell trade was triggered five days later when the price bars broke below the overall trend channel (three parallel up-sloping lines). Let's examine this situation more closely (see Figure 7.18) and check against the similar (but reversed in direction) technical indicators mentioned in the Wave 5 buy for trend reversal confirmations. They are as follows:

- Oscillator divergence: The (5, 34) oscillator measures the momentum of the preceding trend. Here, the Wave 5 oscillator is smaller in magnitude than the Wave 3 oscillator, indicating that the overall trend has ended. Divergence simply means that the price continues to go higher while the Wave 5 oscillator magnitude is getting smaller.

- A price bar must break out of the overall trend channel (three up-sloping parallel gray lines) and close below it. In Figure 7.18, the first price bar that closed below the overall trend channel occurred on 05/14/2004.

- A second price bar broke below the trend channel *and,* more important, it went below the previous Wave 4 support level of $921 the very next trading day. Most Elliott texts say the price always retraces to the previous Wave 4 in a trend reversal. In this case, the Wave 4 support was taken out and a new downtrend was definitely on its way.

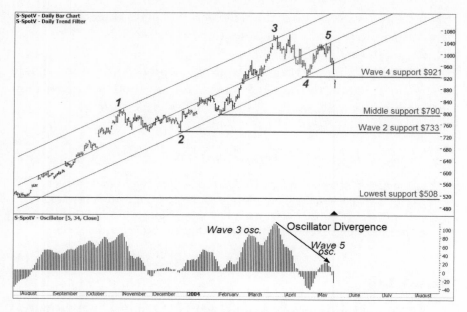

FIGURE 7.18 Soybean futures completed a downtrend 12345 wave sequence on 05/12/2004. The trend reversal Wave 5 sell trade trigger occurred on 05/17/2004.

Source: ProfitSource.

- Measure the RRR, not necessarily as a technical confirmation but as a risk assessor, before entering the trade. Here, the sell entry point was the second breakout bar on 05/17/2004—low at $882.5 and a stop loss at the previous price bar low of $932.5. Normally the Wave 4 support, which is now the resistance, would be used, but since the previous price bar high is higher, the high was used as the trade stop. Also, in a price gapping close, the commodity may fill the gap. The price target for the decline is at the next support of $790 established by a midway pivot between the previous Waves 2 and 4. The RRR using these numbers is 1.85-to-1. Since soybeans had a long bull run, it is possible that the trend reversal may also be a long one. Therefore, let's consider the Wave 2 support of $733 as the second target and the lowest support of $508 as the third target. The trade management plan would be to buy to cover one-thirds at $790 and $733. The remaining third would be a very high RRR of 7.5-to-1 trade exiting at $508. Each time soybean breaks below a support level, that support level becomes the new trade stop.

Figure 7.19 shows what happened to soybeans after the Wave 5 sell trade was triggered. As it turned out, soybeans moved lower to $801 on 06/03/2004, just $11 above the first target of $790.50. It then bounced up for about two weeks but stayed below the previous Wave 4 support, which is now the resistance. Finally, it gapped down past Wave 2 support on 06/22/2004 and continued to trade lower all the way down to $552 on 8/11/2004. This is a bearish trade, which I consider a grand slam. As mentioned before, Wave 5 trend reversal trades are low-probability trades but when they work out, the payoff can be huge.

FIGURE 7.19 Soybean futures trend reversal Wave 5 sell.
Source: ProfitSource.

Summary

Applying the Elliott Wave principles in conjunction with a few other independent technical indicators for directional trading can provide a decisive edge for a trader. The Elliott Wave principles on their own are predictive in nature but lack confirmatory triggers; therefore, it is useful to apply other technical indicators such as price bar breaks outside trend channels or support/resistance levels, oscillator analysis, and reward-to-risk ratios based on previously established support/resistance or Fibonacci extensions/retracements for profit targets and stop-loss levels. Money management is also important to lock in profits as the underlying moves in the right direction by scaling out of positions. Conversely, exiting a trade once a stop-loss level has been triggered is equally important to conserve trading capital.

Key Summary Points

1. Recognize Elliott Wave trade setups: Wave 4 buy, Wave 5 buy, Wave 4 sell, and/or Wave 5 sell.

2. Wave 4 oscillator pullbacks should be at least 90 percent but less than 140 percent for Wave 4 trades. Look for oscillator divergence for Wave 5 trades.

3. Wait for price bar breakouts from trend channels as a trigger.

4. Watch for nearby previous resistance or support levels as additional breakout triggers.

5. Use previously established support or resistance levels as profit targets or stop losses.

6. Use Fibonacci extensions for profit targets and Fibonacci retracements as stop losses.

7. Use combinations of (4) and (5) to measure the most conservative reward-to-risk ratio (RRR). As a guideline, the RRR should be at least 1.6-to-1.0 for the underlying futures trade, which would allow a higher RRR when option strategies are used on the trade setup.

8. Exit the trade when the profit target has been achieved. Scaling out of a profitable trade to lock in profits is a good money management technique, or use a trailing stop. Watch for oscillator slope in the opposite direction or a flattening out for an early indication as the move loses momentum.

9. Exit the entire trade when the stop loss gets triggered.

Options Trading in the Commodity Markets

What Is an Option?

In financial circles, an *option* is referred to as a *derivative*. A derivative is a financial instrument. Its price fluctuates based on the price movements of another security, hence the use of the word *derivative*. In other words, the price of the option is derived from the price of the underlying security. For example, the price of a given soybean option is based primarily on the price of the underlying soybean futures contract.

There are two types of options: *calls* and *puts*. The purchase of a *call option*—also known as a *long call* strategy—gives the buyer the right, but not the obligation, *to buy* a specific futures contract at a specific price until a specific date. Typically, a call option will increase in price as the underlying security rises in price.

The purchase of a *put option*—also known as a *long put* strategy—gives the buyer the right, but not the obligation, *to sell* a specific futures contract at a

option
a trading instrument that enables the buyer to purchase (call) or sell (put) the underlying market at a specific strike price until a specific expiration date.

call
a bullish type of option contract that gives the buyer the right, but not the obligation, to buy a specific asset at a specific price for a predetermined time.

put

a bearish type of option contract that gives the buyer the right, but not the obligation, to sell a specific asset at a specific price for a predetermined period of time.

strike price

a market price at which the commodity (or stock) underlying a call or put option can be purchased (call) or sold (put).

expiration date

the last day on which an option may be exercised.

premium

the actual debit (cost) to buy an option; the amount you are credited as a result of selling an option.

specific price up until a specific date. A put option will increase in price as the underlying security declines in price.

Each option has a specific *strike price* and a specific *expiration date*, and can be bought or sold for a real-time price, or *premium*.

For an option trade to occur, there must be a buyer and a seller who agree upon a price and consummate a trade. The buyer of the option may be either entering into a new long position or closing out a short position he or she already holds. The seller of the option may be either selling a position that he or she already holds or creating a new option by entering a short position in the option. When a new option is created, the seller of the option is also referred to as the *writer* of the option. To write an option means to sell an option that you do not already own.

As an example, let's consider a call option on September corn futures with a strike price of 220. This option will expire at some date prior to the expiration of the September corn futures contract—the exact expiration date is set by the exchange where the option is traded (in the case of corn, that would be the Chicago Board of Trade, or CBOT). Up until that expiration date, the buyer of this call option has the right, but not the obligation, to buy a September corn futures contract at a price of 220. Conversely, the writer of this call option may be called upon to sell a September futures contract at a price of 220 at any time until the option expiration date. As you can see from this simple example, the buyer and the seller of any option acquires certain rights and obligations by virtue of entering into their respective positions. Before discussing the specific rights and obligations conferred upon option buyers and sellers, let's first lay the groundwork and discuss some of the basics of option trading.

Contracts can be bought or sold and are described using the following four factors:

1. The name of the underlying stock (or futures, index, exchange-traded fund, etc.).
2. Whether it is a put or a call.
3. The strike price.
4. The expiration date.

The Basics of Options

In order to succeed in any endeavor in the long run, you need to have a clear understanding of the basic concepts that govern that particular field of endeavor. Option trading is no exception. The realm of option trading has a vocabulary all its own. It is important that you understand the meaning of certain key words and phrases in order to maximize your potential in the long run. While option trading offers a number of unique benefits versus other investment vehicles, the fact remains that it is different in many ways from simply buying or selling short a commodity contract.

Let's say you want to enter a long position in a given commodity. You could buy that contract at the current price, put up your margin money, and then wait to see whether the market moves in your favor. If you buy a soybean contract and it subsequently rises 10 points, then you make $500 (as soybeans trade at a contract value of $50 per point). Conversely, if beans fall 10 points, then you lose $500. While determining when to buy and sell a given commodity can be a complex decision, the act of calculating the profit or loss for a commodity trade is a very straightforward process. This is not necessarily the case with option trades. In option trading, depending on the option or options that you buy and/or sell in order to establish your position, your potential rate of return and your risk exposure can vary greatly.

An Option Lexicon

The usual assumption in using any form of analysis is to identify a specific market that you would want to buy or hold, and when the news turns bad, the investor would then want to exit the trade. With options, however, a market that shows inherent weaknesses can also signal the time to use options in a different way.

In the first hardback book I wrote—*The Options Course* (Wiley, 2005)—I provided a comprehensive exploration of options trading as it related to the stock market. All of the strategies detailed in that book, however, can be applied to the futures markets. If you make the decision to trade options, you must commit yourself to becoming successful by getting educated on the diverse factors that influence option trading. Hence, before we go any further, let's define some of the most common and most important terms associated with option trading.

call option   the purchase of a call option gives the call buyer the right, but not the obligation, within a specified period of time, to buy a given commodity contract at a specific price (the strike price), regardless of how high the price of the commodity contract may rise above the strike price.

put option   the purchase of a put option gives the put buyer the right, but not the obligation, within a specified period of time, to sell a given commodity contract at a specific price (the strike price), regardless of how low the price of the commodity contract may decline below the strike price.

underlying   refers to the commodity contract upon which a given option is based. For example, all soybean options are based on the fluctuations of a given soybean commodity contract. The September soybean commodity contract is the *underlying* contract for September soybean call and put options.

option buyer   the person who buys an option.

option writer   the person who writes or sells an option.

strike price   the price at which the underlying commodity contract can be bought (if a call position) or sold (if a put position) if the buyer of an option chooses to exercise his or her option. If the buyer of a soybean call option with a strike price of 600 chooses to exercise his or her option, he or she will then enter into a long position in soybean futures at a price of 600. If the buyer of a soybean put option with a strike price of 600 chooses to exercise his or her option, he or she will then enter into a short position in soybean futures at a price of 600.

expiration date   the date after which an option is void and ceases to exist is referred to as its expiration date. Expiration dates are set by the exchange at which the given commodity contract and its options are traded.

in-the-money option   a call option is in-the-money (ITM) if its strike price is less than the current market price of the underlying commodity contract. A put option is in-the-money if its strike price is greater than the current market price of the underlying commodity contract. If soybeans are trading at 598, then any call option with a strike price of less than 598 is considered to be in-the-money. Any put option with a strike price greater than 598 is considered to be in-the-money. The amount by which any option is in-the-money is referred to as its *intrinsic* value.

at-the-money option   a call option is at-the-money (ATM) if its exercise price is equal to the current market price of the underlying. At-the-money options have no intrinsic value.

out-of-the-money option   a call option is out-of-the-money (OTM) if its exercise price is higher than the current market price of the underlying. If soybeans are trading at 598, then any call option with a strike price above 598 is out-of-the-money. A put option is out-of-the-money if its exercise price is lower than the current price of the underlying. Any put option with a strike price of less than 598 is out-of-the-money. Out-of-the-money options do not have any intrinsic value.

intrinsic value   the amount by which an option is in-the-money is its intrinsic value. An out-of-the-money option has no intrinsic value. If soybeans are trading at 598, then a call option with a strike price of 590 has 8 points of intrinsic value (598 − 590 = 8). Likewise, a put option with a strike price of 600 has an intrinsic value of 2 points (600 − 598 = 2). So at expiration, an in-the-money option will be worth whatever its intrinsic value is, and any out-of-the-money option will expire worthless.

extrinsic value, or time premium   time premium can be thought of as the amount of money that an option buyer pays to the option seller above and beyond the intrinsic value of the option, in order to induce the writer of the option to enter into the trade. All options lose their time premium value as expiration approaches. At expiration, the option will have zero time value remaining.

- The price of an in-the-money option consists of its intrinsic value plus any time premium.
- The price of an out-of-the-money option consists solely of its time premium as there is no intrinsic value.

> **long** a long position is entered into by purchasing an option contract to open a position.
>
> **short** a short position is entered into by selling, or writing, an option contract to open a position.
>
> **long premium** you enter into a long premium position if you pay more for any option or options you buy than you take in for any option or options you write. This applies to spreads, which we look at a bit later.
>
> **short premium** you enter into a short premium position if you take in more for any option or options you write than any option or options you buy.
>
> **spread** a spread position involves buying one or more options and writing another option or options of a different type, strike price, and/or expiration month.

Understanding Option Pricing Models and Theoretical Value

The theoretical price for an option can be calculated using an option pricing model. The most well-known of these models is the *Black-Scholes model.* While option pricing models can be a highly complex subject, it is possible to get the general idea of how they work fairly easily. It is also possible to understand the most important outputs without a PhD in mathematics.

Black-Scholes model

an options model developed by Fischer Black and Myron Scholes in the early 1970s.

How much is an option worth? In the marketplace, an option is worth whatever a buyer and a seller agree it is worth. But how do these traders know what the proper price is for a given option? They use an option pricing model to calculate the theoretical value (also known as *fair value*) for an option by entering certain variables into the model. Then the buyer or seller of a given option has some frame of reference for determining whether the current market price for a given option is reasonable. The variables that get passed into an option pricing model include:

- The type of option: call or put.
- The strike price of the option.
- The price of the underlying commodity contract.

- The number of days left until the option expires.
- A volatility value (that volatility of the underlying commodity).
- An interest rate (in order to calculate the risk-free rate of return).

For example, with November corn futures trading at 246.25, let's look at the September 250 call option:

- Option type = call.
- Strike price = 250.
- Price of underlying contract = 246.20.
- Number of days until expiration = 37 days.
- Volatility = 29.9 percent.
- Interest rate = 5 percent.

If we pass these variables to an option pricing model, the model will calculate the *theoretical value* for this option. In this case, the theoretical value equals 7.875. The actual market price at the time was 8.00. So in this case, the theoretical price is very close to the actual price. If the actual market price for an option is above the theoretical value, it is considered to be *overvalued*. If the actual market price for this option is below the theoretical value, it is considered to be *undervalued*. Be aware that just because an option is overvalued does not mean that it is destined to decline in price. Likewise, just because an option may be undervalued does not mean that it is destined to rise in price. An over- or undervalued situation simply means that the price of a given option has moved away from the value we might expect it to trade at. Looking at the theoretical value for an option can help traders avoid paying too much to buy a particular option or receiving too little to sell (write) a particular option.

theoretical value
the price of an option based on a mathematical model rather than the actual price in the market.

Implied Volatility

Implied volatility is a term used to refer to the volatility for a given option, or group of options, that is implied by the current market price. This information is generated from an option pricing model; however, the calculation is just a little bit different. This time, instead of passing a volatility value to the option pricing model and having the model calculate the theoretical option value, we pass the actual price of the option to the model and let the model solve for volatility. This output is referred to as *implied volatility*. Let's look again at the September 250 corn call option, with September corn futures trading at 246.25.

- Option type = call.
- Strike price = 250.
- Price of underlying contract = 246.2.
- Number of days until expiration = 37 days.
- Volatility = ? (model to solve for this value).
- Interest rate = 5 percent.
- Actual price of option = 8.00.

**implied
volatility (IV)**
a measure of
volatility that is
derived using an
option pricing
model. IV reflects
expectations
about an asset's
future volatility.

If we pass these variables to an option pricing model, the model will calculate the implied volatility for the September 245 call and return a volatility value of 30.30 percent. Again, this is the volatility of the option implied by the current price of the option in the marketplace. If the option were trading at a price of 9.00 or 10.00, then the implied volatility would be higher. If the option were trading at 6.00 or 7.00, then the implied volatility would be lower. Hence, overpriced options tend to have high implied volatility and underpriced options tend to have low implied volatility.

Smart Trader Tip

To learn more about volatility, check out *The Volatility Course* (Wiley, 2004), a book I coauthored with Tom Gentile. It provides a comprehensive analysis of how to trade volatility in any market using an arsenal of innovative tools.

An alert trader might compare the current implied volatility value to the historical range of implied volatility for options on that particular commodity to determine whether the implied volatility level is presently high or low relative to what it has been in the past. The implications are important for option traders. A *high implied volatility* value means that there is a lot of time premium built into the price of the options for that particular commodity. Conversely, a *low implied volatility* means that there is not a lot of time premium built into the price of the options. Clearly, option buyers would prefer to buy when implied volatility is low, since this means that they will be paying less to buy options than they would be if implied volatility was at the high end of the historical range. However, option sellers would prefer to write options when implied volatility is extremely high, since this means they collect a great deal more time premium than they would if implied volatility was at the low end of the range.

high implied volatility
implied volatility that is at relatively high levels compared to the underlying asset's historical volatility.

low implied volatility
implied volatility that is at relatively low levels compared to the underlying asset's historical volatility.

Figure 8.1 displays the two-year implied volatility history for corn options. As you can see, the implied volatility for shorter-term options is more volatile than for longer-term options. This is generally due to the fact that most speculation occurs in the shorter-term options; thus, these options are more likely to rise and fall sharply. In Figure 8.1, you can see that the implied volatility of shorter-term corn options typically fluctuates in a range from about 15 to 50. So if implied volatility is at the low end of the range—say, 20 percent or lower—a trader might reasonably conclude that corn options are exceptionally cheap. Conversely, if implied volatility is greater than, say, 35, a trader might conclude that corn options are exceptionally expensive. Generally speaking, an astute trader avoids selling premium when implied volatility is exceptionally low and avoids buying premium when implied volatility is exceptionally high.

Smart Trader Tip

Compare current implied volatility to the historical highs and lows for a given commodity to determine whether current levels are presently on the high or the low end of the historical range. Ideally, you will buy premium when volatility is low and sell premium when volatility is high (buy low/sell high).

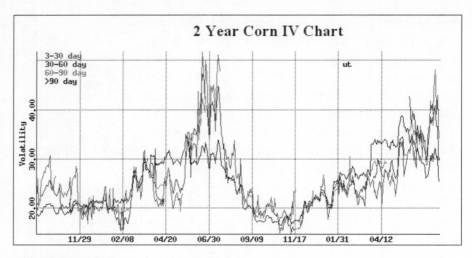

FIGURE 8.1 Implied volatility for corn options.

Source: Optionetics Platinum.

Understanding the Greeks

Another useful output from an option pricing model is a group of values known in options parlance as the *Greeks*. They are referred to this way be-

the Greeks

statistical measures that help to explain the changes in options premiums.

cause each value has a Greek name (delta, gamma, vega, theta) and, more important, conveys unique information about the option in question. The most successful option traders understand the importance and implications of the Greeks, as well as how they can be used to select and adjust trades. Let's take a closer look at the most important Greek values.

Delta

delta

a Greek that measures the change in the value of an option for every point change in the value of the underlying asset.

The *delta* value for an option is the expected change in the price of the option relative to the price of the underlying commodity. In other words, a call option with a delta of 50 would be expected to move half a point if the underlying contract moved a full point. The delta value of a long position in a commodity contract is 100. The net delta for a short position in a commodity contract is −100. The value for the delta of a call option can range from 0 to 100. The delta value for a put option can range from 0 to −100. In our corn example, the September 250 call had a delta value of 46. This means that if the September corn contract advanced 10 points, then the September 250 call option would be expected to advance 4.60 points.

Traders also may look at the delta value of a position in terms of its underlying equivalent. For example, if a trader had bought two September 250 calls, each with a delta of 46, then he or she would have a net delta of 92 (delta of 46 × 2 contracts). As a result, this trader is holding a position that is almost equivalent to a long position in a futures contract (92 versus 100). Of course, delta values change over time due to changes in the underlying price and, to a lesser extent, the effects of time decay and volatility changes.

Gamma

The *gamma* value for an option is the expected change in delta for that option relative to the price of the underlying commodity. It tells you how much delta will rise or fall based on a one-point move in price by the underlying commodity contract. The September 250 corn call option had a delta of 46 and its gamma was 1.6. This means that if the underlying corn contract rose 10 full points, the 250 call option would be expected to gain 16

gamma
a Greek that measures the change in delta in relation to changes in the price of the underlying asset.

deltas (1.6 gammas × 10 points). Thus, we know that if corn rose from 246.25 to 256.25, then the delta for the September 250 call option would increase from 46 deltas to 62 deltas.

Vega

The *vega* value for an option is the expected change in price for that option relative to a change in the volatility of the underlying commodity. In other words, it tells you how much the price of the option should rise or fall if implied volatility rises or falls one full point. The September 250 corn option was trading at a price of 8.00 points and had

vega
a Greek that measures the impact of changes in volatility on option premiums.

an implied volatility of 30.30 percent. It also had a vega of 0.315. This value tells us that if the implied volatility for this option rose or fell 10 full points, then the option would gain or lose 3.15 (0.315 × 10 points) points based solely on this change in volatility. If you were expecting a sharp increase in volatility, it would make sense to consider buying options with high vega in order to maximize your potential. Alternatively, if you are expecting a sharp decline in volatility, it would make sense to consider writing options with high vegas, since they are predisposed to lose the most value if, in fact, volatility declines.

Theta

The *theta* value for an option is the expected change in price for that option relative to the passage of one day of time. It measures how much the price of the option will lose on the current day as a result of time decay. Our September 250 corn call option had a theta value of −0.125 and, if nothing else changes—that is, if corn futures and implied volatility levels were completely unchanged today—the September 250 call option would be expected to lose 0.125 point due solely to the effect of time decay. Theta values for a given option increase as a percentage of the price of the option as expiration draws closer and as time decay accelerates.

theta
an option Greek that measures the impact of time on options premiums.

Smart Trader Tip

Theta is also referred to as time decay. Options lose value over time, and this loss increases exponentially as the option approaches expiration.

Rights and Obligations of Option Buyers and Writers

The Greeks are useful for understanding how options contracts are priced and why prices change from one day to the next. However, the most important factor in determining the value of an options contract is the price of the underlying asset. In addition, option traders should develop a good understanding of the basics of puts and calls, including the rights and obligations inherent in these contracts.

Buying a Call Option

The buyer of a call option enters a *long call* position and obtains the right to buy the underlying futures contract at a specific price through the date that the option expires. No matter how high the price of the underlying futures contract might rise between the time a trader buys a call option and the time that option expires, the buyer of a call option can exercise his or her option and buy the futures contract at the strike price for the option. The only obligation that he or she incurs is paying a premium to buy the option at the time of purchase; the premium is the maximum amount that can be lost in the trade.

long call
the limited-risk strategy that involves the purchase of a call option to open a position.

So let's assume that a trader buys a call option on a soybean futures contract with a strike price of 600. Let's say that the premium to buy this option is $500. Now assume that the price of that soybean futures contract subsequently rises to 650. The buyer of this call option can exercise his or her option and buy the soybean futures contract at a price of 600 anytime up until option expiration. Soybean futures trade at $50 a full point, so the trader in this example could buy soybeans at the strike price of 600 and then sell them at the current futures price of 650 for a profit of $2,500 [(650 − 600) × $50 per point]. If you subtract the $500 the trader originally paid to purchase the options, this trader made a net profit of $2,000 on a $500 investment.

The buyer of a call option has three choices regarding how to exit the trade. He or she can:

- Sell the option prior to expiration, either at a profit or at a loss.

- Exercise the option prior to expiration and thus acquire a long position in the underlying futures contract.

- Hold the option until expiration. If the option is held until expiration, it will expire either *in-the-money* or *out-of-the-money*. This distinction has important implications.

in-the-money
a call option that has a strike price lower than the current price of the underlying asset or a put option that has a strike price higher than the price of the underlying asset.

out-of-the-money

an options contract that has no intrinsic value. A call option is out-of-the-money if its exercise or strike price is above the current market price of the underlying security. A put option is out-of-the-money if its exercise or strike price is below the current market price of the underlying security.

long put

the limited-risk strategy that involves the purchase of a put option to open a position.

If the price of the futures contract at the time of option expiration is below the strike price for the call option, then that option is out-of-the-money and will simply expire worthless. The buyer of the option loses the entire premium paid to purchase the call option in the first place. If the price of the futures contract at the time of option expiration is above the strike price for the option, then that call option is considered to be in-the-money. Call options that are in-the-money at the time of expiration are automatically exercised and the holder of the option no longer holds the option but acquires a long position in the underlying futures contract.

Buying a Put Option

The buyer of a put option enters a *long put* position and obtains the right, but not the obligation, to sell the underlying futures contract at a specific price through the date that the option expires. No matter how low the price of the underlying futures contract might decline between the time a trader buys a put option and the time that option expires, the buyer of a put option can exercise the option and sell the futures contract at the strike price for that option. The only obligation the put buyer incurs is that he or she must pay a premium to buy the option at the time of purchase. Once again, the premium is the maximum amount that can be lost on the trade.

So let's assume that a trader buys a put option on a soybean futures contract and the strike price of the option is 600. Let's say the premium to buy this option is $500. Now let's assume that the price of that soybean futures contract subsequently declines to 550. The buyer of this put option can exercise the option and sell the soybean futures contract at a price of 600. Thus, the trader in this example could sell soybeans at the strike price of 600 and then buy them at the current futures price of 550, for a profit of $2,500 [(600 − 550) × $50 per point]. If you subtract the $500 the trader originally paid to purchase the put, this trader made a net profit of $2,000 on a $500 investment.

Like the buyer of a call option, the buyer of a put option has three choices regarding how to exit the trade. The trader can:

- Sell the option prior to expiration, either at a profit or at a loss.
- Exercise the option prior to expiration and thus acquire a short position in the underlying futures contract.
- Hold the option until expiration. If the option is held until expiration, it will expire either in-the-money or out-of-the-money. This distinction has the same essential implications as with a call option, only in reverse. Allow me to explain.

If the price of the futures contract at the time of option expiration is above the strike price for the put option, then that option is out-of-the-money and will simply expire worthless. The buyer of the option loses the entire premium paid to purchase the option in the first place. If the price of the futures contract at the time of option expiration is below the strike price for the option, then that put option is considered to be in-the-money. Options that are in-the-money at the time of expiration are automatically exercised and the holder of the option no longer holds the option but acquires a short position in the underlying futures contract.

Writing a Call Option

The writer of a call option enters a short position in the option and assumes the obligation to sell an underlying futures contract at a specific price through the date that the option expires. No matter how high the price of the underlying futures contract might rise between the time the trader writes the option and the time that option expires, the writer of a call option is obligated to sell a futures contract at the strike price if the option is exercised. The writer of an option receives a premium equal to the price of the option at the time he or she writes the option. This represents the maximum profit potential. The writer of a call option hopes that the underlying futures contract will be trading at a price that is less than the strike price for that call option at the time the option expires. If this happens, the option will then expire worthless and the trader will pocket the entire premium he or she received at the time the trade was entered. Let's look at an example of how this works.

Let's assume that September soybean futures are trading at 600 and the trader believes that the price for September soybeans will not exceed

625 prior to September option expiration. Based on this belief, the trader might write a September soybean call option with a strike price of 625. The price of the option—and thus the amount of premium he or she will receive for writing the option—will be set in the marketplace based on supply and demand. For this example, let's assume the trader writes the option and collects $250 of premium. As a result, the implications of the position just entered are that the trader has a maximum profit poten-

short call

an unlimited-risk strategy that involves the sale of a call option to open a position.

tial of $250 and unlimited risk. Risk is unlimited because if soybeans started to rise in price and the trader continued to hold the *short call* option position, then no matter how high the price of soybeans might rise, he or she could be called upon to sell a September soybean contract at a price of 625.

So why would anyone write an option? The other part of the equation besides risk is the proba-
bility or likelihood that September soybeans will rise above the strike price of 625. With soybeans trading at 600 at the time the option is written, the trader has probability on his or her side.

Unlike the buyer of a call option who has three choices of how to exit a position, the writer of a call option has only two choices as to how to exit the position. The writer can:

- Buy back the option he or she wrote (also known as a *short* option) prior to expiration.

- Hold the short position until option expiration. If the option is held until expiration, it will expire either in-the-money or out-of-the-money. This distinction has important implications.

If the price of the underlying futures contract at the time of option expiration is below the strike price of the call option written, then that call option is considered to be out-of-the-money and will expire worthless. In this case, the writer of the option keeps the entire premium received at the initial entry of the trade. However, if the price of the underlying futures contract at the time of option expiration is above the strike price of the call option, then that call option is considered to be in-the-money. The writer of that call option is obligated to deliver a long position in the underlying futures contract to the assigned option buyer. This will leave the option seller short one futures contract at a below-market price. To close the risk in this position, the trader will have to buy one futures contract. This would result in a loss for the option writer.

Using our previous example, let's assume that a trader wrote a September 625 call option and collects $250 of premium. The trader then holds the option until expiration, at which time the September soybean contract is trading at 650. Since the price of the futures contract is above the strike price of the option, the option is in-the-money. The option seller will be forced to sell one futures contract at 625. To close that position, s/he will have to buy one futures contract at the current price of 650, thus incurring a loss.

Writing a Put Option

The writer of a put option assumes the obligation to buy an underlying futures contract at a specific price through the date that the option expires. No matter how low the price of the underlying futures contract might decline between the time the trader writes the option and the time that option expires, the put seller must buy a futures contract, or have it "put" to them, at the strike price if the option is exercised. The writer of an option receives a premium equal to the price of the option at the time he or she writes the option. This represents the maximum profit potential. The writer of a put option hopes that the underlying futures contract will be trading at a price that is greater than the strike price for that put option at the time the option expires. If this happens, the option will then expire worthless and he or she will pocket the entire premium received at the time the trade was entered. Let's look at an example of how this works.

Let's assume that September soybean futures are trading at 600 and that a trader believes that the price for September soybeans will not drop below 575 prior to the September option expiration. Based on this belief, the trader might write a September soybean put option with a strike price of 575. The price of the option—and thus the amount of premium received for writing the option—will be set in the marketplace based on supply and demand. For this example, let's assume the trader writes the option and receives a premium of $250. The implications of the position just entered are that the trader has a maximum profit potential of $250 and essentially unlimited risk. Risk is technically limited, but only because the price of soybeans can only fall to zero. If soybeans start to fall in price and the trader continues to hold the *short put* option position, then no matter how low the price

> **short put**
> a high-risk strategy that involves the sale of a put option to open a position.

of soybeans might fall, the trader could be called upon to buy a September soybean contract at a price of 575.

Unlike the buyer of a put option who has three choices of how to exit a position, the writer of a put option has only two choices as to how to exit the position. The trader can:

- Buy back the option he or she wrote prior to expiration.
- Hold the short position until option expiration. If the option is held until expiration, it will expire either in-the-money or out-of-the-money. Once again, this distinction has important implications.

If the price of the underlying futures contract at the time of option expiration is above the strike price of the put option, then that put option is considered to be out-of-the-money and will expire worthless. In this case, the writer of the option keeps the entire premium collected at the initial entry price of the trade. However, if the price of the underlying futures contract at the time of option expiration is below the strike price of the put option, then that put option is considered to be in-the-money and the writer of that put option is obligated to deliver a short position in the underlying futures contract to the assigned option buyer. This means that the trader would be long one futures contract at an above market price, resulting in a loss for the option writer.

For example, let's assume that a trader wrote a September 575 put option and received a premium of $250. The trader then held the option until expiration, at which time September soybeans were trading at 550. Since the price of the futures contract is below the strike price of the option, the option is in-the-money. The writer of the 575 put will be asked to honor the terms of the put and buy the contract at the strike price (575), or above the current market price of 550, thus incurring a loss on the trade.

A quick note on exercise and assignment. Option owners can "exercise" their options by contacting their brokers, or allow in-the-money options to be automatically exercised at expiration. Once the long option is exercised, a trader with a short will be "assigned."

What Is a Risk Curve?

A *risk curve* is a graph that can display how the profit or loss characteristics of a particular option trade will fluctuate based on changes in the price of the underlying security, the passage of time, and changes in volatility. A risk curve can be drawn for any single option position or for any combination of option and/or futures positions. In other words, if you were to enter into a spread whereby you are long certain options and short other options, you could draw one risk curve to display the profit/loss profile for all of these various positions combined.

> **risk curve**
> a chart that shows the potential profit and loss from an option or an options strategy as it reacts to changes in the price of the underlying stock.

Risk curves are an essential tool in helping traders understand how any particular option strategy works. It is critical to understand the implications of a given risk curve if you expect to make money trading options. A risk curve for any given option trade essentially serves as your road map and allows you to plan in advance for various contingencies, including when to take a profit and when to cut a loss. Planning your trades in advance is one of the keys to long-term trading success. A risk curve will display the following information for any options-related positions:

- Position profit or loss based on underlying price fluctuations.
- The effect of time decay.
- Breakeven points.
- Maximum profit and maximum risk.

The risk graph that appears in Figure 8.2 represents the profit and loss outlook for an option strategy known as a *straddle*. The position depicted in the chart was created by the simultaneous purchase of an October crude oil call option and an October crude oil put option, both with a strike price of 75. The price for the underlying October crude oil futures contract appears on the left-hand side of the graph. The bar chart displays the price fluctuations for October crude oil over the past three months.

> **straddle**
> the simultaneous purchase of a call and put option with the same at-the-money strike, expiration date, and underlying market.

As you can see, over the past three months October crude oil has fluctuated between $70 and $77 a barrel. Farther to the right are four lines, or risk curves. Each of these curves displays the expected profit or loss for this particular straddle position as of a certain date. For example,

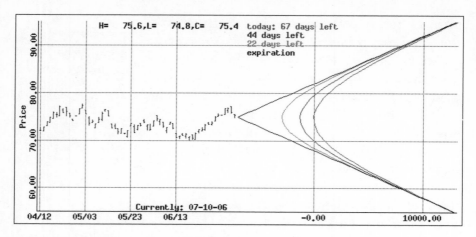

FIGURE 8.2 Risk curves for straddle using crude oil options.
Source: Optionetics Platinum.

the curve farthest to the right represents the expected profit or loss as of the current date of this graph, which was 67 days prior to expiration. Each curve farther to the left represents the expected profit or loss for this position as of a date that is closer and closer to expiration. The curve that is farthest to the left and looks like a sideways "V" represents the expected profit or loss for this position if the trade is held until expiration. The point of the sideways "V" is exactly at the strike price of 75 because if October crude oil were to close exactly at 75 at the time of option expiration, then both the 75 call and the 75 put would expire worthless, thus resulting in the maximum loss. Beyond this, there is much to be learned from this chart.

Underlying Price and Position Profit/Loss

As you can see in Figure 8.2, in order for this trade to make money, crude oil must move significantly in one direction or another. In fact, the most common reason for entering into a straddle is because a trader expects a meaningful price movement but is not sure of the direction of the move. For this particular trade, the October 75 call is purchased at 3.73 (or $3,730) and the October 75 put is purchased at 3.33 (or $3,330). Thus, the cost of this trade is $7,060. This is the maximum risk on the trade and is represented on the chart by the point of the sideways "V."

On the plus side, a straddle has unlimited profit potential on both the upside and the downside. If the price of crude oil keeps rising (or falling), the profit on this straddle can continue to grow; this is the beauty of a *delta-neutral strategy*. For example, if crude oil makes a move beyond $92 to the upside or $68 to the downside, then the profit on this trade could exceed $10,000.

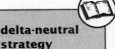

delta-neutral strategy
a calculated ratio of long and short positions so that the overall position is not immediately sensitive to changes in the price of the underlying instrument.

As the price of October crude oil moves higher or lower, the expected profit for this particular trade fluctuates. Since both a call option and a put option have limited risk and unlimited profit potential, a straddle can make money because one side of the trade can earn a profit that is larger than the maximum risk on the other side of the trade.

If the price of crude oil rises significantly, then the October 75 call option will start to make money and the October 75 put option will start to lose money. If crude oil rises far enough, then the amount of profit gained by the October 75 call option will begin to exceed the amount of loss suffered by the October 75 put option. Likewise, if crude oil declines far enough, then the amount of profit gained by the October 75 put option will begin to exceed the amount of loss suffered by the October 75 call option.

If October crude oil rises to 85 at the time of option expiration, then the October 75 call will be worth 10 points and the October 75 put will be worthless. As a result, the October 75 call will be worth $10,000 (10 points × $1,000 per full point) and the October 75 call will be worth $0. The straddle originally cost $7,060 to enter, so the buyer of this straddle earns a profit of $2,940 ($10,000 − $7,060).

Time Decay

time decay
the fact that option premiums have a fixed life and lose value over time.

The risk curves that appear in Figure 8.2 clearly depict the effect of *time decay*. Due to the effect of time decay, both the call and the put options will lose time premium as time goes by. This is clearly illustrated by the fact that on the downside, each successive risk curve moves further into the loss side and the breakeven points move further away from the current price with each successive risk curve. In other words, as time goes by, and as the price of both the call and the put lose time premium, the market must move further in one direction or the other in order to compensate for this loss of time premium. This is important information to consider for virtually any option trade, as time decay is inevitable. Remember, every option will lose all of its time premium by expiration.

Some trades are helped by time decay and others are hurt by time decay. In general, if you are long premium, then time decay will work against you. Conversely, if you are short premium, then time decay actually works in your favor, as the time premium built into option prices erodes over time. In our crude oil straddle example, time decay is clearly working against this trade, as both positions experience more and more time decay with each passing day. It would clearly be advantageous for the buyer of this straddle if crude oil were to make a large movement in price sooner (before a lot of premium is lost to time decay) rather than later.

The Greek value known as *theta* tells you how much time decay a given option is going to experience on any given trading day. And while it can be extremely useful, this value will change as time goes by; time decay accelerates as expiration draws closer. As a result, under the category of "a picture is worth a thousand words," a set of risk curves is the best way to quickly and easily visualize the negative, or positive, effects of time decay on any option position.

Smart Trader Tip

Remember, if you are long premium, time decay is your enemy. If you are short premium, time decay is your friend.

Breakeven Points

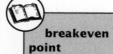

breakeven point

a point where a trade or position does not make any profits or suffer any losses.

Each option-related trade will have at least one *breakeven point*. This is the price, or prices, that the underlying market must reach and exceed in order for the option trade to generate a profit. As you can see in Figure 8.2, a straddle is unique in that it has two breakeven points, one below the current market price (downside breakeven) and one above the current market price (upside breakeven). If this trade is held until expiration, the breakeven prices are 67.94 and 82.06. In other words, October crude oil must be outside that price range at the time of option expiration in order for this trade to show a profit.

Knowing the breakeven point(s) is for a given trade is an extremely critical piece of information. Armed with this piece of information, you can objectively assess the likelihood, or probability, that your trade will ultimately generate a profit. Certain trades may at times sound like good ideas, yet once you analyze your likelihood of success, they may not look so good. For example, if soybeans are trading at 600, you might be able to purchase a call option with a strike price of 650 for maybe 5 points, or in the case of soybeans, $250 (5 points × $50 a point). If soybeans rally to 700, then the call would be worth 50 points, or $2,500. This would result in a profit of $2,250 on an investment of only $250. On the face of it, this may sound like a great bargain. However, what you also need to consider is that your breakeven price is 655 (which equals the strike price of 650 plus the 5 points paid to buy the option). In other words, while the reward-to-risk profile looks good, the fact remains that soybeans must rally significantly, from 600 to 655, in order for this position to generate a profit. Anything less than a major advance in price will result in a complete loss of the premium paid if the option is held until expiration. Breakeven can be thought of as the "worst" price the underlying must reach. In the case of a call, it's the highest price the underlying must reach if the option is held to expiration. Options can be profitable before expiration without reaching the breakeven point.

Again, as with viewing the effects of time decay, analyzing a set of risk curves for a given option position can give you vital information about the likelihood that your trade will result in a profit.

Maximum Profit and Maximum Risk

The maximum risk for a straddle is equal to the amount of the double premium paid to buy the at-the money call and put positions that constitute the straddle. The point of maximum risk is easy to pick out in Figure 8.2. If October crude oil were to be trading exactly at 75 at the time of option expiration, then both the 75 call and the 75 put would expire worthless, resulting in the maximum loss of $7,060. With crude oil at any other price, this straddle will show either (1) a smaller loss or (2) a profit if crude oil is outside the breakeven points of 67.94 and 82.06. A quick perusal of the risk curves in Figure 8.2 also illustrates the fact that a straddle has unlimited profit potential to the upside, and limited (but high) profit potential to the downside. The further crude oil moves outside the breakeven points, the greater the profit potential.

As with the other factors that I have discussed, it is important to understand the potential rewards and risks for any trade before you enter into it. Likewise, the easiest way to assess these potential rewards and risks for any trade is to view a set of risk curves, as this allows you to visualize both the best- and worst-case scenarios. This information can then enable you to make objective and intelligent decisions regarding the wisdom of entering into a given trade.

Beyond just looking at maximum rewards and risks, a set of risk curves also allows you to assess how the overall reward-to-risk scenario might change or is changing for any hypothetical or actual position. By viewing the changes that occur as expiration draws closer, you may at times realize that you are better off not holding a trade until expiration. For example, in our crude oil straddle example, the only way you could experience anything close to the maximum potential loss is to hold the trade until expiration. An astute trader may plan in advance to exit this trade well before option expiration so as to limit the negative effects of time decay and eliminate the risk of experiencing the maximum loss.

Smart Trader Tip

Risk curves allow you to distinguish the forest from the trees. Regardless of the position or positions being held, risk curves boil it all down to the most relevant information including potential profit or loss, the effect of time decay, breakeven points, and maximum profit and maximum risk. Learn how to interpret and use this powerful tool to increase your trading savvy.

The Primary Uses of Options

One of the primary benefits of learning to use options is that option trading strategies offer traders a great deal of flexibility. Through the use of options—either by themselves or in conjunction with futures contracts—you can craft a position designed to meet whatever specific objective you wish to achieve. Most traders use options in one of three ways:

1. To speculate on market direction.
2. To hedge an existing position.
3. To take advantage of a neutral situation.

Speculating on Market Direction

Buying an option gives a trader the ability to control one futures contract. Depending on the cost of the option and the amount of margin required to trade that particular futures contract, buying the option may require less capital than buying or selling short the underlying futures contract itself. Buying a call or put option allows you to enjoy unlimited profit potential with limited risk. When you buy a call or a put option, you pay out however much money is required to purchase the option. This also represents your maximum risk on the trade. However, if you buy a call option on a futures contract and that underlying futures contract rallies, there is no limit to how high the price of the option can rise. You might buy a call (or put) option on a particular commodity contract for any or all of the following reasons:

- You expect the underlying futures contract to rise (call) or fall (put).
- You want to obtain leverage—that is, put up only a little money to control a large position.
- You want to limit your risk in trading a given commodity.

While buying or selling short a commodity contract allows a trader to speculate on market direction and control a large position for a relatively small amount of capital, the big difference is that a commodity position essentially entails the assumption of unlimited risk. In contrast, buying an option affords you the same benefits but without the risk of losing more than the initial premium required to enter the trade.

Interestingly, when trading options on stocks, the cost to purchase an option on a given stock is typically much less than the cost of buying 100 shares of the underlying stock position. This is not always the case when trading options on futures. Since commodities are traded on margin and because *margin requirements* can be relatively low, it is possible that you will pay more to buy a particular call or put option on a given commodity contract

margin requirements
the amount of capital required by a brokerage firm to implement a trade or strategy.

than you would have to put up in margin money to buy or sell short the underlying commodity contract itself. Still, the primary benefit of trading the option is the ability to take a position in a given commodity while holding a limited-risk position. If you buy or sell short a commodity contract and the underlying market keeps moving further and further against you, unless you exit the trade you just keep losing more and more money. However, if you buy a call or put option and the underlying market keeps moving against you, you can never lose more than you put up to buy the option in the first place. This limited-risk aspect of options trading offers traders the opportunity to participate in the commodities markets, where they might be hesitant to participate otherwise.

Hedging an Existing Position

Another unique feature associated with trading options is the ability to hedge an existing position. Hedging an existing position means reducing or eliminating the downside risk on a position currently held. This can be extremely useful in a situation where traders wish to temporarily minimize or eliminate the downside risk of positions that they currently hold, without completely exiting the current positions altogether. This process can be accomplished in a variety of ways.

One of the most straightforward approaches to hedging an existing position in a given commodity is to buy a put option (if long the commodity) or a call option (if short the commodity). If you are holding a long position in a given commodity and you purchase a put option, then up until the time that option expires, your downside risk is limited below the strike price of the put option. This strategy makes sense when a trader wants to continue to hold an existing position in a given commodity for the longer term but is concerned about the downside risk in the shorter term.

For example, let's say that a trader is long soybean futures and is confident that the commodity will ultimately rise to higher prices. However, let's also say that a crop report is due out in the next several weeks and that this trader is concerned that the report could prove to be surprisingly bearish, at least in the short term. The most obvious alternative would be to simply sell the futures contract and wait until after the report is out to reestablish a long position. The problem is that there is an equally good chance that the report will prove bullish for soybeans, thus propelling prices sharply higher. So if the trader exits the long position completely, he or she may miss out on the very move that is presently anticipated. This would be a good time to consider hedging the long position in the futures market using an option position.

Let's assume that this trader is long November soybeans and that November beans are trading at 622. In this example, the trader buys a put option with a strike price of 600, presently trading at a price of 19. In order to enter this hedge position, the trader would need to pay $950 (19 points × $50 a point). This is in addition to maintaining the margin requirement to hold the long position in a soybean futures contract. So at this point the trader would be long a November soybean contract and long a November 600 put option. Figure 8.3 depicts the risk curves for this trade. As you can see, this trader's risk is absolutely limited once soybean prices drop below a price of 600. Likewise, the position still retains unlimited profit potential.

In this example, if the trader is correct and soybeans break out to the upside and rally significantly, the position may reap unlimited profits. At the same time, if the trader is wrong and soybean prices collapse below recent support, the risk is limited by the stike price of the put.

There are other ways to hedge a futures position using options. However, discussing all of the possible ways to hedge or adjust a position in the underlying futures contract using options is beyond the scope of this chapter. Still, this simple example gives you an idea of how easily a certain objective (limiting downside risk) can be achieved via the use of options. Remember that anytime you hedge a position, you essentially give up something in order to gain something else. In this case, the trader is giving up the next 19 points of upside potential (i.e., the amount paid to buy the put as a hedge) in order to completely eliminate the downside risk beyond a certain point.

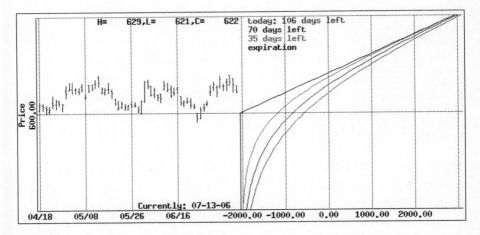

FIGURE 8.3　Risk curve for long soybean position hedged with a long put.
Source: Optionetics Platinum.

Neutral Strategies

The ability to take advantage of a neutral market situation is something that is entirely unique to option trading. Anytime you simply buy a commodity contract, that market must rise in price in order for you to generate a profit. Likewise, anytime you sell short a commodity contract, that market must fall in price in order for you to profit. In other words, the market has to move in the direction you expect it to. If it doesn't, you will either suffer a loss or, at best, break even. Yet the fact remains that commodity markets often spend a great deal of time fluctuating in trading ranges.

uptrend
a prolonged move higher in the price of an underlying asset.

downtrend
a prolonged move lower in the value of a security.

whipsaw market
a market that does not trend higher or lower, but makes frequent moves back and forth.

As previously discussed, trading range is a range of prices with an identifiable low point, also known as support, and an identifiable high point, known as resistance. Many traders find it difficult to make money when a commodity market is stuck in a trading range. Typically, by the time they feel that an *uptrend* is being established, the market is reaching the upper end of the trading range, and then fails to break out to the upside. Likewise, just when it appears that a *downtrend* is being established, the market is reaching the lower end of the trading range, and then fails to break out to the downside. This can be extremely frustrating for traders and often leads to *whipsaw markets*, whereby the trader bets on the market to move in a particular direction and it quickly reverses back to the other direction.

Through the use of options, however, it is possible to craft a position that will make money if the underlying commodity remains above a given price, below a given price, or between two prices, depending on your objective. This is an opportunity that is completely unique to option traders. When utilized properly, these types of option trading strategies can greatly enhance the returns for a commodity trader by allowing the individual to make money when he or she normally might not (i.e., when there are few discernible trending opportunities in the commodities traded).

Option Trading Strategies

The spectrum of option trading strategies is extremely wide. There are strategies that will allow you to profit if a market moves above a specific price, moves below a specific price, stays within a certain price range, moves outside of a certain price range, and any number of other possibilities. Since there is no way to adequately cover all of these possibilities in one section, for now I will focus on a handful of the most useful and commonly utilized option trading strategies. This can prove to be valuable because, although the trading strategy spectrum is wide, most successful option traders ultimately wind up focusing on just a small handful of strategies. The key is to specialize in the strategy or strategies that you are most comfortable with and to become very good at using those strategies. These are the strategies that we will discuss in this section:

- Long calls
- Long puts
- Bull call spread
- Bear put spread
- Butterfly spread

The Long Call Option

A long call option position is entered into simply by purchasing a call option on a given commodities market. The only reason a trader would ever have for buying a call option is that he or she thinks the price of the underlying futures market is going to rise. If the trader did not expect the market to rise, there would be no reason to buy a call option. The reason a trader would buy a call option instead of the underlying futures contract itself is because a long call position provides limited risk, unlike a long position in a futures contract. As previously mentioned, when you buy a call option, you pay a *premium*, which is simply the cost of the option contract at the time you buy it (option price × dollars per point). This represents your total maximum risk for the trade. If you hold the call option until expiration and it is out-of-the-money at that time, the option will expire worthless and you lose the entire premium you paid to purchase the call originally. This is true no matter how far the underlying futures contract might fall in price.

So, for example, let's say you bought a call option on soybeans and paid $600 to buy that option. Subsequently, the underlying soybean futures contract falls 100 points in price. At a contract value of $50 per point, this would represent a decline in value of $5,000 (100 points × $50 per point) for the futures contract itself. However, in this example the buyer of the call option could never lose more than the $600 he or she paid to buy the option. This type of limited-risk trade can often allow traders to have more staying power in the face of an adverse price movement. Now let's look at an actual example of a long call position.

Figure 8.4 displays the risk curves for a long call option position in crude oil. The risk curves depict the expected profit or loss for the October 75 call option purchased at a price of 3.73 points. For crude oil, each full point is worth $1,000, so it would cost a trader $3,730 to purchase this call option.

As you can see in Figure 8.4, this position will make money if, and only if, crude oil rises in price. In fact, a long call position has unlimited profit potential. As long as the crude oil price keeps rising, the price of the option can continue to rise with it. The expected profit or loss as of option expiration is depicted by the leftmost risk curve, which resembles a hockey stick tipped up on its blade.

The other risk curves in Figure 8.4 clearly depict the effect of time decay on a long call position. Remember that anytime you enter a long call position, you pay time premium on top of any intrinsic value (if the option is in-the-money; otherwise, the price of the option consists solely of time premium). As option expiration draws closer, this time premium starts to evaporate. This is simply a function of time decay. Remember, an option will have no time premium left as of option expiration. So as you can see in the Figure 8.4, the risk curves move up and to the left. This means that because of time decay, the underlying market must move further to the upside as time goes by in order to compensate for this loss of time premium. Remember that time premium is the enemy of all option buyers, as time decay is inevitable.

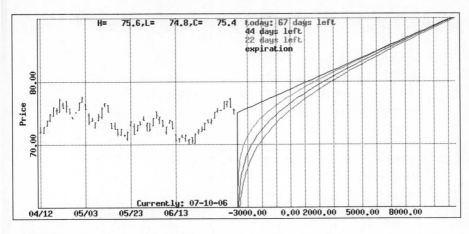

FIGURE 8.4 Risk curves for October crude oil 75 call.
Source: Optionetics Platinum.

For this crude oil option trade, the breakeven price at expiration is 78.73 based on the October crude oil futures contract. For a long call position, the breakeven price is calculated as follows:

(Strike price of option + premium paid to purchase option)

So in this example we add the strike price of 75 and the option price of 3.73 to arrive at a breakeven price of 78.73. This means that if you hold this call option until expiration, the price of October crude oil futures must be above 78.73 in order for you to generate a profit. If crude oil were to close at exactly 78.73 at the time of option expiration, the option would be worth exactly what you paid for it originally (3.73); thus, you would have no profit or loss and would simply break even. At any price above 78.73, the option will be worth more than 3.73 and you will earn a profit. For example, if October crude oil closed at 80, the 75 call option would be worth 5.00 points and you would have a profit of 1.27 points, or $1,270 [(5.00 − 3.73) × ($1,000)]. Conversely, at any price below 78.73, the option would be worth less than the 3.73 you paid to purchase it, thus resulting in a loss. However, even if crude oil happened to fall below the strike price of 75, the most you could lose is the $3,730 you paid to purchase the option.

underlying instrument
the trading instrument from which an options or futures contract derives its value. Soybeans are the underlying instrument for soybean futures.

Long Call

Strategy: Buy a call option.
Market Opportunity: Look for a bullish market where a rise above the breakeven is anticipated.
Maximum Risk: Limited to the premium paid for the call.
Maximum Profit: Unlimited as the price of the underlying instrument rises above the breakeven.
Breakeven: Call strike + call premium.
Margin: None. Option paid for in full.

Smart Trader Tip

Remember that a long call position gives you unlimited profit potential and limited risk. The higher the strike price of the option you buy, the greater the profit potential but also the higher the probability that the option will expire out-of-the-money and thus worthless.

The Long Put Option

A long put option position is entered into simply by purchasing a put option on a given commodities market. The only reason a trader would ever have for buying a put option is that he or she thinks the price of the underlying futures market is going to decline. If the trader did not expect the market to decline, there would be no reason to buy a put option. The reason a trader would buy a put option instead of selling short the underlying futures contract itself is that a long put position entails limited risk, unlike a short position in a futures contract. When you buy a put option, you pay a premium, which is simply the cost of the option contract at the time you buy it. This represents your total maximum risk for the trade. In other words, if you hold the put until expiration and the option is out-of-the-money at that time, the option will expire worthless and you will lose the entire premium you paid to purchase the put originally. This is true no matter how far the underlying futures contract might rise in price.

So, for example, say you bought a put option on soybeans and paid $600 to buy that option. Subsequently, the underlying soybean futures contract rises 100 points in price. At a contract value of $50 per point, this would represent a loss of $5,000 had you sold short the futures contract itself. However, the buyer of the put option in this example could never lose more than the $600 he or she paid to buy the option. Once again, this type of limited-risk trade can often allow traders to have more staying power in the face of an adverse price movement. Now let's look at an actual example of a long put position.

Figure 8.5 displays the risk curves for a long put option position in crude oil. The risk curves depict the expected profit or loss for the October 75 put option purchased at a price of 3.33 points. For crude oil, each full point is worth $1,000, so it would cost a trader $3,330 to purchase this put option.

As you can see in Figure 8.5, this position will make money if, and only if, crude oil declines in price. In fact, a long put position's profit potential is limited only by the fact that crude oil can only fall to zero. As long as the price of crude oil keeps falling, the price of the option can continue to increase. The expected profit or loss at option expiration is depicted by the leftmost risk curve. In this example, it resembles a hockey stick tipped over on its handle.

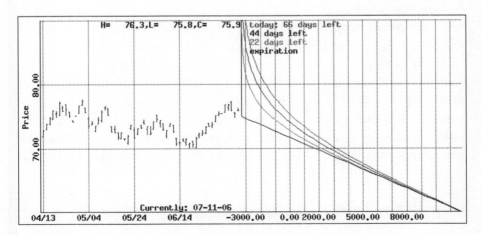

FIGURE 8.5 Risk curves for October crude oil 75 put.
Source: Optionetics Platinum.

The other risk curves in Figure 8.5 clearly depict the effect of time decay on a long put position. Remember that anytime you enter a long put position, you pay time premium on top of any intrinsic value (if the option is in-the-money; otherwise, the price of the option consists solely of time premium). As option expiration draws closer, this time premium starts to evaporate simply as a function of time decay. Remember, an option will have no time premium left as of option expiration. So as you can see in Figure 8.5, the risk curves move down and to the left as time goes by. This means that because of time decay, the underlying market must move further to the downside as time goes by in order to compensate for this loss of time premium.

For this crude oil option trade, the breakeven point or price is $71.67 basis the October crude oil futures contract. For a long put position, this price is calculated as follows:

(Strike price of option − premium paid to purchase option)

So in this case, we take the strike price of 75 and subtract the option price of 3.33 to arrive at a breakeven price of 71.67. This simply means that if you hold this put option until expiration, the price of October crude oil futures must be below 71.67 in order for you to generate a profit if held until expiration. If crude oil were to close at exactly 71.67 at the time of option expiration, the option would be worth exactly what you paid for it originally—3.33; thus, you would have no profit or loss (i.e., you would simply break even). At any price below 71.67, the option will be worth more than 3.33, and thus you will earn a profit.

For example, if October crude oil closed at 70, the 75 put option would be worth 5.00 points and you would have a profit of 1.67 points, or $1,670 [(5.00 × 3.33) × $10 for each 0.01]. Conversely, at any price above 71.67, the option would be worth less than the 3.33 you paid to purchase it, thus resulting in a loss. However, even if crude oil happened to rise above the strike price of 75, the most you can lose is $3,330.

Smart Trader Tip

Remember that a long put position gives you unlimited profit potential and limited risk. The lower the strike price of the option you buy, the greater the profit potential but also the higher the probability that the option will expire out-of-the-money and thus worthless.

Long Put

Strategy: Buy a put option.

Market Opportunity: Look for a bearish market where you anticipate a fall in the price of the underlying below the breakeven.

Maximum Risk: Limited to the premium paid for the put.

Maximum Profit: Limited as the stock price falls below the breakeven to zero.

Breakeven: Put strike – put premium.

Margin: None. 100 percent cost of option. Paid in full.

Bull Call Spread

A *bull call spread* is established by buying a call option with a lower strike price and selling another call option with a higher strike price and the same expiration date. A bull call spread is entered into in a ratio of 1-to-1. Therefore, if you buy one lower strike call, then you sell one higher strike call. If you buy 10 lower strike calls, then you sell 10 higher strike calls, and so on. This debit strategy should be used only if you expect the underlying commodity to rise by the time of option expiration. In other words, it is a bullish strategy.

bull call spread

a trade that involves the purchase of a call option and a sale of a call option with a higher strike price, both with identical expiration dates.

Like a long call position, a bull call spread is a limited-risk position. However, unlike a long call position, which enjoys unlimited profit potential, a bull call spread has limited profit potential. The risk on a bull call spread is limited to the net amount paid to enter the trade in the first place. The maximum loss occurs if the underlying commodity was trading below the strike price of the option you bought at the time of option expiration. The maximum profit on a bull call spread is limited to the difference between the two strike prices minus the amount you paid to enter the trade. The maximum profit will occur if, at the time of option expiration, the underlying commodity contract is trading above the strike price for the option you sold.

Typically, a bull call spread is used when you are moderately bullish on a given market. If you were extremely bullish on a market, it might make more sense to simply buy a call option or trade the underlying commodity market itself. Ideally, a bull call spread should use options with at least 45 days (preferably more) left until expiration. This gives the trade an adequate amount of time to work out.

Figure 8.6 depicts the risk curves for a bull call spread using October gold options. At the time this trade was entered, the October gold futures contract was trading at $649.90. This example involves buying an out-of-the-money bull call spread and is established by purchasing the October 670 call at $27.20 and simultaneously selling the October 680 call at $24.00. The cost of this trade is $320 [(27.20 – 24.00) × $100 per point]. This represents the maximum risk on the trade that will occur if October gold futures are trading at 670 or below at the time of option expiration. The maximum profit potential on this trade is $680. This is calculated as follows: [(higher strike price – lower strike price) – cost to enter trade]. So for this gold bull call spread, the numbers work out as follows: (680 – 670) – 3.20 = 6.80 points × $10 a point = $680. This maximum profit will be achieved if October gold futures are trading at or above the higher strike price of $680 at the time that the October options expire.

As you can see in Figure 8.6, the curvature of a risk curve changes significantly with the passage of time due to the effects of time decay. As expiration draws closer and as the trader's options lose their respective time premium, the risk curves essentially lose some of their curvature with each passing day. At expiration the position will show a maximum loss of $320 if gold is at a price of 670 or below. The profit then rises in a straight line to the upper maximum profit of $680, and flattens out at that level if gold is at a price of 680 or above. Prior to expiration, however, gold futures must make a much larger move in order to generate anything approaching the maximum profit or maximum risk.

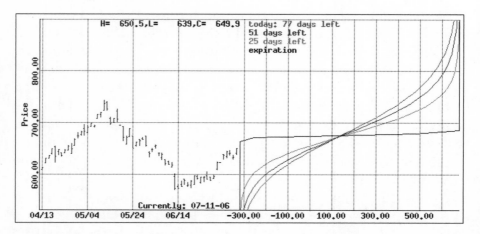

FIGURE 8.6   Risk curves for gold bull call spread.
Source: Optionetics Platinum.

On the downside, although the maximum risk is $320, prior to expiration, gold would have to fall well below $600 in order for this bull call spread to suffer a loss approaching that maximum level. This represents another potential benefit of a bull call spread. In many cases, a trader can set a stop-loss trigger level for the underlying futures contract and basically say, "If the underlying contract drops below this price, I will cut my loss." In most cases, if the underlying market does, in fact, take out that designated price prior to expiration, the trader can exit the bull call spread with a loss that is much smaller than the maximum loss the trader might have suffered had the trade been held until expiration without the underlying ever rebounding.

One other advantage of a bull call spread is the ability to invest small amounts of capital and still enjoy a very favorable reward-to-risk ratio. For example, a trader who is bullish on October gold could simply buy the October 670 call at 27.20 and enjoy unlimited profit potential. However, he or she would be risking $2,720 on this trade. If this trader had entered instead into the 670/680 bull call spread that we just discussed, the trader's profit potential would be limited, but the maximum risk would be only $320, just a fraction of the risk associated with the long call position.

So remember, if you are absolutely bullish on a given market, you should enter into a position that will allow you to maximize your profitability. However, if you are anything less than wildly bullish, you should at least consider the possibility of entering into a bull call spread as a way to generate a profit on a relatively small move by the underlying, without committing large amounts of capital.

Bull Call Spread

Strategy: Buy a lower strike call and sell a higher strike call with the same expiration dates.
Market Opportunity: Look for a moderately bullish market where you anticipate an increase in the price of the underlying above the price of the short call option.
Maximum Risk: Limited to the net debit paid for the spread.
Maximum Profit: Limited. [(Difference in strikes – net debit) × multiplier].
Breakeven: Long strike price + net debit paid.
Margin: Normally, the debit is paid for in full.

Bear Put Spread

bear put spread
a strategy that consists of buying a put and selling a put with a lower strike price.

A *bear put spread* is established by purchasing a put option with a higher strike price and selling another put option with a lower strike price with the same expiration date. A bear put spread is entered into in a ratio of 1-to-1. In other words, if you buy one higher strike put, then you sell one lower strike put. If you buy 10 higher strike puts, you then sell 10 lower strike puts, and so on. This debit strategy is used when you expect the underlying commodity to move moderately lower between now and expiration. In other words, it is a bearish strategy.

Similar to a long put position, a bear put spread is a limited-risk position. However, unlike a long put position, which enjoys unlimited profit potential, a bear put spread has limited profit potential. The risk on a bear put spread is limited to the amount paid to enter the trade in the first place. You would experience the maximum loss if the underlying commodity was trading above the strike price of the option you bought at the time of option expiration. The maximum profit on a bear put spread is limited to the difference between the two strike prices minus the amount you paid to enter the trade. The maximum profit will occur if, at the time of option expiration, the underlying commodity contract is trading below the strike price for the option you sold.

Typically, a bear put spread is used when you are moderately bearish on a given market. If you are extremely bearish on a market, it might make more sense to simply buy a put option or trade the underlying commodity market itself. Ideally, a bear put spread needs options with at least 45 days left until expiration to give the trade an adequate amount of time to work out.

Figure 8.7 depicts the risk curves for a bear put spread using October gold options. At the time this trade was entered, the October gold futures contract was trading at 649.90. This example involves buying an out-of-the-money bear put spread and is established by purchasing the October 630 put at 24.80 and simultaneously selling the October 620 put at 20.50. The net cost of this trade is $430 [(24.8 − 20.50) × $10]. This represents the maximum risk on the trade and will occur if October gold futures are trading at a price of 630 or better at the time of option expiration. The maximum profit potential on this trade is $570. It is calculated as follows: [(higher strike price − lower strike price) − net debit × cost to enter trade] or (630 − 620) − 4.30] = 5.70 points × $10 a point = $570. This maximum profit is achieved if October gold futures are trading at or above the higher strike price of 680 at the time that the October options expire.

As you can see in Figure 8.7, the risk curves change quite a bit with the passage of time. This is due to the effects of time decay. As expiration draws closer and as these put options lose their respective time premium, the risk curves essentially lose some of their curvature with each passing day. At expiration, the position will show a maximum loss of $430 at 630 or above. The profit then rises in a straight line to the lower maximum profit of $570, and flattens out at that level at any price of 620 or below. Prior to expiration, however, gold futures must make a much larger move in order to generate anything approaching the maximum profit or maximum risk.

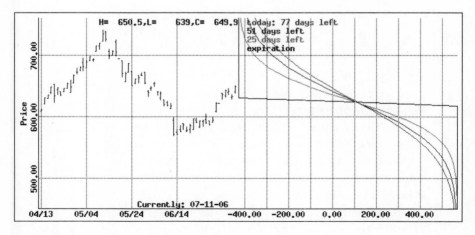

FIGURE 8.7 Risk curves for gold bear put spread.
Source: Optionetics Platinum.

On the risk side, although the maximum risk is $430, prior to expiration, gold would have to rise beyond 750 in order for this bear put spread to suffer a loss approaching that maximum level. This represents another potential benefit of a bear put spread. In many cases, a trader can set a stop-loss trigger level for the underlying futures contract and basically say, "If the underlying contract rises above this price, I will cut my loss." And in most cases, if the underlying market does, in fact, take out that designated price prior to expiration, the trader can exit the bear put spread with a loss that is much smaller than the maximum loss he or she might have suffered had he or she held the trade until expiration.

One advantage of a bear put spread is the ability to invest small amounts of capital and still enjoy a very favorable reward-to-risk ratio. For example, a trader who is bearish on October gold could simply buy the October 630 put at 24.80 and would thus enjoy unlimited profit potential. However, remember that the trader would be risking $2,480 on this trade. If this trader had instead entered into the 630/620 bear put spread that we have just discussed—while the trader's profit potential would be limited—the maximum risk would be only $430, just a fraction of the risk associated with the long put position.

So remember, if you are absolutely bearish on a given market, you should enter into a position that will allow you to maximize your profitability. However, if you are anything less than wildly bullish, then you should at least consider the possibility of entering into a bear put spread as a way to generate a profit on a relatively small move by the underlying, without committing large amounts of capital.

Bear Put Spread

Strategy: Buy a higher strike put and sell a lower strike put with the same expiration date.

Market Opportunity: Look for a moderately bearish market where you anticipate a modest decrease in the price of the underlying asset below the strike price of the short put option.

Maximum Risk: Limited to the net debit paid.

Maximum Profit: Limited. [(Difference in strikes – net debit) × multiplier].

Breakeven: Long strike price – net debit.

Margin: Usually, the cost of the spread or the debit paid for in full.

The Butterfly Spread

One opportunity that is unique to option traders is the ability to take advantage of a neutral market situation. For example, it is possible to make money while a market trades in a narrow price range. One of the most useful strategies for taking advantage of a going-nowhere market is the *butterfly spread*.

butterfly spread
an advanced options strategy that involves selling at-the-money options (the body) and buying out-of-the-money options (the wings).

A call butterfly spread involves buying a call option at one strike price, writing two calls at a higher strike price, and buying one more call at an even higher strike price. A put butterfly spread involves buying a put option at one strike price, selling two put options at a lower strike price, and buying one more put at an even lower strike price. A butterfly spread is always entered into in a ratio of 1:2:1. For example, this type of spread would be entered in a ratio of 1:2:1, 2:4:2, 3:6:3, 4:8:4, and so on. A properly constructed butterfly spread can allow a trader to enjoy a very high probability of profit combined with minimal dollar risk.

Strategists should look for several key elements when looking for butterfly spreads. The first and foremost is an underlying commodity market that is trading in a range with easily identifiable support and resistance levels. That is, the best market is one that is presently fluctuating within a particular trading range. The hope is that that market will remain in that range long enough for the butterfly spread to generate a profit. Now please note that just because a market is presently stuck within a given trading range and just because it has meaningful support and resistance levels does not mean that it cannot or will not break out to new highs or lows. Nevertheless, the point is that you are better off betting on the market that is currently trading in a range to continue to do so than betting that a market that is trending strongly in one direction or the other will immediately top its current trend and begin to drift sideways.

Also, if there is identifiable support and resistance, very often a market will move to one of those levels, only to fail and move back into the range. This is ideal market action for the holder of a butterfly spread, as a butterfly spread profits from having the underlying market stay in a range and also profits from the passage of time.

The implied volatility of the options on the underlying security is also an important consideration. Since the butterfly spread makes money via time decay, when entering a neutral butterfly spread (i.e., centered around the current underlying price), it makes sense to do so in a market where implied volatility is on the high end of its historical range. This allows you to take in a great deal of time premium, thus enhancing your profit potential.

When you are looking to enter a neutral butterfly spread, it is best to use options with no more than 30 to 45 days left until expiration. Remember, a neutral butterfly spread makes money via time decay. Since the most pronounced effects of time decay occur in the last month of trading, it makes sense to focus on those options that are either within that period or will soon be within that period.

The best thing about a butterfly spread is that if you enter the position properly, you can enjoy an exceptionally high probability of profit as well as a limited (and in many cases very low) dollar risk. The best way to put all of these factors together and illustrate them is through an example. So let's look at an example using options on soybeans.

At the time of this trade, August soybeans are trading at 99.50 and the August soybean options have 36 days left until expiration. As you can see in Figure 8.8, August soybean futures have been trading in a range between about 570 and 650 for more than nine months. This is the optimum type of market action for trading a butterfly spread.

Figure 8.9 displays the implied volatility for soybean options with varying times left until expiration. As you can see, the shorter-term options (3 to 30 days) are presently trading at the higher end of the typical range for implied volatility. This suggests that it may be a good time to sell premium. Remember that the higher the implied volatility for a given option or group of options for a given market, the more time premium there is built into the price of the option or options. When selling premium, higher premium is definitely better.

So what we should do is craft a position that will allow us to profit if August soybeans continue to trade within the current trading range. Let's say it's mid-June and we want to take make money if soybeans continue to trade within a range over the next two months. In order to do this, we will look at the following trade:

- Buy 1 August 560 call at 42.50.
- Sell 2 August 600 calls at 18.50.
- Buy 1 August 640 call at 7.75.

The risk curves for this trade appear in Figure 8.10.

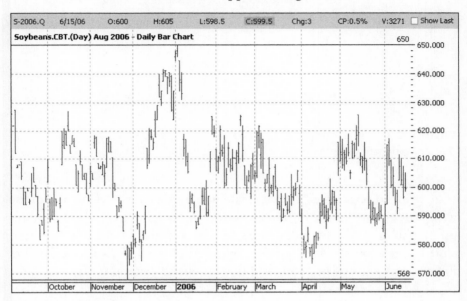

FIGURE 8.8 August soybeans trading in a range.

Source: ProfitSource.

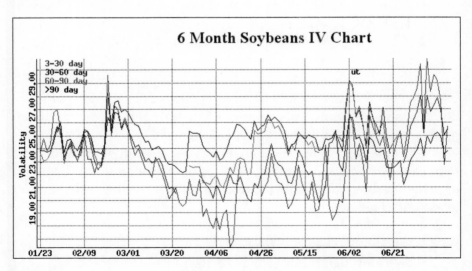

FIGURE 8.9 Implied option volatility for soybean options.

Source: Optionetics Platinum.

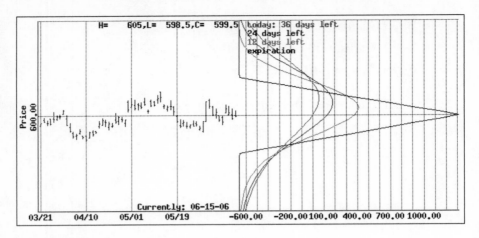

FIGURE 8.10 Risk curves for soybean butterfly spread.
Source: Optionetics Platinum.

Before discussing all of the possibilities for this trade, let's first examine what would happen if this trade was held until expiration. The maximum profit potential for this trade is $1,315.07 and would occur if soybeans closed at exactly 600 on the day of option expiration. This is calculated as follows: If August soybeans close at 600 on option expiration day . . .

- August 560 call bought at 42.50 would be worth 40.00, a loss of 2.50.
- August 600 call sold at 18.50 would be worth 0.00, a profit of 37.00 (18.50 × 2).
- August 640 call bought at 7.75 would be worth 0.00, a loss of 7.75.

The net result is a profit of 26.75 points (−2.50 + 37.00 − 7.75) = 26.75 points. Soybean options trade at $50 per point, so the maximum profit would be 26.75 points × $50, or $1,337.50.

The total cost for this trade is equal to the amount of premium paid to buy the two wings, or outer options, of the spread, minus the amount of premium received to write the middle option. For this trade, the cost works out as follows:

- Bought one August 560 call at 42.50.
- Sold two August 600 calls at 18.50.
- Bought one August 640 call at 7.75.

So the cost to enter the trade is calculated as follows:

$$(42.50 - (18.50 \times 2) + 7.75) = (42.50 - 37.00 + 7.75) = 13.25 \text{ points.}$$

$$13.25 \text{ points} \times \$50 \text{ a point} = \$662.50.$$

The cost of the trade is also equal to the maximum risk for the trade. So once this trade is entered, the most that we can lose is $662.50. This maximum loss would be realized if at the time August options expired, the August soybean futures were trading below the lower strike price of 560 or above the upper strike price of 640.

The breakeven prices for this trade at expiration are 573.25 and 626.75; if August soybean futures are trading between these two prices at the time of option expiration, then this trade will show some profit. A maximum profit of $1,337.50 occurs when soybeans reach a price of 600 and the short calls expire worthless.

So now we know what can happen to this position if we hold it until expiration. But another question that needs to be asked is, "What can happen prior to expiration?" There are a number of possibilities. In reality, the purpose of putting on a butterfly spread is not to attempt to achieve the maximum profit, as enticing as it may look on a risk curve. The problem is that the maximum profit can be achieved only if the underlying commodity closes exactly at the middle strike price on the day the options expire. The odds of this happening are low. The real purpose of entering a butterfly spread is the anticipation that the underlying futures contract will continue to fluctuate within the breakeven points for the trade and that over time an acceptable profit will accumulate. For example, this soybean butterfly spread could show a profit in excess of $400, or about 60 percent, if August soybeans are anywhere between about 588 and 612 two weeks prior to option expiration. So as you can see, the underlying market can move within a fairly large range and still generate an excellent rate of return.

There is good news on the risk side also. Prior to expiration, the underlying security would have to move far outside of the current range in order to generate a significant loss. This is due to the fact that the risk curves will not begin to narrow and rise until option expiration draws closer. What this means is that even if soybeans were to move outside of the 560 to 640 range, a trader might be able to give the market a little more time to reverse back into the range before he or she has to worry about adjusting or exiting the trade.

Long Butterfly Spread

Strategy: Buy one lower strike option, sell two higher strike options, and buy one higher strike option (all calls or all puts) with the same expiration. Profit exists between breakevens.

Market Opportunity: Look for a range-bound market that is expected to stay between the breakeven points.

Maximum Risk: Limited to the net debit paid.

Maximum Profit: Limited. (Difference between strikes – net debit) × multiplier.

Upside Breakeven: Highest strike – net debit.

Downside Breakeven: Lowest strike + net debit.

Smart Trader Tip

Take advantage of a range-trading market by entering butterfly spreads in order to profit from time decay and/or declines in implied volatility.

Summary

As you have seen in this chapter, there are many potential benefits to trading options on futures. Options on futures offer traders a number of different possibilities and opportunities not available to traders who trade only futures. At the very least, buying calls or puts affords you the opportunity to generate large profits while limiting your risk, unlike the futures markets themselves. Likewise, alert traders can find opportunities to cover trades that not only offer limited risk but are also very inexpensive to enter (bull call and bear put spreads). The combination of low cost of entry and limited risk can allow traders to diversify their portfolios far beyond what they might normally feel comfortable with if trading only futures contracts.

Beyond simply speculating on price direction, option traders can also take advantage of opportunities to hedge existing futures positions. These types of maneuvers can allow them to lock in profits and/or limit or, in some cases, completely eliminate downside risk. This can be done by purchasing options (e.g., buying a put option to hedge a long position in the underlying futures contract), selling options (e.g., writing a covered call against a long position in the underlying futures contract), or some combination thereof.

Last but not least, the opportunity to be able to take advantage of neutral situations is unique to option trading. The simple fact of the matter is that overall markets tend to spend a lot of time moving sideways (i.e., trading within a range rather than trending in a given direction). Only through trading options can a trader take advantage of this fact of life. The utilization of a neutral strategy (such as a butterfly spread) enables the astute trader to make money despite the fact that the underlying commodity market is essentially not gaining or losing much ground (see Table 8.1).

TABLE 8.1 Strategy Matrix

Market Behavior	Option Strategy	Strategy Outlook	Order Type	Profit Potential	Risk Potential	Time Decay
Bullish Market	Long call	Bullish	Debit	Unlimited	Limited	Hurtful
	Bull call spread	Bullish	Debit	Limited	Limited	Mixed
	Bull put spread	Moderately bullish	Credit	Limited	Limited	Mixed
	Call ratio backspread	Very bullish	Credit at-even	Unlimited	Limited	Mixed
Bearish Market	Long put	Bearish	Debit	Unlimited	Limited	Hurtful
	Bear put spread	Bearish	Debit	Limited	Limited	Mixed
	Bear call spread	Moderately bearish	Credit	Limited	Limited	Mixed
	Put ratio backspread	Very bearish	Credit at-even	Unlimited	Limited	Mixed
Volatile Market	Long straddle	Nondirectional	Debit	Unlimited	Limited	Hurtful
	Long strangle	Nondirectional	Debit	Unlimited	Limited	Hurtful
	Long synthetic straddle	Nondirectional	Debit	Unlimited	Limited	Hurtful
	Calendar spread	Volatile / sideways	Debit	Unlimited	Limited	Helpful
Sideways Market	Long butterfly spread	Stable	Debit	Limited	Limited	Helpful
	Long condor spread	Stable	Debit	Limited	Limited	Helpful
	Long iron butterfly spread	Stable	Debit	Limited	Limited	Helpful
	Collar spread	Stable	Debit	Limited	Limited	Mixed

A full discussion of all the factors that affect option trading and the full array of strategies available is beyond the scope of this book (you may want to peruse *The Options Trading Course*). Nevertheless, from the material in this chapter, you should by now have a sense of the power and usefulness that options offer to you as a commodity trader. I encourage you to explore this area more fully.

Key Summary Points

1. A derivative is a financial instrument whose price fluctuates based on the price movements of another security.

2. A call option gives the buyer the right to buy a specific futures contract at a specific price up until a specific date. A put option gives the buyer the right to sell a specific futures contract at a specific price up until a specific date.

3. A call option is in-the-money if its strike price is below the current market price for the underlying commodity contract. A call option is out-of-the-money if its strike price is above the current market price for the underlying commodity contract.

4. A put option is in-the-money if its strike price is above the current market price for the underlying commodity contract. A put option is out-of-the-money if its strike price is below the current market price for the underlying commodity contract.

5. The price of an in-the-money option consists of intrinsic value—that is, the amount by which it is in-the-money—plus any time premium. The price of an out-of-the-money option consists solely of time premium.

6. A fair value price for any given option can be calculated using an option pricing model. This fair value gives you some idea whether the price of a given option is presently overvalued, undervalued, or fairly priced.

7. The implied volatility of a given option, which is calculated by an option pricing model, can tell you whether the amount of time premium built into the option price is presently relatively high or low. When buying options, low implied volatility is preferable. When writing options, high implied volatility is preferable.

8. An option's delta value tells you how much the option will move if the underlying commodity contract moves one full point. For example, a call option with a delta of 70 would be expected to gain 0.70 points if the underlying commodity contract rose 1.00 point.

9. Certain strategies allow you to profit from a rise in the price of the underlying contract (buying a call option and buying a bull call spread).

10. Certain strategies allow you to profit from a decline in the price of the underlying contract (buying a put option and buying a bear put spread).

11. Options can also allow you to take advantage of a neutral or range–bound market (butterfly spread).

Chapter 9

Money Management: Staying in the Game

Veteran commodity traders commonly assert that proper *money management* represents the keys to the kingdom. But what does this statement mean, and what exactly is money management? These are critical questions to be answered, not only for veteran traders but especially for novice traders who are just getting started in commodities trading. Before these questions can be answered, however, it is important to first have a full understanding of exactly how commodity futures are traded and the risks involved and potential rewards that are available. Yet, although we have already discussed many of the risks and rewards of commodity futures, the issue of money management should come first. What is money management? In its most succinct definition, money management involves deploying trading capital in a manner that minimizes risk as much as possible, while simultaneously affording maximum profit potential.

> **money management**
> the act of deploying trading capital in a manner that minimizes as much as possible the risks that you are exposed to, while simultaneously affording you maximum profit potential.

Since most new commodity traders originally start out trading in the stock market, it is important to understand the differences in the mechanics involved in trading stocks versus commodities and the inherent risks involved. The best way to gain an understanding of these important differences is through an example comparing a commodity trade to a stock trade.

The majority of individual investors have few reservations about buying and selling individual stocks or mutual funds. These vehicles are perceived to be investments, which have tangible value and are likely to produce profits in the long run. On the other side of the coin, many individuals are led to believe that commodity trading is risky, as it involves speculation, with no tangible value attached to it. In reality, these assertions are incorrect. Owning a stock gives you a small piece of ownership in a publicly traded company. In theory, you are entitled to some portion of the profits generated and any dividends paid by that corporation. In reality, the company may or may not pay a dividend. Ultimately you will profit from a company's earnings growth only if another investor is willing to pay more to buy your shares later at a higher price. However, if you buy a soybean futures contract, you inherit the right to control 5,000 bushels of soybeans; the price of soybeans will never go to zero. Meanwhile, a company might go out of business. If you own the stock, it leaves you holding shares worth nothing. In other words, a physical commodity will always have some value, which isn't always true with stocks

So why are stocks considered to be an investment and commodities speculation? Many individuals have been led to believe that commodities are too risky due to volatility and the unpredictability of commodity prices. In reality, this assertion is only partially correct. The perception that there is risk associated with buying and selling short commodity contracts is certainly true. However, the notion that there is some sort of inherent price volatility that makes trading commodities more risky than trading other investment vehicles is completely untrue. While there is no question that commodity prices can be volatile at times, the markets are not nearly as volatile as many people seem to think. In any event, it is typically not the volatility of commodity price movements that causes speculators to lose money. What can cause commodity trading to be risky is the amount of potential leverage involved, as we will explore momentarily. Even more to the point is the fact that many traders begin speculating in commodities without a full understanding of the leverage involved. In essence, many individuals simply blow it by not taking the time to fully understand just what they are getting into. To make sure you don't follow in their footsteps, let's look at how a stock trade compares to a commodity trade.

Understanding the Money Game

There is no question that trading commodities involves risk. Sometimes those risks are exaggerated, however. Many investors lose money trading commodities due to a poor understanding of margin and the leverage it offers. In short, understanding the mathematics associated with the trading instrument you choose to trade is an essential part of sound money management.

The Mathematics of Buying a Stock or Mutual Fund

The majority of individuals who enter into commodity trading have had prior experience in trading stocks and/or mutual funds. Buying a stock or a mutual fund is a fairly straightforward process. If you wish to buy 1,000 shares of a stock that is trading for $30 a share, you need to invest $30,000 (1,000 shares × $30). The same math holds true for a mutual fund. If you wish to invest $30,000 in a mutual fund, the fund company will divide your $30,000 by the net asset value (NAV) of the fund at the time of your purchase, and you will purchase that number of shares. For example, if the NAV of the fund is $20 a share, you will purchase 1,500 shares ($30,000 ÷ $20). If the price of the stock or the mutual fund changes, the amount of capital required to buy that security will rise or fall depending on whether the price of the stock or fund goes up or down. This is not necessarily the case when trading commodities. In fact, in some respects a commodity trade is a completely different animal.

The Concept of Margin in Commodity Trading

initial margin

the minimum amount of money that a trader must put up in order to enter into a trade in a given commodity, whether long or short.

Commodity trading involves the use of margin. The *initial margin* is the amount of money that a trader must put up in order to enter into a trade in a given commodity, whether long or short. Each commodity exchange sets a minimum margin requirement that a speculator must put up as a good faith deposit in order to enter into a trade in a given commodity at that exchange. Various brokerage houses may at times require their customers to put up a greater amount of margin than the exchange minimum, but they cannot allow their customers to put up less than the exchange-required minimum.

The minimum margin requirement can be raised or lowered for any market at any time by the exchange at which that market trades. However, changes tend to happen infrequently. Upward changes in margin requirements will typically occur during periods of extreme volatility and/or large price movements. In these circumstances, margin requirements may be raised; when things quiet down, margin requirements are often lowered again. Table 9.1 displays a number of markets and the margin requirements as of a given date. In the future, these values may be higher or lower than what is indicated here.

As you can see in Table 9.1, the margin requirement for wheat traded at the Chicago Board of Trade (CBOT) is $945 (in June 2006). This implies that as long as you have at least $945 in your commodity trading account, you can buy long or sell short one contract of wheat. However, this doesn't mean that your maximum risk is $945 or that you won't be called upon to put more money in your account if the trade moves against you. To illustrate this important concept, let's assume that July wheat is trading at $4.07 a bushel. A standardized wheat contract is for 5,000 bushels of wheat, and each price movement of one penny, or $0.01, is worth $50. So at the moment, a trader who puts $945 into her account and buys one wheat contract now controls $20,350 worth of wheat (407 cents times $50 a cent = $20,350). If wheat subsequently rises $0.10 to $4.17 a bushel, this trader will have an open profit of $500 (10 cents times $50 a cent = $500).

Now let's say the trader exits this trade with a $500 profit; after she exits the trade, the price for wheat rises another $0.10 a bushel. Once the trader exits the trade, she can withdraw $500 from her account, once

TABLE 9.1   Margin Requirements

Market	Initial Margin	Maintenance Margin
Dollar index	$1,463	$1,100
British pound	$1,755	$1,300
Canadian dollar	$1,755	$1,300
Japanese yen	$2,700	$2,000
Swiss franc	$1,755	$1,300
EuroFX	$2,835	$2,100
T-bonds	$1,350	$1,000
10-yr. T-notes	$878	$650
5-yr. T-notes	$540	$400
Corn	$540	$400
Wheat	$945	$700
Soybeans	$1,013	$750
Soybean meal	$810	$600
Soybean oil	$540	$400
Dow Industrials	$12,188	$9,750
eMini Dow	$2,438	$1,950
S&P 500	$19,688	$15,750
eMini S&P 500	$3,938	$3,150
Nasdaq 100	$18,750	$15,000
eMini Nasdaq	$3,750	$3,000
Live cattle	$1,148	$850
Live hogs	$1,215	$900
Feeder cattle	$1,485	$1,100
Pork bellies	$1,620	$1,200
Gold	$5,386	$3,990
Silver	$8,079	$5,985
Copper	$12,150	$9,000
Cocoa	$1,120	$800
Coffee	$2,520	$1,800
Sugar	$1,120	$800
Orange juice	$1,960	$1,400
Cotton	$1,260	$900
Crude oil	$4,725	$3,500
Heating oil	$6,075	$4,500
Natural gas	$11,475	$8,500
Unleaded gas	$7,425	$5,500

again leaving only $945 in the account. If she so desires, she can buy or sell short another contract of wheat by once again putting up just $945, despite the fact that the contract itself is now worth $21,350 (427 cents times $50 a cent = $21,350), or $1,000 more than it was when she originally bought the first contract at $4.07 a bushel. Unless and until the CBOT raises or lowers the minimum margin requirement, the trader can continue to buy or sell short a contract of wheat for $945, regardless of the underlying value of the contract.

This is a key difference between trading stocks and trading commodities. As the price of a stock rises or falls, the amount of money required to purchase the stock will rise or fall commensurately. The price for entering a commodity trade (i.e., the margin requirement) will change only when the exchange at which that market is traded raises or lowers the margin requirement, regardless of how much the price for that commodity may rise or fall in the interim.

maintenance margin

the minimum amount of money that a trader must maintain in his or her account in order to continue to hold a trade in a given commodity.

So far, we have been talking only about initial margin. There is another type of margin that traders need to be aware of, and this is referred to as *maintenance margin*. Maintenance margin represents the minimum amount of money that a trader must have in his or her trading account in order to be allowed by the exchange and/or brokerage firm to continue to maintain an open position in a given market. In our wheat example, let's assume that this trader literally had only the minimum margin of $945 in her account when she originally entered a long trade and that the price of wheat subsequently declined after the trade was entered. If at some point the trade was to move far enough against her, the trader would then be required to post additional funds to maintain the position.

margin call

a brokerage firm's request for additional funds in a customer's trading account.

In this example, the initial margin requirement is $945 and the maintenance margin is $700. This means that the trader can open a new long or short position in wheat with just $945 in her account. However, if at some point the amount of money in the account declines below $700, she will receive a *margin call* from her brokerage firm to add more money to the account to restore the account to the initial margin of $945 or more. If she fails to meet this margin call, then the brokerage firm will automatically liquidate the position on behalf of the trader. In reality, trading commodities using minimum margins and very low account balances is typically an invitation to disaster. Still, it is important to understand the raw and minimal requirements of trading.

In any event, anyone who has ever traded stocks or mutual funds will recognize that the arrangement I have just described for funding a commodity trade via the use of margin is very different from the method used to buy stocks or mutual funds. To illustrate this important difference more thoroughly, let's compare a hypothetical stock trade to a hypothetical commodity trade.

Smart Trader Tip

Before entering any position, be certain that you understand the concept of margin and the fact that you can lose more than the amount initially required to enter a commodity trade.

A Futures Trade versus a Stock Trade

Let's look at an example that compares putting a particular dollar amount into a commodity trade versus putting a particular dollar amount into a given stock. Let's assume that July soybeans are trading at $6.00 a bushel. The standardized soybean contract sets an arbitrary value of $50 for every penny. At this price, the total contract value for soybeans is $30,000 (calculated by multiplying 600 cents times $50 a cent). Now, if commodities traded like stocks, you would be required to put up the full amount of $30,000 in order to buy or sell short one contract of soybeans. However, the exchange minimum for soybeans may be $1,000 (minimum requirements can change from time to time based on the price and volatility of a given contract). In other words, instead of putting up 100 percent of the value of the contract in order to trade it, in this example a speculator needs to put up only 3 percent of the value of the contract ($1,000 ÷ $30,000 = 3.0 percent) in order to enter a trade. This is referred to as *leverage*. A person who buys $30,000 worth of stock and puts up $30,000 in order to do so has leverage of 1-to-1. A trader

leverage
using small amounts of capital to control large amounts of a commodity or other asset. Margin is an example of using leverage.

who buys a soybean contract worth $30,000 and puts up only $1,000 to do so is obtaining leverage of 30-to-1.

You are probably already getting a sense of the importance of money management. Anytime you are dealing with leverage, you need to be aware that you are dealing with a double-edged sword, especially when you start talking about leverage of 30-to-1. To better appreciate the magnifying effect of leverage, let's compare a stock trade to a commodity trade using the full amount of leverage available. Let's say both Trader A and Trader B have $30,000 of trading capital available.

- Trader A invests $30,000 and buys 1,000 shares of stock XYZ at $30 a share.

- Trader B buys 30 soybean contracts at a price of $6.00 a bushel and puts up $30,000 of margin money.

In the process, while both traders have invested $30,000, Trader A holds $30,000 worth of stock, while Trader B actually controls $900,000 worth of soybeans (600 cents × $50 a cent × 30 contracts). Now let's assume that both the price of XYZ stock and the price of soybeans decline by a modest 3 percent, and compare the outcomes for each trader.

If the price of XYZ stock declines 3 percent, from $30 to $29.10 a share, Trader A will lose $900, or exactly 3 percent. In other words, the trader will lose 90 cents per share times 1,000 shares (1000 × 0.90 = $900 and $900 ÷ $30,000 = .03 or 3 percent). However, if the price of soybeans declines 3 percent, from $6.00 a bushel to $5.82 a bushel, Trader B will lose $27,000, or a full 90 percent of his initial margin deposit. How is this possible? Because Trader B is using 30 times as much leverage as Trader A. Trader B loses $0.18 per contract times $50 a cent times 30 contracts, or $27,000 (−18 × $50 × 30 = −$27,000).

This example clearly illustrates the potential danger associated with using too much leverage. In this example, the commodity trader basically overreached by using too much leverage. Unfortunately, this type of overreach is more common among commodity traders than among stock traders. The obvious question remains, "Why is this so?" Why do commodity traders have a greater propensity to overleverage themselves and thus expose themselves to the risk of catastrophic loss? There are two basic answers. The simple answer is "Because they can." The more complicated answer involves the fact that too many individuals simply do not fully understand the amount of leverage they are using when they buy or sell short a commodity contract.

If you give a person a choice between putting up $30,000 to buy $30,000 of a particular investment, whatever it may be, or putting up just $1,000 to buy $30,000 of a particular investment, a certain number of people are going to say, "Hey, why put up a lot of money when I can put up only a little?" By itself, putting up a small amount of money is not necessarily a good thing or a bad thing. If a person understands that he or she is buying $30,000 worth of something and might ultimately lose more than the original $1,000 used to enter the trade, this type of leverage can be used to generate extremely high rates of return. However, if a trader puts up $1,000 to buy or sell short $30,000 of something and assumes that the $1,000 is the most that he or she can lose (when that is absolutely not the case), the trader is set up for a devastating loss. The first thing any trader needs to understand is just what buying or selling short a particular commodity really entails.

Here is the key point to remember about futures trading: Your maximum potential risk on a commodity trade is *not* limited to the amount of margin money you need to put up in order to enter the trade. Any commodity trader who fails to understand this reality is unlikely to survive in the long run. If you buy a soybean contract, putting up the minimum margin of $1,000, and the next day soybeans gap lower by $0.30, you will suddenly find yourself with an open loss of $1,500. If you had no additional money in your account, your brokerage firm would issue a margin call requiring you to immediately deposit $500 into your account to cover the deficit.

Understanding the Risks Involved in a Commodity Trade

By now you should clearly understand that buying or selling short a commodity does not entail the same financial risks as buying a stock. While you are required to put up a certain amount of money in order to establish the position, the amount of potential risk that you are actually taking on is almost always more than the initial margin requirement. But how does one measure risk? There are several important measures to consider. Among them are the amount of leverage you are actually using, the magnitude of price movement you can normally expect from a given market, and what that equates to in terms of dollars, as well as the largest gap experienced by the commodity you are trading. Let's examine these potential risks one at a time.

Price Movements in Dollars

As you can see in Figure 9.1, in a matter of just 13 trading days, July wheat rose from a closing price of $3.60 a bushel to $4.23 a bushel. In the chart, the prices are multiplied by 100 to reflect point movement. Now, if this were a stock and the price moved from 360 to 423, we could easily figure out that the stock rose $63 a share (423 − 360 = 63). If we had bought 100 shares of stock, then we would have a profit of $6,300. But with commodities, you first need to know the dollar value of a point move for the market you are trading before you can calculate actual profit or loss. Since a standardized wheat contract is for 5,000 bushels of wheat, each penny in price is worth $50. So in this example, if a trader had bought one wheat contract at 360 and sold it at 423, he or she would have made 63 cents, for a profit of $3,150 (63 cents × $50 per cent).

Table 9.2 displays some examples for 10 heavily traded commodity futures. For each market, the table lists:

- A recent price at which that market traded.
- The amount of margin required in order to enter a new trade in that market.
- The actual dollar value of the contract based on that price.

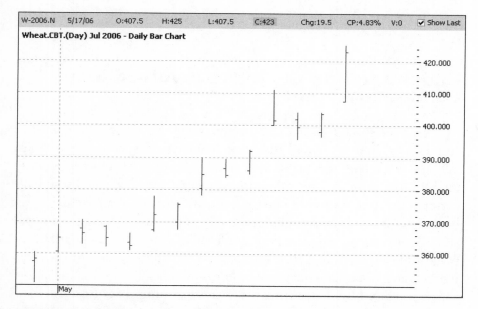

FIGURE 9.1   Wheat contract gains 63 cents, or $3,150.
Source: ProfitSource.

TABLE 9.2 Contract Dollar Value, Margin, and Leverage

Commodity	Price	Contract Value ($)	Margin ($)	Margin as a % of Contract Value	Leverage
Crude oil	69.47	$69,470	$4,750	6.8%	14.6-to-1
Gold	703.00	$70,300	$6,250	8.9%	11.2-to-1
Silver	1350.00	$67,500	$9,400	13.9%	7.2-to-1
Soybeans	603.00	$30,150	$1,000	3.3%	30.1-to-1
Wheat	407.00	$20,350	$745	3.7%	27.3-to-1
Corn	259.00	$12,950	$450	3.5%	28.8-to-1
Live cattle	77.65	$31,060	$945	3.0%	32.8-to-1
Coffee	101.80	$38,175	$2,520	6.6%	15.1-to-1
Sugar	17.11	$19,163	$1,400	7.3%	13.7-to-1
Cotton	51.40	$25,700	$1,400	5.4%	18.3-to-1

- The initial margin requirement as a percentage of the total contract dollar value.
- The amount of leverage obtained.

All the numbers in Table 9.2 will change as market prices and margin requirements change for each market. Still, the values in this table can give traders some idea of exactly what they are getting into when they buy or sell short a given commodity contract. Using the numbers as they appear in Table 9.2, you can see that the market with the lowest contract value is corn, at $12,950. The market with the highest contract value is gold, at $70,300. Since gold recently experienced an extremely large price movement and much price volatility, the margin requirement is presently 8.9 percent of the contract value, thus resulting in leverage of 11.2-to-1. The leverage factor is arrived at by simply dividing 100 by margin as a percent of contract value ($100 \div 8.9 = 11.2$).

Smart Trader Tip

Determine roughly how much a given commodity is likely to fluctuate in terms of dollars and be certain that that amount of risk fits into your own trading capital restraints. Margin requirements and information regarding contract specifications can be found at the exchange where the futures contracts are traded.

Average True Range

average true range

essentially measures the average amount of day-to-day fluctuation in points and/or dollars for a given commodity contract. A handy tool for estimating relative risk between two commodities.

Table 9.3 looks at price and margin data in another useful way. This table includes *average true range* (ATR), a trading tool that enables traders to get a handle on the amount of risk involved in trading a given commodity. Before looking at this data, let's look at what average true range actually measures.

To calculate the true range for a single trading day, you would employ the following steps:

- *To calculate today's true high*, compare today's high price and yesterday's closing price. Today's true high is equal to whichever of these two values is higher. In other words, if corn closed yesterday at $2.12 per bushel and today's high is $2.14 per bushel, then today's true high is $2.14 per bushel. However, if corn opened at $2.10 per bushel and that turned out to be the high of the day, then today's true high would be equal to yesterday's closing price of $2.12 per bushel.

- *To calculate today's true low*, compare today's low price and yesterday's closing price. Today's true low is equal to whichever of these two values is lower. In other words, if corn closed yesterday at $2.12 per bushel and today's low is $2.09 per bushel, then today's true low is $2.09 per bushel. However, if corn opened at $2.14 per bushel and that turned out to be the low of the day, then today's true low would be equal to yesterday's close of $2.12 per bushel.

- *To calculate the daily true range for any market*, subtract that day's true low from that day's true high. In utilizing true range values, most traders use an average of the daily true range readings over a previous number of days. Figure 9.2 displays cocoa prices with the 25-day average true range value plotted below it. As you can see, the average true range is 24.755. Since cocoa futures trade at $10 a point, this means that in terms of dollars, the average daily range over the past 25 days has been $247.55. Obviously, on some days the dollar fluctuation will be greater and on other days it will be less. As you can also see, this average ATR value will fluctuate over time as market volatility rises and falls.

Table 9.3 displays the average ATR for the same 10 markets that are listed in Table 9.2.

FIGURE 9.2 Cocoa with 25-day average true range (ATR).

Source: ProfitSource.

		TABLE 9.3	Average True Range	
Commodity	ATR (points)	ATR ($)	Margin ($)	ATR as a % of Margin
Crude oil	1.82	$1,820	$4,750	38.3%
Gold	16.02	$1,602	$6,250	25.6%
Silver			$9,400	
Soybeans	9.62	$481	$1,000	48.1%
Wheat	8.40	$420	$745	56.3%
Corn	5.03	$252	$450	56.0%
Live cattle	1.18	$472	$945	49.9%
Coffee	3.01	$1,128	$2,520	44.8%
Sugar	0.45	$504	$1,400	36.0%
Cotton	0.82	$410	$1,400	29.3%

Gaps

price gap
the difference between the opening price today for a given commodity and yesterday's closing price.

Another factor that commodity traders need to consider in their trading plans and decisions is the fact that commodity market prices can fluctuate widely while the market exchanges are closed. Price changes that take place while the exchanges are closed are referred to as *price gaps*.

Regardless of where a trader might place a stop-loss order, it's possible for markets to gap far beyond any stop-loss order. Table 9.4 displays the largest overnight gap experienced by a variety of heavily traded commodity futures. In virtually every case, the largest gap is well in excess of the margin requirements that appeared in Table 9.1. This simply means that if you choose to trade a market using minimum margin requirements, it is conceivable that you will enter a trade today and that by tomorrow morning your open loss on the trade will exceed your margin and you will be subject to a margin call from your broker. Likewise, the information in Table 9.4 alerts you to the fact that while you may enter a stop-loss order to get out of a given trade, there is always the possibility that the market could open the following day well beyond your stop-loss point.

TABLE 9.4   Largest Opening Gaps in Dollars

Commodity	Largest Overnight Gap ($)
Crude oil	$7,500
Gold	$5,040
Silver	$5,105
Soybeans	$2,412
Wheat	$2,412
Corn	$1,500
Live cattle	$800
Coffee	$13,838
Sugar	$3,898
Cotton	$1,940

In theory, gaps are not necessarily as much of a danger as they used to be. This is because with the advent and expansion of electronic trading in recent years, many markets trade around the clock, though not necessarily 24 hours a day. For example, soybeans and other grain products have for years traded on the floor of the Chicago Board of Trade from 9:30 A.M. central time until 1:15 P.M. central time. This means that once the market closed at 1:15 one day, there could be no more trades made in these markets until 9:30 in the morning of the next trading day. Now, the grain markets also trade electronically from 6:30 P.M. central time until 6:00 the following morning. So in this case, there is now overnight trading available should traders wish to avail themselves of that opportunity. Still, the grain markets are closed between 6 A.M. and 9:30 A.M. and between 1:15 P.M. and 6 P.M. This still leaves plenty of opportunity for a gap to occur.

Smart Trader Tip
Use average true range and gaps to estimate your worst-case loss for any given position.

Dealing with Risk

By now you have seen examples of the profit potential and also the risk of loss that are associated with futures trading. The key to success then is to manage your trades in a manner that allows you to minimize your risk and maximize your profits. Due to the low levels of margin required in order to trade a given commodity contract, properly capitalized commodity traders have a great deal of flexibility in deciding how many markets to trade at one time and in what quantity. The first thing that intelligent traders must do is insulate themselves from the risk of catastrophic loss. We will get into a more comprehensive list of issues in a bit, but let's first talk about the last line of defense for any single trade: the stop-loss order.

What Is a Stop-Loss Order?

stop-loss order

an order placed to exit an open trade in an attempt to limit the risk on that particular trade to a given amount.

A *stop-loss order*, as its name implies, is an order that you place after entering a trade, which attempts to limit the maximum loss on that trade to a predetermined amount. This amount should be equal to or less than the maximum amount that the trader is willing to risk on that particular trade. Let's illustrate this concept with an example. Suppose a trader expects cocoa prices to rise and wishes to enter into a long position in order to profit from what he expects will be a subsequent rise in price.

Let's assume that he looks at the double bottom that has formed in Figure 9.3 and decides to enter a long position in July cocoa once the price reaches 1,482. Let's further assume that the most he is willing to risk on this trade is $500. Cocoa futures trade at a point value of $10 per point. So the trader in this example could afford to risk 50 points in the price of cocoa. If the trader buys a long position of one contract in cocoa at a price of 1,482, he would then need to place a stop-loss order at 1,432, in order to attempt to limit his risk on the trade to $500 $\{[(1,482 - 1,432) \times \$10] = \$500\}$.

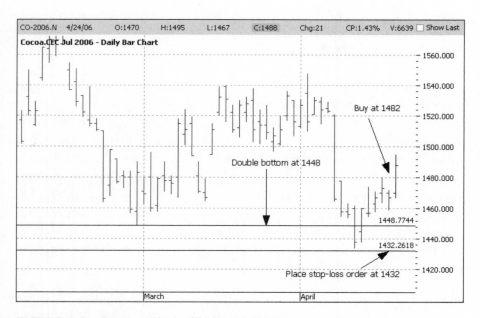

FIGURE 9.3 Cocoa with double bottom pattern.
Source: ProfitSource.

In this example, the trader hopes that the price of cocoa will rise after entering a long position and that the subsequent sale of the contract at a higher price will generate a profit. However, in the case that the long position in cocoa does not work out, the trader has now entered an order that will hopefully allow him to limit his risk to just $500 per contract.

Still, traders need to be aware of the following truth: Placing a stop-loss order does not guarantee that your loss will be limited to a certain amount. There are several limitations to the effectiveness of stop-loss orders including the following three basic potential problems:

1. Gaps.
2. Slippage and running of stops.
3. Fast markets.

Let's take a look at all three of these potential stop-loss obstacles.

More on Gaps

As discussed earlier, a gap occurs when a market closes one trading session at a given price and opens the next trading session at a different price. Typically, there will be some amount of gapping when a new trading session begins. In other words, more often than not a market will not begin trading a new session at exactly the same price at which it closed the last. Usually there will be at least a small difference between the old session's close and the new session's open. The problem that can arise—as you saw in Table 9.3—is that from time to time this gap can be unexpectedly wide.

While the gaps in Table 9.3 represent the most extreme and rare examples of gaps in each commodity market, Figure 9.4 displays the kind of extreme gap that can occur much more commonly. For example, let's say soybean futures closed at $5.905 a bushel. On the next trading day, soybeans opened at a price of $6.13 a bushel. As soybeans have a point value of $50 a cent, this gap of 22.5 cents equates to $1,125. Let's put this into perspective. If you were long soybeans at the close of trading one day, at the open of trading the next day you would instantly have garnered a gain of $1,125 per contract. Likewise, if you happened to be short soybeans at the close of that trading day, then at the next day's open your position would instantly be worth $1,125 less than it was at the previous close. Traders need to factor these kinds of possibilities into their risk management decisions.

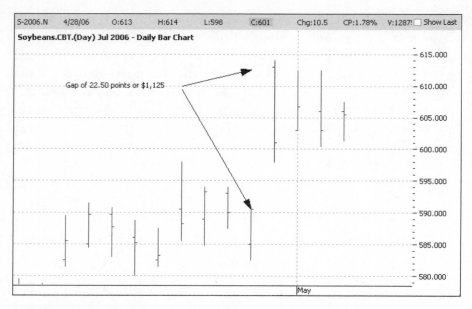

| S-2006.N | 4/28/06 | O:613 | H:614 | L:598 | C:601 | Chg:10.5 | CP:1.78% | V:1287! ☐ Show Last |

Soybeans.CBT.(Day) Jul 2006 - Daily Bar Chart

Gap of 22.50 points or $1,125

FIGURE 9.4 Soybeans gap 22.50 cents, or $1,125.
Source: ProfitSource.

For example, let's assume that a trader had decided to sell short soybeans at the open of the day prior to the gap that is highlighted in Figure 9.4. Let's further assume that she has a $60,000 trading account and is willing to risk 5 percent of her trading capital on a single trade. Finally, let's assume that she wants to exit this short trade if soybeans exceed the prior eight-day high price of 598 and will place a stop-loss order to buy at 599 in order to limit her risk. Now, if the trader expects to sell short at a price of 585, then she needs to determine how many contracts she can trade without exceeding her 5 percent per trade risk limit.

Risk Calculations

- Sell short price = 585.
- Stop-loss price = 599.
- Risk per trade = 14 points at $50 a point equals $700 per contract.
- Maximum allowable risk per trade is 5 percent of $60,000, or $3,000.
- Number of contracts to trade = ($3,000/$700), or four contracts.

So the trader sells short four soybean contracts at 585 and then places an order to buy four soybean contracts at a price of 599 in an effort to limit her risk to less than 5 percent of her trading capital. Let's say the market gaps higher the next day to open at 613. At this point, because the trader entered a stop order to buy at the market as soon as the price of 599 was reached or exceeded, she will buy four soybean contracts at the open price of 613. As a result of this gap, instead of losing $2,800 as was deemed an acceptable risk, the trader lost $5,600, or a painful 9.33 percent of her trading capital.

Trade Summary
Sell short price = 585.
Actual buy price = 613.
Loss in points = 28.
Loss in $ = 28 points × $50 a point = a loss of $1,400 per contract.
Total loss = $1,400 × 4 contracts, or $5,600.

Clearly, traders must give careful consideration to the potential for any market they are trading to gap, as well as the likely size of any such gaps. Without taking this into account, traders may inadvertently set themselves up for unexpectedly large losses.

Slippage and Running of Stops

Slippage describes a situation where a trader expects to get filled on an order at one price and ends up getting filled at a different price. For example, if a trader enters a stop order to buy sugar at a price of 650 but ends up getting filled at a price of 652, then the trader has suffered 2 points of slippage. Since each point in sugar is worth $11.20, this trader is said to have suffered $22.40 of slippage.

Slippage happens for a variety of reasons, and a little bit of slippage is not entirely unexpected, particularly in nonelectronic markets. Some traders perceive that any slippage is the result of people doing unscrupulous things to profit for themselves. Typically, however, slippage occurs as the result of market prices moving quickly in one direction. If a broker standing in a trading pit has a number of orders in hand and prices start quickly moving higher (or lower) through the prices at which the broker is supposed to execute these trades, the fact of the matter is that he can only act so fast. So by the time he is physically able to execute a given order, it is possible that the market price will have already moved past the desired price for that order. This can happen despite the best efforts of a floor broker to fill the order in a timely manner.

Slippage is most likely to occur when a trader uses a stop order in an open outcry market. A stop order becomes a market order once the stop price stated in the order is hit. Once it becomes a market order, the broker in the trading pit is obligated to execute the trade *at the market* (i.e., the best price available at that moment). In other words, the broker has no discretion in this case to wait and try to fill the order at a better price. So a situation can arise where a number of stop orders are bunched together at a particular price—say, just above the previous day's high price. Once this price is hit, all of these stop orders are triggered at once. This can create a flood of market orders all attempting to buy that commodity at the same time. This type of situation can create a surge of demand. Commodity prices are ultimately determined by supply and demand. As a result, this surge of demand will likely propel prices higher in fairly short order. Likewise, the greater the amount of buying taking place, the larger the likely move in price.

It is often suggested that at times traders who deal in large volume will attempt to *run the stops*. If they can discern that there might be a lot of orders placed at a particular price or within a particular price range, they will attempt to move prices to that level in order to trigger the stops. They will then attempt to trade the other side of the market. Let's look at an example to better understand this phenomenon.

Let's assume that a large-volume soybean trader determines that there are a lot of buy stop orders just above yesterday's high price. If the price of soybeans today starts to get close to that level, the trader may start buying aggressively in an effort to push prices up to the area of those buy stops. If she succeeds and the buy stops are hit, then the large-volume trader has instant demand for the contracts she bought on the way up and now wishes to sell. If all of the buy stops are triggered, one of two things will typically happen. Either the rally will build momentum and carry on to still higher prices or the rally will fail once all of these buy stops are filled. At this point the market will usually reverse back to the downside as demand dries up. The large trader, having bought a large position and then having sold that position into the rally triggered by the buy stops, will monitor the market for signs of weakness. If the rally appears destined to fail, the large trader may begin to sell short aggressively in an effort to push prices lower, knowing that there are no buy orders left in the market, since they were already triggered as the market moved higher.

The advent of electronic trading can help alleviate slippage to some extent. In an electronically traded market, orders are matched electronically and instantaneously. As a result, the slippage that can occur in an open outcry market by virtue of the physical limitation that a broker can execute only so many orders at a particular time is, in essence, alleviated. Likewise, it is often more difficult for traders outside of a trading pit, seated at a computer terminal, to know where stop orders are bunched. Nevertheless, traders in electronic markets should not think that they are immune from experiencing slippage or from a large trader attempting to run the stops.

Fast Markets

Another situation that can cause slippage is known as a *fast market*. A fast market is defined as a financial market that is experiencing a combination of high volatility and heavy trading. This can often lead to chaotic trading, and even real-time price quotes may not be terribly accurate. Typically, this type of situation occurs when some sort of news event triggers a strong movement by a market in one direction or the other. While the direction of the market may appear obvious—either sharply higher or sharply lower—the problem is that in chaotic market conditions, the spread between the bid and ask prices may

fast market
a market may be designated as a *fast market* by the exchange it is traded on if it is presently experiencing high volatility and heavy trading. It may be difficult to get filled at a specific desired price during a fast market.

widen substantially as market makers try to protect themselves. As a result, even though the overall trend may be down, sharp countertrend rallies can occur. Once traders see prices jump, they may be quick to climb on board in hopes of riding a quick rebound. Their buying may help to propel prices higher still. The hoped-for rally may work out, however, if the advance is based mainly on someone buying at an unusually high ask price, a new wave of selling that hits the unusually low bid price can quickly cause this short-term rebound to reverse completely.

During a fast market, your only real defense is simply not to trade. If you have an order in the market, you typically have little control over what price you are filled at, unless you use a limit order. The problem with using a limit order, however, is that your order is more likely to be bypassed altogether as prices tend to move in large increments.

Smart Trader Tip

Remember that gaps, fast markets, and normal slippage can all work against you and plan accordingly to deal with these adverse events.

Money Management from the Top Down

All of the things discussed so far are basically the nuts and bolts of money management. Now we need to get down to putting the major building blocks together to form a comprehensive money management approach designed to minimize risk and maximize profitability. The very first step that any commodity trader needs to take is to realistically assess his or her own ability to tolerate risk. An individual who has never traded anything before, and likewise does not grasp the effect of leverage as it is involved in commodity trading, is the candidate least likely to succeed. This is simply because until you find yourself on the wrong side of a trade that is losing money in greater quantity and/or more quickly than you had anticipated, you cannot adequately prepare yourself for the sick feeling in the pit of your stomach that accompanies such an experience. This type of experience can cause even the most experienced trader to react emotionally and abandon all discipline, and to do so at the worst possible moment. However, an individual who is willing to tolerate a reasonable risk and who also understands that there are certainly going to be losses along the way—and takes steps to minimize the risk of serious losses—has the highest likelihood of achieving long-term success as a commodity trader.

In some respects, trading is like war. Your ultimate goal is to win (in this case, to profit). However, just as in a war, it is also critical to your success that you recognize and acknowledge that you are unlikely to win every battle. Along the way you may take some casualties (losing trades) and at times you may have to retreat (trading smaller during a bad stretch). These are simply the realities not only of the battlefield, but of the marketplace. At the same time, no matter the situation, when the opportunity presents itself to move forward aggressively, you must stand ready to act at a moment's notice. Simply put, you have to know when to stay the course and when to cut and run. Also, like a good soldier, there will be times when your training and discipline will be tested. In these cases, how you react to adverse situations and how much you capitalize on favorable situations will ultimately determine your success or failure.

How Much Money Do You Have Available to Commit?

Before you enter into your first commodity trade, there are a number of questions to be asked and answered. The first decision that you must make prior to trading is to determine how much capital you will commit to trading. Some brokerage firms will allow you to open a commodity trading account with as little as $5,000, and some possibly with less. As we have already discussed, once your account is open, you could, if you so desired, keep only the minimum amount of margin required in your trading account. The advantage to this approach is that it allows you to invest any excess money elsewhere, thus affording you other moneymaking opportunities. The downside to this approach, however, can be fatal to many individuals' trading accounts. The primary problem is that this involves adopting the mind-set of a gambler. Picture the scenario: You open a commodity trading account with the minimum amount of money required and then draw out any excess, leaving just enough to trade. As long as you are making money, it's not a problem. But ultimately, as you experience the inevitable losing trades, you may start getting margin calls. On a regular basis you find yourself wiring money into your account in order to continue trading, then later wiring money back out as profits accumulate, only to have to wire more back in the next time a trade or two goes against you. The stress of doing this alone is something that most individuals are ill equipped to handle. Therefore, the best suggestion is to adopt the mind-set that your commodity trading account is no different from any other investment. You need to view it as an investment—not a speculative crapshoot.

Often critics will try to equate commodity trading to gambling. However, there is a critical difference between trading and gambling that negates this argument. When you make a bet in gambling, be it blackjack, craps, or pulling the lever on the slot machine, once you make your bet you must wait for the outcome before determining whether you win or lose. Likewise, there is rarely a chance to decrease your bet if the hand starts to look like a loser. Compare a gambler who bets $1,000 on a hand of poker and a trader who is willing to risk up to $1,000 on a given trade. If you are playing poker and have been dealt a bad hand, the odds are starting to work against you. Your only risk control choice is to fold and thus avoid throwing good money after bad. But in this case you still lose the $1,000.

This is not the case with commodity trading. If you enter a long trade in corn and the corn market starts to fall apart and move against you, you can sell immediately and completely avoid any additional risk. Likewise, if everything starts to unfold as you thought it would and corn starts to move higher, you can buy more corn and essentially increase your bet while the odds are in your favor. This ability to control not the action, but your exposure to the action in the middle of a hand, is something that is not available in gambling. So again, it is important to adopt an investor's mind-set and not that of a gambler.

In order to start yourself on the right road, it is suggested that you determine how much money you are going to commit to commodity trading and then open an account with that full amount. So if you decide to commit $25,000, you should open an account and fund the account with the full $25,000. With commodity accounts, you do not earn interest on the uninvested portion. However, you can purchase T-bills with the uninvested portion. You can then apply the bulk of the value of the T-bill toward your margin requirements while you earn interest on the T-bill.

Money Management as Part of Your Trading Plan

In developing a trading plan, many first-time traders spend virtually all of their time attempting to devise trading systems or methods that they hope will have a high probability of generating winning trades—which is ultimately what commodity trading is all about. The fact of the matter, however, is that there is more to the game than simply generating buy and sell signals. In the game of basketball, the goal is to score baskets. Yet if a team had a group of players who were very accurate shooters but who could not dribble, run, jump, or play defense, they would likely never win a game, let alone the championship. So it is critically important to understand that while generating winning trades is essential, there is more to the game of commodity trading than simply generating accurate buy and sell signals.

Within your trading plan, you need to lay out several critical components. One of the first questions to answer is "What type of trading do you plan to do?" The choices are many. On one end of the spectrum there are traders who day-trade, constantly moving in and out of the market, often using one-minute bar charts to determine when to buy and sell. These traders may be long a market one minute, short that market the next, and long again the minute after that. This type of trading requires a certain mentality and a personality willing to focus entirely on the market's action as it unfolds. At the other end of the spectrum there are traders who might trade only once a month, preferring to simply follow the longer-term price trends of one or more commodities. And then, of course, there is everyone else in between.

It is essential to your long-term success that your style of trading fit your personality and situation. For example, if you work full-time during the day, then your likelihood of success as a *day trader* is very low. You simply will not be able to follow the markets closely enough to react when the time is right to take advantage of opportunities and still do your job. Likewise, day traders tend to be more comfortable with a frenetic pace. They are able to quickly adapt to changing situations; successful day traders have no real problem with going long, exiting that long trade with a small

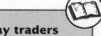

day traders
short-term speculators who buy and sell frequently throughout the trading day.

loss, and reversing to a short position all within a matter of moments. Not everyone possesses these traits. This is not necessarily a good thing or a bad thing. What is important is that you recognize your strengths and weaknesses as a trader and adapt your trading style in a way that maximizes your strengths and minimizes your weaknesses. Just because someone you talk to claims to be making a killing by "scalping beans," does not mean that you will necessarily be able to emulate that individual's supposed success.

You also need to think about how mechanical you want the trading process to be. Again, the choices run the gamut. At one end of the spectrum you can completely make it up as you go along, simply trusting your instincts to determine when to enter and exit as the markets twist and turn. This approach is fraught with peril, as there are many ways to go wrong. The markets can mess with your mind at times by doing exactly the opposite of what you think will happen. Not everyone reacts to these types of surprises in a positive manner—particularly when there is money on the line. A couple of quick, unexpected losses can leave any traders second-guessing themselves the next time around, which might cause them to miss the next big winner. That being said, there are individuals who are able to thrive using a completely discretionary style of trading.

At the other end of the spectrum, there are traders whose trading is completely automated. They develop or acquire a trading system (or systems) and simply allow the system to generate the trading signals for them. All they do is place the orders. Like everything else, this approach offers certain advantages and disadvantages. The obvious advantages are that this approach requires a lot less work and analysis once the systems are put into place. Likewise, this approach can greatly reduce the amount of mental stress that traders might feel if they were using a discretionary approach. Instead of internalizing a losing trade and saying, "That loss was my fault"—a fact that might cause you to question your own judgment on some subsequent trade—you can say, "That loss was the system's fault." And the system will continue to work exactly the same way in the future as it did in the past, completely unencumbered by any emotional baggage acquired as a residual effect from a particularly bad trade or series of trades.

The downside to this approach, however, is that your profit potential is limited to whatever the system itself can produce. If you take yourself completely out of the equation, you eliminate the risk of gumming up the works by yourself; however, you also limit your ability to use your own acquired knowledge and experience to enhance your returns. Like everything else, you need to consider carefully where you wish to be along this trading method spectrum.

There are two other questions that need to be asked and answered regarding your trading method:

1. What criteria will you use to exit a trade at a loss?
2. What criteria will you use to exit a trade with a profit?

The one thing you must recognize about trading commodities is that there will be losing trades. The trick is to keep those losses manageable. Although it may seem counterintuitive at first, in a way a losing trade can be viewed in a positive light. If you get on the wrong side of a market and exit the trade quickly with only a small loss, you may save yourself from suffering a larger loss that might have seriously affected your trading account adversely.

One thing that separates a winning trader from a losing trader is the ability to know when to exit a trade—whether at a profit or at a loss. We will have further discussions on exiting a trade at a loss in a bit; however, suffice it to say that one of the things to remember is that your willingness and ability to cut your losses short will have a profound effect on your long-term success or failure as a commodity trader. While the need to exit losing trades is fairly obvious, the question of when to exit a winning trade is a more complex issue than many traders realize at first. In large part, the answer to the question of when to exit with a profit depends on the type of trading that you are doing.

If you are scalping a market using a one-minute bar chart, chances are that you will be taking small profits and (hopefully) small losses, with the expectation that you will have many more winning trades than losing trades. However, if you are trading using a long-term trend-following approach, then it will likely be imperative that you capture an occasional large profit in order to offset the small losses that will occur along the way. This means that you will need to let your profits run, which can also be interpreted to mean that you must do nothing, even though you are dying to take a profit and put that money in the bank.

In a nutshell, holding onto a winning trade can at times be a very difficult thing to do. If you have just had a series of small losses and suddenly find yourself with a winning trade, the temptation can be great to take your profit early. Unfortunately, if your trading plan involves the need to let your profits run in order generate an occasional big winner, then you must fight the urge to cash out too soon. Do not underestimate how difficult this may be at times.

Beyond simply deciding what criteria you will use to buy and sell various commodities, there are a number of important money management decisions that need to be a part of your comprehensive trading plan. As you will see, these questions have nothing to do with the actual generation of buy or sell signals. Yet when taken together, they can ultimately have more effect on your long-term profitability than the actual method you use to generate your trading signals. For example, consider these important questions:

- What markets do you plan to trade?
- How many positions will you hold at one time?
- How much will you risk per trade?
- How much risk are you willing to assume at one time for all positions combined?

Smart Trader Tip

Put all of your money management criteria into writing as part of your overall trading plan. This will force you to follow your predesigned plans more closely. Plan your trade and trade your plan!

Let's consider these questions one at a time. Deciding which markets you are going to trade is an important question to answer and in some ways will depend on your experience level, the amount of trading capital that you have to commit, and the method that you are going to use to trade. As with most things in trading, there is an entire spectrum of possible choices. At one end of this spectrum are traders who specialize in trading just one market. For example, someone might decide to strictly trade stock index futures or Treasury bonds or soybeans or some other market. Typically, traders will do this if they feel that they have an edge or some level of expertise in that particular market. The advantage is that you can focus all of your attention on that one market. The disadvantage is that you have no diversification that might allow you to offset losses in that one market with profits generated by trading other markets.

At the other end of the spectrum, there are large traders that might trade a wide variety of markets worldwide. For example, there are commodity funds that trade 80 or more markets across a variety of worldwide exchanges. The advantage to this approach is that you can achieve maximum diversification and you also have the opportunity to profit wherever markets are moving. The disadvantage is that the time and capital required to utilize this approach are typically out of the reach of the average individual trader.

Another important consideration is determining the trading method or methods that you are going to use. If you have a systematic approach that can be run across a variety of markets, you can basically scan each market, determining where the action is at any given point in time, and direct your trading capital to those markets. In this scenario, you are essentially letting your system or method decide which markets you are going to trade and when. This leads directly to the next question you need to answer: How many positions will you hold at one time?

If you are going to focus on only one market, then it's pretty simple; at any given point in time, you will hold either a long position, a short position, or no position at all in that market. However, if you are going to trade a variety of markets, then you need to decide how many you can realistically trade at one time. There are two primary factors involved in this decision: time and money. The more markets you wish to trade, the more time you will need to devote to managing your open positions, open trading orders, and new trading possibilities for each market. Likewise, each position you hold adds to the amount of risk you are exposed to. Therefore, the more positions you plan to hold at one time, the more trading capital you will need to have in your trading account in order to avoid exposing yourself to the risk of an unacceptable loss.

Keep in mind that utilizing a mechanical trading approach that enables you to backtest can be extremely useful. Backtesting allows you to develop some idea of the profits and losses you are likely to face along the way and can help you determine more accurately just how many positions you can hold at any one point in time.

Another issue to decide is how much of your trading capital you are willing to risk on any single trade. The most common and typically most effective rule of thumb is to risk some percentage of your trading capital on each trade. What that percentage should be depends on the type of trading that you are going to do and the size of your trading account. For example, say you feel comfortable risking 2 percent of your trading capital on any given trade. If you have a $100,000 trading account, this allows you to risk up to $2,000 on each trade. However, if you have only a $10,000 account, then you can risk only $200, which in almost all cases will require you to trade using extremely tight stops and will likely result in your getting stopped out much more frequently than if you were able to use a wider stop. On the flip side, if you decide to risk 10 percent of your trading capital on each trade, then a string of four consecutive losses could leave you with a loss of 40 percent of your trading capital. This type of drawdown can prove psychologically devastating and can severely impair a trader's ability to continue trading, both financially and psychologically. Utilizing a mechanical trading approach—which allows you to backtest and develop some idea of the profits and losses you are likely to face along the way—can be extremely useful in helping you to answer these important questions. For example, if your backtesting tells you that the average losing trade using your approach is $600, then it is fairly simple to determine that risking only $200 per trade is simply not going to work in the long run. You will continually be getting stopped out of trades that might ultimately prove to be winners in order to adhere to your $200-per-trade risk constraint. Because of the potential benefits, let's take a closer look at how the use of a mechanical approach to trading can be helpful.

The Role of a Mechanical System

Determining money management guidelines and rules is much easier to do if you have some idea of what you can realistically expect from your trading method. There are several measurements that can be very useful on a single market basis. These include:

- Expected percentage of winning trades.
- Expected percentage of losing trades.
- Average profit of winning trades.
- Average profit of losing trades.

One of the most basic measurements that a trader can make regarding profit and loss involves the following calculation: (% winning trades ÷ % losing trades) × (average $ profit ÷ average $ loss). This formula generates what is known as the *profit factor*. In order to simply break even, the profit factor must not be less than 1.00. Anything above 1.00 suggests that the method has a positive expectation for profit. Anything less than 1.00 suggests that the approach is a long-term loser. Let's look at a couple of examples.

- *System A* generates 80 percent winning trades and 20 percent losing trades, and makes $250 on the average winning trade and loses $250 on the average losing trade. If we plug these values into the earlier formula, we get a profit factor of 4.0, as follows: (80 ÷ 20) × (250 ÷ 250) = 4 × 1 = 4.0.

- *System B* generates only 40 percent winning trades and 60 percent losing trades. However, it earns a profit of $1,200 on the average winning trade and loses $200 on the average losing trade. If we plug these values into our formula, we get a profit factor of 4.0, as follows: (40 ÷ 60) × (1,200 ÷ 200) = 0.67 × 6 = 4.0.

As you can see, System A and System B are quiet different in the way they go about generating returns, yet they have the same profit factor. System A generates a lot of small losses and a lot of small profits, but the profits outnumber the losses by a factor of 4 to 1. As a result, it has a positive expectation as indicated by a profit factor value above 1.0. System B generates only 40 percent winning trades. However, the average winning trade is six times greater than the average losing trade. As a result, this method has the same profit factor as System A.

System A is probably a short-term method that gets in and out quickly, taking a lot of small profits along the way. System B is probably a trend-following method that experiences more losing trades than winning trades but compensates for that by making a lot of money on the winning trades. There is no way to say which system is best for any given trader. Each trader needs to decide which type of approach fits his or her own trading style. The real point of this discussion is simply to point out the usefulness of being able to generate this type of profit and loss data in order to get a handle on what to expect from a given trading approach.

Other data that might be generated by a *mechanical trading system* that can be extremely useful in setting expectations are monthly returns data and maximum drawdown values. By looking at monthly returns over a period of time, it is possible to quantitatively estimate how much capital traders should have in order to utilize a particular trading approach, without exposing themselves to too much risk. A *drawdown* is any loss of equity that occurs between any two peaks in equity growth. For example, if Trader A makes $10,000, then loses $5,000, then makes another $10,000, she will have a net profit of $15,000 and a maximum drawdown of $5,000. Had Trader A started trading at exactly the worst time, she would have first suffered a loss of $5,000, before her trading approach began generating new profits. Therefore,

> **mechanical trading system**
> a set of specific rules that govern buy and sell decisions with the intention of removing emotion from the decision-making process.

had Trader A started trading at exactly the wrong time and with only $5,000 in her trading account, she would have run out of trading capital before her trading approach began generating new profits. Thus, she now knows that a $5,000 trading account is too small for what she is planning to trade.

Having a realistic idea about your expected maximum drawdown is critically important to understanding what to expect from your trading approach. This value basically gives you an idea of what your worst-case scenario might look like. Setting realistic expectations and being prepared to deal with the adverse things that can happen along the way are other factors that separate the winners from the losers in the commodity trading game.

Consider what might happen if a trader did no analysis of what the expectations were for his trading approach in advance of starting to trade. The trader just assumed that things would work out in the long run. Let's further assume that the trader opened a trading account with $10,000 and only watched while the system he decided to use made $10,000 in paper profits. At that point, he is thinking, "Wow, my trading approach just generated 100 percent return on what I have in my account." Brimming with confidence, the trader then decides to take the plunge and start trading and immediately suffers a drawdown of $5,000. He would then be sitting there saying, "Holy cow, I'm 50 percent in the hole!" Whether or not he would continue to trade, and thus make the next $10,000 profit generated by his trading method, is hard to say. Many traders who see their risk expectations exceeded develop that "deer in the headlights" syndrome and find it difficult or impossible to continue trading. This is a danger that always applies to all traders. And it is for this reason that generating some idea of reasonable expectations is critically important to your long-term success.

> ### Smart Trader Tip
>
> A mechanical trading method removes emotion from your trading decisions and may also allow you to generate historical trading results, which can be useful in calculating proper capital requirements.

Tools for Controlling Risk and Maximizing Profits

Due to the amount of leverage involved, there are inherent risks in commodity trading. Therefore, it is imperative to achieving long-term success that a trader take all steps necessary to minimize this risk and protect against an extremely adverse event. Fortunately, there are many risk management tools available to commodity traders. By utilizing these tools in combination, traders greatly enhance their probability of success. Beyond simply minimizing their overall risk, traders can also develop a tremendous amount of confidence in their trading efforts, knowing that the downside is being managed. This peace of mind can allow traders to trade as aggressively as they are comfortable with, thus offering them the opportunity to maximize their long-term profitability. There is an old adage in commodity trading: "If you take care of the losing trades [i.e., by minimizing the number and magnitude of losing trades], the winning trades will take care of themselves." This is basically another way of saying that the most important thing you can do today is to make sure that you can still continue to trade tomorrow.

The greatest risk in commodity trading is the risk of suffering a catastrophic loss. The second greatest risk in commodity trading is suffering a loss that is big enough to cause you to stop trading just in time to miss the rebound that would have allowed you to make back all of the money that you had lost plus more. As a result, anything that can be done to reduce the magnitude of equity fluctuations reduces both of these risks and increases the odds of long-term success. It's not bad for a trader's peace of mind, either.

Risk Management Tool #1: Diversification among Markets

The first tool that a trader can use to control risk is to actively trade more than one market. As I discussed earlier, there are many traders who feel more confident simply by focusing on one particular market. And if an individual feels that he or she truly has an edge in trading this single market, then it makes sense to specialize. However, from a strict risk management point of view, there is much to be gained by *diversifying* your trading among different commodity markets. The trader who focuses on one market is basically engaging in an all-or-nothing endeavor. In other words, the trader is either making money in that one market or not. If the trader goes through a period of not making money, there are no other positions that might offset those losses.

diversification
a risk management technique that mixes a wide variety of investments within a portfolio in order to minimize the impact of any one security on the overall portfolio.

From a risk management perspective, the ultimate goal of trading a diversified portfolio is to reduce the volatility of the overall portfolio. To put it as unscientifically as possible, this idea revolves around the theory of "zigs and zags." Some markets trade similarly to others (for example, soybeans and soybean meal will typically rise and fall in tandem), while others do not. The degree to which two markets trade in a similar manner is referred to as their *correlation*. Furthermore, there is a statistical function known as the *correlation coefficient*, which measures just how closely two markets track one another in terms of their respective price fluctuations. A correlation coefficient can range from +1.00 to –1.00. A value of +1.00 indicates that two markets trade in exactly the same manner. A correlation coefficient of –1.00 indicates that two markets trade in an exactly inverse manner (i.e., each time one market rises, the other market falls by a similar magnitude). A correlation coefficient of 0 indicates that the two markets trade in a completely independent manner. A lack of correlation between markets can allow astute traders to minimize the fluctuations of the equity in their trading accounts.

As you can see in Figure 9.5, soybeans and soybean meal trade in a highly similar manner. In fact, the correlation coefficient between these two markets is 0.87, confirming the fairly obvious fact that there is a high degree of correlation between these two markets.

If traders were to trade only these two markets, the odds are great that if they are making money in one market, they are also making money in the other market. Conversely, if they are losing money in one market, they are also likely to be losing money in the other market. This can have the effect of exaggerating the swings in equity that they will experience. For example, take a look at Figure 9.6, which displays prices for lean hogs and corn.

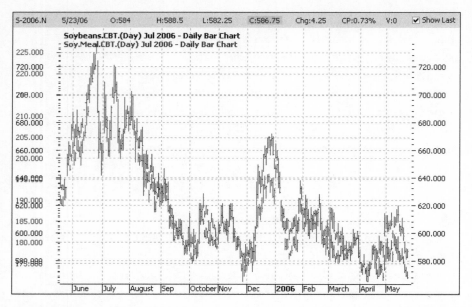

FIGURE 9.5 Soybeans and soybean meal trade in virtual lockstep.
Source: ProfitSource.

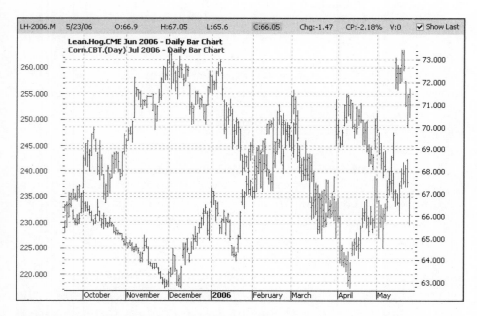

FIGURE 9.6 When lean hogs zig, corn typically zags.
Source: ProfitSource.

As you can see in Figure 9.6, lean hogs and corn tend to trade in a fairly dissimilar manner. The correlation for these two markets is –0.04. Thus, a trader who is trading hogs and is presently losing money might be making enough money in corn to completely or partially offset losses in hogs, and vice versa.

Consider a trader who is interested in reducing the overall volatility of his portfolio. Do you suppose this goal would be better achieved by trading a portfolio of soybeans, soybean meal, and soybean oil, or a portfolio of soybeans, lean hogs, and cocoa? By trading a variety of markets using a trading method that you believe will ultimately generate profits in the long run, there will be periods when some markets are making money while others are losing money. As long as the gains are exceeding the losses, the net result is a steady increase in equity.

Risk Management Tool #2: Diversification among Different Trading Methods

There are a multitude of methods that can be used to trade commodities. The possibilities are virtually limitless. One trader might rely on fundamental supply and demand data. Another might use technical analysis and use chart patterns or moving averages to find promising trades. Some might use a trend-following approach; others, a countertrend method. Still others will day-trade using overbought and oversold indicators. As I said, the possibilities are limitless.

What typically happens to traders new to commodities trading is that they test out a number of different approaches and eventually settle on the one method that they expect will generate the most profit. And, of course, it intuitively makes sense to want to focus your trading capital on the method about which you are most confident. Still, commodity trading is about money as much as it is about markets. So it is worth considering the notion that utilizing more than one approach to trading can offer some interesting and unique benefits.

Let's face it: There is more than one way to skin a cat. If you trade coffee using a long-term trend-following method and coffee embarks on a long-term trend, then you stand to make money. If you trade coffee using a short-term, countertrend method, you may end up losing money by trading against a strong trend. However, if you trade coffee using a long-term, trend-following method and coffee prices begin a choppy, trendless period of trading, chances are you will not make money as long as that choppy period persists. If you use a countertrend method to trade during this period, you may perform exceedingly well. This raises the obvious question of which approach is better: trend following or countertrend? In reality, both approaches can perform equally well over the long term. The only difference is the manner in which profits accumulate. The trend-following method may make a lot of money every once in awhile, with choppy periods in between. Conversely, the countertrend method may generate a lot of small profits along the way but only an occasional loss. These differences raise another question: Why choose between the two? In reality, it doesn't necessarily need to be an either/or proposition.

Consider the following possibility: Instead of using a trend-following approach or a countertrend approach, why not use them both simultaneously? The downside is that at times these two approaches cancel one another out and no money can be made. Still, this is not necessarily all bad, because these occasional offsets serve to lessen the volatility of the fluctuations of equity in your trading account.

Let's consider what happens if you combine two systems using very dissimilar trading methodologies. Let's further assume that either system can be long, short, or flat at any given point in time. Now let's look at the possibilities listed in Table 9.5 for the positions that may be held at any given point in time.

TABLE 9.5 Possible Positions Using Two Trading Methods

System #1	System #2	Net Position
Long	Long	Long 2
Long	Flat	Long 1
Long	Short	Flat
Flat	Long	Long 1
Flat	Flat	Flat
Flat	Short	Short 1
Short	Long	Flat
Short	Flat	Short 1
Short	Short	Short 2

As you can see in Table 9.5, if the two systems are in agreement, then the trader will be in the maximum allowable position of long two or short two. Under any other circumstance, either the trader will be trading a 1-lot long or short or the trader will be out of the market altogether. This simple two-system combination actually has a certain elegance and sophistication to it. If you think about it logically, you want to have maximum exposure only when you are most likely to make money. In this case, that would be when both of your trading methods are signaling either long or short positions. If the two methods that you have chosen to use to generate your trading signals are not in agreement, it makes a great deal of sense to trade a smaller position or to avoid that market altogether.

commodity trading advisor (CTA)
a licensed trading advisor who specializes in the trading of commodities.

You should be aware that many professional commodity traders—such as *commodity trading advisors* (CTAs) and *commodity pool operators* (CPOs)—spend a great deal of time devising trading systems with a positive expectation of generating profits in the long run as well as methods for combining multiple systems that result in the smoothest equity curve that they can achieve. Just as certain markets have a high correlation or a low correlation with other markets, the same is true of the equity curve generated by various trading methods. As a result, it is possible to greatly reduce the volatility of the changes of equity in your trading account not only by diversifying among different markets, but also by employing a variety of trading systems.

commodity pool operator (CPO)
an individual or firm that operates one or more commodity pools. A commodity pool is a trust or syndicate that trades commodity futures or option contracts.

Risk Management Tool #3: Determining Capital Requirements and Proper Account Sizing

As discussed at the outset of this chapter, determining capital requirements for trading stocks is relatively straightforward. If you want to buy $30,000 worth of a given stock, you put up $30,000 (or $15,000 in a margin account, which allows the investor to borrow up to 50 percent from his or her broker). However, buying $30,000 of a given commodity is a different proposition. Each contract has its own dollar-per-point value, its own contract size, its own price at which it is presently trading, and its own margin requirement. Typically, to enter into a commodity trade, you need to put up anywhere from 3 percent to 20 percent of the underlying contract value. Hence, it's often difficult for traders to determine whether they are overleveraged, underleveraged, or leveraged just about right. Let's look at some objective ways to get to the proper level of leverage for your account, looking at the problem from both a single market perspective and a portfolio-wide perspective.

Capital Requirements for a Single Market   When considering each particular market that you intend to trade, there is certain information that you can combine to get a handle on your realistic risk, thus your realistic need for capital. It is most helpful to have some backtested history trading this market with your chosen trading approach, even if the numbers are only hypothetical. Three numbers that you can use are:

- Current margin requirement.
- Largest overnight gap.
- *Maximum drawdown* experienced using your selected trading approach.

maximum drawdown
the greatest amount of capital loss that a trader is willing to withstand within his or her trading account.

You can get the current margin requirement for a given market from your broker. The largest overnight gap for most markets can be found in Table 9.4. The maximum drawdown figure is something you must derive on your own. If you cannot arrive at a maximum drawdown number, you can default to using margin and gap figures to arrive at a reasonable trading capital requirement figure.

A simple formula for estimating the amount of capital you should have in order to trade one contract of a given market is the following: $\{[(\text{margin requirement} \times 3) + \text{largest gap} + \text{maximum drawdown}] \div 3\}$.

Let's look at an example using soybeans and let's assume that we are using a mechanical trading system that experienced a maximum drawdown of $6,000 at one point trading a single contract of soybeans.

- Current margin requirement = $1,000 (this may change from time to time).
- Largest overnight gap = $2,412.
- Maximum drawdown = $6,000.

Plugging these values into our formula works out as follows: $\{[(1,000 \times 3) + 2,412 + 6,000] \div 3 = \$3,804\}$. So according to this formula, the minimum amount of your trading capital that you should apply to trading one contract of soybeans is $3,804. Now in reality, if you were going to trade only soybeans, you would probably have to consider using more capital because the suggested amount is less than the maximum drawdown suffered using the trading approach selected for this example. In other words, if you started trading a 1-lot of soybeans with $3,804 in your account and suffered a repeat of the maximum drawdown of $6,000, then you would need to add more money to your account in order to continue trading.

Still, the purpose of this chapter is to enlighten you about the benefits of trading a variety of markets and, if possible, to utilize a variety of trading methods as well. As a result, the simple method I have just described for determining the capital requirements for a given market using a specific approach is best used across a portfolio of markets, as we will discuss next.

Capital Requirements for a Portfolio There are two ways to estimate capital requirements for a portfolio of commodities. The first approach is to go market by market and sum up the capital requirements for each market using the method just detailed. The other approach is to look at the fluctuations in equity generated by the overall portfolio, if that data is available.

Method #1 would be accomplished by first selecting a group of markets that you plan to trade. Since we are seeking diversification, it makes sense to trade a given market or handful of markets from each of the general categories listed in Table 9.6 (to the extent that your trading capital allows). Quite obviously, a trader with a large trading account will be able to trade more markets than a trader with a smaller trading account.

TABLE 9.6   Major Commodities by Group

Group	Market
Grains	Soybeans
	Soybean meal
	Soybean oil
	Corn
	Wheat
Metals	Gold
	Silver
	Copper
	Platinum
Meats	Live cattle
	Lean hogs
Softs	Coffee
	Cocoa
	Sugar
	Cotton
	Orange juice
Energies	Crude oil
	Heating oil
	Unleaded gas
	Natural gas
Rates	T-bonds
	10-yr. T-notes
	5-yr. T-notes
Indexes	S&P 500
	Nasdaq 100
	Dow Industrials
Currencies	British pound
	Swiss franc
	Canadian dollar
	Dollar index
	Japanese yen
	EuroFX

Once the markets to be traded are selected, a trader can employ the simple calculation just described to arrive at a *suggested* capital requirement for each market by determining the margin requirement, largest gap, and maximum drawdown for each. The next step is simply to add up the capital requirements suggested for each market and arrive at a grand total.

Let's look at the example portfolio that appears in Table 9.7. Five markets—one from each of five different groups—appear in the table. For each market, a margin requirement is listed (remember, these will change from time to time), as well as the largest overnight gap for that market and the maximum drawdown experienced (using the trading method we decided to use to trade each of these markets). The dollar amount that appears for each market in the "Capital Requirement" column is arrived at by using the formula discussed earlier.

By summing up the capital requirements for each of the markets listed in Table 9.7, we arrive at a capital requirement for this portfolio of $31,062. Another way to arrive at a useful capital requirement figure for a given portfolio of commodities can be accomplished if you have monthly returns data for the overall portfolio. In order to do this, you need some type of software that can calculate this data, or previous monthly statements from actual trading. Using this data can allow you to tailor your account size to achieve a certain balance between percent profitability and percent volatility. One method for doing so works as follows:

1. Calculate the standard deviation of monthly returns in dollars for your portfolio of futures markets.

2. Multiply the standard deviation of monthly returns by 3 and divide the result by 0.1.

TABLE 9.7 Example of Capital Requirements for Trading a Hypothetical System

Market	Margin	Max. Gap	Maximum Drawdown	Capital Requirement
Soybeans	$1,000	$2,412	$6,000	$3,804
Gold	$6,250	$5,040	$7,000	$10,263
Live cattle	$945	$800	$5,000	$2,878
Sugar	$1,400	$3,898	$4,500	$4,199
Crude oil	$4,750	$7,500	$8,000	$9,917
Total				**$31,062**

one-standard-deviation move
a move in the price level of a security that is one standard deviation from the mean or average.

two-standard-deviation move
a move in the price level of a security that is two standard deviations from the mean or average.

What do we accomplish with these calculations? For a given set of data, a *one-standard-deviation move* above and below the average encompasses two-thirds of the data under consideration. A *two-standard-deviation move* encompasses 96 percent of all data, and a three-standard-deviation move above and below the average encompasses 99 percent of the data. By multiplying the standard deviation of monthly returns by 3, we arrive at a dollar figure that encompasses 99 percent of all monthly returns. By dividing this value by 0.1, we are attempting to ensure that there is a 99 percent chance that we will not experience a monthly loss in excess of 10 percent. This, of course, assumes that further results will be similar to past results. In essence, we are attempting to insulate the portfolio as a whole from experiencing a larger-than-tolerable drawdown.

Now let's assume that for the portfolio that appears in Table 9.7, the standard deviation of monthly returns has been $1,500. If we multiply this value by 3, we get $4,500. If we then divide this figure by 0.1, we get a suggested capital requirement of $45,000. This is a higher figure than the $31,062 we calculated using the "one market at a time" method. So which method is correct? The truth is that there is no right or wrong answer. Traders must decide for themselves. At this point, traders must accurately assess their own tolerance for risk.

Let's assume Trader A decides to trade the portfolio listed in Table 9.7 using $31,062 and Trader B chooses to trade the same portfolio with $45,000. Let's further assume that both Trader A and Trader B take exactly the same trades in the exact same quantities. In this case, they will both make or lose the exact same amount of money. The only difference then will be the fluctuations of the equity in their accounts as a percentage of starting equity.

For example, let's say that this portfolio first generates a profit of $12,000, then suffers a drawdown of $8,000, and finally garners another profit of $10,000. Let's look at how the traders would view the fluctuations in their respective trading accounts (see Table 9.8).

Portfolio $ +(−)	Trader A Equity	Trader A % Swing	Portfolio $ +(−)	Trader B Equity	Trader B % Swing
	$31,062			$45,000	
+$12,000	$43,062	+38.6%	+$12,000	$57,000	+26.7%
(−$8,000)	$35,062	(−18.6%)	(−$8,000)	$49,000	(−14.0%)
+$10,000	$45,062	+28.5%	+$10,000	$59,000	+20.4%
Net % Gain		**+45.1%**			**+31.1%**

TABLE 9.8 Percent Equity Swings Using Different Amounts of Trading Capital

As you can see in Table 9.8, the only difference experienced by Trader A and Trader B is that each swing in equity represented a larger percentage of gain or loss for Trader A than it did for Trader B. The trade-offs that any individual must consider in this case are as follows.

If you trade using the smaller account size:

- If you are profitable, you will make a higher-percentage rate of return.
- You will suffer larger-percentage *drawdowns* and you must be absolutely certain that the expected swings are not so large that they might cause you to stop trading altogether, thus eliminating your potential for recouping temporary losses.

drawdown
losses in a trading account.

If you trade using a larger account size:

- Your rate of return will not be as great as if you had devoted less capital to commodity trading. Likewise, the extra money that you devote to commodity trading could have been invested elsewhere, so there is potential opportunity cost.
- The inevitable drawdowns will always be a lower percentage of your equity than if you had traded using a smaller, more aggressive amount of trading capital. As a result, you may experience less of the type of anxiety that might cause you to abandon your trading approach.

Note the importance of psychological factors in trading. Although Trader A and Trader B will experience the exact same fluctuations in terms of dollars, it is the percentage of the fluctuations that would ultimately trigger a negative emotional response that could adversely affect their trading.

Smart Trader Tip

Diversifying among markets and trading systems can greatly reduce your overall risk. Calculating realistic capital requirements and properly sizing your account afford you the best chance of avoiding your maximum pain threshold.

Risk Management Tool #4: Margin-to-Equity Ratio

Determining an appropriate capital requirement in order to trade a given portfolio of commodities is a critical step that too many traders ignore. The reason that traders benefit from arriving at a reasonable account size is obvious. If your trades utilize too small an amount for your account (i.e., if you do not use enough leverage), you will not generate the rate of return that you are hoping to. Conversely, if your trade is too big for your account (i.e., you are using too much leverage), you run the risk of suffering a drawdown that is in excess of what you can handle. This can, in turn, lead you to stop trading altogether. Hence, we see the value in achieving a reasonable balance. While the methods that I have detailed previously are quite useful, for simplicity's sake there is a quick and easy way to estimate your present risk level. This measure is referred to as the *margin-to-equity ratio*. To calculate your margin-to-equity ratio, simply add up the margin requirements for all of your open positions and then divide the sum by the total value of your trading account.

margin-to-equity ratio
the amount of margin presently committed to commodity positions divided by the total amount of capital in your trading account.

The key point to remember here is that there are no magic cutoff levels regarding the margin-to-equity ratio. That being said, the most commonly quoted guideline regarding the margin-to-equity ratio is around 30 percent. In other words, anytime you find yourself trading with a margin-to-equity ratio that is greater than 30 percent, you must recognize that you are trading aggressively and that large-percentage fluctuations in your trading account are quite likely.

Another key point is to emphasize efficiency in your trading. For example, let's assume that Trader A and Trader B each have $50,000 in their respective trading accounts, that they use two entirely different methods to generate trade entry and exit signals, and that both made 50 percent in their trading accounts. The one difference is that Trader A uses an average margin-to-equity ratio of 10 percent and Trader B uses an average margin-to-equity ratio of 40 percent. Who is the more efficient trader? That would be Trader A, simply because she is committing less capital at all times than Trader B, yet is still generating the same returns. Likewise, who is more likely to experience a major drawdown or even to blow up completely? That would be Trader B simply because he is always assuming more risk than Trader A.

So again, a low margin-to-equity ratio is not necessarily good, nor is a high margin-to-equity ratio necessarily bad. However, the use of a low margin-to-equity ratio might mean that you miss profit opportunities that you could have benefited from if you'd been using a higher margin-to-equity ratio. By using a high margin-to-equity ratio, you may suffer larger drawdowns than you would by using a lower margin-to-equity ratio. The main thing that this useful ratio tells you is, essentially, how heavily you have your foot on the gas pedal. This ratio can fluctuate from time to time for an individual trader. If you feel that you have an advantage and want to attempt to maximize your profitability, it might make sense to devote more margin to a given trade. You just have to remember not to floor it.

If we go back to the five-market portfolio listed in Table 9.7, we find that the total margin requirement to trade one contract of all five markets at the same time is $14,345. So a trader who uses the market-by-market account size of $31,062 would be looking at a maximum margin-to-equity ratio of 46.2 percent. The trader who uses the portfolio-wide method using monthly returns of $45,000 would be looking at a maximum margin-to-equity ratio of 31.9 percent. One more time, let me emphasize that there is no right or wrong amount. What is critical is that you understand and appreciate the potential fluctuations that you are likely to experience and that you are willing and able to withstand the heat when things don't go as planned. The margin-to-equity ratio is just one more tool to help you assess the level of risk you are exposing yourself to at any given point in time.

Risk Management Tool #5: Stop-Loss Orders

We discussed stop-loss orders earlier, but they still need to be mentioned here in the context of risk control. In this context, a stop-loss order acts as sort of a last line of defense. There are many considerations involved regarding the use of stop-loss orders, including where to place them and whether to enter open orders or use mental stops, just to name a few.

Ideally any stop-loss order that you place will be beyond some meaningful price level that, by virtue of that price being hit, clearly indicates that you were wrong in your expectation for that market. For example, traders typically try to place stop-loss orders beyond a recent support level (if holding a long position) or resistance level (if holding a short position).

Smart Trader Tip
Cutting your losses and keeping them small is one of the keys to trading commodities successfully.

Look at the chart of wheat in Figure 9.7. Let's assume a trader is interested in buying wheat at the current price of $372.25. As you can see in the chart, there is a fairly obvious support level at $350.50. It makes intuitive sense to think that if wheat were to fall below that support level, then a bullish stance would no longer be reasonable. So a trader might logically consider placing a stop at some price below $350.50.

But there are other considerations as well. If a trader places a stop at, say, 350.25—just one tick below the support level of $350.50—chances are he will have a lot of company. In other words, it is quite likely that there will be a lot of sell stop orders bunched up just under this obvious support area. This could potentially lead to the situation of *running the stops* that I discussed earlier, whereby the price of a market moves to an area where there are many stop orders bunched together. Then, once those orders are triggered and all of the selling is out of the way, the market goes back in the other direction. One possible solution for an astute trader might be to place a stop at a price that is less likely to get hit. For example, instead of placing a sell stop order at $350.25, the trader might place a stop at $349.25, or $348.25, or $347.25. By placing this stop further away from the obvious level chosen by most traders, he is forcing the wheat market to do more than just poke through support before taking out his position. As a result, if the wheat market were to fall to, say, $349.75—thus taking out a lot of sell stop orders bunched up under the 350.50 support level—and then reverses back to the upside, the trader would still have his long position intact, rather than having to scramble to buy back in after having gotten stopped out at a lower level.

As with everything else in commodity trading, there is a trade-off. If you place your stop further away from an obvious support or resistance level, you do, in fact, reduce the likelihood of getting stopped out on a simple retest of that critical price level. The obvious trade-off, however, is that you assume more risk. If you place a sell stop in wheat at $347.25 instead of $350.25, you assume $150 more risk per contract (three points × $50 per point). So you also need to factor in how much you are willing to risk on a given trade before placing your stop. And this brings us to an important point.

All traders ideally strive to place their stop-loss orders so that they won't get hit. However, the main thing to remember is that when you boil it all down, the primary purpose of a stop-loss order is to try to keep you from suffering a loss that is larger than you can handle, whether financially or psychologically or both. So ultimately you should place your stops wherever they need to be from a risk control point of view, depending on your own circumstances. Let's illustrate this reality with an example using the wheat trade shown in Figure 9.7.

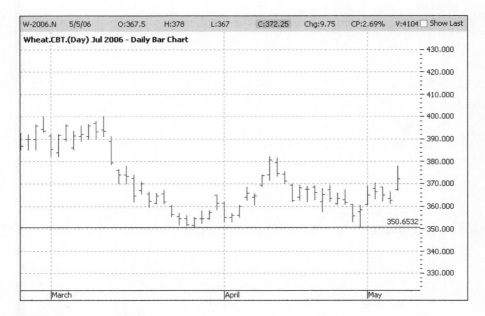

FIGURE 9.7 Wheat with support level.
Source: ProfitSource.

Trader A has $25,000 in her account and is willing to risk 5 percent of her capital on a single trade. Trader B has $10,000 and is willing to risk 10 percent of his capital on a single trade. The net effect of these account sizes and self-imposed restrictions is that Trader A can risk $1,250 per trade ($25,000 × .05) and Trader B can risk $1,000 per trade ($10,000 × .10). If Trader A bought wheat at $372.25, with $1,250 to risk, she could place her stop as far away as $347.25, or three full points below the support level of 350.25.

However, if Trader B bought wheat at $372.25 and was willing to risk only $1,000 per trade, he would need to place his stop-loss order no further away than $352.25 (20 points × $50 a point = $1,000). As a result, in order to adhere to his risk control constraints, the trader would actually have to place his stop above the recent support level. While this is not ideal, these kinds of considerations and hard choices are the reality of trading and risk control.

Again, the important thing to keep in mind is that the stop loss is designed to help mitigate losses if the assumptions underlying the trade are wrong. When the stop is hit, it can prove emotionally painful. We all hate to take losses. For that reason, it can be tempting to move the stop loss while the market is approaching that price level in order to avoid feeling the pain associated with the loss. However, this is self-defeating behavior. Avoid the temptation of moving the stop loss. If anything, get out sooner and before the stop loss is hit. Don't move the stop and hope that the market will turn around in your favor.

Smart Trader Tip

Determine what percentage of your trading capital you are willing to risk on any given trade and then stick to it, with no exceptions. It is good to get into the habit of using stop-loss orders to make sure your maximum risk threshold is not exceeded.

Determining How Many Contracts to Buy

There are no absolute rules for determining how much to risk on a single contract, nor how many contracts to buy or sell short at one time. Still, a simple example can give you an idea about the thought process that you should be going through in making these critical decisions. Let's assume that a trader has a $50,000 trading account and is willing to risk no more than 3 percent on any single trade. This means that on any single trade she is willing to risk $1,500. This also means that she could risk $1,500 on a single contract, $750 each on two contracts, $500 each on three contracts, and so on. How does a trader make this decision? There are several choices available, so let's discuss two possibilities. One is determined on a trade-by-trade basis, and the other is determined on more of a macro basis. In either case, you must first consider what percentage of your trading capital you are willing to risk, and work from there. This is accomplished using the following formula: dollars to risk per trade = (trading capital × percent of capital to risk per trade). So if a trader has a $40,000 trading account and is willing to risk 2 percent on a trade, she can then risk $800 per trade. Likewise, if she is willing to risk 5 percent on a trade, she can then risk $2,000 per trade. Once this dollar risk figure is determined, a trader can then proceed to figure out how many contracts to buy.

Method #1

For any given trade, the trader will determine the price at which she expects to enter the trade and the price at which she expects to get stopped out if the trade goes against her. The trader would then calculate the dollar value of a price movement of that magnitude. This price move in dollars would then be divided into the total amount she is willing to risk on the trade. Let's assume that a trader with a $40,000 trading account is willing to risk 5 percent of her trading capital on one trade and that she expects to buy corn at $2.53 a bushel and will place a stop-loss order at $2.40 a bushel after the trade is entered. As a result, here is what she is looking at:

- Dollars to risk per trade = $2,000 ($40,000 × .05).
- Dollars to risk per single contract = $650 [($2.53 − $2.40) × $50 per cent].
- Number of contracts to trade = 3 ($2,000 ÷ $650).

So in this example, a trader would buy three corn contracts at $2.53 a bushel and then place a stop-loss order to sell three contracts of corn at $2.40 a bushel. Hopefully, corn will advance in price and the trader will earn a profit. However, if this trade does not go as planned, and if her stop-loss price of $2.40 is hit, she will lose $1,950 on the trade ($650 loss per contract × three contracts). This is within the tolerable risk limit she had previously established.

Method #2

If you are using a systematic approach to trading that allows you to back-test previous trades, or if you have been trading a market using a given approach for some time and have established a history of wins and losses, there is another way to ensure proper risk control. We will use the same formula as earlier, but substitute the dollar value of the difference between the entry price and the anticipated stop-loss price with the dollar amount of the largest losing trade that has previously been experienced. This allows traders to build some worst-case scenario protection into their strategy of risk control. Let's assume that the trader in the previous example is using a system to trade corn that previously had experienced a worst-case loss of $900 on a single contract of corn. The formula that she will apply is as follows: (Account size × percent to risk per trade) ÷ largest losing trade.

- Dollars to risk per trade = $2,000 ($40,000 × .05).
- Dollars to risk per single contract = $900 (previous worst-case loss).
- Number of contracts to trade = 2 ($2,000 ÷ $900).

Hence, using the previous worst-case loss results in trading only two contracts instead of three (as in the previous example).

Other Considerations in Setting Stops

Regardless of which method a trader prefers, there are several other important considerations to keep in mind. First off, the determination of how much capital you will risk on a given trade is critically important. The trade-offs between being too aggressive and not aggressive enough are large. Let's illustrate this with two extreme examples.

Trader A is a gunslinger and expects to set the world on fire trading commodities. Due to the confidence in his trading approach, he decides that he will risk 30 percent of his trading capital on each trade. The trader believes so much in his market-timing ability, he intends to use tight stop-loss orders and thus chooses to set stops on a trade-by-trade basis, based on how much he actually figures to risk per trade.

Trader B has also decided to trade commodities but is extremely timid about taking risk, almost to a fault. Since her first concern is minimizing risk (as opposed to maximizing profit), she decides to risk no more than 2 percent per trade. And likewise, because she is concerned about her ability to trade through large losses, she decides to set her stops using the "largest previous loss" method.

Now let's assume that both traders have $100,000 in their accounts. Let's also use the corn trade example where corn can be bought at $2.53, and the previous worst losing trade for the methods used by Trader A and Trader B is $900 for a single contract. Trader A feels strongly that corn is about to rise, so he decides to use a tight stop of just $0.05.

Trader A

- Dollars to risk per trade = $30,000 ($100,000 × .30).
- Dollars to risk per single contract = $250 ($0.05 × $50 per cent).
- Number of contracts to trade = 120 ($30,000 ÷ $250).

Trader B

- Dollars to risk per trade = $2,000 ($100,000 × .02).
- Dollars to risk per single contract = $900 (previous worst loss).
- Number of contracts to trade = 2 ($2,000 ÷ $900).

Just in these numbers alone you can see the profound impact that risk control decisions can have, completely aside from any buy and sell signal criteria. Trader A is now long 120 corn contracts, while Trader B is long only 2 contracts. So let's look at what happens if corn is bought at $2.53 a bushel and is later sold at $2.73 a bushel.

Trader A

- Profit = [($2.73 − $2.53) × $50] × 120 contracts.
- Profit = $120,000, or 120 percent of his total account.

Trader B

- Profit = [($2.73 − $2.53) × $50] × 2 contracts.
- Profit = $2,000, or 2 percent of her total account.

As you can see, by using a most aggressive set of risk controls, Trader A earned a whopping 120 percent on his entire trading account on just this one trade. Conversely, by trading very conservatively, Trader B settled for a profit of 2 percent. So now we know the potential benefit of trading aggressively. Now let's look at what might have happened in a worst-case scenario.

The largest overnight gap for corn has been $1,500 per contract. So let's see what would happen if Trader A and Trader B had entered into their respective trades and on the following day corn had experienced a massive gap to lower ground.

Trader A

- Loss = (−$1,500) × 120 contracts.
- Loss = $180,000, or −180 percent.

Trader B

- Loss = (−$1,500) × 2 contracts.
- Loss = $3,000, or 3 percent.

This example clearly illustrates the dangers of being overly aggressive. By aggressively going for it all, Trader A put himself in a position where not only did an adverse price movement wipe out his entire trading account of $100,000, but he also now needs to pony up another $80,000 to cover his excess loss. Trader B suffered a 3 percent loss; this percentage exceeded her desired maximum loss of 2 percent per trade. Still, because she was so conservative in her application of leverage, the net result is that this loss will not affect her ability to continue trading, unlike Trader A.

So which is better: going for the gusto or playing it safe? The truth is that there is no definitive answer to this question. For most traders, the answer probably lies somewhere in between. The main point here is that you need to make thoughtful, conscious decisions regarding the amount of risk you can truly accept. If you bite off more than you can chew, you run the risk of suffering a devastating loss of capital. If you bite off less than you can chew, you run the risk of generating returns far inferior to what you might have generated with even a slightly more aggressive approach.

Summary

Novice traders tend to focus the bulk of their time attempting to fine-tune their buy and sell criteria. The thinking is that if the timing of their buy and sell signals is precise enough, profits are sure to follow. And technically this is true, to a point. However, the goal of completely eliminating losing trades is little more than a pipe dream. The reality of commodity trading is that the traders who deal most successfully with the losing trades are the ones most likely to profit in the long run. This is why when you read interviews with successful commodity traders, they often seem to spend an inordinate amount of time discussing money management rather than specific trading methods. This occurs because successful traders have learned that commodity trading is as much a game of money management and risk control as it is simply speculation.

As you have seen in the examples contained in this chapter, the way in which you allocate your capital—how many markets you trade, how many contracts you buy or sell at a time, how much margin money you risk at any one time, and so on—will have at least as much (and in most cases, more) impact on your long-term success as the method you ultimately use to time your trade entries and exits. It is tempting to focus on generating precise buy and sell signals and leave that boring money management stuff until later. It is also a fatal mistake for most traders who fall into this trap. By thinking through and integrating money management throughout your trading plan, you act to minimize your risk and greatly increase your long-term profit potential before you even enter the first trade.

Key Summary Points

1. Money management involves deploying your trading capital in a manner that minimizes as much as possible the risks that you are exposed to, while simultaneously affording you maximum profit potential.

2. Successful veteran traders recognize that proper money management is the key to long-term success.

3. Each commodity has its own contract size and dollar value per point. Be aware of how much a given market is likely to fluctuate on any given day as well as over time.

4. In assessing risk, you must look at how much a given contract typically fluctuates in terms of dollars and also consider how big an overnight gap could occur.

5. Price gaps, slippage, and fast market conditions can all work against you. Rather than hoping that you don't encounter these situations or pretending that they are not a risk, you need to plan in advance for such possibilities and build risk control measures into your trading plan.

6. How much capital you will commit to trading, how much you will risk per trade, and how many markets you will trade at any one time are all important elements of the trading plan you should develop before you start trading, and which you should adhere to once you have money on the line.

7. There are a number of methods that can be employed to minimize risk and maximize profits:

   • Diversification among markets.
   • Diversification among trading methods.
   • Proper account sizing.
   • Tracking margin-to-equity ratio.
   • Stop-loss orders.

Chapter

10

Psychology 101:
Winning the Mind Game

I s a winning trade always a good thing? On the face of it, the obvious answer is yes. Yet depending on circumstances, it is not at all uncommon for traders to view a particular trading win in a less than positive light. How can this possibly be so? Consider the following example. Suppose a trader is thinking about buying soybean futures but is nervous about taking the plunge. As the trader watches and tries to muster the courage to enter a long trade, soybeans rally from 550 to 560. As beans touch 565, the trader finally pulls the trigger and buys soybean futures at 565. Beans subsequently rally to a high of 585 before starting to back off. But in this example, the trader is hoping for more, so he holds on. A few weeks later he finally exits the trade at 570 and thus garners a profit of $250 on the trade. But is this trader happy to have made $250? Quite possibly not, for if he is like many people, he will instead be kicking himself for having waited so long to get in and so long to get out and missing out on a much bigger profit. As a result, not only does he come away with a negative thought about a profitable trade, but he also runs the risk of having this experience negatively impact his judgment in the future. The next time he is contemplating a trade, he may be too quick to enter or exit, not wanting to miss a move as he did with the soybean trade.

Is a losing trade always a bad thing? Once again, on the face of it, the obvious answer is yes. Since we trade in an effort to make money, it seems fairly logical to conclude that a losing trade is a bad thing, as it works against the trader's ultimate goal of accumulating profits. Still, consider the following situation. A trader buys gold at $510 an ounce in anticipation of an immediate move to higher prices. A few days later, gold has declined to $505 an ounce and our trader decides to cut her loss at this point, thus losing $500. The next day, gold gaps lower by $8 to $497 and continues to plunge all the way down to $490 an ounce. Had our trader not acted when she did to cut her loss, the loss would have ended up being much higher. So in this circumstance, the trader might actually feel pretty good about this particular trade. In other words, by acting when she did, she saved herself an additional loss of $1,500. So despite the fact that the trade ended in a loss, the trader could in her mind view it as a good loss.

So now we've seen an example of a trader who made money on a trade and felt negative about it and another trader who lost money on a trade and came away feeling positive about it. Ultimately, it comes down to your perspective—how you think about things makes all the difference in the world.

In a sense, trading is a microcosm of life itself. In life, good things and bad things happen along the way. Ultimately, it is how you prepare for, interpret, and react to these events that determines the quality of your life. If you are unprepared for or react in an overly negative way to the inevitable bumps along the way, you are destined to live a less full life than a person who makes a few contingency plans in advance, then reacts appropriately. Likewise, if you take time to savor the good things that come along and enjoy the pleasurable moments, again, you are far more likely to be a happy person than someone who is always looking at things in a negative way. All of these things can be applied to your trading approach.

crowd psychology

a large group of people behaving in a similar manner or sharing the same (occasionally misguided) notion.

The financial markets are ultimately a barometer of *crowd psychology*. This holds true for the stock market, the bond market, and also for the commodities markets. The crowd goes from feeling bearish about a given market as it declines in price and then bottoms out to being bullish about that same market as it advances in price and then tops out. The pendulum just keeps swinging back and forth. And from this perpetual swing of investor emotions—from bullish to bearish and back again—springs both opportunity and danger.

Traders who recognize and embrace this ebb and flow of crowd psychology and who do not let their emotions get the best of them stand to profit handsomely by continually adjusting their stance as needed. However, traders who do let their emotions dominate their trading ultimately sail in very dangerous waters. They are far more likely to drift with the tide and be surprised by every twist and turn in the market. Being willing to part company with the crowd—even when it is uncomfortable to do so—and to think for yourself will go a long way toward determining your ultimate success as a trader.

Smart Trader Tip

Crowd psychology is typically right during the middle of trends but wrong at the tops and bottoms. Pay close attention to crowd psychology that leans too far bullish or bearish. This can be a sign of an impending reversal.

The First Step toward Trading Success: Setting Realistic Expectations

It is virtually impossible to pick up a financial publication or watch a financial program without viewing some overhyped advertisement for the next brilliant idea certain to allow you to get rich quick. Here's the problem. Deep down, most of us would welcome the opportunity to make a great deal of money in a short period of time. As a result, advertisers—whose job it is to generate sales—recognize that anything that can press investors' hot buttons is quite likely to generate a response. This explains the tendency for investment advertisements to be overhyped. In turn, the more investors read overhyped ads and the longer this goes on, the more they begin to believe—even if only subconsciously—that it's possible to get rich quick. After all, people are out there doing it all the time. Therein lies the irony. In fact, it is possible to make a lot of money quickly in the commodities markets, and in addition, yes, there is always someone making a killing in the markets. The catch is that a person making a sudden fortune trading commodities is the exception rather than the rule. Most people who accumulate great wealth trading commodities do so over time and are not the beneficiaries of some lucky windfall profit. Likewise, most of these people did not get into commodities with the expectation of getting rich quick (rich, yes, but not necessarily quickly). These people became wealthy because they had a solid plan and they executed that plan successfully. So, the first key to trading success is to set realistic expectations.

Due to the leverage involved, commodity trading offers traders the potential for great profit, as well as great risk—more so than many other investment vehicles such as stocks and bonds. As a result, it can be easy for budding commodity traders who believe that their trading methods will be successful to develop overly optimistic expectations. The fact is that these overly optimistic expectations can ultimately be the traders' undoing. We can all remember situations in life where we went in with exceedingly high expectations—whether on a date, a new job, or a sporting event—and things did not go as well as we had hoped. That's bad enough, but because our expectations were so high we had the added letdown that accompanies deflated expectations. This can leave us even more demoralized than we might have been if we had entered that situation with more realistic, less optimistic expectations. This can definitely be a problem for the first-time commodity trader, both on a trade-by-trade basis as well as on a cumulative basis.

Smart Trader Tip

If you set overly optimistic expectations for your trading results, you run the risk of being disappointed and making unwarranted changes to your trading approach, even though you are actually doing well.

In commodities trading, there are quite simply many ways to go wrong from a psychological standpoint. Remember, it is possible to come away from a winning trade thinking negative thoughts like "I should have made more money" and come away from a losing trade thinking positive thoughts such as "I was smart to get out when I did." Likewise, there is a great danger to entering into any investment or trading program with high expectations. Ironically, it is typically a much better approach to expect bad things to happen. This forces you to prepare for a variety of contingencies. If you go into any endeavor with overly inflated expectations, you run the risk of being that much more disappointed if and when things don't go as well as you had hoped. When there is money on the line—especially *your* money—this can be problematic.

Many people open commodity trading accounts in the anticipation that they are going to make a lot of money. This is only natural. No one would open a commodity trading account if they didn't hope they were going to make a lot of money. Still, problems arise when traders do not spend enough time assessing possibilities and making contingency plans designed to deal with those occasions when they are not making (or losing) a lot of money. Traders who fall into this category ultimately experience the following cycle:

1. *Overly optimistic expectations.* Traders focus most of their attention on how much money they are going to make while ignoring the realities of trading and the possibility of losses. This is usually due to a lack of planning and is based on hope.

2. *Disappointing results.* For virtually all traders, a losing period is a natural part of trading, is to be expected, and must be dealt with, both financially and emotionally. Unfortunately, traders who are focused only on profitability and not on risk control stand to feel much more disappointment than other traders who adequately prepared themselves psychologically to deal with these events in advance.

3. *Immediate aftermath.* Unprepared traders are far more likely to take losing trades personally and suffer more psychological angst than traders who took all the proper steps and implemented risk controls prior to starting to trade. Common effects are anger, frustration, uncertainty, and a tremendous feeling of disappointment. All of these effects are obviously things that people would prefer to avoid feeling if they could help it. In addition, not only are these unpleasant things to deal with in the here and now, they can also have negative effects on your trading performance in the long run.

4. *Longer-term residual effects.* Traders who have unrealistic expectations can become very disenchanted when their expectations are not met. They may begin to second-guess everything they are doing and can end up carrying around a great deal of excess psychological baggage. For example, they may find themselves focusing on any or all of the following negative thoughts:

   - I should have bought sooner.
   - I should have sold sooner.
   - I should have held on longer.

- I should have traded more contracts.
- I should have cut my loss sooner.
- I should have traded fewer contracts.
- I should have skipped that trade altogether.

If they let their emotions get the best of them, this can have a domino effect as time goes by. These traders will be far more likely to make mistakes based solely on emotional responses to previous negative experiences. They may be far more likely to exit a trade too soon or skip what turns out to be a winning trade simply because they second-guess their own trading methods. Clearly, this type of emotionally driven random behavior is unlikely to produce winning results in the long run.

So if you expect to get rich quick trading commodities, beware. There is work to be done. One essential tool for all commodity traders is to create a concrete plan for what they will do if a trade starts to move the wrong way. To avoid an emotional response to a negative event, you must be prepared ahead of time for an adverse outcome. In fact, I take this to an extreme. When I get into a trade, I simply assume that it will be a loser, and as a result I am forced to determine what my worst-case scenario is right then and there. Also, by doing this I am prepared mentally to handle a losing trade and I ensure that I will not exceed my maximum pain threshold. The bottom line is that underinflated expectations work best in commodity trading.

Smart Trader Tip

Often traders who set overly optimistic expectations end up trying to double up or take on too much risk in order to break even if their initial results are unfavorable. This can lead to even larger losses, which is why realistic expectations are essential.

How the Commodity Markets Can Fool You

Like any investment vehicle, the commodities markets try to fool you at times. For a while, a market will be screaming higher, and all indications will point to a continuation of that trend. The headlines will scream out that higher prices are imminent and the pundits will trot out myriad justifications for why such-and-such a commodity may soon be reaching new highs. At such a time, traders who have missed the boat stand on the sidelines and comfort themselves with the notion that it's too late or that they will catch the next big trade. Eventually, however, the desire to jump in and participate becomes overwhelming. Unfortunately, once a trend is completed—especially an unusually strong trend—the reversal can be surprisingly swift and severe.

Consider the movements in the price of silver that appear in Figure 10.1. After bottoming at a price just below 7,000 at the end of August, silver then doubled in price over the next seven and a half months. But note how the advance seemed to be "two steps forward, one step back" in nature, until about early March. Between the August low and March of the following year, silver advanced almost 50 percent in price. Still, it is not difficult to envision a lot of wary traders sitting on the sidelines trying to decide whether the advance was for real. Now consider what happened next. After steadily climbing 50 percent higher over six-plus months, silver exploded higher in March and April, advancing another 50 percent in price in just over a month.

This parabolic advance is the type that:

- Allows some traders to make a great deal of money.
- Drives some traders crazy as they sit and watch the market soar, and bemoan all the money they did not make by getting on board.
- Causes some traders to jump in too late because they just can no longer bear to watch the market move higher without them.

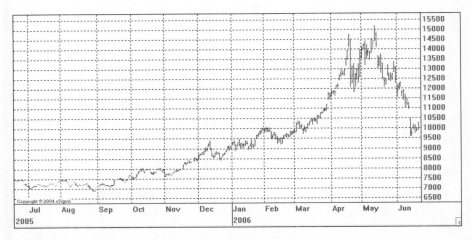

FIGURE 10.1 Silver with long rally and fast decline.

Source: eSignal.

Now consider the slightly longer-term effects for traders in each group. Traders in Group A have the chance to garner huge profits if they happen to sell at the right time. First, of course, they needed the foresight or good fortune to be in the market as the advance unfolded. Traders in Group B are left muttering "woulda, shoulda, coulda" for a long time and are susceptible to beating themselves up psychologically over the money they feel they should have made but did not. Finally, traders in Group C run the risk of losing a great deal of money. As markets move higher in a virtual straight line—sometimes referred to as a *parabolic* advance—they typically are setting the stage for an imminent decline of equally sharp proportions. And very often this decline occurs in much less time than it took for the original up move to play out.

Let's look again at the silver market (see Figure 10.1). Between August and the following May, silver prices rose from 687 to 1,520—a total of 833 points. However, note the decline that followed the May high. In just 22 trading days, silver gave back two-thirds of the advance that had previously taken eight and a half months to unfold. The markets giveth and the markets taketh away. Unfortunately when the markets take away, they often do so in a much quicker and unrelenting fashion.

In this example, the aforementioned problem of inflated expectations rears its ugly head. As silver creeps higher and higher over a period of months and as more and more explanations and justifications for this rise appear in the financial press, traders adjust their mind-set from bearish or neutral to bullish. And when silver explodes to sharply higher prices, the consensus swings almost completely to the bullish side. Traders read stories about the silver spike of 1980 and wonder, "Could it be happening again"?

Finally, with their eyes fixed firmly on the stars, a number of traders plunge into silver with the expectation that they are about to participate in a historic rally—right before the bottom drops out, and silver plummets 37 percent in just over a month. This pattern repeats itself over and over in the commodities markets. Bearishness gives way to bullishness, them rampant bullishness, then the market in question tops out and many late-blooming bulls get their heads handed to them. As the decline continues, bullishness gives way to bearishness, then rampant bearishness, then downright fear—and then that market bottoms out. And all of those who sold or sold short in a panic are left to scramble as the market rallies, leaving them in the dust. And so it goes.

Smart Trader Tip

Be aware that the markets will try to fool you at times by giving you the impression that it is easy to make money in them. Typically, once a large number of traders come to believe that all they need to do is pile on to the latest trend for a given market, that particular market tends to reverse sharply.

Cut Your Losses

One of the things that can make trading success so difficult to achieve is the fact that much of what needs to be done runs counter to *human nature* and in opposition to many customs that most of us have had ingrained in us from a very young age. In most endeavors in life, we are told that if we just persevere, things will work out in the end. In the big picture, that tenet does in fact apply to commodity trading, but it does not necessarily apply on a trade-by-trade basis. For example, let's assume that you have done a great deal of analysis—whether technical, fundamental, or some combination thereof—on the coffee market and have determined that a major price advance is in the offing. Based on this thorough analysis and with great confidence, you enter a long position in coffee in anticipation of a big winning trade. But for whatever reason, coffee refuses to cooperate. Little by little at first, coffee prices start to tick lower. Then suddenly the price begins to break more sharply. So what should you do? Your upbringing and professional experience in other fields have taught you to have confidence in your beliefs and to hang in there when the going gets tough. Is this good advice? Therein lies the paradox. In most situations in life, perhaps this is good advice. In the case of trading commodity futures—no way! In the face of a clearly adverse price movement, the number one, two, and three priorities are simply:

human nature traits that are innate to most human beings. Most important, in trading the markets, these traits can work against you.

1. Cut your loss.
2. Cut your loss.
3. Cut your loss.

In a sense, trading can be viewed as being at war. The goal of war is to control ground and to endlessly advance in order to control more ground. In trading, your goal is to make money, then hold onto that money and move forward and make more money. However, in any war it is unrealistic to expect to win every battle. Obviously, you have to win more than your enemy and you certainly need some big victories along the way in order to defeat your opponent. However, from time to time the ebb and flow of events might favor the enemy. In those situations, it is not only necessary but prudent to simply retreat, regroup, and prepare for the next battle. This is an apt analogy for trading. While you need to have your share of winning trades, and you also need some big winners along the way, there are times when things simply will not go as you had hoped. In those cases, the only prudent thing to do is to retreat—that is, cut your loss.

Smart Trader Tip

If you focus the bulk of your efforts on minimizing risk and controlling losses, the winners will take care of themselves. Your primary responsibility to yourself as a trader is to make sure that you can continue trading tomorrow.

Risk Management

As I mentioned earlier, managing your expectations is one of the keys to your long-term success as a commodity trader. There was a broker who, upon opening a new account, would offer the new client his guarantee: "I guarantee you that if you trade commodities, there will be losing trades." Chances are that not many traders were thrilled to hear that little piece of information. But in the end, this broker did his customers a great service by properly setting their expectations. Let's face it, the only reason anyone opens a commodity trading account is because they expect, or at least hope, to make money. So being told that the only thing you can know for sure is that from time to time you will lose money can be a bitter pill for many people to swallow. But the truth is that they are better served by knowing what they can realistically expect.

In Jack Schwager's book *Market Wizards* (HarperCollins, 1993), the author interviews a number of world-class traders about their experiences and successes. It is most interesting to note how much time these traders—traders who collectively have generated billions of dollars of trading profits—devote to managing risk and how much emphasis they place on the importance of cutting losses. Somewhere along the way, these ultra-successful individuals recognized that trading—particularly commodity trading with its increased leverage—involves risk and that the active management of their exposure to risk was what would ultimately determine their success or failure. They also realized that trading success is more about money management—in other words, making a lot when you win and limiting your losses to a tolerable amount when you lose—and less about specific entry and exit criteria designed to achieve uncanny accuracy. If risk control—and an understanding that losing trades are a part of the price you pay along the way to trading success—is the primary consideration for the world's greatest traders, it should go without saying that it needs to be your primary concern as well.

Smart Trader Tip
The more you envision and prepare yourself to deal with the adverse events that will inevitably come up, the greater the likelihood that you will deal successfully with these events.

Winning and Losing Streaks

Consider an automated trading system that historically generates 60 percent winning trades. Generally speaking, 60 percent winning trades is pretty good for an automated commodity trading system. However, it is essential that traders realize that this is not the same as saying that for every 10 trades they make, 6 will be winners. Automated trading systems are often known to experience *streaks*—an extended series of either winning or losing trades. Noted market analyst John Bollinger, the creator of Bollinger bands, recently discussed the fact that an automated trading system that generated 60 percent winning trades—in other words, 6 out of every 10 trades would show a profit—could still be

streak
a run of consecutive winning or losing trades. Traders must be prepared mentally to trade through losing streaks and must not become overconfident during a long winning streak.

expected to experience up to 11 consecutive losing trades at some point in time. Stop and ponder that for one moment.

There you are, trading a system with 60 percent accuracy, accumulating profits, everything operating just as you would expect. And then, out of the blue, you suffer three consecutive losing trades. "Well, these things happen," you tell yourself, and muddle on. Then losing trades 4, 5, and 6 follow. At this point, most traders have one of two reactions. Either they stop trading altogether, figuring the system is broken, or they double up on their positions, figuring that a big winner just has to be around the corner. In reality, either of these reactions is a mistake because both involve ditching a well-thought-out plan and acting solely on the basis of an emotional response to an adverse event. But let's say a courageous trader musters the will to keep trading as is. Then the losing trades—7, 8, and 9—pile on. How many brave souls could carry on at this point? And even if they did, what about when losing trades numbers 10 and 11 unfold? In reality, this would be the very best time to start taking trades. But once an individual has been knocked around from pillar to post and beaten down by losing trade after losing trade, his or her thoughts are focused on making the pain stop, rather than on an objective analysis of the big picture.

So let's think about this rationally. Traders who understand the realities of trading and recognize the possibility of extended winning and losing streaks should never fall prey to a string of losing trades. In reality, they should take these possibilities into account as they develop their trading plans and likewise should size their accounts and diversify their portfolios so as to be able to withstand what is sometimes referred to as a *two-sigma* event (i.e., a situation that does not occur very often but most assuredly can occur from time to time). Once these contingency plans are in place, an extended string of losing trades should be viewed as dispassionately as possible. Unfortunately, this type of nonemotional trading is difficult to achieve. In fact, it is almost impossible to achieve if you are not actively making an effort to try to achieve it. What this means is simply that too many traders try to make it up as they go along and end up reacting to current events rather than following a well-thought-out, predetermined plan. This phenomenon is due to the fact that we are all mere mortals and as such are subject to the laws of human nature. There are several obstacles that are notably applicable to commodity trading.

The Three Great Obstacles to Trading Success

There are three great psychological obstacles to trading success: fear, greed, and ego. Virtually every individual who has ever traded anything has at one time or another been stymied by one or more of these obstacles. All traders must continually fight to overcome these obstacles.

Since human nature is what it is, the truth is that these three obstacles are essentially unavoidable. That is not to say that you have no choice but to fall victim to them. What it means is that you cannot help but encounter them because they are simply a part of human nature. The key is to train yourself to work around these obstacles rather than succumbing to them. But make no mistake: These three foes will weigh on you regardless of the trading method you choose to utilize and no matter how long you have been trading. While experience can teach you the importance of avoiding these pitfalls, you nevertheless always remain susceptible to their influence. These three emotional obstacles are typically intertwined; however, they can be addressed one at a time. So let's look at some example situations and see how a trader might work around these problems.

Fear

For most traders, *fear* typically manifests in one of two ways. The first way is the fear of losing money (or more accurately, the fear of losing more money than you've already lost) and the fear of missing out on a moneymaking opportunity. If you look at historical bar charts for any market, you will find times when that market created a "V" bottom. A "V" bottom is formed by a sharp sell-off followed by an immediate rally. This type of bottom is typically caused by fear. As a market starts to break, more traders become fearful. As that decline accelerates, still more traders who are holding long positions decide to throw in the towel and sell. This selling often causes the decline to accelerate even more, thus triggering yet more fear and more selling. Eventually the panic selling runs out of steam and

> **fear**
> in the markets, fear is manifested as a fear of losing money and/or as a fear of missing out on making money.

there is nobody left to sell, so the market reverses quickly to the upside. Those who sold near the bottom must now decide if they want to pile back into the long side at higher prices.

The other type of fear is the type that I described in Figure 10.1—the fear of missing out. When a market movement begins to accelerate, the desire to participate seems to grow exponentially. The more convinced traders become that a given movement is likely to continue in the long run, the more willing they can become to chase a current run. As we saw in Figure 10.1, the stronger the initial move, very often the more swift and violent the eventual retracement. This can cause the late plungers not only to lose a great deal of money, but to do so very quickly.

These experiences can have a devastating long-term effect on any individual. Most people work hard for their money, so losing any portion of it can be difficult. However, losing a lot of it in a very short period of time is like a punch to the head that leaves people wondering what the heck just happened and how in the world they did not see it coming. In addition, the real problem is that this can cause them to be too slow (or too quick) to pull the trigger in the future in either entering or exiting a trade, for fear of experiencing that pain again. And this invariably results in less profit being generated than they might have had they not been influenced by this one adverse event. This feeling of falling behind can ultimately lead to the next main obstacle: greed.

Greed

For most traders, *greed* manifests itself in a desire to continue to try to milk more profit out of an opportunity that has already run its course or

greed
in the markets, greed manifests as a desire to make more money than is reasonably possible, given a trader's particular approach to trading.

to try to make up for an adverse event as quickly as possible. In a rational moment, virtually any individual would agree that these are bad ideas, which are almost certainly prone to blow up in a trader's face. And that is, in fact, the case. Nevertheless, it is not really the rational moments that we need to worry about. After a particularly painful loss, most traders who are going to react badly do so in one of two ways. Some simply pull back or withdraw from trading for a while and try to regain their emotional equilibrium. Others decide to try to make back their losses in a hurry. They might start trading more actively, trading more contracts, trying to take profits more (or less) quickly, or cutting losses more (or less) quickly, all in an effort to quickly recoup a big loss. Unfortunately, assuming you have a trading plan, you cannot cause your plan to make money more quickly without altering the reward-to-risk profile. In other words, what these traders typically do is throw their trading plan or system out the window and take on more risk. Of course, as you might guess, this is no way to generate long-term successes. In fact, taking on more risk and flying by the seat of your pants is the quickest way to become an ex-trader.

The other typical manifestation of greed occurs when traders pile into a certain position with the expectation that they are going to make a killing. If you knew for certain that you were going to be correct about the future price movement for a given commodity, it would make sense to take on as large a position as possible in order to maximize your profitability. Unfortunately, it is impossible to ever be certain about a future price movement. As a result, loading up on a given position almost invariably increases your risk beyond your maximum pain threshold. Once you exceed your maximum pain threshold, you run the risk of falling victim to fear, and the cycle repeats itself.

Ego

Fear and greed are the two elements of human nature that get talked about the most when people discuss which human frailties most often cause traders to fail. But there is one other trait of human nature that can create problems for traders: *ego*. Too often, traders make not only a financial investment but also an emotional investment in every trade. They hope to make money, but they also want to be vindicated and have it be recognized (even if only in their own minds) that they were right. Let's face it, everybody likes to appear smart, which is why traders most like to tell stories about their greatest successes. And just as much, traders don't really like to talk about their failures.

ego
in the market, ego is typically manifested as a desire to be right, even if the markets and your own trading approach suggest you are wrong.

Actually, this is true in any endeavor. The problem here is that when the ego gets in the way of trading, the result can be a great loss of money. It's one thing to be wrong about something; we've all been there countless times. But it is a whole other matter to not only be wrong but also lose a great deal of money as a result. That combination can make you feel foolish. Likewise, since most traders crave making as much money as possible, there is a natural tendency at times to want to hang on to winning trades as long as possible. This desire to ride the big winner is what often causes traders to hold on to a winning trade long after the top (or bottom) has occurred, and to ultimately give back much of their profit.

Refusing to cut a loss and allowing it to mushroom into something that can inversely impact your ability to trade in the future—whether because you are sure you are right (and thus that the market itself is wrong) or because you just can't stomach taking a big loss—is the deadliest sin among commodity traders. You need to develop a plan to make sure that this situation—as well as many other potentially adverse situations—never arises.

The Importance of Having a Trading Plan

To succeed in any endeavor in the long run, you must have confidence. In trading, especially, this confidence cannot simply be bravado or false confidence. The only kind of confidence that will work in the trading arena is the kind you get from being mentally prepared. And this confidence is not something innate, by which I mean that no one is simply born with the ability to successfully trade commodity futures. The confidence you need to have in order to successfully trade commodity futures can come only through relentless preparation. In other words, the more prepared you are for as many of the twists and turns as you will undoubtedly experience during the course of trading, the greater your likelihood of long-term success. So how does one go about preparing relentlessly to succeed as a commodity trader? The key is to develop a *trading plan* and let it serve as your road map.

trading plan
a preset group of rules or guidelines (preferably put into writing) that serve as a road map to help you in making all trading-related decisions.

If you want to get somewhere but you're not quite sure how, what do you do? Well, if you are driving somewhere, you look at a map. If you were planning to start a new business, it is quite likely that prior to starting up you would develop a very detailed business plan. In fact, it is highly unlikely that you could succeed without carefully planning out the steps you intend to take in order to achieve that success. In business, your business plan serves as your road map. The purpose of a road map is twofold. The main goal is to help you get to where you want to go. The other equally important purpose is to keep you from getting lost on the way to getting where you want to go.

We are all familiar with the joke about how men, when they're driving, never want to stop and ask for directions. Most of us have encountered someone who got lost driving somewhere because he refused to consult a map before leaving and was unwilling to ask for directions along the way. This analogy is particularly applicable to commodity trading. The sad fact is that too many individuals start trading commodities without adequately preparing themselves. Likewise, too many traders rely on their gut feelings to make trading decisions, rather than executing a well-thought-out plan. Since the majority of new commodity traders have previously traded stocks or mutual funds, they simply assume that "trading is trading" and figure that if they had success trading other vehicles, they will certainly have success trading commodities. On the flip side, if they'd had a little success in other investments, they might decide to try something else. Does this sound like a recipe for success? Not by a long shot. Now imagine a person who decides to start a business without making any serious plans ahead of time. What is the likelihood of this person's long-term success? Obviously, it is quite low. This is true in business, and it is also true in trading commodities. If you want to succeed in trading, you need to treat it as you would any other business that you might start: Proceed slowly and methodically, with a comprehensive business plan in hand.

The only way to avoid many of the potential pitfalls in trading is to plan ahead to deal with them before they arise or, preferably, avoid them completely. Thus, the first step toward trading success is to develop a trading plan. By having a well-thought-out trading plan, traders can:

- Develop a great deal of confidence in their ability to succeed in the long term.
- Avoid many of the psychological pitfalls that afflict too many traders and cause them to fail.

> **Smart Trader Tip**
>
> Fear, greed, and ego are the enemies of all traders—from the most successful on down. Regardless of experience level and previous success, all traders run the risk of falling victim to these three pillars of human nature. This is why following a well-thought-out trading plan is vital to your success.

The Key Elements of the Trading Plan

As in any business endeavor, there are many key considerations to take into account and many critical questions that need to be asked and answered both prior to starting and along the way as conditions change. The discussion that follows is not intended to be in depth. The primary goal is to make you aware of some of the critical decisions that must be made, how these decisions will affect your trading, and how a trading plan can give you confidence by serving as your foundation for all that follows.

> **Smart Trader Tip**
>
> The more well-thought-out, detailed, and realistic your trading plan is, the greater your likelihood of long-term success.

Important Questions That Need Answers

Here are five important questions that you should answer when formulating your trading plan.

1. *How much do I have to invest?* Bottom line, the more capital you have to commit to trading, the greater your likelihood of long-term success. This is true simply because more capital affords you more flexibility, and in the world of commodities, that means a lot. More capital allows you to trade more markets at one time. It also affords you the opportunity to employ more than one trading method and also to trade a larger size, thus increasing both

your level of diversification and your profit potential. The more flexibility you have, the more opportunities you can take advantage of. Likewise, being in a position to risk $2,000 on any given trade offers you a much greater likelihood of success than being able to risk only $500 per trade (because you will be getting stopped out less often).

2. *How much will I risk per trade?* This is a critical decision and must be decided individually. Traders who are risk averse might risk as little as 1 percent of their trading capital per trade. Very aggressive traders might choose to risk 10 percent or more per trade. As with all things, there are trade-offs. Traders who risk 10 percent per trade clearly have a greater profit potential since they can trade more contracts per trade. However, they are also far more likely to suffer a major hit. If they were to have five consecutive losing trades, they would lose 50 percent of their trading capital. So the key is to be as close to what works for you as possible. For novice traders who are not used to large equity swings, a risk of 2 percent to 5 percent per trade is the most common and most manageable range.

3. *What criteria will you use to enter a new long or short position?* There are as many potential answers to this question as there are traders. Some traders are comfortable scalping the markets, moving in and out very quickly. At the other end of the spectrum, many traders prefer to utilize long-term trend-following methods that reverse positions only occasionally. And then there is every strategy in between. Clearly the trading strategy spectrum is wide. With such a wide range of possibilities to choose from, there are two key thoughts to keep in mind here.

   The first is that whatever method you choose to use in generating new trades, it has to fit your personality and your lifestyle. If you try to trade more actively or less actively than you are comfortable with, you will ultimately fail, simply because you are not playing to strengths of your own personality. The other possibility to consider is that of utilizing more than one trading approach. As I discussed in Chapter 9, on money management, the idea of combining multiple trading methods can serve not only to enhance your returns but, just as important, to reduce the overall volatility of your returns.

The only way to develop realistic expectations about a particular trading method is to see how it trades. Whatever method or methods you ultimately decide to use, it is important to be able to do some sort of testing on that method's performance results. This may involve backtesting the method using previous data or tracking it on paper in real time in order to determine the expected nature of the ebb and flow of the equity in your account. There are two conflicting problems here. On the one hand, if you've built enough rules into a system, you could theoretically fit the past price data to perfection. This is known as *curve-fitting*; typically, a method that is overfit will not perform as well in real-time trading. Still, some degree of curve-fitting is necessary in order to generate any useful performance data. It is not difficult to see that the "I've got this really neat idea and I'm going to test it in real-time trading with my own hard-earned money to see if it actually works" method is fraught with peril.

So the bottom line here is that you need to take however much time is needed to develop a trading approach that you are comfortable with and in which you have a high degree of confidence. Anything less is simply not going to work in the long run.

4. *What criteria will you use to exit at a profit?* The decision regarding when to exit a trade with a profit can have a profound impact on your long-term success for both financial and emotional reasons. Clearly, if you develop a method for taking profits at opportune times (times that maximize your profitability), you will benefit by making more money on your trading account. That is the obvious financial consideration. The other consideration, however, is the long-term psychological impact. Here is why this is a consideration: No one always sells at the top or buys at the bottom. This means that in many of your commodity trades, you will exit too soon. In other words, you will be holding a winning position, your trading plan criteria will tell you to exit the trade, you will exit the trade, and the market in question will keep right on going. If you are like most people, you will start adding up all the money that you didn't make because you sold too soon in your head. This can cause you to start second-guessing your methods down the road. Eventually, you may start holding onto positions too long.

The key is to develop the best set of profit-taking criteria you can and stick with it trade after trade after trade. Second-guessing will only cause problems in the long run. The basic choices are to take profits while the market is moving in your favor, to use a *trailing stop* in order to follow a trend as long as it continues, or some combination thereof. The idea of taking a profit on part of your position (once an acceptable profit is established) and then using a trailing stop to protect the remaining position (while still allowing yourself to profit more if the trend continues) is definitely worth exploring. This approach allows you to put money in the bank while still allowing profits to run on a portion of your position.

trailing stop
a stop-loss order that moves along with the price of the commodity price. For example, a sell trailing stop order can be placed below the price of long position.

5. *What criteria will you use to exit at a loss?* Interviews with dozens of the world's best commodity traders almost all ultimately come down to a discussion of risk management. Sizing an account properly so as not to assume too much risk is critical. Good entries and exits are important, and skillful profit taking can greatly enhance your profitability. But the answer to this single question may be simpler: the long-term success or failure of a commodity trader. It's vital to keep each loss to a manageable amount. You have to make sure the market won't clobber you with that one big hit that sets you back not only financially, but also emotionally. This kind of risk management is at the very heart of commodity trading success.

Most top commodity traders risk a particular percentage of their capital per trade. Whether it's 1 percent or 15 percent, when they enter into a trade, if the market goes against them far enough to trigger a loss of that magnitude, there is no debate, no second-guessing, no holding out just a little longer because they are sure the market is about to turn back in their favor. They simply cut their loss and move on to the next trade. If you truly wish to be successful, you need to train yourself to do the same.

Smart Trader Tip

Traders who exceed their maximum tolerance for risk are the most likely to fail in the long run. We all want to make as much money as possible. Remember, if you run with your eyes on the stars, you are much more likely to stumble and fall.

The Primary Tenets of a Trading Method

When you sit down to determine the actual method or methods that you are going to use to enter and exit trades, it can be helpful to keep in mind the basic tenets that have been consistently used by highly successful commodity traders:

- Go with the trend.
- Cut your losses.
- Let your profits run.
- Don't let big winners get away.
- Maintain trading discipline (i.e., follow your trading plan).

There are two basic reasons to consider basing your trading around these ideas. The first one is that many successful traders have followed these principles and made a great deal of money in the process. The other reason is that when times get rough, you will always be able to retain your confidence in your core trading principles. When the going gets tough, it is much easier to stick to your trading plan when you know that the foundation is solid.

Periodic Checkups

Now here is something of a paradox. Once you establish your trading plan, you have to stick with it through thick and thin, right? Well, the answer here is "yes, but." The trap that most traders who ultimately fail fall into is that they simply don't adhere to their trading plan. The second most common trap, however, is tinkering too often with their trading plan. The third most common trap is never tinkering with their existing trading plan.

The dangers of the first trap are fairly obvious and have been discussed elsewhere. Suffice it to say, if you develop a plan for anything and then don't follow your plan, you can't be surprised if you ultimately fail to achieve your objective. As for the second trap, it is easy to see how this can happen. Every time a trader experiences a losing trade or gets in too late or out too early, or whatever, there is a natural tendency to want to make a change to try to make things better. The change or changes may be small and at times may actually prove useful in the long run. The problem here is that if you are always tinkering with your trading plan, then you will never feel confident in it. You will always feel like something else needs to be changed.

The problem presented by the third trap—that of never revisiting your trading plan—is that if you are an astute trader, you will learn things along the way. I keep a log of every trade that I ever take, noting why I entered the trade, what my plan was for getting out, how the trade turned out, and my thoughts on why the trade did or did not work out. By carefully analyzing and reviewing your trades, you will find ideas that can improve the performance of your trading approach. Thus, if you never revisit your trading plan, you are never able to apply that newfound knowledge. So what to do? The best advice is to review your trading plan on a scheduled basis, whether it is yearly, quarterly, or monthly. At that time you can review each element of the plan and assess whether there might be useful changes that could be made to improve long-term results. What is equally important, however, is that this review not be done in the heat of battle, while you are presently feeling emotional about your trading results. A completely unemotional quarterly review can allow you to fine-tune your methods without constantly tinkering and also allows you to avoid the danger of simply reacting to the latest losing trade.

How to Handle the Daily Fluctuations of the Commodity Markets

If you are like most successful commodity traders, the bulk of your trading days will tend to eventually melt into one another. That is, each day is essentially in and of itself a nonevent. Some days you make some money; other days you lose some money. On occasion, however, you will experience days that are completely exhilarating, as you make more money than you can believe. And then there are those days that contain little but sheer terror. The keys to dealing with this pattern are:

- To develop the patience to deal with the majority of quiet days.
- To develop the discipline to not increase your expectations during the great days.
- To prepare ahead of time to deal with the bad days.

The Quiet Days

As I mentioned at the outset, setting realistic expectations is absolutely essential to success as a commodity trader. While commodity trading has a reputation as being a volatile, wild, and crazy ride, the truth is that most traders experience a lot of trading days during which their account equity fluctuates within a pretty normal and unexciting range. This is especially true for traders who use some sort of automated trading system, because few people will employ an automated trading system that causes their account equity to fluctuate wildly from one day to the next. Most people use trading systems to try to achieve just the opposite effect. So it is important to prepare yourself for the possibility that there may be little net change in your trading account for extended periods of time. Actually, plenty of things will happen during this time. Markets will rise, markets will fall, the headlines will suggest continuations and/or reversals, and so on. The markets will continue to fluctuate from day to day just as they always do. You will see opportunities pass by without making any money on them. During these times, frustration can rise to a particularly high level and the urge to do something different will be great. This is the exact time when you must remember to adhere to your trading plan and not abandon it simply because you haven't made a new equity high in a while. Patience and confidence go hand in hand at this point. If you have confidence in your trading plan, then you must exhibit the patience required to let it work.

The Great Days

There is nothing quite like the rush that a trader feels on those days when everything seems to be going right. When you are used to earning money the old-fashioned way—working hard day in and day out to get it—the experience of a huge windfall in the commodity markets can almost be a shock to the system. You may find yourself saying, "Wait a minute, this can't be happening." It's easy to get seduced by that feeling of making easy money. You may find yourself extrapolating today's profit into the future. "Let's see, if I make money at this rate for an entire year, I will make roughly three billion percent!"

While it's only natural to want to enjoy those days when everything falls into place, there is also a greater danger involved. Great days—let me define that a bit more as days when you make far more money than you normally do—can easily lead to inflated expectations. Like a mountain climber who has been to the summit and can't wait to get back, or the surfer forever in search of that perfect wave, it is easy to get addicted to the rush of making fast money. The danger is that you may ignore your trading plan in an effort to recapture that feeling. In most cases, this involves assuming more risk than you normally would. This is a mistake and can set you up for a bigger than expected, or even potentially catastrophic, loss.

In theory, you should never allow emotion to influence your trading. Likewise, in theory, you should not be excited about making money nor should you be demoralized about losing money. You should simply take each day as it comes. However, since we are all captives of the forces of human nature, this is virtually impossible. Once again, the antidote is preparation and discipline.

Within your trading plan, you should have some rules or guidelines for handling windfall profits. Whether it involves selling part of your position or utilizing a trailing stop or some other technique, it is important to make sure that you don't let the big winners just vanish. Experiencing the joy of holding a big winning trade and then watching that profit vanish is just another in a long list of things that might happen to a trader that can have devastating long-term effects. In terms of discipline, it's okay to feel elated over a favorable development, but it is essential that you don't let your emotions get the best of you and cause you—whether because of greed or ego—to allow a good trading day to affect your judgment moving forward.

The Bad Days

Bad days are an inevitable part of commodity trading. They may involve steady showers or something more severe, but just like rain and wind, they are essentially unavoidable. Once you acknowledge that you will experience bad days now and then, the trick is to take steps in advance to ensure that your bad days are not also devastatingly bad days. This may seem like an exercise in semantics, but there is a key difference between a bad day and a devastatingly bad day. A bad day leaves you wondering why you ever started trading in the first place. A devastatingly bad day leaves you wondering when you will be able to trade again (whether emotionally, financially, or both).

The trick to successfully dealing with the bad days is to plan for them in advance. This is often easier said than done. Traders who jump into commodity trading with high expectations have a tendency to downplay the likelihood, magnitude, and residual effect of any bad days. This typically leaves them unprepared financially and emotionally to deal with the aftermath of a bad day. As I said, in order to be effective, preparations must be made in advance. There are two key elements to consider in this preparation: proper money management and setting realistic expectations.

Start Small

As strange as it may sound, one of the best things that any trader can do is to fear the markets. I don't mean to fear them in a terrifying, paralyzing way, but, rather, that you make sure that you have a reverence and a healthy level of respect for how quickly the markets can take away your hard-earned money from you if you don't take proper care. Think of a prizefighter who is preparing to fight a challenging opponent for the first time. This fighter can either develop a complete disdain for the danger that his opponent presents or acknowledge the other fighter's strengths and prepare physically and mentally to overcome those obstacles. Which approach do you believe is the better course? It is exactly that way in commodity trading as well. You can tell yourself that you are going to beat the market, but if you are not prepared to withstand what the market can hit you with from time to time, you run the risk of getting flattened.

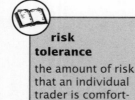

risk tolerance
the amount of risk that an individual trader is comfortable assuming.

The better approach is to carefully consider all of the things that your opponent might hit you with and then make plans in advance to deal with potential problems. The place to start for most traders is to carefully assess their own *risk tolerance*. Due to the leverage involved in commodities trading, extremely risk-averse individuals should probably think twice before even getting involved. For anyone else, the first few questions are simply these:

- How much do I have to invest?
- How much am I willing to risk before I stop trading?
- What percentage of drawdown would likely cause me to stop trading?

I cannot emphasize enough how foolhardy it is to start trading without first providing yourself with firm answers to all of these important questions. Likewise, you need to answer these questions as honestly as possible. For example, if you tell yourself that you can keep trading through a 25 percent drawdown but then later lose your nerve and stop trading after a 15 percent drawdown, you have done yourself a great (and costly) disservice. If you have never traded commodities before, the very best thing you can do for yourself when starting out is to trade small. In other words, don't go into this endeavor expecting to make huge money from day one. Like anything else, it will take a while to get used to the ebb and flow of the markets and the ebb and flow of the equity in your account. If you are going to learn any lessons, it is best to learn them when you are not risking huge amounts of money.

Adopting an overly optimistic assessment of your own ability to tolerate risk is one of the biggest mistakes you can possibly make as a commodity trader. Be humble, respect the markets, and don't overestimate your ability to tolerate pain.

Applying Proper Account Sizing

While *account sizing* is a more technical topic and is discussed in more detail in Chapter 9, it is worthy of a mention here. Amateur commodity traders spend the bulk of their time attempting to perfect their trading methodology in an effort to generate more accurate buy and sell signals. And while good entries and exits are important, this approach essentially amounts to looking at the trees and not the forest. On the other end of the spectrum, professional commodity traders understand that the techniques used for entering and exiting trades are just one piece of the puzzle. In fact, these traders

> **account sizing**
> determining the appropriate amount of trading capital needed to trade a given group of markets using a given trading approach, without exceeding one's own risk tolerance level

spend the bulk of their time analyzing the expected fluctuations of the equity in their accounts and devising ways to minimize the downward fluctuations that will occur along the way. These traders understand that commodity trading is simply about making money and not about proving to everyone how prescient they are in pinpointing tops and bottoms. This type of analysis is done in an effort to make sure that they never face a worst-case scenario. In commodity trading, knowing how much margin you need to put up in order to enter and/or maintain a particular position is not the same thing as knowing how much you are actually risking. Any data that you can generate to better assess or estimate the type of equity fluctuations that you can expect in your account can prove extremely valuable.

For example, if you determine that the maximum drawdown you could withstand and still continue to trade is 20 percent, it is absolutely imperative that you take steps to ensure that this does not happen. If you likewise determine that the method you are planning to use is likely to generate a 25 percent drawdown at some point, then you need to either (1) allocate more capital or (2) alter your trading plan in some way to trade smaller. By properly allocating your capital, you start managing risk even before you enter your first trade.

Trader's Enemy #1: A Lack of Discipline

Theoretically, when you trade commodities, you should feel no emotion—no highs, no lows—just each trade executed one after the other in an objective, nonemotional manner. And then, of course, there is the real world. In the real world, there is an endless stream of information that tugs at your emotions day in and day out. First, information on the markets can be found from any number of sources. Some say a particular commodity is due to rise; others say that a decline in price is imminent. This crosscurrent of information can cause doubt and angst even among the most steely-eyed traders.

Then there is your own analysis. You might have spent countless hours devising your trading methods, but what if you have just experienced three losing trades in a row? Now the potential for doubt and second-guessing begins to creep in. Is my system falling apart? Should I skip the next trade and see if things pick up? Should I double up and quickly try to make back my losses plus more?

Then there are the markets themselves. They fluctuate from day to day, sometimes in patterns that you seem to read like the back of your hand. At other times the markets drift aimlessly or worse, whipsawing back and forth in a violent fashion, almost daring you to try to outsmart them. At times the markets will try to fool you and when that happens, again doubt and second-guessing can be the by-product.

Finally, there are fluctuations of the equity in your trading account. By simple fact of human nature, you feel good when you are making money—especially when you are making it fast and easy. Conversely, when you are losing money, nothing in the world seems quite right. You just can't figure out how you could be so wrong or how your hard-earned money could disappear so quickly. And you always wonder when the drawdown will finally end. The longer the drawdown lasts and the deeper into the red it goes, the greater the risk that fear might take over and cause you to significantly alter your trading approach or just stop trading altogether.

All of these factors can conspire against you as you trade. Any of these factors can cause you to act in violation of your well-thought-out trading plan. All of these factors can cause a lack of discipline. And it is always easy to justify a lack of discipline. "I have to do something" is the common refrain. Whether it is something to maximize profitability or something to stop the flow of red ink, the easiest thing to do in all of trading is to second-guess a trading signal. Unfortunately, it is also one of the biggest mistakes. Once you abandon your trading plan and start flying by the seat of your pants, you set yourself up for failure.

The Trader's Paradox

Assuming you have risk controls in place designed to eliminate your risk of ruin, then in the long run it is better to follow your trading plan and experience a losing trade than to violate your plan and experience a winning trade. As contradictory as it may sound, the reason this is a mistake is that although you come out ahead in the short run (a winning trade rather than a losing trade), you have now opened a Pandora's box that allows you to second-guess your trading plan at any time, because "what the heck, I was right that one time." A lack of discipline in your trading can put you on the road to failure.

Summary

It is commonly estimated that far fewer individuals trade commodities than, say, stocks or mutual funds. Likewise, it is commonly estimated that the majority of individuals who trade commodities ultimately lose money. This is sort of a sad (but instructive) comment on the impact of human nature in the world of speculation. Yet the real question remains: Why is life like this? Why is it that commodity trading often seems to be relegated to second-level status in the financial world? Why do fewer people succeed in this realm than in other investment vehicles?

The fact of the matter is that many people are just not suited emotionally and/or psychologically to deal with the rigors of commodity trading. The variety of markets that can be traded at any point in time, the lack of a long-term upward bias—as is evident in the stock market—and the all too often unanticipated effects of leverage can be overwhelming for many novice traders to conquer. Let's consider each of these key differences between stock trading and commodity trading.

While there are far more stocks available to trade than there are commodities, the fact remains that stocks, by and large, ultimately trade based on earnings (or at the very least, the investment public's perception of earnings). To paint an even broader picture, we can state that in the long run an individual stock fluctuates based on the answer to the question "How's business?" If a company is successful at selling its products and generates profits over time, we can reasonably expect that the price of its stock will ultimately rise. In contrast, a commodity will fluctuate based on the present outlook for future supply and demand for that commodity. If a company develops a new product that is likely to be a big seller for years to come, analysts will adjust their sales and earnings forecast for that stock for the next five years. And while five-year forecasts for individual stocks are admittedly prone to error, still it is possible for each of us to make our own commonsense assessment of a given company's prospects simply by thoroughly analyzing the products or services the company sells.

This type of analysis is possible, yet highly questionable in something like soybeans, for which the supply picture can change dramatically from year to year based on something as random as surprise changes in weather patterns. While there are analysts who generate long-term supply and demand forecasts for various commodities, it is easy to be skeptical of such forecasts. Heck, meteorologists typically can't predict the weather correctly for the next week—how are we supposed to believe their forecast for the next five years? The net effect is that the stock of an individual company can experience a long-term advance based essentially on one event (i.e., the release of a new product that swells sales and earnings for years to come). This is typically not the case with most commodities, for which supply and demand factors often change from year to year. As a result, over the past 150 years we have witnessed an upward bias in the stock market as companies continue to develop new and innovative ways to improve their businesses and as the methods for quickly and profitably delivering goods and services improve. Overall, commodity prices also tend to rise over time. However, this is primarily due to inflation and the occasional swing between paper assets (stocks and bonds) and hard assets (commodities). Still, the trend is less predictable when you start looking at each individual commodity.

Many individuals buy and hold stocks or stock mutual funds for the long term and watch their assets grow over time (or at the very least, they perceive that they can). A much smaller percentage of individuals would consider buying and holding a variety of commodity markets for the long term. The net effect of all of this is that the stock market is typically viewed as an investment and the commodities markets are viewed as speculation. Right or wrong, this perception definitely colors people's thinking.

The other primary difference between commodities and other investment vehicles is the amount of leverage involved. There are too many individuals who start trading commodities without fully understanding how leverage works in the commodities markets. There is almost no chance that these people will generate profits in the long run. So now we have identified two of the biggest problems for commodities traders: the lack of a reliable long-term uptrend to count upon (as in the stock market) and the double-edged sword of leverage.

So how do the winners overcome these problems and separate themselves from the rest of the field? They recognize these two problems and adapt their trading to minimize the potential negative effects while maximizing the positive effects. For example, most stock traders never sell short a stock; they focus solely on the long side of the market. Given the long-term upward bias of the stock market, this approach is understandable. Still, one of the benefits of trading commodities is that it is just as easy to sell short a contract as it is to go long. As a result, a successful commodities trader may have many more moneymaking opportunities than a stock trader. In the face of a major bear market decline in the stock market, the average trader will either go to cash or simply hold on and hope for a bounce. If a particular commodity goes into a bear market, traders can profit just as easily as they might from a bullish move simply by selling short a commodities contract. So what most traders find unnatural (i.e., selling short) is a primary source of opportunity for successful commodity traders.

Successful commodity traders also learn how to harness the power of leverage without pushing the pedal all the way to the floor. They realize that by using the leverage associated with commodities trading they can increase the bang for their buck, and thus greatly increase their profitability. Equally important, however, they recognize the dangers associated with using more leverage than is prudent and take steps to make sure that their risk exposure never exceeds their predetermined maximum at any given point in time. This critical form of risk control is at the foundation of what allows them to follow their trading plan day in and day out—through the quiet days, the great days, and the bad days.

So what are the key things that winners do to separate themselves from the crowd? First, they establish a trading plan to develop a clear idea of how they are going to achieve success before they start trading. They determine how much capital they have to devote to commodity trading and how much they are willing to risk at one time, on a single trade and on a portfolio-wide basis. They also develop objective criteria for determining when to exit with a profit and when to exit with a loss.

Then they follow their trading plan. Through thin and through thick, they follow the rules and guidelines that they established for themselves. They don't second-guess things every step of the way. Likewise, they don't spend all of their time tinkering with their trading plan. On occasion, they will sit down and dispassionately examine their trading results to see if they might have learned something along the way that would lead to greater profitability in the future. If they identify a useful change, they will adjust their trading plan accordingly and then go back to working the plan. All along the way, they remain aware of the reality that unexpected things will happen to set them back. The commodity markets are too unpredictable to think otherwise. The key is not to hope that difficult times will not arise, but, rather, to make plans—both financially and emotionally—to deal with those situations as they arise.

Successful commodity traders set realistic expectations, and then make concrete plans to achieve these expectations. If they can do it, so can you.

Smart Trader Tip

A lack of discipline—as in a failure to follow your trading plan—is always a mistake, as each breach of discipline makes it easier to ignore your trading plan the next time. Very few people who make it up as they go along in trading succeed in the long run. Don't expect to be the exception to this rule.

Key Summary Points

1. The first step toward trading success is setting realistic expectations.

2. The markets have a way of preying on human nature. Long, steady price advances can be followed by quick and very sharp downside reversals, which often catches investors unaware.

3. Adverse events can have negative psychological ramifications that can last a long time. Thus, preparing for such eventualities and learning that sometimes the markets will go against you is critical to your long-term success.

4. Losing trades are simply a part of commodity trading. The key is to cut your losses and keep them small.

5. The three great obstacles to trading success are fear, greed, and ego. Each is affected differently in varying situations, but each must be held in check.

6. In order to succeed in trading, you must develop and follow a well-thought-out trading plan that addresses each of the following key elements:

   • How much do I have to invest?
   • How much will I risk per trade?
   • What criteria do I use to enter a new position?
   • When do I take a profit?
   • When do I cut a loss?

7. Without answers to these key questions, the markets will inevitably cause you to make a costly mistake, via fear, greed, or ego.

Chapter 11

Trading Commodity-Related Growth Stocks

Trading an existing *secular* trend in a commodity-related stock can be very profitable. *Growth stocks*, however, often have even stronger technical moves than stocks that are just riding the trending cycle for no other reason than they are directly involved with the underlying commodity. This chapter focuses on how traders can successfully trade this special breed of stock. Initially, I'll define some of the key components of growth—both fundamental and technical—and then explore the idea of growth outside of the traditional commodity-based sectors. The chapter concludes with an exploration of a few real-world case studies.

Defining Growth

In the most basic sense, a growth stock is a company that is experiencing above average increase of its earnings per share in comparison with companies in its sector or the broader market at large.

secular
a market that trends for several years or more and goes beyond the length associated with normal cyclical markets.

growth stock
shares of companies that are expected to show above-average increases in revenues and earnings in the future. In order to continue growing and expanding, these companies will retain most of their earnings in order to reinvest in operations.

Typical growth stocks that relate to commodities include such companies as Alcoa, U.S. Steel, Exxon Mobil, Southern Peru Copper, and Newmont Mining. In all of these companies, the constraints of supply versus demand are key; expectations that this relationship will continue to tighten invariably lead to higher prices in the underlying product. That's fantastic news, of course, for trend traders looking to profit, as this type of development can translate into extraordinary gains. In fact, many large and well-respected companies that are responsible for bringing commodities to market (like the ones just cited) have seen their stock prices soar over the past couple of years. It seems that many highly cyclical businesses have pushed into the realm of a secular bull run.

In recent times, many companies owe their success to the price surges experienced in the underlying commodities. Of those, a few smaller companies are in a position to profit as the result of an innovative product or perhaps an unfulfilled or underappreciated niche. Early prospectors of these stocks stand to realize stronger gains than might be realized in those *larger-capitalization* stocks. Don't get me wrong, traditional investing or trading of steel, oil, aluminum, gold, or other commodity stocks can be very worthwhile. However, for those traders who go the extra mile by identifying growth stocks within a secular trend, the potential for even larger gains is possible.

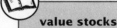

large capitalization
publicly traded companies whose market values are in excess of $10 billion.

Growth Factors

value stocks
stocks that appear to be bargains because they are priced lower than their calculated worth.

When looking to trade growth, finding a promising candidate depends on a myriad of factors. To prevent you from becoming a growth trader trapped in a *value stock* portfolio, we're going to emphasize factors that are known to be of importance to other traders, which include innovative or untapped products, as well as fundamental and technical criteria.

On more than one occasion, I've heard some words of wisdom that emphasize the idea that as traders we trade other people, not stocks. This seems to make particular sense as it relates to growth stocks. The message I hear is that you have to know what drives other traders to make a decision that ultimately benefits your own foresight into a particular opportunity. While it's great to spot a growth stock on paper, if other investors aren't appreciative of that same analysis, there's a good chance that your selection will be more defined by a potential value trap. To be successful, it's vital to see the very real effects of momentum-based growth—the equivalent of striking gold when it comes to trading. So let's get down to some of those factors that should help us in our selection process and possibly find the next gem before it's unearthed.

Smart Trader Tip
When looking to trade growth stocks, make sure there have already been signs of interest on the charts through increased and sustained volume and prior moves in the stock that point to the ability to trend strongly.

Earnings Growth

What makes a stock a growth candidate worthy of that designation and possibly worthy of trading? Heading up my list of what's important is *earnings growth*, a measurement of how well a company is adding to its bottom line. Popular methods of looking at this figure include looking at how earnings are growing from one quarter to the next (sequentially) as well as the year-over-year (YOY) basis. These quarterly and yearly comparisons better reflect any seasonal/cyclical factors that might make certain reporting periods weaker or stronger on average.

earnings growth
the rate of sequential profit improvement for a company or business.

While growth traders typically expect to see a year-over-year minimum increase of 15 percent for the current quarter's results, a 25 percent increase or more is preferred. Furthermore, it's important to look for companies that have been meeting this earnings growth benchmark for at least three quarters. This type of screening will help determine that a trend is being established, rather than perhaps a one-time earnings aberration. Typically, growth traders will look at the prior five years' performance and want a benchmark of 15 percent earnings-per-share (EPS) growth. However, for commodity-based growth, if the trend has been in place for a shorter amount of time—such as our current situation in early 2006— then this percentage doesn't really figure into our analysis. Bottom line, Wall Street will pay up for consistent growth stories in commodity-related businesses, as early developing trends suggest earnings momentum. As institutional money is rotated into those names, multiple expansions (price/earnings = multiple) and soaring stock prices in the form of technical momentum or *relative strength* (RS) are the net effect as traders anticipate further strong results going forward into the cycle.

relative strength

a technical tool used to calculate the price difference between two securities over a certain period in an effort to determine weakness or inherent strength.

postearnings drift

the fact that a positive earnings surprise can lead to an upward price tendency in the stock until the next report.

When screening for growth standouts, it's important to make comparisons to the stock's peers as well as noting whether the company has beaten expectations or surprised Wall Street in recent quarters. In fact, upside earnings surprises can be a very important characteristic of trading growth stocks. According to Richard W. Miller (www.triplescreen method.com), a well-known statistician of this group's characteristics, a positive earnings surprise typically develops into an upward bias for the stock until the next report. This observable fact is called *postearnings drift*. This phenomenon is further validated by a recent Merrill Lynch survey of institutional money managers. Of the nearly 200 participants surveyed, 26 elected an earnings surprise as their top priority when looking to build positions. However, an earnings surprise isn't the proverbial green light to go long a stock. The process can be bumpy when a stock is in this exciting stage of growth. Some of this price volatility is due to institutional buying and large investors trying to participate in a positive fundamental story but at price levels determined to be of value or below the new growth standard set by the latest report. In addition, since most of these stocks have small capitalizations and quite often lighter volume, traders should be prepared for more volatile and quick moves in the stock price. Shares of small growth companies tend to experience greater volatility than large-cap value plays.

Smart Trader Tip

Try looking for pullback entries, as a strongly trending stock tests technical supports such as the 50-day simple moving average (SMA) after an upside earnings surprise. Institutions tend to make their own purchase decisions around this popular moving average.

Earnings information is readily available from the Internet. For instance, Zachs.com, Yahoo Finance, and Google all offer earnings-related content that's free for traders and very convenient for finding the type of information mentioned here. Marketwatch.com is another free site where relative strength leaders and laggards within sectors can be evaluated. The *Wall Street Journal (WSJ)* and *Investor's Business Daily (IBD)* are popular business periodicals and shouldn't be overlooked. Stocks highlighted on the pages of these widely read publications do attract extra attention, and those issues might be expected to produce stronger momentum moves when conditions are considered to be favorable. Finally, subscription-based charting software packages such as *ProfitSource* and *ValueGain* offer a great combination of financial and technical data that can be sorted by a multitude of criteria set up by the user. This is my preferred method for scanning the market.

Price-Earnings/Growth Ratio

The *price-earnings/growth (PEG) ratio* puts those raw earnings figures that we might come across into a simple number that is used to determine a stock's potential value.

PEG Ratio = (Stock Price ÷ Earnings per Share)
÷ EPS Growth

The PEG ratio has become increasingly popular because rather than just following a stock's *price-earnings (PE) ratio*, this number reflects growth. For instance, two stocks can share an identical PE multiple of 20, but command drastically different PEG results—the lower of the two being the more attractive to the growth strategist. This same analysis can also lead traders to realize that a high-multiple PE can also be underpriced relative to a stock with a much lower PE. As with any numbers, traders should be aware of which growth

ProfitSource

a sophisticated financial market analysis program designed to help traders identify winning trades by harnessing the power of Elliott Wave Theory as well as advanced scanning and searching functionalities (www.profitsource.com).

ValueGain

a stand-alone software program that makes use of a data feed to provide the most current financial metrics available. Also offers pre-computed scans categorized by investment styles—growth, value, and income—based upon fundamental approaches used by leading analysts including Benjamin Graham, Warren Buffett, and Peter Lynch (www.valuegain.com).

price-earnings/ growth (PEG) ratio

the PEG ratio compares a company's earnings growth rate to its PE ratio.

price-earnings (PE) ratio

a PE ratio is computed by dividing the stock price by earnings per share.

revenue growth

the rate of sequential sales improvement for a company or business.

estimates are being used in this calculation. For instance, the EPS growth used in the preceding calculation can be determined by using forward estimates, a trailing or historical percentage, or possibly a mix of the two. There is no right or wrong here, but the numbers can often produce different results, which traders should be aware of before making any assumptions.

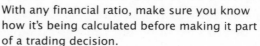

Smart Trader Tip

With any financial ratio, make sure you know how it's being calculated before making it part of a trading decision.

Revenue Growth

Bottom line, while Wall Street pays the most for earnings that are growing, strongly trending revenues are very important if a stock is to be truly considered a growth story. Traders are looking for minimum percentage (25 percent) increases in *revenue growth* similar to those outlined for EPS growth, as well as consistency with those numbers (as previously stressed). Strong revenue is considered so important that many growth investors insist that its trend must confirm the earnings growth picture and that its percentages need to be equally robust. While either raising prices or cost cutting is a means to achieving higher earnings, those methods (particularly cost cutting) can only last so long. It's the increased demand for a product that is measured through a company's revenues or sales that keeps growth traders involved and looking for additional upside appreciation in the stock price.

David Beats Goliath

While size does matter when it comes to growth stocks, it's often best to look for smaller-capitalization companies. Smaller players can generate incredible percentage gains for investors as a result of offering the right product or service within a new business trend. Due to their size, the net result can be explosive *EPS growth*; ultimately, that's what growth stock traders are on the lookout for. Hence, a $30 million order for mining gear means a lot more to the bottom line (earnings) of a company with a market cap of $700 million than for one valued at $15 billion. Hence, a good *market capitalization* range for companies that are potentially just entering a powerful growth cycle is from $500 million to approximately $10 billion. Most small-, all mid-, and some lower-value large-capitalization companies make up this range. This is seen as being attractive overall for trading/liquidity purposes, as well as being in the "sweet spot" for market capitalization with the capacity to ramp higher. On a side note, many *initial public offerings* (IPOs) start in this capitalization bracket. As such, relevant names might fit in nicely with some of the important sizing factors discussed and be considered attractive growth candidates.

EPS growth
the rate of sequential profit-per-share improvement for a company or business.

market capitalization
the total value of a company computed as the number of shares outstanding multiplied by the current stock price.

Institutional Momentum

Growth stocks with stellar fundamentals need to have the support of institutional players—such as mutual funds, pensions, and even the so-called fast money hedge funds—if they are truly going to achieve a price momentum that matches or even usurps what the company is doing on paper. This is referred to as *institutional momentum*. What we're looking for is increased interest by hedge funds, mutual fund managers, pension funds, and other large players. Those statistics are readily available on any of the aforementioned web sites. At a minimum, if the absolute ownership is small, we'd like to see a noticeable rise in the number of institutions owning the stock. For instance, if only a handful of funds are involved (under 15), we'd like to see that number double, along with healthy and increasing average daily volume (which we'll discuss next).

initial public offering (IPO)
a company's initial sale of shares to the public.

institutional momentum
buying interest on the part of large players such as pension funds, mutual funds, and portfolio managers that can cause rapid upward movement in a stock price.

Another method that traders use to track this group's interest is through the percentage of shares available to trade in the open market, or *float*. Institutional interest of 25 percent to 30 percent in a stock's float is seen as a minimum threshold in weeding out possible candidates. Remember, without the involvement of the larger players, potential momentum in a stock is greatly reduced. Simply by looking at price charts, traders can visually determine when interest is picking up or is already strong enough to be considered. It's thought that a stock worthy of institutional support will foster further meaningful and sustainable momentum.

float

a stock's amount of shares available (the supply) to trade in the open market. The smaller the float, the easier it is for demand in the stock to lead to outsized gains.

Smart Trader Tip

With all else being equal between two companies, the stock with the smaller tradable float tends to have stronger momentum and overall price volatility. In general, stocks with less than 30 million shares may be thought to be small-float issues. This can be a double-edged sword; traders should take care to understand the extra risks involved. Making sure that the average daily volume meets your own requirements is one precaution to take in trading this caliber of stock.

Unlike you or me, institutions can't just walk into a stock and expect to be filled on their order. When growth stocks within our capitalization range begin to attract these players, it can take days or even weeks of working buy-side orders before they have the sizing they require without totally influencing the stock into a feeding frenzy. These guys want growth momentum, but not before they've positioned themselves at levels that still afford value within the momentum phase. This means stocks that average less than 300,000 shares daily are less likely to attract an institutional following. However, traders might do well by monitoring a stock with compelling fundamentals if its only flaw looks to be *volume* related. If over the course of a few weeks or months the average daily volume starts to rapidly increase, this can be a powerful

volume

the amount of trading activity associated with a specific investment or market. Stock volume is measured in shares. Futures and options volume is based on number of contracts.

early signal. It could imply that a dormant growth stock is now seeing an infusion of institutional money ready to build on the company's existing fundamentals.

> ### Smart Trader Tip
>
> Looking for increased volume levels on the weekly chart perspective is a great visual means for determining when activity is picking up at the institutional level. Using a 30- or 50-day moving average (MA) on volume to see if it slopes upward is another tool that can help you visualize this tendency.

Price-Sales Ratio

This ratio compares the current share price of a stock to its per-share sales for the past 12 months. *Price-sales ratio* can be a better determinant for value than the more popular price/earnings (PE) ratio with growth stocks. Earnings may have yet to turn the corner for the smaller cap, but for a growing company, growth geared toward being involved

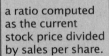

price-sales ratio
a ratio computed as the current stock price divided by sales per share.

in the momentum phase needs to account for this. In general, a figure below 1.5 to 2 is the domain of the value-oriented investor, but we also don't want to get caught dreaming too much of a product that hasn't seen any enthusiasm in the form of sales. Hence, for our purposes, a ratio between 2 and 5 is interpreted as being a good range for this type of growth candidate.

Concept Factor

The smaller the capitalization of a company, the more you might be able to forgo some fundamentals in appreciation of what may be in store for future EPS growth. While it's exciting to see new or innovative products unfold, some of these companies may also be labeled *cash burners*. Without positive operating cash flows, a company is inherently more risky. For growth stocks, this can be a tricky point. Savvy traders seek to find balance between a competing mind-set of both prudence and objectivity, and the ability to see the possibilities that lie ahead. So, what can you do? First, traders should allow themselves to dream big once in a while. Remember, even healthy and more widely followed growth-based companies are subject to optimistic projections that might end up pinching the portfolio. However, in keeping to the spirit of concept growth (but also respecting money management), allocating less money to this group and employing limited-risk strategies with listed options is a commonsense approach worth heeding.

Return on Equity and Cash Flow

return on equity (ROE)

an indicator of a company's profitability. It is computed by dividing net income for the past 12 months by common stockholders' equity. The result is expressed as a percentage.

Return on equity (ROE) and *cash flow* are two common figures used to measure the health of a company. The ROE is simply a percentage figure that demonstrates how efficient a business is with its shareholder equity (i.e., a company's assets less its liabilities). ROE is calculated using the following formula:

$$(\text{Net Income} \div \text{Shareholder Equity}) \times 100 = \text{ROE}$$

Many growth traders like to use the benchmark of 15 percent (15 cents of assets are created for each $1 invested). If the figure is under 15 percent, other methods for confirmation include looking to see whether the percentage is above the prior quarter's level and/or is trending higher for the last couple of quarters.

cash flow

the amount of net cash generated by an investment or business during a specific period of time. Also, the money received by a business minus the money that is paid out.

Cash flow simply asks how much a company has left over at the end of a period after paying all of its expenses. Without operating cash flow, the alternatives are adding to debt or using up existing cash. Neither of these solutions matches up to a debt-free and profitable concern. However, there simply isn't one hard-and-fast rule on this issue. For instance, renowned growth investor Ken Fisher will allow for negative cash flow if there's enough cash to cover three years. Other traders want to see positive cash flow greater than the current earnings of the company so that financial obligations during tougher periods can be met.

Smart Trader Tip

Check out what each of these fundamentals was doing just prior to an event of technical interest, such as a powerful weekly breakout. Find out if there's a pattern that emerges from these ratios that can help concentrate your search efforts.

Commodity-Related Areas and Current Growth

So far we've familiarized ourselves with a few factors that are relevant to growth stocks. Before we get into the nuts and bolts of trading this group, however, let's move into some areas of commodity-related growth that have done very well and should continue to outperform their more traditional and larger-capitalization peers. Keep in mind that technologies and names are always changing, so this is by no means an end-all for traders. That said, Table 11.1 details a list of companies and sectors that have demonstrated both the fundamental and the technical wherewithal to be labeled growth stocks. I've also offered a few that are still flying under the radar and not yet profitable, but could be the next big growth story if the commodities cycle continues its run into secular territories.

TABLE 11.1 Growth Stocks with a Commodity Base (10-2006)

Alternative Energy/ Conservation Solutions	Powershares Clean Energy Index (PBW), Suntech Power (STP), MEMC Materials (WFR), Pacific Ethanol (PEIX), Archer Daniels Midland (ADM), SunPower (SPWR), Itron (ITRI), Medis Tech (MDTL), Evergreen Solar (ESLR), Energy Conversion (ENER), Ormat Tech (ORA), Hoku (HOKU), MGP Ingredients (MGPI), Echelon (ELON), Color Kinetics (CLRK), Sulphco (SUF), Sunopta (STKL), Rentech (RTK), Hydrogenics (HYGS), FuelCell (FCEL), Ballard (BLDP), GrafTech (GTI)
Machinery or "Picks and Shovels" and Related Services	Dynamic Materials (BOOM), Joy Global (JOYG), Bucyrus (BUCY), Terex (TEX), Oil States (OIS), Lufkin (LUFK), Hydril (HYDL), World Fuel Services (INT), Mine Safety (MSA), Symyx (SMMX)

(continued)

TABLE 11.1 (continued)	
Specialty Metals/ Composites	Alleghany (ATI), Zoltek (ZOLT), AMCOL (ACO), Titanium Metals (TIE), RTI International (RTI), Hexcel (HXL), Cytec (CYT)
Infrastructure	Fluor (FLR), Jacobs (JEC), Shaw Group (SGR), Chicago Bridge (CBI), Encore Wire (WIRE)
Transport	Burlington (BNI), FreightCar America (RAIL), Teekay (TK), Overseas Shipping (OSG), Norfolk (NSC)
Coal/Nuclear	Peabody (BTU), Arch Coal (ACI), Headwaters (HW), Cameco (CCJ), KFx Inc. (KFX), USEC (USU)
Financial	U.S. Global Investors (GROW)

Growth Technicals

I like to trade growth stocks, as I expect them to outperform their peers when times are good (i.e., trending strongly). Let's start by exploring a few examples and then discuss those factors involved in two of the simpler technical bases used by many growth traders. From there, the analysis gets a lot more exciting with the help of some charts that depict how some of the more complex patterns play out in the real world of commodity-related growth stocks. Finally, I'll leave you with a discussion of a couple of growth stocks that are currently developing and show you the characteristics of what to look for while they're happening. This exploration is designed to better prepare you to take advantage of powerful moves notorious for attracting other growth traders and the associated momentum. Let's get started.

flat base pattern
a type of chart pattern that occurs in the midst of an advance or decline when prices trend sideways for a period of time. It is considered a continuation pattern because it is a pause during an advance or decline.

The *flat base pattern* (see Figure 11.1) is an easily defined formation that is typically seen as a continuation trigger within the existing trend. Classic characteristics include development after a run-up of 15 percent to 25 percent from a larger base such as a cup-with-handle (see case study later in this chapter). As the name suggests, the base is essentially lateral, as it digests the prior gains, typically in a trading range of 10 percent to 15 percent. The pattern is also the shortest of all the

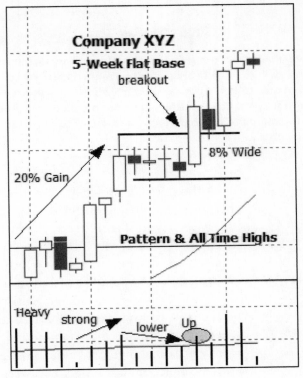

FIGURE 11.1 Flat base weekly.
Source: ProfitSource.

weekly chart base structures that attract growth traders. Standard prac-
tice is to demand a minimum of five weeks, but it's thought that there is
some room for time allowance if the conditions of the day merit it, as
well as the characteristics of the pattern itself. For instance, in the preceding example, we find that there are four easily defined and tight (8
percent) weekly bars seen as part of the base-building process after a
fresh all-time-high is made. The breakout that occurs in week 5 might
be viewed as being a little early. However, we also have to take into account the weekly chart action leading into the four-week pause and the
strong volume characteristics throughout the process (strong, drop, and
pop). The entry during week 5 would be allowable based on our extra
analysis for confirmation.

Smart Trader Tip

Growth breakouts from proper bases can happen very fast and quite often move swiftly. So be fastidious in tracking your top picks. It can take a lot of time to find a good opportunity. So once you have one, don't lose sight of it. Then, putting stop-limit orders on the stock or a limited-risk option position before the breakout occurs will turn your hard work into a well-conceived trade.

ascending base pattern

the least common of the continuation pattern groupings. Angular wedging over a 9- to 16-week period with the deepest wave or trough being less than 20 percent in width is key. Three full waves need to develop, along with constructive volume characteristics during the base building, in order to qualify and before a breakout entry might be confirmed.

Although it is much less common than the other formations being outlined, the *ascending base pattern* (see Figure 11.2) deserves some attention as well. However, according to research from *IBD*, when it does develop, it is seen as being a reliable base structure. The specifics include a series of narrowing weekly waves within an existing uptrend. Each successive wave or pullback begins with a higher high pivot than the prior one and ends with a higher low. Some might see this as a wedging or pennant type of action, but it does have very specific requirements that must be met. Aside from the aforementioned characteristics, the deepest any of the three waves can be is 20 percent and each one, as implied, contracts against the prior one. Second, the length is seen as taking 9 to 16 weeks—much longer than the minimum requirement shown in the flat base. And finally, during this process, the breakout (and all the work put into its making) needs to demonstrate sufficient strength in institutional

Smart Trader Tip

Making sure a proper ratio of 3:1 in favor of accumulation can help in the process of determining stronger bases before they break out. When distribution is evident, see if the weekly price bars actually demonstrate strength. Was the closing price for the five-day period in the upper quartile of the week's trading range? That's one sign for spotting buyers in action that might otherwise be labeled distribution.

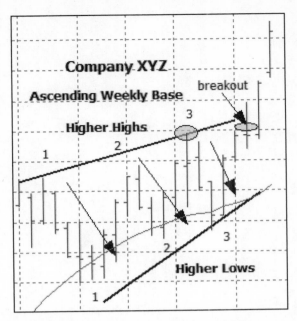

FIGURE 11.2 Ascending weekly base.
Source: ProfitSource.

sponsorship. A sufficient edge in the form of buyers during uptrending weeks should be evident versus those weeks in which any above-average distribution might occur.

Nuts and Bolts

Now we're ready to get into the nuts and bolts of commodity-related growth stocks. The following charts and analysis highlight the kind of growth characteristics that I like to see from both a technical and a fundamental perspective. We'll start with some recent triggers related to the current commodities boom and then work into some developing growth stocks that are exhibiting some very interesting patterns right now (in the summer of 2006).

MEMC Electronic Materials, Inc. (WFR)

MEMC Electronic Materials (WFR) is involved in the manufacturing and sale of wafers and intermediate products for both the semiconductor and the solar industries—two hot sectors (see Figure 11.3). However,

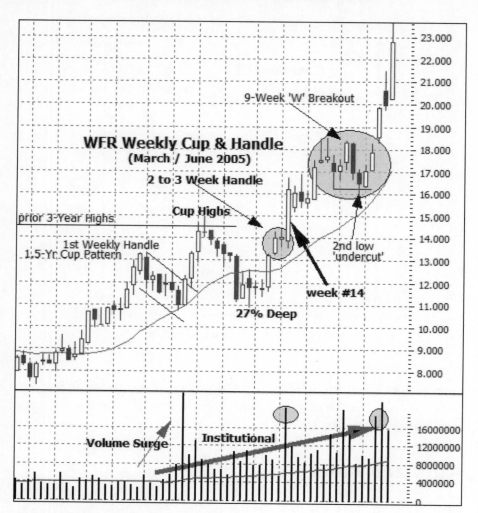

FIGURE 11.3   MEMC (WFR) weekly chart.

there's a high degree of cyclicality in its business model, as both the energy markets (solar) and the volatile semiconductor industry are involved. That said, the company is well-established, with an $8 billion market cap, and has been consistently profitable for more than three years. As of mid-2006, WFR maintained a PEG ratio of 1.3 and had a projected five-year EPS growth estimate of 16.2.

Looking at the WFR weekly chart, some early prospecting started back in mid-2005 from a three-month *cup-and-handle pattern*. This formation is very popular among intermediate traders who rely on weekly charts for entering into growth/momentum stocks. The basics of the pattern include weekly base development of at least six, and preferably seven, weeks to exist. Depth is also important. Retracements from the pattern high to low shouldn't run deeper than 35 percent (corrective activity) in a healthy market where the broader averages are enjoying a rally of intermediate significance. Next, after a weekly qualified low has been established, the stock will have to muster up some buying power (stronger volume) so that it can develop price action into the right side of its base. At that time, growth traders are looking for a slight pause and lighter activity, which is commonly known as a *handle*. This consolidation is five or more days in length and within 15 percent of the cup highs. The handle should also be in proportion to the cup, or the corrective phase of the pattern. This can be done by a simple visual inspection of the chart. What you don't want is a cup base and handle that look disproportional to one another. Figure 11.3 labels all of these characteristics, which fit comfortably into the trade criteria.

> **cup-and-handle pattern**
> a chart pattern that lasts from 7 to 65 weeks. The cup is in the shape of a "U" and the handle is usually more than one or two weeks in duration. The handle is a slight downward drift with low trading volume that develops within 15 percent of the cup highs and in the upper half of its weekly base.

In the case of WFR, 13 weeks had passed before the breakout triggered from a nine-day handle on explosive upside volume. It should also be noted that this pattern occurred after three-year highs were established and while the semiconductor sector was down more than 25 percent during this same period. The interpretation is that institutional traders were sending an overall message of relative strength and potential further growth in this solar-semiconductor stock as energy prices continued their yearly advance higher.

In fact, back in late April 2005 the company reported solid year-over-year results based on growing its cash flow to more than $73 million. That number, when compared to its operating income of $63 million, is one way for some growth traders to see the company as being fundamentally sound. Furthermore, during that period, it did push its EPS up by more than 40 percent compared to the previous year. However, all wasn't rosy according to the numbers and whispers. The company actually fell shy of estimates by .02 cents when it delivered earnings of .23 cents. Interestingly enough, the supposed disappointment looks to have been very much anticipated by the institutional players and ended up marking the weekly low (4/29/05) of our cup-with-handle base.

Smart Trader Tip

"Do as we do, not as we say." The market's a funny place, so try to appreciate some imperfections from the background evidence. In fact, if the evidence looks too perfect, be extra defensive in making any trade decisions.

Remember the discussion about positive earnings drift and how surprises are important, but that you shouldn't rest on your laurels just because of a supposed surprise? Well, this is a great reverse case study demonstrating why the charts and an ability to read between the lines ("do as we do") go a long way toward enabling you to profit in the market. With energy prices just off their all-time-highs, a still very healthy-looking financial statement (keep in mind the dual cyclicality we're dealing with) and institutional support for the stock (weekly closing upper range and higher volume 4/29/05 and 27 percent corrective depth) despite the earnings alarm, monitoring for an eventual breakout pattern made sense. Even though growth in the strictest sense wasn't there, part of the growth equation was staring investors in the face via the chart. This feeds back into what I stressed earlier about undervalued growth on paper and holding on to an issue that might never see the share price catch up to the earnings momentum before some negative development occurs.

Returning to the technical picture, the monitoring of institutions and the realization that a proper base could have been developing off the late April earnings paid off in the form of a handle in the right side of its weekly base—one that developed perfectly after nearly two weeks on decreased trade, before exploding higher through the pivot of the consolidation. Remember how institutional participation has been stressed, as such involvement is ultimately what defines the vast majority of successful growth stock breakouts? Well, look at what the institutions were saying with their money back in early 2005—*volumes*! As with any pattern breakout trigger, confirmation of volume in excess of 150 percent of the stock's average daily trading activity is considered a necessary rule. As you can easily see in Figure 11.3, WFR handily passes that condition. In fact, the surge witnessed can only be attributed to the big boys piling money into the stock. Remember that when they do, it's usually more than just another one-night stand. Clearly, a trend (rising energy prices and alternative solutions) was developing and WFR was very much a part of it.

Proper growth investing is equal parts digging to find strong numbers and/or a compelling theme or business niche and being technically savvy enough to recognize when those money managers are clearly showing interest by putting their money to work in a meaningful and powerful way.

Joy Global Inc. (JOYG)

Joy Global is a *picks and shovels* provider of the commodities boom. Just as during the California gold rush of the 1800s, many of the most profitable players weren't the ones doing the digging; rather, they were providing the equipment. With an offering of both underground and surface mining equipment used in bringing coal, copper, iron ore, and other minerals to market, Joy Global is a key provider in making the commodities business possible for others and profitable for their shareholders. Most recently, the company announced an earnings surprise of .05 cents and revenue growth of about 17 percent on a YOY basis and forecasted 12-month revenue growth of 16 percent to 29 percent. After seeing the stock drop into a very hard corrective base slightly more than 50 percent deep, the announcement catapulted the stock higher by more than 21 percent. It also helped to establish a slew of fresh upgrades by analysts apparently caught off guard by the better-than-expected report and a not-dead-yet commodities boom (see Figure 11.4).

Let's go back in time a little bit more than a year. Right before a 200 percent run-up in the stock, a mischievous bout of necessary profit taking occurred. Still in its growth phase, Joy Global displayed a formation known as the W base, or a high *double bottom pattern*. The common double bottom basing pattern has at least seven weeks (typically more) to develop and a depth of no more than 35 percent when the broader market is trending higher. Typically, the pattern will see the second pivot in the base undercut the original low. Generally, that additional weakness is seen as a stronger low than one that doesn't make a hard test because this action shakes out the last remaining weak hands. However, most technicians also realize the limitations of strict pattern analysis. As we've emphasized earlier, volume and what the institutions

double bottom pattern
price action of a security where it has declined two times to approximately the same level, indicating the existence of a support level and a possibility that the downward trend has ended. The double bottom is confirmed when the price of the security moves through its midpoint pivot, ideally with handle development in place.

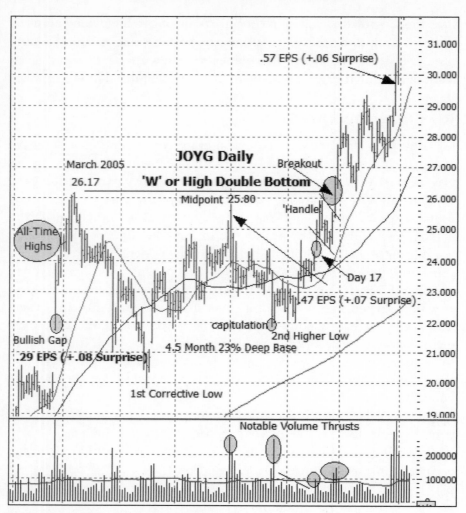

FIGURE 11.4   Joy Global (JOYG) W base breakout.
Source: ProfitSource.

are doing on a case-by-case basis take precedence. This is important because the situation is rarely presented as black or white. Your job as a trader is to interpret the clues, be they price, volume, earnings surprises, or a combination of all three and more.

Key points of activity, and the characteristics associated with the double bottom basing formation, are visible in the daily chart of Joy Global (see Figure 11.4). From the March inception to the first corrective low of 23 percent to the midpoint at $25.80—all told, JOYG is establishing a solid potential base. But then "stuff happens," if you will, which makes the analysis somewhat more complex. JOYG establishes its midpoint on the heels of an upside surprise. This would seem to be a good thing, of course. But if most traders are already anticipating the better-than-expected news, unless it truly surpasses those raised expectations, the stock will typically be vulnerable. The smart money operators that bought in leading up to the announcement will also invariably need to exit if the numbers don't trounce the estimates. Remember that, on average, stocks with positive surprises will ultimately see upward price drift leading into their next earnings cycle. That said, Joy Global's move lower also stresses some of the bumps in the road. It depicts another common condition of an earning's high flier: When price action runs up in the three- to four-week period ahead of the anticipated surprise, it becomes more prone to profit taking, even if the result was supposed to be stronger than expected.

As growth stock traders not yet involved, our interest should be on future price and volume action. It's not until later that month and into July that the stock raises our awareness level that a bullish pattern could still be developing. At that point, a second session of hard selling hits the stock, which we call *capitulation*—and which couldn't be determined with any efficacy until more clues were presented. However, over the next three to four weeks, that event became much more credible and fostered the interpretation that we had a higher low version of the double bottom, or W, pattern developing. The key for growth stock breakout players truly became evident 17 days later when a bullish gap on volume offered up the start of handle development.

capitulation
when investors, in disgust, throw in the towel on an investment. This is often followed by a reversal and rebound in the price of the security.

Proper handle development takes one week, at a minimum, to confirm a larger base pattern such as a W or the already discussed cup-with-handle. The six-day count for JOYG barely meets that requirement. Other requirements, though, such as downward-sloping price action on lighter volume, confirmed the construction nicely. That key element is indicative that holders at this stage are comfortable with the price action and aren't going to pressure the stock further. The last ingredient necessary to qualify the structure is for a *breakout* on volume that's 150 percent above average (i.e., 450,000 versus 300,000 average). On that measure

breakout
a move in a security above a resistance level or below support. A breakout accompanied by heavy volume is generally an indication that a market is ready to make a significant move higher or lower.

as well, Joy Global confirms the breakout and shows why picks and shovels do quite well in a commodities boom.

Ormat Technologies, Inc. (ORA)

This one is going to be our little secret. Ormat Technologies (ORA) is listed as a utility company—a sector that has benefited from the rise in energy-related commodity prices. But unlike an industry that has merely benefited due to being able to raise prices, Ormat has a couple of other powerful factors that make it a truly exciting candidate going forward. It's an alternative-energy-providing utility engaged in developing and operating geothermal power plants as well as selling the electricity. Now that's exciting stuff! In addition, the combination of fundamentals and technicals makes this company really compelling as a trade or investment.

Fundamentally, Ormat has been a consistent grower, with current 2006 estimates approaching 45 percent. It's also delivered an average earnings surprise of more than 50 percent during the past year, which just goes to show you that green power innovations really can work. But what's even more exciting to me from a trading vantage point is the current technical picture (see Figure 11.5) being carved out in the summer of 2006. First, what you might not know by looking at the chart is that Ormat is a very recent IPO, having made its debut less than two years ago. As mentioned earlier, IPOs can be a great place to locate growth stocks. An IPO in and of itself doesn't represent growth, but if you find a promising candidate, it does put an additional very positive variable into any potential breakouts. The reason is that ownership in the stock hasn't been saturated by the very same institutional owners that we want to back up the current price action. Next, the weekly chart shows us that, in fact, Wall Street has just begun to notice ORA in the past few months. Look at the decisive pickup in volume as we move toward the right side of the chart. The average daily volume has more than doubled, delivering sufficient liquidity as the institutions start to accumulate shares in a still young, publicly traded company, and it lends itself to the idea that we're on the same side as the early smart money.

The technical icing on the cake is the last six months of pattern development—a potentially very bullish formation. I've labeled the consolidation as being either a W or a bullish flag pattern. Irrespective of which title is decided upon, the focus point for a breakout is defined by the midpoint on the weekly chart. Did I say icing on the cake? Actually, the only thing that would make Ormat more perfect would be some listed

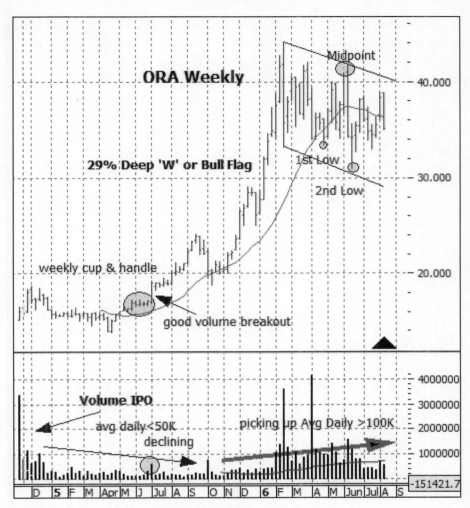

FIGURE 11.5 Ormat Technology (ORA) weekly IPO, 2005.
Source: ProfitSource.

options before, and if, the current pattern triggers an institutional break-out that speaks volumes about its potential!

World Fuel Services Corporation (INT)

With soaring energy prices, World Fuel is another one of those very prof-itable pick-and-shovel businesses that have seen solid double-digit earn-ings and revenue growth as well as a stock price that's soared over 1,600 percent in the past five years. The company offers both aviation and ma-rine fuel services (such as the provision of market intelligence/access to marine fuel deposits), cost and price hedging, procurement, and quality control services. It also acts as a reseller of fuel on its own behalf.

Like any stock that's had a price run of World Fuel's magnitude (and most don't), the expectation is that profit taking will be an inevitable part of the picture at some point. When dealing with commodity-based stocks, of course, the underlying product is going to have a strong influence on when this process kicks in. However, many leading growth stocks also lead the market—in this case, the price of oil—to both the upside and the downside. This looks to be the case with World Fuel during the summer of 2006.

The current analysis of the weekly chart (see Figure 11.6) is based on a more advanced strategy that looks to combine a few technical concepts while finding one of those bottoms that everyone loves to point out after the fact. Before we move forward, though, a couple of points should be addressed. As previously mentioned, a 35 percent correction is seen as being healthy for many growth stocks as they consolidate some of those extraordinary gains in a healthy market climate. However, most market leaders will eventually fall 72 percent from their peaks! Further, 50 percent of growth stocks never end up fully recovering, according to analysis at *IBD*. Summed up, we don't want to catch a falling knife that might not ever recover. That's why solid confirmation techniques and, hopefully, a limited-risk strategy utilizing options should be stressed.

Several weeks before crude oil hit a new high, INT ran up to an all-time high (ATH) of $53.45 in June and then started to pull back. It then made a weekly rally attempt into both July and early August before falling apart aggressively from the one-month double top (which had been setting up the framework for a W with a handle at $49.59). That activity is marked by A through C in the weekly view shown in Figure 11.6. The next couple of weeks were surely difficult for some shareholders, as a very hard corrective move (with a nasty daily gap) occurred. In the aftermath of all this movement, a combination of pattern development and hard corrective activity was close to producing a confirmation of a major low in the making, which is considered great news for advanced pattern and reversal traders.

Mind you, we don't know how this is going to turn out. But, like our analysis of Ormat, this information is intended to help you understand some of the factors involved in locating a strong candidate for bottoming before we know the outcome. While it would be great if the individual trade ultimately makes us look smart, the analysis is presented so that you can walk away with some valuable concepts and tools for your own trading down the road.

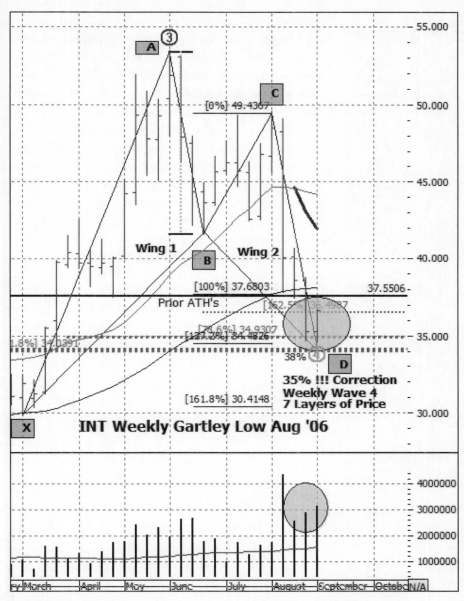

FIGURE 11.6 World Fuel (INT) weekly reversal low (advanced).
Source: ProfitSource.

What exactly is so compelling technically that a bottom and a reversal of the current downtrend is anticipated? The potential low contains the elements of *Fibonacci* pattern analysis, Elliott Wave Theory, and volume and depth (or corrective) analysis for growth stocks. Admittedly,

Fibonacci

a twelfth-century mathematician who identified certain ratios to be a common factor throughout the natural world, such as in DNA, music, architecture, and nature. In the financial markets, technicians use these ratios (for instance, 50 percent and 62 percent) in an attempt to locate key support or resistance levels that mark extremes in crowd behavior and price action.

Gartley

a type of advanced pattern that attempts to find trend reversals using pivots and retracement levels.

retracements

a move counter to the prevailing trend. Technical analysts consider 33 percent, 50 percent, and 61.8 percent retracements to be significant.

some of this analysis is more advanced than can be explained at this time, but it's important to note that the combination of factors is interpreted as powerful enough. I'd be remiss if I failed to show you how various technical tools and strategies work together to form bottoms of significance.

Referring again to the weekly chart of INT, note how a pattern has been drawn over the price action. This formation is known as a bullish *Gartley*, and it's my primary motivation for anticipating a reversal of the current trend. The Gartley is a Fibonacci-based pattern that contains multiple levels of *retracement*, extension, and projection analysis (in this case, going all the way back to 2001). These levels, or layers, represent a support zone. More than three layers are considered strong. In this example, my analysis determined six, plus the prior highs, for a total of seven levels of zone support. The bullish Gartley is defined by the letters X, A, B, C, and finally D. I've drawn in lines outlining these pivots—also referred to as *wings*—in Figure 11.6; point D is the final pivot. In the case of INT, the price action still needs to fully develop into a swing low on the weekly chart.

Pattern Calculations

- X = Pattern inception pivot low.
- A = Pattern pivot high.
- B = Pivot low that ideally measures from a 38 percent to a 62 percent retracement of X:A.
- C = Pivot lower high that ideally measures from a 38 percent to a 78 percent retracement of A:B.
- D = Final pivot of the Gartley. The D pivot low must complete as a 62 percent to a 78 percent retracement of X:A.

Next, the Elliott Wave (see Chapter 7) is attempting to find a potential Wave 4 bottom. Using ProfitSource, the weekly signal line (a proprietary measure) was still removed from the current price action (the line near $42). Nonetheless, it's another factor that suggests a bullish outcome could be looming. Our next piece of evidence is the huge levels of volume over the past four weeks. The most recent week took out the prior week's trading lows by a mere .08 cents and then reversed to the upside on heavier trading (while maintaining the integrity of the aforementioned support and pattern analysis). That action is interpreted as a capitulation on the part of sellers.

Finally, what I'll refer to as *proper depth* or *corrective testing* has also taken place. Remember, growth stocks, with their often outsized gains (and surely INT's 1600 percent qualifies), will have periods of countertrend activity. When this kind of natural market ebbing occurs, corrective moves up to 35 percent are seen as being healthy in the normal course of business. As this percentage relates to INT, the weekly low is a near perfect 35 percent decline from the highs of 53.45. This becomes another point of confirmation and helps to explain why we're carefully monitoring World Fuel as a trade candidate for a very promising bottom.

Summary

This chapter covered a lot of ground on growth stocks. Unlike merely trading a trend in commodities—whether it's with a futures contract or perhaps a listed ETF—traders need to realize that there are meaningful differences. When the intricacies of growth stocks are fully appreciated and understood, stronger opportunities than would otherwise be possible become available to traders.

This chapter provided a host of key concepts and factors that can help you to identify promising growth stocks, including the following:

- Fundamental analysis and ratios associated with growth stocks.
- Benchmarks used in determining a growth stock's attractiveness.
- The importance of institutions and volume.
- Emphasizing suppliers and innovators when locating growth stocks.
- Powerful price patterns.
- Recognizing and interpreting growth potential with imperfect information.

There's a lot to be learned through further exploration of key fundamentals like earnings growth, cash flow, and positive surprises, to technical concepts such as classic formations like the W pattern. The study of more advanced pattern analysis, which combines a myriad of techniques, will no doubt increase your trading know-how exponentially.

As important, if not more, this chapter is designed to help the reader go beyond just taking a number and thinking that it's mysteriously going to catapult the stock into a growth story that will appreciate in your trading account. The analysis of several case studies that involve a varying range of factors is provided to give you a better understanding of how, why, and when growth stocks become growth stocks worthy of your investment dollars.

Key Summary Points

1. Growth stocks are expected to show above-average increases in revenues and earnings in the future and be already delivering on those expectations.

2. Earnings growth of 15 percent minimum is mandatory, but 25 percent for three or more quarters is preferred.

3. Smaller-capitalization companies up to $10 billion on a whole have a built-in earnings growth advantage when involved in an expanding market segment.

4. Fundamental and technical criteria need to be weighed and balanced when assessing the prospects for a growth stock position.

5. By sizing up the charts for institutional interest, you can try to avoid value traps that never fulfill the promise of price momentum.

6. Be cognizant of earnings surprises, warnings, and the price action before and after the report's release. "Do as we do, not as we say" is a much stronger growth-oriented approach to trading than strict fundamental analysis.

7. Institutional support is a necessary catalyst for a growth story to be fully valued as a growth stock. Twenty-five percent or more of the float should be held by this group. Institutional ownership should be increasing handily. Average volume of at least 300,000 shares also provides needed liquidity.

8. Locating early signs of institutional interest with strong numbers on paper is a solid sign that growth stock momentum is beginning.

9. PEG Ratio = (Stock Price ÷ Earnings Per Share) ÷ EPS Growth. Lower ratios are typically more attractive. Revenue growth is necessary for strong earnings growth. Benchmarks should be similar to earnings rules.

10. Price-sales ratios between 2 and 5 are the domain of many growth stocks.

11. Return on equity (ROE) and cash flow measure financial health. ROE of 15 percent or more and a positive cash flow figure, quarterly increases, or enough free cash on hand for three years are common gauges.

12. Innovators, early achievers, and pick-and-shovel companies equate stronger growth success to sales achievements rather than cost cutting and heavy reliance on commodity pricing.

13. Growth stock technical development comprises identifiable weekly chart price and volume characteristics.

14. Two classes of tradable patterns are identified: continuation and reversal patterns.

15. Classic continuation patterns include the flat base, ascending, cup-and-handle, and W, or double bottom bases. Specific depth and duration characteristics for each are readily apparent in determining a qualified pattern. Common characteristics of each include accumulation within the base based on weekly chart and/or less visible distribution.

16. Breakouts from continuation bases must be confirmed by heavy volume. A common benchmark is 150 percent of a stock's average daily volume.

17. After a breakout, lighter volume retracements to key technical levels such as the 50-day SMA are a popular trend method for entering growth stocks.

18. Reversal or contratrend entries are associated with more advanced technical techniques. Incorporating principles of Elliott Wave, Fibonacci, and volume analysis to identify strong reversal pivots and the use of limited-risk spreads are emphasized.

Chapter
12

Seasonal Commodity Patterns

Entire textbooks have been written about the seasonal patterns that influence the commodity markets. Most of these books, however, only touch the surface of how commodity markets react during certain times of the year to seasonal factors. One of the most comprehensive sources for the analysis of seasonal patterns can be found in the *CRB Commodity Yearbook*. Published by the Commodity Research Bureau each year and long considered the bible of commodity research, the CRB Commodity Yearbook includes current seasonal patterns as well as data from the past 10 years. In this chapter, I will provide a synopsis of my favorite seasonal patterns and how they affect commodity markets.

Smart Trader Tip

Seasonal factors have an impact on the performance of various commodities year-round. While traders can't always plan their trades around seasonal factors, it would be unwise to ignore them, as commodities are obviously affected by weather changes (oil in wintertime, utilities in summertime, etc.).

What Is a Seasonal Pattern?

Seasonal patterns are identified by associating various interactive factors throughout a year, month, or even a day. A seasonal pattern can be a short-term pattern, which I would identify as an intraday pattern (within a day), a weekly pattern, or even a monthly pattern. The events that affect the price of a commodity on a consistent basis identify the pattern itself. The trick is to translate this information into trading or investment profits.

For example, the sun rises and sets each day; this is a pattern we can all bank on. If you could get paid $100 each time this happens, this would be a great investment pattern. However, patterns in commodities are just not that simple—if they were, everyone would be using them. Everyone would be rich.

long straddle

a delta-neutral options strategy created by the simultaneous purchase of an at-the-money call and put with the same expiration date.

Let's explore a weekly pattern you might see in a commodity. Each Thursday, reports are released that affect the energy markets. The numbers that are released can cause wide price swings up and down (i.e., a lower-than-expected crude oil inventory number drives prices up, while a higher-than-expected crude oil inventory number drives prices down). So how can we use this scheduled event to make a profitable trade? Well, since this up-and-down movement increases the volatility of the options, a strategy such as a *long straddle* could be used to benefit from this pattern.

How Are Seasonal Patterns Identified?

catalyst

an event that causes a reaction in the price of an asset. For example, an earnings report can be a catalyst for a big move higher or lower in a stock price.

One way to identify a monthly pattern is by monitoring the monthly reports of an agricultural commodity. These reports can serve as a *catalyst* for the commodity. That is, once the numbers are released, investors react and the price of the commodity begins to move. The best patterns are identified by looking for catalysts that directly drive the prices of a commodity up or down. It is an event that makes people, traders, investors, or anyone react in such a way that they want to buy or sell something. This, in turn, increases demand as more people want to own the commodity or decreases demand as more people want to sell it.

- Positive catalyst = increased demand = higher prices.
- Negative catalyst = decreased demand = lower prices.

For example, gold prices were very volatile in 2006 and generally trended up for much of the year, reaching a high of just around $732 before having a significant down move from the highs for the year. When prices move up or down significantly, you need to ask yourself, "What is the catalyst?" There will always be one! Smart commodity traders put the odds in their favor by identifying markets with catalysts that create trends and patterns.

In 2006, a great deal of the buying was attributed to the expansion of the economies in China and India, as well as speculative buying by the hedge funds. These were the catalysts that created the upward pressure in buying that pushed the prices up significantly in 2006—from approximately $520 an ounce to $732 per ounce.

Smart Trader Tip

The phrase *hedge fund* is sometimes misunderstood by traders and investors. A hedge fund, in its most basic form, is typically a group of investors who pool their money for a specific purpose such as investing in stocks, commodities, real estate, or any other vehicle. Let's say we get 10 friends together to form a partnership to invest in a piece of real estate and each of us puts in $10,000; we could call ourselves a hedge fund. Hence, the term *hedge fund* does not necessarily mean that the partnership is using hedging techniques to reduce the risk. Bottom line, not all hedge funds are hedged, but some use hedging as a way to reduce risk.

What goes up fast can come down just as fast. In the gold market, the move down was even faster than the move up, driving prices down to a low of $555 in June 2006. So what was the negative catalyst? As mentioned before, catalysts drive the markets in both directions. As everyone was jumping on the gold bandwagon to the upside, one big day of down prices scared the pack; everyone jumped off and the party was over, at least momentarily.

Smart Trader Tip
The term *hedging* describes the process of reducing the risk of an investment by using techniques that can mitigate its financial impact if you are wrong about the direction of the investment. For example, when you buy car or house insurance, you are hedging. If you have an accident or if a fire were to destroy your home, you are hedged, as the insurance will reduce the negative financial impact. Let's say you buy a gold futures contract. If it goes down in price, you can use a protective options position—such as buying a put option on the gold futures contract—to act like insurance.

Seasonal and nonseasonal patterns are identified by looking back in time using commodity price charts to see if any identifiable patterns stick out. Additionally, historical price data can be used to go back and see if any patterns stick out. Remember that it is historical data that creates the charts. Some traders like to use the prices (as numbers) as opposed to a chart to do the analysis. Since most people are more visual by nature, looking at a chart often makes more sense. Check out the charts in Figures 12.1 through 12.3 to see whether you can find and/or identify patterns.

Figure 12.1 shows a definite upward trend pattern in oil prices.

Figure 12.2 shows the definite seasonal trend in natural gas prices.

FIGURE 12.1 Crude oil monthly pride chart.

Source: ProfitSource.

Figure 12.3 shows dramatic price movements thanks to a catalyst in the form of a supply shortage at the end of 2003, followed by a dramatic move to the downside in 2004.

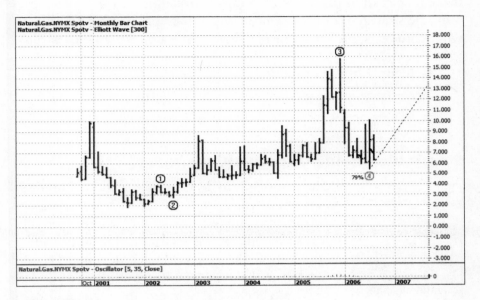

FIGURE 12.2 Natural gas monthly price chart.
Source: ProfitSource.

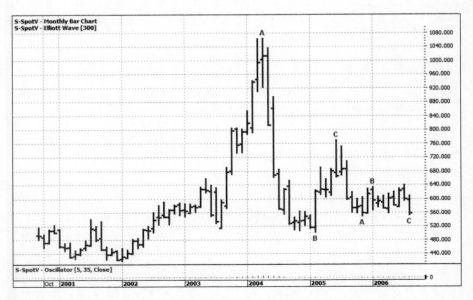

FIGURE 12.3 Soybeans monthly price chart.
Source: ProfitSource.

Three Steps to Success

Once you've identified a pattern you like, it's time to identify ways to make money from this pattern. If it's a seasonal pattern or a trend pattern, the strategy is as important as seeing the opportunity. As I like to tell my students, success in the markets is really a three-step process:

1. Identifying opportunities.
2. Selecting a strategy that matches the opportunity.
3. Managing the investment once it is made.

Step 1: Identifying Opportunities

trending market
a market that is moving either up or down in an identifiable manner. For example, if oil prices rise from $50 to $70 a barrel, it's an uptrending market. If sugar prices fall from 16 cents to 10 cents a pound, this is an example of a downtrending market.

The first step is to decide where to put your money to work. If you haven't identified a promising opportunity, then your money isn't working for you. It is sitting idle. Catalysts can help identify trading opportunities because prices are moving in one direction or the other. However, without catalysts, prices are likely to stay in a trading range. Certain strategies that fit range-trending markets can be used when there are no foreseeable catalysts and prices are expected to trade in a range. In sum, different types of opportunities exist in different types of markets.

Important note: Markets do not trend forever nor do *nontrending markets* trade in ranges forever. As a commodities trader, you need to understand that market characteristics are in constant fluctuation.

Step 2: Selecting the Strategy That Matches the Opportunity

Once you've identified a promising market, the next step is action. Have you ever come up with an idea and thought, "Wow, I could make a lot of money on this," but then never acted on the idea—only to see the product sold on TV later? It has happened to me, and I have to say, it doesn't feel very good. Bottom line, if you don't enter, you can't win. Ideas are a dime a dozen. Hence, the implementation of an idea is the next critical step to success.

Applying this talking point to the commodity markets, let's say you think oil prices are rising (the opportunity). Which action is best to implement?

> **nontrending**
> a market where prices have a tendency of moving in between two price points for a period of time. For example, if gold trades between $600 and $650 for a six-month period, it would be identified as a nontrending or sideways-moving market.

1. Buy oil and store it.
2. Buy crude oil futures contracts.
3. Buy crude oil futures contracts with a hedge (buy puts to protect).
4. Buy crude oil call options.

To determine which strategy best takes advantage of the opportunity (oil prices rising), evaluate the risk and reward potential. Then, integrate your findings with whatever approaches you feel most comfortable with as a trader. I prefer to employ actions 3 and 4, my two favorite strategies.

Smart Trader Tip

Before implementing any investment strategy, make sure you understand the risks and the rewards of that strategy. Trading involves risk, and you need to be aware of these risks before trading commodities of any sort. It is advisable to only use money you can afford to risk.

Step 3: Managing the Trade

Once you find a promising market and determine which strategy to employ, decide how to strategically proceed during the life of the trade. Have an exit plan. Sometimes knowing when to sell or close a position is more challenging than knowing when to buy or open it. You may want to ask some of the following questions:

- How long are you going to keep the trade?
- Do you have a maximum loss you are willing to accept (stop loss)?
- Do you have a profit objective?

- What will tell you when the trend has changed?
- Will you add to or subtract from your position over time
- Will you use a trailing stop?

In the final chapter of this book, we will review these questions (and more) to assist you in reconciling all your trading objectives and ultimately putting it all together.

My Favorite Patterns

Entire books have been written about trends and seasonal patterns. Since I have limited space here, I want to focus on a few of my favorite seasonal patterns. Let's start out with the Natural Gas Winter Pattern.

What Is Natural Gas?

Before you start trading commodity futures contracts, it's vital to really understand the instruments you are trading as well as the risks inherent in the trading process. One of the biggest mistakes new traders make is to not accurately comprehend exactly the instrument or market they are trading. Remember that in commodity futures trading, you are using a small amount of money (i.e., margin) to control the futures contract, which controls the underlying trading asset.

One way to become familiar with natural gas, as well as other energy markets, is to visit the New York Mercantile Exchange web site (http://www.NYMEX.com). For example, the description (entitled "Henry Hub Natural Gas") featured on the next page comes from the NYMEX web site.

The next step is to understand what you are controlling. The NYMEX web site offers traders access to the specifications of whatever contract you are trading, providing additional information on the product—say, natural gas. For example, the site would clue you in to the fact that each $1 move in natural gas is equal to $10,000. That is a lot of money. So if natural gas is trading at $6, this would represent a $60,000 contract; if natural gas is trading at $10.50, it's a $105,000 contract. At the time of this writing, natural gas (symbol: NGF) is trading at $6.06, which means that one futures contract would control $60,600 of natural gas. This price fluctuates second by second as traders buy and sell and supply and demand drives prices up and down.

Henry Hub Natural Gas

Natural gas accounts for almost a quarter of U.S. energy consumption, and the NYMEX Division natural gas futures contract is widely used as a national benchmark price. The futures contract trades in units of 10,000 million British thermal units (mmBtu). The price is based on delivery at the Henry Hub in Louisiana, the nexus of 16 intra- and interstate natural gas pipeline systems that draw supplies from the region's prolific gas deposits. The pipelines serve markets throughout the U.S. East Coast, the Gulf Coast, the Midwest, and up to the Canadian border. An options contract and calendar spread options contracts provide additional risk management opportunities.

Two financially settled natural gas (HH and HP) contracts are available for trading on the CME Globex system. The HH contract settles on the same date as the physically delivered NG contract, and HP is a penultimate contract. Both contracts are listed for 72 months.

The spread between natural gas futures and electricity futures—the spark spread—can be used to manage price risk in the power markets.

Because of the volatility of natural gas prices, a vigorous basis market has developed in the pricing relationships between Henry Hub and other important natural gas market centers in the continental United States and Canada. The exchange makes available for trading a series of basis swap futures contracts that are quoted as price differentials between approximately 30 natural gas pricing points and Henry Hub. The basis contracts trade in units of 2,500 mmBtu on the NYMEX ClearPort trading platform. Transactions can also be consummated off-exchange and submitted to the exchange for clearing via the NYMEX ClearPort clearing web site as an exchange of futures for physicals or exchange of futures for swap transactions.

The NYMEX miNY natural gas futures contract, designed for investment portfolios, is the equivalent of 2,500 mmBtu of natural gas, 25 percent of the size of a standard futures contract. The contract is available for trading on the CME Globex electronic trading platform and clears through the New York Mercantile Exchange clearinghouse.

Smart Trader Tip

Although seasonal and other patterns may have occurred in the past, this does not guarantee in any way that these seasonal patterns will occur in the future. No representation is being made that the seasonal patterns described here will recur in the future.

My Favorite Natural Gas Pattern

There is one pattern I've seen occur year after year: a spike in natural gas prices that always comes when it gets cold in winter. As we get closer to spring, natural gas prices drop quickly. This pattern is pretty consistent. The main question is how high will it spike and how low it will go? Figure 12.4 shows a monthly chart of natural gas. Can you see a pattern?

The chart in Figure 12.4 shows us that at the end of each year, prices go up; at the beginning of the next year, prices go down. Some years the prices go higher than others and some years the prices go lower. However, all in all, the winter seasonal pattern is consistently visible just by eyeballing the charts. Let's break this down into a smaller time frame. The weekly chart of natural gas is shown in Figure 12.5, which is the time frame I prefer to use to spot patterns.

Figure 12.5 shows a distinct natural gas pattern of a jump in the August/September time frame and then a steep fall in price at the end of the year as traders start looking forward to the spring. Traders typically look ahead a few months (unless there are periods of extreme cold and heat, and then they think in the present). However, you can see the distinct oscillations of the prices as they swing up and down in natural gas futures traded at the NYMEX.

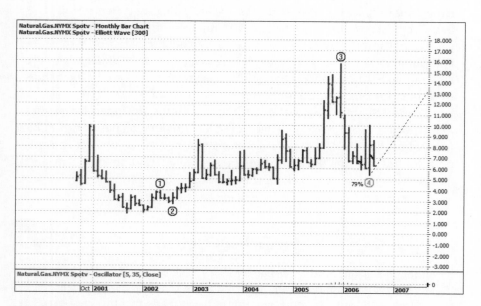

FIGURE 12.4 Natural gas monthly price chart.
Source: ProfitSource.

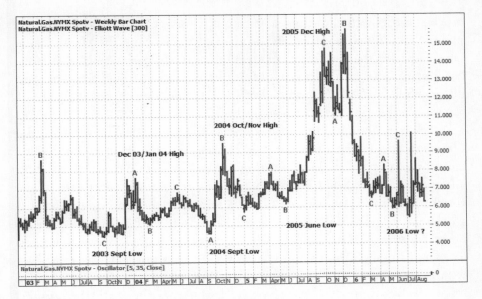

FIGURE 12.5 Natural gas weekly bar chart.
Source: ProfitSource.

Soybeans by Season

Soybeans are one of the most widely known and heavily traded of all physical commodities. A soybean contract can be bought and sold at the Chicago Board of Trade; a single contract represents 5,000 bushels of soybeans. As a result of this contract size, a one-cent move in the price of soybean futures represents a fluctuation of $50. So, for example, if soybeans rise in price from 500 to 510, this implies an increase from $5.00 a bushel to $5.10 a bushel. Since each penny represents a contract value of $50, then this move would result in a profit of $500 (10 cents times $50 a cent) to a trader holding a long position, and a $500 loss to a trader holding a short position.

As a physical commodity, soybeans that have already been harvested can be stored for a period of time. Ultimately, however, they must be grown anew and harvested every year. In the United States, soybean seeds are typically planted in most soil in May and June. In July, August, and September, the plants will bloom. In late September, the soybean plants begin to mature. Between mid-October and November, the soybeans will be ready to be harvested. As you would likely guess, the weather has a large impact on the quantity and quality of soybeans that grow and are harvested in any given year. Many things can go wrong in the process. If there is too much moisture, this can delay planting and make the planting process more difficult, thus affecting the quantity of beans that get planted. Too much hot weather can damage the soil and the plants themselves. Locally, the level of insects and/or weeds that grow among the soybean plants can also adversely affect the quantity of soybeans that are ultimately harvested. Any and all of these factors can impact the price of soybeans either positively or negatively.

Like any commodity, soybean prices ultimately fluctuate based on the supply and demand for the commodity itself. As a result, anything that increases the supply (i.e., ideal planting and growing conditions followed by a bountiful harvest) will ultimately serve to depress soybean prices. Conversely, anything that might decrease the supply (poor planting conditions, a drought, or unseasonably wet weather) will serve to inflate the price of beans. So at first blush, it seems pretty straightforward. Good weather leads to a large supply of beans and thus lower soybean prices. Conversely, bad weather leads to a smaller supply and higher soybean prices. So a trader might easily assume that by keeping track of the weather as it relates to the growth of soybeans, he or she can profit from the resulting boom or bust.

But there is a catch: Financial markets tend to act as discounting mechanisms. This simply means that market prices tend to anticipate what is likely to unfold in the future. Thus, the trader who waits for all of the relevant fundamental information to become apparent before making a decision runs the risk of missing the actual price movement that that fundamental information portends.

This is surprisingly true in the soybean market—for while the plants don't go into the ground until May or June, as it turns out, the most reliable rally of the year typically occurs during the months of February, March, and April. It is during these months that concerns for the upcoming growing season tend to run highest. This is the time of year when concerns about a small harvest manifest themselves among users and producers. As a result of these concerns, a lot of buying typically takes place in an effort to hedge against a bad year for soybean crops. Figures 12.6 and 12.7 illustrate this phenomenon during 2004 and 2005.

On the flip side, by the time the actual crop conditions are readily apparent, most of the anticipatory buying done to hedge against higher bean prices has already taken place. As a result, and as is the case with any market, once the buying dries up, prices typically have nowhere to go but down. In the soybean market, this unwinding typically takes place in the summer months. Over the past 30 years, soybean prices have registered consistent net declines in price during the months of July and September.

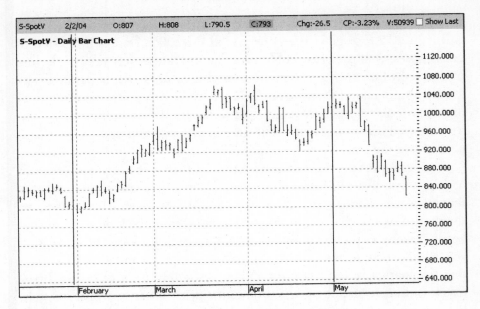

FIGURE 12.6 Soybeans, February through April 2004.

Source: ProfitSource.

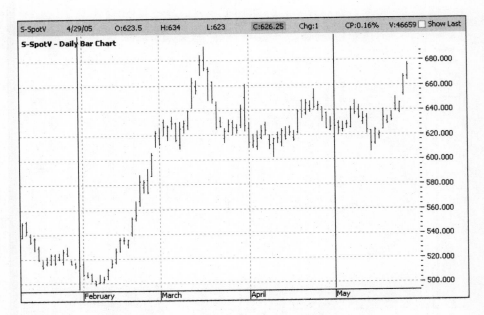

FIGURE 12.7 Soybeans, February through April 2005.

Source: ProfitSource.

Figure 12.8 displays the July through September period for 2004, and Figure 12.9 displays the same period for 2005. Traders interested in utilizing seasonal patterns should note that markets rarely rally or decline in a straight line during seasonally favorable or unfavorable periods. The key is to understand that the tendency to move in a given direction during a particular time frame exists and to focus on playing that market in the expected direction during that time in order to take advantage of and profit from the seasonal trend.

One important thing to keep in mind is that seasonal patterns can have a strong historical tendency to work, but there is still no guarantee that they will work in any given year. So, just because it happens to be the month of March does not mean that you should be long a ton of soybeans. Likewise, just because it happens to be July does not mean that you should take a huge short position in soybeans and simply assume that the market has to head lower. The best application of seasonal patterns is often to use them in conjunction with other forms of analysis. For example, if soybeans are starting to break or are clearly trending lower as July or September approaches, then it makes a great deal more sense to play the short side aggressively than it does if bean prices are screaming higher at that time.

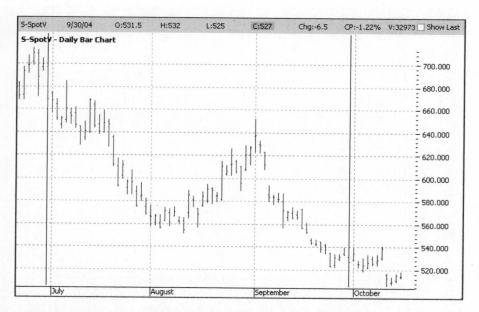

FIGURE 12.8 Soybeans, July through September 2004.
Source: ProfitSource.

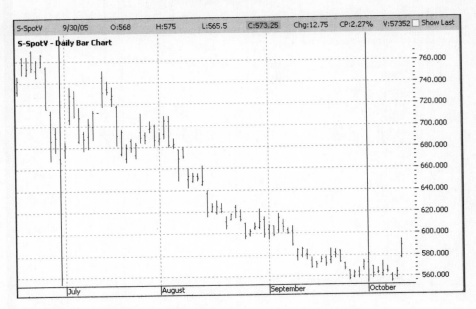

| S-SpotV | 9/30/05 | O:568 | H:575 | L:565.5 | C:573.25 | Chg:12.75 | CP:2.27% | V:57352 ☐ Show Last |

FIGURE 12.9 Soybeans, July through September 2005.
Source: ProfitSource.

A Seasonal Play in Live Cattle

Live cattle is another market that has displayed a definite seasonal pattern over the years. In a nutshell, cattle prices have displayed a clear tendency to decline in the spring months and to rally in the late summer and fall. This appears to be related in some ways to the fact that the amount of cattle raised in a given year correlates inversely to the price of corn. Corn is a primary source of feed for live cattle; thus, if the anticipation is that corn prices will be very high, farmers have a disincentive to raise an abundance of cattle, since the more cattle they raise the more corn they must buy in order feed their herds. Conversely, as corn prices fall, or if there is an expectation that corn prices will be low, then farmers have a greater incentive to raise more cattle, since their production costs will be less thanks to the lower price of corn.

Fears of sharply higher corn prices tend to start abating as the key planting season of spring and early summer comes to an end. As these fears abate, then concerns of higher levels of cattle being raised increase, thus depressing live cattle prices. As a result, live cattle prices have displayed a strong tendency to decline during the April-through-June time frame. This three-month period has witnessed a decline in live cattle

FIGURE 12.10   Live cattle, April through June 2005.
Source: ProfitSource.

prices in 19 of the past 23 years. The chart in Figure 12.10 displays the action of the August 2005 live cattle contract between the end of March and the end of June in 2005.

On the opposite side of the coin, live cattle has also shown a definite bullish seasonal pattern over the years. The most reliably bullish time of the year for live cattle is between the months of August and November. This contiguous four-month period has witnessed an advance in live cattle prices in 18 of the past 22 years since 1983. The chart in Figure 12.11 displays the rally that occurred between August and November of 2005.

To better appreciate the potential profits and risks associated with seasonal patterns, take a look at the charts that appear in Figures 12.12 and Figure 12.13. The chart in Figure 12.12 depicts an equity curve displaying the growth of equity achieved by trading one contract of live cattle and holding a long position each year between July 31 and November 31, since 1983.

The chart in Figure 12.13 depicts an equity curve displaying the growth of equity achieved by trading one contract of live cattle and holding a short position each year between March 31 and June 31, since 1983.

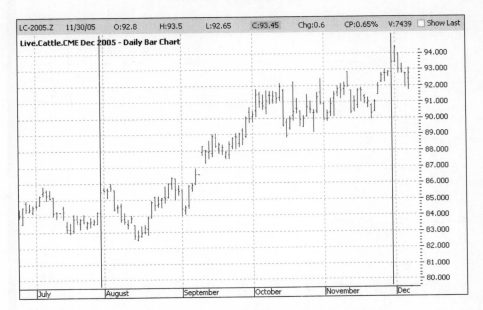

FIGURE 12.11 Live cattle, August through November 2005.

Source: ProfitSource.

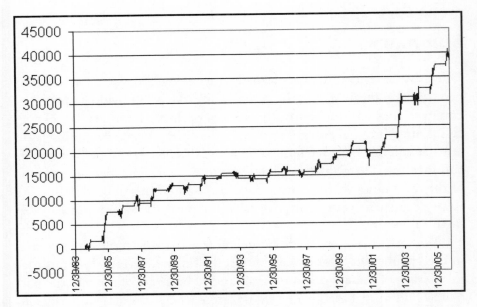

FIGURE 12.12 Equity curve for live cattle holding a long position during August through November.

Source: ProfitSource.

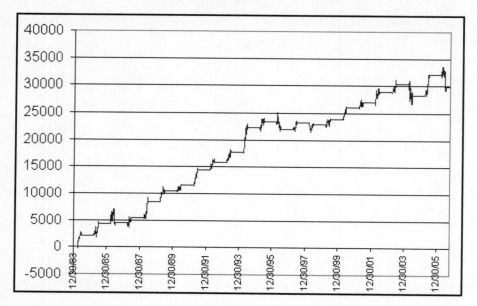

FIGURE 12.13 Equity curve for live cattle holding a short position during April through June.

Source: ProfitSource.

Summary

Once you have identified a seasonal pattern, you'll need to analyze how best to take advantage of the opportunity. Many individuals prefer to employ a limited number of strategies to optimize their chances of success. I am a firm believer that specialization is the key to becoming good at what you do. Doctors and lawyers specialize, so why shouldn't traders and investors? Specializing enables you to become an expert using some of the techniques we have mentioned throughout this book. Finding the strategies that fit your comfort level will typically lead to a much better financial result.

Unfortunately, there are no guarantees that the trends highlighted in this chapter will continue to exist in the future. Nevertheless, it is useful to learn of these types of patterns and to be aware of them as the particular bullish or bearish time frame approaches. It is also important to determine why a particular seasonal pattern seems to work, such as the ones identified in this chapter. If there is a solid basis for the pattern to exist (impending cold weather, as in the case of natural gas; fear of a poor harvest, as in the case of soybeans; or fear of high production costs, as in the case of live cattle), then you should pay much more attention to that pattern than to something that seems to occur for no explainable reason.

Key Summary Points

1. Many commodities are affected by weather and by the influence of other commodities that may be affected by the weather. As a result, the influence of seasonal patterns in various commodity markets has a solid fundamental underpinning.

2. Remember that in almost all cases, seasonal factors that decrease the supply of a given commodity will also serve to raise the price of that commodity. Conversely, seasonal factors that increase the supply of a given commodity will serve to lower the price of that commodity.

3. When identifying seasonal patterns, not only must you determine whether a given catalyst is going to be bullish or bearish for a given commodity, you must also determine when investors are likely to react to this catalyst. Cold temperatures are bullish for natural gas prices; however, the time to anticipate impending cold weather appears to be during the August/September time frame. Ironically, once the truly cold weather actually arrives, natural gas prices typically top out.

4. The same type of anticipatory buying and selling occurs in several grain markets, including soybeans. For example, bean prices tend to rally in late winter/early spring, even before the year's crops are planted. Additionally, bean prices tend to top out and head lower just when the hottest weather typically arrives. Most traders intuitively expect the opposite, thus giving the seasonally aware trader a distinct advantage.

5. Some commodities have established definite tendencies to rally or decline during a given time of year. For example, live cattle prices typically decline in the spring months and rally in late summer and into fall. While nothing is ever guaranteed, savvy traders should be aware of such trends and should examine ways to exploit any such advantages.

Chapter 13

Brokers and the Online Revolution

Finding the right broker is an essential part of becoming a successful commodities trader because the broker represents an important link between you and the financial markets. Once an order is entered, the broker sends it to the appropriate marketplace. Obviously, traders want an honest and reliable firm to handle this important part of the trading process. There is a lot of trust involved in this relationship.

While finding the right broker is important, it isn't always easy. There are hundreds of different firms to choose from. The fees or commissions will vary from one to the next. Some offer tools such as charting, research, and analysis. Others simply focus on providing cheap execution of orders and not much else. How do you find the right broker? This chapter is designed to help you narrow your search and find the right one.

Ask Your Friends

I really can't recommend any one broker. While there are clearly some that are better than others, without knowing you and your experience, goals, and financial resources, it is impossible to offer any sort of specific recommendation. While remaining broker neutral, I'll try to give you some of the facts and information that might help make your decision a bit easier.

Obviously, most brokerage firms try to win your business. These companies make their profits by generating commissions from trades and charging fees. The more customers who open accounts and trade, the more revenues and the greater the profits these firms can generate. It would be highly unlikely that one brokerage firm would recommend the products and services of another, even if it might be in your best interest.

So if we can't recommend a broker and the brokerage firms themselves are probably not the most objective sources of information, where can new commodities traders turn when looking for suggestions?

One place to start is with people you know. Do you have a friend who trades commodities? Does your brother-in-law? How about that loudmouth coworker who is always bragging about his pork belly trades? If you know people who are already trading commodities, ask them which broker they use. It is important that the person be someone you trust—and someone who gives convincing signs of being an intelligent life form.

If you don't know anyone who trades commodities, you might check with a firm that you have done business with in the past. Some of the larger stock brokerage firms also offer commodities trading. Obviously, you should be happy with the firm's performance in the past before asking whether they want your commodities business. In short, if you are happy with your stock brokerage firm, ask them if they also trade commodities!

It is important to note that commodities and futures are regulated separately from stocks. Before making a transaction in the futures or options markets, traders must first open an account through a Series 3 licensed commodity brokerage representative. Stockbrokers require a Series 7 license. So if your brokerage firm offers both stock and futures trading, you might need to open a separate account to begin trading. If you already trade stocks, stock options, or index options, ask your brokerage firm if they offer trading in commodities and futures. If so, can you get an information package and the documents necessary to open an account?

Smart Trader Tip

Brokers are required to pass licensing exams before buying or selling investment securities on behalf of customers. However, obtaining a license does not necessarily mean that the broker has the knowledge and skills to deliver profitable results. The exams require a certain level of knowledge regarding investments, but not the ability to trade or invest successfully. Brokers who consistently deliver solid results will have a big book of business and will be able to give you names of satisfied customers.

Another place to look for information on brokerage firms is on the web sites of the exchanges. The Chicago Mercantile Exchange (CME) and the Chicago Board of Trade (CBOT) have free find-a-broker search tools on their web sites (www.cme.com and www.cbot.com). These systems allow users to search for commodities brokers based on a specific criterion such as location or type of commodity traded. The net result is a list of brokerage firms that can be considered for closer examination.

If you want to deal with a live broker and not just trade online, find a broker in your area and set up an appointment to meet him or her in person. It is a good idea to call first and arrange a meeting because a good broker will almost always be busy, especially during market hours. Ask the broker to send you an information packet about himself/herself and the company if you need more to go on. Ask for references and be sure to check them out prior to the meeting.

Many traders today don't use the services of a live broker. Instead, orders are entered electronically using web-based or stand-alone electronic trading platforms. However, during system or power outages, traders sometimes need to pick up the phone and talk to a live broker. When the trade is placed through a live broker, it is called a *broker-assisted* trade. Some online firms charge extra for the assistance of a broker. If this is important to you, ask potential brokerage firms what their policy is regarding broker-assisted trades.

> **broker-assisted**
> when the trade is placed through a live broker, it is called a *broker-assisted* trade. Some online firms charge extra for the assistance of a broker.

Remember, you are looking to establish a long-term and successful relationship with the broker. Conduct the interview carefully and make sure that the broker is someone you can trust. There must be a high comfort level. You might need to contact several brokers before you find one who is right for you.

Assess Your Needs

Once you have a list of firms, you can find a lot of information about their products and services on their web sites. This includes important information such as commissions and fees, margin requirements, and minimum deposits. If you trade often, the cost of each trade will have an important effect on results.

However, commissions and fees are not the only consideration when searching for a broker. Each trader has a different set of needs.

Some trade very often and require little help from the brokerage firm. These active traders often seek low commissions or fees and speedy execution, but not much else. Others are less concerned with commissions and want more help from their brokerage firm; this might include assistance from a live broker, research, and charts. Find out what the commissions are before opening an account and keep in mind that sometimes firms will give breaks to traders who execute a large number of trades during each month or quarter.

Smart Trader Tip

Many traders are lured to a brokerage firm because of low costs or commissions. A commission is the amount a trader pays to buy or sell a security. Over the years, competition has forced commissions to historical lows. However, while low commissions can help boost returns, other factors are equally important. For example, getting good execution, or *fills*, can affect long-term results as well. Talking to other traders and asking around can help you find a broker who offers both low commissions and good execution.

fills

"getting filled" is a term traders sometimes use when talking about the execution of an order. For example, if XYZ Futures were bought at 1,500, the trader was filled at 1,500. Traders want to get good fills on the orders because they want trades executed at the best prices possible.

What types of products are traded? If your trading involves mostly exchange-traded funds (ETFs) or stocks, then you don't need the services of a futures or commodities broker. Instead, an account with a stock brokerage firm (which you might already have) will fit your needs just fine. A review of various stock brokerage firms that offer online trading is available in the Broker Review section at www.optionetics.com. However, as noted earlier, if you are trading futures and futures options, you must first open an account through a Series 3 licensed commodity brokerage representative.

It makes sense to do business with a live broker when you are looking for advice, especially in the early stages of your trading career. If so, don't trust just anyone. Find out as much as you can about that individual. Try to get referrals and check their track record. If they guarantee that you will never lose money, run away. No reputable broker can guarantee success all of the time.

Most of the students we teach don't rely on recommendations from others, but do their own homework instead. The brokerage firm merely executes orders. These do-it-yourself investors need little hand-holding or advice, but spend more of their time doing research and finding good trading opportunities. These traders also do most of their trading online and pay less in commissions or fees.

So a final consideration is what, if any, type of online trading does the firm offer? Another way to look at it is to ask what type of firm you are dealing with.

Full-Service Brokerage

A full-service brokerage firm is a type of firm that offers a wide range of services including advice, research, and market data. A representative is assigned to your account and might contact you with investment suggestions or ideas. So the trading strategies you implement are often a joint effort between you and the representative. Transaction fees will generally be higher because of the extra information and attention. But if you're new to commodities and futures trading, you might feel more comfortable with the extra attention that a full-service brokerage offers.

Introducing Broker (IB)

An introducing broker is a type of full-service broker, usually specializing in futures, that executes orders on the commodity exchanges through another well-known and established firm. The established firm is a clearing member of one of the commodities exchanges. Although the introducing broker might not have a familiar name, it can provide the same attention to your account as a full-service firm. So if you find an introducing broker that seems to offer the products and services you need, find out more about the firm, including the name of its clearing firm. This can be a practical solution, especially in smaller cities where large firms do not yet have a presence.

Discount Brokerage

If you make all of your own decisions, you probably want to use a discount brokerage firm. This type of firm allows you to make all the decisions about how to trade your account and then executes the trades on your behalf. You only need to go online or call the firm, place an order, and then the firm executes the trade. You do all of the research and strategy selection. However, most discount firms do offer some information, research, and charts. Nevertheless, support is limited, but the commissions and fees should be less.

Understanding Margin

A final consideration when evaluating brokers is margin. We have covered the topic more than once in the book and apologize for the repetition. But it is extremely important! Margin with futures is different from margin with stocks. When buying stocks, traders can borrow money from their broker. The amount that is used to pay for stocks (minus the money that is borrowed) is known as margin. The government sets the margin rate for stock trades (which is currently 50 percent).

In futures, however, the initial margin is not partial payment for the product at all. It is a good faith amount deposited to ensure performance in the event that the market moves against the trader the next day. In effect, the margin is an estimate of a maximum possible next day's losses, which is escrowed in advance. Since there is no way to anticipate market direction, both buyers and sellers post margin. The process instills confidence among traders because if the market moves in their favor, those gains come directly and immediately from the opposite side of the market.

If the market makes a big move against the trader after money from the brokerage account moves through the exchange to the other side of the trade, there may not be enough left in the account to incur any potential losses on the following trading day. If so, the trader will get a *margin call*, which requires that more money be deposited in the account or the position is closed. Maintenance margin is the amount of initial margin that must be maintained for that position before a margin call is generated.

Table 13.1 shows some examples of initial and maintenance margin requirements. Let's consider an example here to illustrate how it works. The initial margin required to buy or sell a specific commodity contract is $1,000 and the maintenance margin requirement is $750. If losses on the open positions reduce the funds in the account to $700, the account will receive a margin call for the $300 difference. This would restore the account value to the initial $1,000. If the excess funds are not in the account, that position creates a margin call—then the account holder needs to either immediately add funds or have the position liquidated to cover the margin call.

Table 13.1   Initial and Maintenance Margin Requirements

	Initial	Maintenance
Livestock		
Feeder cattle	$1,350	$1,000
Live cattle	$945	$700
Lean hogs	$1,080	$800
Frozen bellies	$1,620	$1,200
Foods/Fibers/Softs		
Cocoa	$840	$600
Coffee "C"	$2,520	$1,800
Cotton #2	$1,400	$1,000
Orange juice FCOJ	$980	$700
Sugar #11	$1,400	$1,000
Lumber	$1,650	$1,100
Metals		
Copper	$8,100	$6,000
Gold	$3,038	$2,363
Platinum	$2,700	$2,000
Palladium	$2,700	$2,000
Silver/5,000 oz	$9,000	$6,750
Energies		
Crude oil	$4,725	$3,500
Unleaded gasoline	$8,100	$6,000
Heating oil	$6,750	$5,000
Natural gas	$12,150	$9,000

Margin is a double-edged sword. It can give traders great leverage when trading commodities and it can also expose traders to greater risk since large amounts of commodities can be controlled with relatively little capital. It is an extremely important concept to understand before trading. Make sure that you find out any potential brokerage firm's policy with respect to margin calls and have them walk you through some examples.

The Online Trading Revolution

In more than 20 years of trading, I have seen an incredible shift in how you, as an investor/trader, can participate in the commodities markets.

Commodities have been trading for a very long time. There is some evidence that commodities trading occurred as long as thousands of years ago in China and Japan. Many records point to rice as being the first commodity market to trade. However, there was trading in live animals such as sheep or goats as well as agricultural commodities such as wheat and other food-related products. Some of the rules that were used many years ago have made their way into trading in the modern world of pit-traded commodities.

In the United States, commodities and futures trading started in the mid-nineteenth century. The CBOT was founded in 1848 by 82 merchants in Chicago, Illinois. Shortly thereafter, in 1849, the first futures contracts—then referred to as *to arrive contracts*—came into use. These contracts were for the future delivery of flour, timothy seed, and hay. Futures trading was primarily pit traded until 1998, which was the year that the CBOT began a transition to its electronic trading platform via an agreement with the CME to provide clearing and services to electronic trading of its products. To further increase the CBOT's move into electronic trading, in August 2006, the exchange opened side-by-side trading for CBOT agricultural products. It was historic because now the electronic markets would trade while the trading pits were open. That, in turn, would open the markets to many players worldwide who were interested in the electronic trading of the CBOT products. (Additional information can be found on the CBOT's website at www.CBOT.com. It's a fantastic site for getting information on the commodity markets.)

Smart Trader Tip

Side-by-side trading refers to the simultaneous trading of commodities and futures contracts in a trading pit occupied by floor traders who make a market to buy and sell, as has been done over hundreds, if not thousands, of years, along with the computer trading of the same contracts with a matching system of buyers and sellers. This allows for market buyers and sellers to meet through more than one way, and it is projected that this will allow the commodity markets to gain broader acceptance and accessibility worldwide.

The platform that the CBOT uses for its electronic trading is known as e-CBOT. According to its web site, "The Chicago Board of Trade selected LIFFE CONNECT as the e-cbot trading engine because of its robust functionality and superior technical architecture. Functionally, it will give e-cbot enhanced trading capabilities, better reporting, more flexible matching algorithms, and the ability to accommodate anticipated future trading needs."

The trading of electronic contracts is a highly sophisticated order-matching system that requires high speed as well as accuracy to ensure that market participants get the fairest price execution. Commodities trading on the CBOT electronic platform include those shown in Tables 13.2 and 13.3.

		Futures Symbol	Futures Hours	Options Symbol	Options Hours	Clearing Code
TABLE 13.2　Agricultural Products						
Product						
Corn	Open auction	C	9:30 A.M.– 1:15 P.M.	CY/PY	9:30 A.M.– 1:15 P.M.	C
	Electronic	ZC	6:30 P.M.– 6:00 A.M. and 9:30 A.M.– 1:15 P.M.	OZCC/ OZCP	6:32 P.M.– 6:00 A.M.	C
Mini-size corn	Open auction	YC	9:30 A.M.– 1:45 P.M.	n/a	n/a	YC
	Electronic	n/a	n/a	n/a	n/a	
Soybeans	Open auction	S	9:30 A.M.– 1:15 P.M.	CZ/PZ	9:30 A.M.– 1:15 P.M.	S
	Electronic	ZS	6:31 P.M.– 6:00 A.M. and 9:30 A.M.– 1:15 P.M.	OZSC/ OZSP	6:33 P.M.– 6:00 A.M.	S
Mini-size soybeans	Open auction	YK	9:30 A.M.– 1:45 P.M.	n/a	n/a	YK
	Electronic	n/a	n/a	n/a	n/a	
Soybean oil	Open auction	BO	9:30 A.M.– 1:15 P.M.	OY/OZ	9:30 A.M.– 1:15 P.M.	07
	Electronic	ZL	6:31 P.M.– 6:00 A.M. and 9:30 A.M.– 1:15 P.M.	OZLC/ OZLP	6:33 P.M.– 6:00 A.M.	07
Soybean meal	Open auction	SM	9:30 A.M.– 1:15 P.M.	MY/MZ	9:30 A.M.– 1:15 P.M.	06
	Electronic	ZM	6:31 P.M.– 6:00 A.M. and 9:30 A.M.– 1:15 P.M.	OZMC/ OZMP	6:33 P.M.– 6:00 A.M.	06

(continued)

				TABLE 13.2 (continued)		
Product		Futures Symbol	Futures Hours	Options Symbol	Options Hours	Clearing Code
South American soybeans	Open auction	BS	9:00 A.M.–1:15 P.M.	n/a	n/a	30
	Electronic	ZK	6:31 P.M.–6:00 A.M. and 9:00 A.M.–1:15 P.M.	n/a	n/a	30
Soybean crush	Open auction	BCX	n/a	BC/BP	9:30 A.M.–1:15 P.M.	n/a
	Electronic	n/a	n/a	n/a	n/a	
Wheat	Open auction	W	9:30 A.M.–1:15 P.M.	WY/WZ	9:30 A.M.–1:15 P.M.	W
	Electronic	ZW	6:32 P.M.–6:00 A.M. and 9:30 A.M.–1:15 P.M.	OZWC/OZWP	6:34 P.M.–6:00 A.M.	W
Mini-sized wheat	Open auction	YW	9:30 A.M.–1:45 P.M.	n/a	n/a	YW
	Electronic	n/a	n/a	n/a	n/a	
Ethanol	Open auction	AC	9:30 A.M.–1:15 P.M.	n/a	n/a	EH
	Electronic	ZE	6:36 P.M.–6:00 A.M. and 9:30 A.M.–1:15 P.M.	n/a	n/a	EH
Oats	Open auction	O	9:30 A.M.–1:15 P.M.	OO/OV	9:30 A.M.–1:15 P.M.	O
	Electronic	ZO	6:33 P.M.–6:00 A.M. and 9:30 A.M.–1:15 P.M.	OZOC/OZOP	6:35 P.M.–6:00 A.M.	O
Rough rice	Open auction	RR	9:30 A.M.–1:15 P.M.	RRC/RRP	9:30 A.M.–1:15 P.M.	14
	Electronic	ZR	6:33 P.M.–6:00 A.M. and 9:30 A.M.–1:15 P.M.	OZRC/OZRP	6:35 P.M.–6:00 A.M.	14

Source: Chicago Board of Trade web site www.cbot.com.

		TABLE 13.3 Metals				
Product		Futures Symbol	Futures Hours	Options Symbol	Options Hours	Clearing Code
100-oz. gold	Open auction	n/a	n/a	n/a	n/a	
	Electronic	ZG	6:16 P.M.– 4:00 P.M.	OZGC/ OZGP	6:18 P.M.– 4:00 P.M.	38
CBOT mini-size gold	Open auction	n/a	n/a	n/a	n/a	
	Electronic	YG	6:16 P.M.– 4:00 P.M.	n/a	n/a	63
5,000-oz. silver	Open auction	n/a	n/a	n/a	n/a	
	Electronic	ZI	6:16 P.M.– 4:00 P.M.	OZIC/ OZIP	6:18 P.M.– 4:00 P.M.	39
CBOT mini-size silver	Open auction	n/a	n/a	n/a	n/a	
	Electronic	YI	6:16 P.M.– 4:00 P.M.	n/a	n/a	61

Electronic Trading at the CME and Globex

The leader in the computerization of trading is another Chicago-based commodity and futures exchange, the Chicago Mercantile Exchange (www.CME.com). As with the CBOT, anyone interested in commodities and futures trading should dig into the web site, as there's a great deal of useful information to be found there. On June 25, 1992, the CME launched the first global electronic platform, Globex, used by many of the exchanges to electronically trade a large number of their products. Globex is a matching system that allows both professional traders and nonprofessionals to trade. The CME made Globex access available to everyone in the year 2000. As long as you have an account open with a futures commission merchant (FCM) or introducing broker (IB) and you have access to a CME Globex authorized system to trade, you can set sail and start trading.

> ### Smart Trader Tip
>
> A futures commission merchant (FCM) is an organization or individual licensed by the Commodity Futures Trading Commission (CFTC). For the readers who have stock accounts, FCMs are similar to stockbrokers, as they usually hold your money in an account for your benefit. You can check with the CFTC (www.CFTC.gov) for additional licensing requirements and regulations. The CFTC is the governmental body that regulates the futures industry, and it's a great resource for all commodity traders.
>
> An introducing broker (IB) is an individual or an organization that makes an introduction to a licensed FCM that will typically pay a fee to the IB from the fees that are earned. IBs may service your account, but they do not hold your funds for trading.

What Is Globex?

Globex, in its simplest form, is a fully computerized order-matching system for buyers and sellers. Unlike the trading pits that use the open outcry system (whereby traders communicate by yelling out orders and using their own version of sign language), Globex has an electronic format where traders place their buy and sell orders in an order queue. They are then matched with another party, in an anonymous manner, and the trade is reported back to the trader (see Table 13.4).

Globex trading allows the trader to trade in a number of commodity and noncommodity-related products. Noncommodity-based products include stock index futures, interest-related products, foreign exchange products, and, starting in 2006, even real estate–related products. For a complete listing and description of the products at the CME, visit www.CME.com.

Electronic Trading at the New York Mercantile Exchange

When many people think of commodities, they think of the products that are traded at the New York Mercantile Exchange (otherwise referred to as the NYMEX). The NYMEX lists and trades some of the most popular commodities worldwide including the energy and metal products.

TABLE 13.4 CME Globex Commodities

CME Globex Hours
Scheduled Maintenance
Commodities 4:00–5:00 P.M., Fertilizer 3:15–5:00 P.M., GSCI 4:00–5:00 P.M.

Product	RTH Hours Mon.–Fri. (CST)	Weekday Openings	Sunday/ Holiday Openings	All Closings
CME butter	9:30–13:10			
CME butter options	9:30–13:12			
CME butter spot call	11:05 between 11:07 and 11:21			
CME cash-settled butter		9:30		13:10
CME cheese spot call	10:45 between 10:47 and 11:01			
CME milk class III	9:40–13:10	9:40		13:10
CME milk class III options	9:40–13:12			
CME milk class IV	9:20–13:10			
CME milk class IV options	9:20–13:12			
CME DAP		17:00	17:00	15:15
CME feeder cattle	9:05–13:00	9:05		13:00
CME feeder cattle options	9:05–13:02			
CME frozen pork bellies	9:10–13:00	9:10		13:00
CME frozen pork bellies options	9:10–13:02			
CME lean hogs	9:10–13:00	9:10		13:00
CME lean hogs options	9:10–13:02			
CME live cattle	9:05–13:00	9:05		13:00
CME live cattle options	9:05–13:02			
CME nonfat dry milk	9:25–13:10			
CME nonfat dry milk options	9:25–13:12			
CME nonfat dry milk spot call	10:45 between 10:47 and 11:01 See note.			
CME random-length lumber	9:00–13:05			
CME random-length lumber options	9:00–13:07			
CME UAN		17:00	17:00	15:15
CME urea		17:00	17:00	15:15
CME ethanol		9:05		13:30
CME GSCI	8:45–13:40	14:00	17:00	13:40
CME GSCI Options	8:45–13:40			
CME GSCI excess return		14:00	17:00	13:40

Source: Chicago Mercantile Exchange web site, www.cme.com.

The energy products include crude oil (traded as light sweet crude), natural gas, heating oil, gasoline, electricity, propane, and coal. The metal products include gold, silver, copper, aluminum, platinum, and palladium. These products may be traded in the pits as well as on the Globex platform.

In 2006, the NYMEX also became an exchange committed to allowing its products to be open to traders through Globex and the trading pits. This side-by-side trading allows those traders interested in trading the commodities at the NYMEX to get better access to the market makers and other traders interested in the energy and metals markets. Hence, the year 2006 was a very important landmark for traders desiring to trade electronically; as the NYMEX and other exchanges open the world to electronic trading, it appears to be the mainstay for the future of trading (see Table 13.5).

TABLE 13.5 NYMEX Products Listed on CME Globex	
Full-Size Products *(Physically Settled)* *After-hours trading is available* *Aug 6, 2006 (notice)* *Day trading is available* *Sep 4, 2006 (notice)*	**Full-Size Products** *(Financially Settled)*
Light sweet crude oil futures (CL)	Crude oil financial futures (WS)
Henry Hub natural gas futures (NG)	Heating oil financial futures (BH)
Heating oil futures (HO)	RBOB gasoline financial futures (RT)
RBOB gasoline futures (RB)	Natural gas (penultimate) financial futures (HP)
Propane futures (PN)	Natural gas (last-day) financial futures (HH)
Platinum futures (PL)	Brent crude oil financial futures (BB)
Palladium futures (PA)	
NYMEX Europe Products	**NYMEX miNY Products**
Brent crude oil futures (SC)	NYMEX miNY crude oil futures (QM)
NYMEX Europe miNY Brent Futures (QB)	NYMEX miNY Natural Gas Futures (QG)
Gasoil futures (GR)	NYMEX miNY heating oil futures (QH)
	NYMEX miNY gasoline futures (QU)
	NYMEX miNY platinum futures (PQ)
	NYMEX miNY palladium futures (LQ)

Source: New York Mercantile Exchange, www.NYMEX.com.

Other Products

The previous sections described only three of the worldwide commodity exchanges. As more and more exchanges around the world turn to electronic trading, a greater number of products will be available for you to trade via computer. This will allow you to trade faster and cheaper over time, as the buying and selling through an electronic format is a more efficient and cost-effective way for the exchanges to execute your trades. These efficiencies and the lower cost can then be passed on to you, the trader.

Selecting a Broker to Trade Electronically

Most licensed commodity brokers can provide you with access to electronic trading. You can search for brokers on the Internet and you can go to the commodity exchanges, which also provide links and information on finding brokers. For example, the CME has a search page for brokers by market type (products), location, or broker name. Before opening an account, ask the broker about electronic capabilities to trade commodities as well as commissions charged for executing trades. In this age of electronic trading, commissions keep dropping. This is a highly competitive market in which brokers will compete on commission costs, as execution of orders on electronic platforms will likely be fairly standard.

Noncomputerized Commodities and the Future

Even in this age of computers and computerized trading, there are still some holdout commodity exchanges that do not have their products listed on an electronic platform. Sugar, coffee, and cocoa are three of the commodities that many traders would like to see on a computerized platform, but have not yet been listed for electronic trading. However, with the trend toward computerized trading, it won't be long before these products become available for traders around the world. It only makes sense, as this will allow for more liquidity in the contracts by establishing longer trading hours as well as easy access to traders worldwide.

Summary

The world of trading commodities, futures, and stocks is moving to the computer. It is in your interest as a trader to move in this direction, as trading of commodities is presently a 24/6 market (closed from Friday late afternoon to early evening Sunday). Will trading of commodities become 24/7 one day? More than likely, the answer is yes. No doubt, it is only a matter of time before all commodity and futures products will be traded primarily electronically, given the many benefits such as virtual 24-hour trading, worldwide access, and cost efficiencies, as well as the greater interest of the larger traders and hedge funds to trade electronically as they develop proprietary trading systems.

Finding the right commodities or futures broker is not always easy, but it can be done effectively, given a little focused time and effort. Keep in mind that this should be viewed as an important and long-term relationship that will affect your trading performance. If you are relatively new to trading, then it makes sense to use a full-service broker. If so, make sure to get as many references as possible and choose carefully. If you are a do-it-yourself investor, then look for a reputable firm that offers online tools and research as well as low commissions. Ask your friends and fellow traders whom they choose. Some of the traders we know use some of the firms listed here.

Commodities/Futures Brokers (Examples)

Lind-Waldock
141 W. Jackson Blvd., Chicago, IL
(800) 445-2000
www.lind-waldock.com

Man Financial-Retail Division
440 South La Salle Street, Chicago, IL
(800) 621-3424
www.manfutures.com

Interactive Brokers
Two Pickwick Plaza, Greenwich, CT
(877) 442-2757
www.interactivebrokers.com

R.J. O'Brien
222 South Riverside Plaza, Chicago, IL
(312) 373-5000
www.rjobrien.com

AG Edwards
1 North Jefferson, St. Louis, MO
314-955-3050
www.agedwards.com

Key Summary Points

1. Finding the right broker is an important part of becoming a successful commodities trader.

2. There are several places to turn when beginning a search, including friends, coworkers, and other people you know who already trade commodities.

3. Your stock brokerage firm might also offer commodities trading. If you are happy with them, ask if they do.

4. The Chicago Board of Trade (cbot.com) and the Chicago Mercantile Exchange (cme.com) have find-a-broker features on their web sites.

5. When looking at individual firms, there are several important factors to consider, including commission rates, experience, and execution.

6. A lot of traders use online brokers but like to have the ability to talk to a live broker as well. When a broker executes the trade, it is a broker-assisted trade and will sometimes cost more.

7. While many traders focus on commission costs, getting good fills is equally important.

8. A visit to the brokerage firm's web site will probably get you a lot of information you need, including the minimum amount needed to set up an account, the type of research available, commissions, and margin requirements.

9. Margin is a double-edged sword because it can increase leverage returns, but it also involves more risk.

10. Margin allows traders to take large positions with relatively little capital.

11. Electronic trading has helped smaller traders play on the same field as the big commodities players.

12. The CBOT, the CME, and the NYMEX have been instrumental in developing electronic markets for trading in futures.

13. The trend today is clearly toward computerized and electronic trading, which has made it easier and more cost effective for investors to access the commodities and futures markets.

Chapter 14

Putting It All Together

This book explores both the tremendous rewards and the risks associated with the trading of commodities. The commodity markets are one of the last places that someone who takes the time to learn how these markets work can take a small trading account and achieve incredible financial gains. Yes, there are significant risks and anyone interested in trading the commodity markets needs to be fully aware of these associated financial risks. However, by being aware of these risks, commodity traders can use caution and risk management techniques to successfully trade these exciting markets. Let's face it, we encounter all kinds of risks every day without even recognizing most of them; however, by identifying specific risks, we can endeavor to manage some of them to our benefit.

A number of professional money managers have for many years beat the markets by trading in commodities. While many might think it is pure luck, statistics show that when someone can beat the markets year after year, it's more than luck. The successful money managers have created a systematic approach to beating the markets; a haphazard method could never be that consistent. Hence, in the long run, those who enter the commodity markets in a random manner just dreaming of the financial rewards are more likely to end up on the losing end of the markets. If you take the time to read *The Market Wizards* (by Jack Schwager), you'll see that those very successful traders all felt that managing risk was the most important element contributing to their success. In addition, developing a method that helped them manage their trades in the markets was invaluable. Risk management and effective systematic trading appear to be the most important characteristics of a successful trader in the commodity markets.

Chapter Review

Let's review the book chapter by chapter to see how all of this information fits together. I encourage you to read this book again and again to grasp the breadth of information that has been provided. There is a wealth of information within this text that can assist you in becoming a successful trader in commodities as well as other markets.

Chapter 1: What Is a Commodity?

Chapter 1 provides a comprehensive introduction to the commodity markets. All of us encounter commodities every day—at the gas pump, at the grocery store, heating your home, buying a cup of coffee, and so on. Are these markets important? Definitely! They drive the amount of money you will have in your pocket at the end of each day, week, month, and year. Daily consumption of commodities impacts all of us financially year after year. If you're reading this book, it's obviously time to find a way to profit from this knowledge. Hence, my main objective in this chapter is to perk your interest with just the right amount of information about commodities that you'll be inspired to read the whole book; if you are reading these words, then perhaps I have succeeded.

Chapter 2: How the Commodities Markets Work

The second chapter teaches you how these markets really work. Many individuals enter the commodity markets blindly and do not clearly understand the mechanics of them. You wouldn't drive a car if you didn't know how to start it; turning it on demands understanding what a key is for. Likewise, you have to know why the markets were created, how they trade, and who the participants may be.

Many individuals' first glimpse of the commodity markets comes from television and movies, such as in Eddie Murphy's film *Trading Places*.

That's obviously not enough. Yes, there are plenty of opportunities in trading orange juice futures, but you better know what you're doing and understand why people enter this market, or you'll lose your shirt. True knowledge is power.

Chapter 3: Commodity Trading in the Stock Market

Most individuals get their start in the stock market, hear about the commodity markets, and want to learn more. Chapter 3 explores how some stocks relate to the commodity markets and how to profit from this knowledge. Traders can then take this knowledge and set up trades in the underlying stocks that deal in commodities in one way or another. In sum, Chapter 3 is designed to help you integrate your stock market knowledge with the commodity markets to create a much stronger knowledge base on how they work together. I encourage you to explore the plethora of opportunities that exist in the commodity markets using stocks that deal in commodities.

Chapter 4: Commodity Trading in the Index Markets

The index market is one of the fastest-growing ways for traders to profit in the markets. Chapter 4 introduces the concept of trading index markets using knowledge acquired from the commodity markets. A commodity index is a diversified way to trade in commodities or commodity-related stocks. The largest traders—institutions and hedge funds—like to trade indexes as a way to gain immediate diversification without having to buy a large number of commodities or stocks. This is also why every investor should know about indexes, as it may be one of the best ways to trade in commodities. I highly recommend exploring these markets.

Smart Trader Tip

If you would like to learn a great deal more about the index markets, I recommend picking up a copy of a book I coauthored with Tom Gentile, entitled *The Index Trading Course* (Wiley, 2006). This book offers a wealth of practical information, as well as an in-depth look at the tools and techniques of trading index markets.

Chapter 5: Fundamental Analysis of the Commodities Markets

Chapter 5 explores fundamental analysis and how it can be used to capture profits in the commodity markets. Fundamental analysis can assist traders who seek to gain an edge in the commodity markets—either over the short term or over the long term—by helping them to understand what drives each market. For example, although supply and demand drives inventories of commodities, other factors also make a contribution— such as expected new production and weather. While some traders pick and choose which information they believe will lead to higher profits, many traders miss the boat altogether by ignoring this information completely. Others may be behind in the information flow, giving those who have access to current data an advantage.

In your own trading, it's vital to understand what type of fundamental analysis works best for the markets you want to trade. I recommend investigating the fundamental reports that affect your markets and creating a calendar for the commodities you trade to see how they react to reports as they come out. You can get a lot of this information by visiting the web sites of the commodity exchanges in which you choose to trade.

Chapter 6: Technical Analysis of the Commodities Markets

Chapter 6 explores several technical analysis tools that traders can use to try to capture price movements and make profits in the commodity markets. While a multitude of books have been written about technical analysis, I wrote this chapter to introduce you to some of the techniques I like the best and show you how I recommend employing them.

Some technical analysts exclude all fundamental analysis because they believe that the price of a commodity has the fundamentals already built in; bottom line, they believe that technical analysis is superior to fundamental analysis. My belief is that in the short term, technical trends outweigh fundamentals; however, in the long run, the fundamental trends usually take over. Day traders are purely short-term oriented and may choose not to look at fundamentals. I believe this is a mistake because in any given day a fundamental report might come out that could damage their trading accounts or allow for large profits. Therefore, a good commodity trader will most likely become a hybrid trader, knowledgeable in both fundamental and technical analysis, to gain as much of an advantage as he or she can, especially if trading longer-term positions.

Chapter 7: Elliott Wave Trading for Commodities

Chapter 7 examines one of the most useful technical tools in the trading of commodities: Elliott Wave Theory. Some very successful traders use this technical tool to create significant and consistent profits. If you have never been introduced to Elliot Wave trading, you might think, as you read this chapter, that it is too difficult and technical for you; however, when you break it down, Elliott Wave trading is simply based on five waves. Some waves are better to trade than others, as these waves tend to be more consistent and longer, which usually allows for more profits. I prefer to trade Wave 5s, as they signal reversals and I can then use low-risk and high-reward options strategies, as described in Chapter 8. I have been a reversal trader for many years, especially when there is a strong positive or strong negative catalyst in place. I highly recommend learning as much as you can about Elliott Wave trading, picking a few markets, and seeing how you can employ this technical tool to increase your trading profits in the commodity markets.

Chapter 8: Options Trading in the Commodities Markets

In Chapter 8, I explored my favorite instruments to trade any market: options. I have been teaching options trading throughout the world for more than a decade through Optionetics seminars, books, and CDs. After teaching thousands of people how to use these exciting trading instruments, I am more convinced than ever of the many ways that options can be of benefit to you as a trader. In their simplest form, options are a way to control an asset with less money than actually buying the asset— whether it is a stock or a commodity.

Call options offer traders a way to buy assets with less money, while put options enable traders to sell the underlying commodities or assets. Options can also be sold to create additional income by taking advantage of an option's premium. If you want to become a successful commodities trader, make sure to get to know the options markets relating to the commodities you want to trade. Research the strike prices, the expiration periods, and the seasonal patterns and see if you can devise low-risk, high-reward option strategies to make profits in the commodity markets.

Smart Trader Tip

I have written numerous books and, through Optionetics.com, continue to teach classes on trading options. I suggest you read one of my books, *The Options Course*, to study how options can help you trade successfully. While I have written many others (*The Stock Market Course, The Volatility Course*, and *The Index Trading Course*), this is a great book to help you learn what you need to know to trade options profitably and responsibly in any market.

Chapter 9: Money Management: Staying in the Game

The objective of Chapter 9 is to introduce you to the very important topic of money management. While this may be the last thing most beginning commodity traders want to think about, it could be the most important lesson of all. Perhaps it's just human nature to be more inclined to get excited by creating wealth than by preserving wealth, but it's also one of the biggest mistakes beginning traders, as well as experienced traders, make.

To become a successful trader, it's vital to acquire a basic understanding of money management from the onset of your trading journey. In your quest to develop the skills to create future wealth, you need to make sure you take the appropriate steps to preserve your starting capital as well as wealth captured along the way. Many successful traders admit that it wasn't until they began to pay attention to money management that a very positive turn in their trading occurred.

Chapter 10: Psychology 101: Winning the Mind Game

Chapter 10 takes a look at the important subject of trading psychology. Although I do not have a degree in psychology, after many years of trading my own accounts and teaching thousands of people to trade worldwide, I feel I have earned a virtual PhD in the psychology of trading. In speaking to traders still trying to reach a level of success they feel comfortable with, I often ask what they think is their biggest problem. Many reply that they have yet to feel comfortable as traders and this greatly affects their trading profits.

One of the most important steps to becoming successful is to match your personality to the markets and strategies you use. This is accomplished by performing a detailed inventory of your personality to improve your ability to prevent the market from taking control of your emotions. This is a very difficult thing to do, especially when you are first beginning to trade. You will more than likely feel as though you are on an emotional roller coaster until you reach a level of confidence that comes with trading success. The key is to make consistent profits using limited-risk strategies to gain experience in combination with strong money management techniques.

Chapter 11: Trading Commodity-Related Growth Stocks

Chapter 11 takes a look at commodity-related growth stocks and how you can utilize your knowledge of commodities to make profits. As you begin to learn about various commodity markets, study a few of the companies in your selected areas. By combining your stock market knowledge with your knowledge of these commodities, you can enhance your timing expertise. I recommend using your fundamental and technical analysis knowledge in tandem to hunt for the optimal conditions to structure low-risk and high-return trades. In fact, an effective options strategy can be tailored to take advantage of almost any market condition.

Chapter 12: Seasonal Commodity Patterns

Chapter 12 focuses on seasonal patterns and their effects on commodity markets. Identifying patterns that occur season after season, year after year, enables traders to increase their chances of trading success. As a trader, you can often look at price charts and spot patterns that enable you to make knowledgeable decisions about trading those markets. For example, natural gas is one of my favorite commodity markets. In addition to becoming highly volatile going into the winter months, natural gas is also very volatile in the summer months, thanks to the hurricane season (when hurricanes form, they often move into the Gulf of Mexico, home to the majority of the natural gas production facilities).

While there are a wide variety of seasonal patterns, I recommend finding one really steady pattern and developing effective ways to play this pattern year after year. In learning to spot and profit from seasonal patterns, make sure to explore low-risk and high-profit strategies that use options on futures to benefit from these seasonal patterns.

Chapter 13: Brokers and the Online Revolution

If you are a new trader, Chapter 13 is definitely one of the most important as your choice of brokers is a crucial element in your trading success. Not all brokers are equal by any stretch of the imagination, and finding a broker to meet your particular investment needs can be challenging. There is a multitude of important considerations to be evaluated when choosing a broker. What type of brokerage is it? How does it make money? Does it specialize in one type of investment—such as options or commodities—or does it provide a wide range of services such as credit cards, loans, and other nontrading activities? Commissions and fees also matter. Commissions will generally be higher for full-service brokers who offer specific advice to investors and lower rates for those discount brokers who simply execute buy and sell orders at the lowest cost possible but do not offer any sort of financial advice.

The brokerage industry has changed a lot in recent years. During the late 1990s, as the tech sector boomed and investors turned to online trading rather than traditional firms, the number of online brokerages mushroomed. Today, most online brokers operate as discount brokers. Additionally, advances in computer technology as well as the speed at which exchanges can deliver data to you have changed the investing business forever. Over the many years I have been trading, I always dreamed of the day that this would occur. Although data was available via computer (in a limited way), traders experienced a significant time lag in how long it took to get information. Additionally, the turnaround time to get a trade executed was very slow. Imagine getting an idea, picking up the phone to tell some broker what you want to do, and having to wait for the broker to get a price. If the price is right, then the trade is executed, and then they tell you the final price. This might take all of 30 seconds, but it can seem like a lifetime when the markets are moving fast. These days, thanks to the advent of the Internet, the playing field has leveled for you in relation to large traders, floor traders, market makers, and hedge funds. With *Globex* and *e-cbot* and other electronic platforms, you can trade like a pro at very reasonable costs and lightning speeds. Keep an eye on these technological

Globex
an electronic exchange that offers trading in futures and options. Today, it is available almost 23 hours a day, five days a week.

e-cbot
the electronic trading platform on the Chicago Board of Trade (CBOT) that offers trading in futures on various commodities and financials.

advances, as these are truly revolutionary in nature and will, no doubt, provide you with a multitude of promising trading opportunities.

The Three Steps to Trading Success

Over many years of teaching people to trade, I have learned that the main tendency is to overcomplicate the markets. Many individuals begin trading without any previous exposure to stock, futures, options, or commodity markets. Since they are starting a new career, they want to absorb as much information as possible, as quickly as possible.

Unfortunately, too much information too quickly often leads to a problem I like to call *analysis paralysis*. It encourages traders to look for that perfect trade when everything just lines up and there is no way they can lose. This just doesn't happen too often. If you wait for the moon and the stars to create the perfect pattern, then you'll probably be waiting forever. However, you can put the odds in your favor by using many of the techniques and suggestions in this book.

analysis paralysis
when too much information is taken in, leaving an investor confused and unable to make any sort of investment decision.

Over the years during which I have taught and written numerous books, I have found that trading boils down to essentially three steps:

1. Identifying the opportunity.
2. Selecting the trade.
3. Managing the trade.

Step 1: Identify the Opportunity

The very first step in the commodity markets, or in any market, is to use your knowledge to identify a promising opportunity to capture future profits. Many traders try to make money in a haphazard way and really don't find the right timing to make a trade. It's a lot like a cheetah who can chase down any animal it desires thanks to its amazing speed; however, a cheetah still likes to wait for injured prey to attack. The cheetah, like the trader, is best served by carefully identifying the optimal opportunity for success. Using your knowledge of technical and fundamental analysis will help you find these opportunities.

In addition, some of the greatest opportunities can be found when a catalyst is in place that will likely move the market in one direction or the other. For example, some commodities are heavily influenced by seasonal trends. Weekly and monthly reports are great resources for identifying catalysts. It's important to watch the markets you are interested in trading and create a calendar that notes every time each market trades very fast to find out why this occurred. Identifying the catalyst provides a clue to profiting in a specific market in the future.

Step 2: Select the Trade

The second step in the success cycle is to select the right trading strategy to fit the opportunity you identified in Step 1. This refers to matching the time frame and price ranges of a specific market to the identified opportunity. For example, after having done your fundamental and technical analysis of the crude oil market, you determine that crude oil (trading at $70 a barrel) might drop $5 in price in the next 30 days. To create a successful trade, it's vital to match the market's scenario to the optimal strategy to reap the best chance of making a profit. The time frame in this case is 30 days. The price move is a decline of $5. The combination of these two issues means that you are looking for a bearish strategy that can capture this $5 move for maximum reward with low risk. An analysis of the appropriate strategies finds that buying a put option with an expiration of 60 days is most appropriate under these conditions. While the outcome is never certain, you have created a limited-risk strategy (risk is limited to the cost of the put premium) with limited, but high, profit potential (limited, as the underlying can only fall to zero). While it may take a while, it's important that you do your homework to find the optimal trade. In this case, buying puts on April crude oil futures may give you the best risk and reward at this time.

This is just a simple example of how to match a strategy to an opportunity. If you selected a put that would expire in 10 days, then you wouldn't have enough time until the put expired for the trade to make a profit. Additionally, you have to assess your own time constraints. If you have a nine-to-five job and cannot look at the market all day, it would not be advisable to short a crude oil futures contract, as this would require intense vigilance because the market can quickly make a move against you. Thus, it's important to make sure that you carefully match the strategy to the opportunity by looking at the timing of the trade as well as price projections within a given time frame. In addition, don't forget to use strategies that match your personality for risk, reward, and time availability.

Step 3: Manage the Trade

Once you have selected the strategy for the opportunity, you need to manage the trade through the exit. There are a host of steps you can take to maximize your profits while limiting your risk. This includes many of the steps revealed in Chapter 9 on money management. Take the time to ask yourself the following questions:

- How long will I be in this trade?
- Do I have a profit objective?
- Do I have a stop loss to get me out of the trade if I am wrong?
- Can I adjust the trade and lock in some profits by adding or subtracting new positions?
- Are there any technical or fundamental reasons why I should exit the trade?

The answers to these questions will help you to know when to take profits off the table or exit the trade when you are wrong. Knowing when to exit a trade is just as important as knowing the best time to enter the trade.

Specialization

What is the most important element that makes a trader successful? While this question is nearly impossible to answer, if I had to choose one thing, I would say to find a commodity market in which you wish to specialize. Specializing in one commodity market is not easy for beginning traders. After all, how can you specialize when you really don't know what's out there? Don't you need to test-drive a few markets before finding a specialty? The answer is absolutely yes. Most traders take a while to find the right market to specialize in day after day. However, to become consistently profitable, you need to identify something that gives you an advantage over other traders in that specific market.

So kick a few tires and see what excites you. One way to determine which market to specialize in is to take a look around and find the commodity markets that have the biggest impact in the city or region in which you live. If you live in Texas, the energy markets would be the easy choice. If you live in Kansas, then maybe the wheat markets would work best. If you can get information that others can't readily find, you may have an edge in trading that market. Most important, specialize in markets you can get excited about when you wake up each morning. Loving what you do is the key to excelling at it.

Final Summary

I hope you have learned a great deal from this book, and I hope that one day you will be as excited about trading commodities as I am. Before putting your money at risk, study these chapters carefully and take the time to understand all of the core concepts. While I've provided a summary of each chapter here, ultimately, it is up to you to study, understand the ways to trade the commodities markets, identify opportunities, execute the plan through the best broker, and then adjust the position as needed. Remember, the final goal is to implement the three steps outlined in this chapter: Identify the opportunity, select the trade, and manage the trade.

In addition, I want to stress that risk management and effective systematic trading are two of the most important techniques that successful traders share. In that respect, it is also paramount that you understand your risk tolerance and establish a plan that will limit the stress, in the event that some early trades turn against the trading account. Also, try to find a systematic trading approach that works well on paper before actually putting your hard-earned money on the line.

While it's important to explore a variety of markets, new traders should specialize in one or two markets first. Choose a market that excites you and motivates you to learn more about that commodity. Leverage your previous experience to find markets where you might have unique knowledge—an edge.

Finally, never stop learning. One of the most rewarding aspects of becoming a full-time trader lies in knowing that there is always something new to learn. It is impossible to know everything; the markets are always changing and evolving. Trading is an exciting and financially rewarding journey that requires patience, passion, and perseverance. I sincerely hope this book helps you find your way to a successful career trading commodities.

Appendix

Contract Specifications

Margin Requirements

Strategy Reviews

Additional Reading List

Contract Specifications of Commodities

Contract	Symbol	Exchange	Trading Hours*	Contract Months	Contract Size	Price Quote	Point Value	Minimum Tick
Corn	C	CBOT	9:30–1:15	Mar, May, Jul, Sep, Dec	5,000 bu	c/bu	50.00	1/4 c = $12.50
Dow Jones Index	DJ	CBOT	7:20–3:15	Mar, Jun, Sep, Dec	10 × Index	1 point	10.00	1 pt = $10.00
Gold, Kilo	YG	CBOT	7:20–1:40	Feb, Apr, Jun, Aug, Oct, Dec	33.2 troy ounces	$/oz	33.20	10 c = $3.32
Oats	O	CBOT	9:30–1:15	Mar, May, Jul, Sep, Dec	5,000 bu	c/bu	50.00	1/4 c = $12.50
Rough Rice	RR	CBOT	9:15–1:30	Jan, Mar, May, Jul, Sep, Nov	200,000 lbs	c/cwt	2.00	5 pts = $10.00
Silver	SI	CBOT	7:25–1:35	Mar, May, Jul, Sep, Dec	5,000 troy oz	$/oz	0.005	0.005
Soybean Meal	SM	CBOT	9:30–1:15	Jan, Mar, May, Jul, Aug, Sep, Oct, Dec	100 tons	$/ton	1.00	10 pts = $10.00
Soybean Oil	BO	CBOT	9:30–1:15	Jan, Mar, May, Jul, Aug, Sep, Oct, Dec	60,000 lbs	c/lb	6.00	1 pt = $6.00
Soybeans	S	CBOT	9:30–1:15	Jan, Mar, May, Jul, Aug, Sep, Nov	5,000 bu	c/bu	50.00	1/4 c = $12.50
T-Bonds	US	CBOT	7:20–2:00	Mar, Jun, Sep, Dec	100,000	1/32	31.25	1/32 = $31.25
T-Notes 10-Year	TY	CBOT	7:20–2:00	Mar, Jun, Sep, Dec	100,000	1/32	31.25	.5/32 = $15.63
T-Notes 2-Year	TU	CBOT	7:20–2:00	Mar, Jun, Sep, Dec	100,000	1/32	31.25	.5/32 = $25.63
T-Notes 5-Year	FV	CBOT	7:20–2:00	Mar, Jun, Sep, Dec	100,000	32nds/pt	31.25	.5/32 = $25.63
Wheat	W	CBOT	9:30–1:15	Mar, May, Jul, Sep, Dec	5,000 bu	c/bu	50.00	1/4 c = $12.50
Feeder Cattle	FC	CME	9:05–1:00	Jan, Mar, Apr, Aug, Sep, Oct, Nov	50,000 lbs	$/cwt	5.00	2.5 pts = $12.50
GSCI	GI	CME	7:15–2:15	Feb, Apr, Jun, Aug, Oct, Dec	250 × Index	100ths/pt	2.50	.10 pt = $25
Live Cattle	LC	CME	9:05–1:00	Feb, Apr, Jun, Aug, Oct, Dec	40,000 lbs	$/cwt	4.00	2.5 pts = $10.00
Lean Hogs	LH	CME	9:10–1:00	Feb, Apr, Jun, Jul, Aug, Oct, Dec	40,000 lbs	$/cwt	5.00	2.5 pts = $12.50
Lumber	LB	CME	9:00–1:05	Jan, Mar, May, Jul, Sep, Nov	110,000 ft	$/m/bd ft	1.10	10 pts = $11.00
Milk	DA	CME	8:00–1:10	Feb, Apr, Jun, Jul, Aug, Sep, Nov	50,000 lbs	c/lb	5.00	2.5 pts = $12.50

Name	Symbol	Exchange	Hours	Months	Contract Size	Quote	Tick	Tick Value
Pork Bellies	PB	CME	9:10–1:00	Feb, Apr, May, Jul, Aug	40,000 lbs	c/lb	4.00	2.5 pts = $10.00
S&P 500	SP	CME	8:30–15:15	Mar, Jun, Sep, Dec	250 × S&P 500	100ths/pt	2.5	.10 = $25
E-Mini S&P 500	ES	CME	8:30–15:15	Mar, Jun, Sep, Dec	50 × S&P 500	100ths/pt	0.5	.25 = $12.50
Copper	HG	COMEX	7:10–1:00	Jan, Mar, May, Jul, Sep, Dec	25,000 lbs	c/lb	2.50	5 pts = $12.50
Gold	GC	COMEX	7:20–1:30	Feb, Apr, Jun, Aug, Oct, Dec	100 troy oz	$/oz	1.00	10 pts = $10.00
Silver	SI	COMEX	7:25–1:25	Jan, Mar, May, Jul, Sep, Dec	5,000 troy oz	c/oz	0.50	50 pts = $25
Wheat, Kansas City	KW	KCBT	9:30–1:15	Mar, May, Jul, Sep, Dec	5,000 bu	c/bu	50.00	1/4 c = $12.50
Cocoa	CC	NYBOT	7:30–12:30	Mar, May, Jul, Sep, Dec	10 metric tons	$/metric ton	10.00	1 pt = $10.00
Coffee	KC	NYBOT	8:15–12:35	Mar, May, Jul, Sep, Dec	37,500 lbs	c/lb	3.75	5 pts = $18.75
Sugar	SB	NYBOT	8:30–12:20	Jan, Mar, May, Jul, Sep, Oct	112,000 lbs	c/lb	11.20	1 pt = $11.20
Cotton	CT	NYBOT	9:30–1:40	Mar, May, Jul, Sep, Dec	50,000 lbs	c/lb	5.00	1 pt = $5.00
Dollar Index	DX	NYBOT	7:20–2:00	Mar, Jun, Sep, Dec	1,000 × Index	100ths/pt	10.00	1 pt = $10.00
Orange Juice	OJ	NYBOT	9:15–1:15	Jan, Mar, May, Jul, Sep, Nov	15,000 lbs	c/lb	1.50	5 pts = $7.50
Crude Oil	CL	NYMEX	8:45–2:10	All months	1,000 bbl	$/barrel	10.00	1 pt = $10.00
Gasoline	RB	NYMEX	8:40–2:10	All months	42,000 gals	c/gal	4.20	1 pt = $4.20
Heating Oil	HO	NYMEX	9:05–1:30	All months	42,000 gal	c/gal	4.20	1 pt = $4.20
Natural Gas	NG	NYMEX	9:00–1:30	All months	10,000 MMBtu	$/MMBtu	10.00	1 pt = $10.00
Palladium	PA	NYMEX	7:30–1:00	Mar, Jun, Sep, Dec	100 troy oz	$/oz	1.00	5 pts = $5.00
Propane	PN	NYMEX	8:55–2:00	All months	42,000 gal	$/gal	4.20	1 pt = $4.20

*Many contracts trade electronically and outside of the normal pit trading hours.

All times are central time zone and are subject to change.

Contract specifications often change. Consult your broker for the latest information.

Margin Requirements

Name	Symbol	Exchange	Initial Margin	Maintenance
Corn	C	CBOT	$1,012	$750
Dow Jones Index	DJ	CBOT	$4,875	$3,900
Gold	ZG	CBOT	$2,734	$2,025
Oats	O	CBOT	$675	$500
Rough Rice	RR	CBOT	$742	$550
Silver	ZI	CBOT	$4,658	$3,450
Soybean Meal	SM	CBOT	$675	$500
Soybean Oil	BO	CBOT	$540	$400
Soybeans	S	CBOT	$1,012	$750
T-note, 10-year	TY	CBOT	$810	$600
T-note, 2-year	TU	CBOT	$472	$350
T-note, 5-year	FV	CBOT	$540	$400
Treasury bonds	US	CBOT	$1,215	$900
Wheat	W	CBOT	$1,688	$1,250
CBOE Volatility Index	VIX	CFE	$2,250	$1,800
Feeder Cattle	FC	CME	$1,634	$1,210
GSCI	GI	CME	$5,250	$3,500
Lean Hog	LH	CME	$1,215	$900
Live Cattle	LC	CME	$1,262	$935
Lumber	LB	CME	$1,898	$1,265
Milk	DA	CME	$972	$720
MSCI	EFE	CME	$3,250	$3,250
Pork Bellies	PB	CME	$1,863	$1,380
S&P 500 Index	SP	CME	$19,688	$15,750
S&P 500, E-Mini	ES	CME	$3,938	$3,150
Copper	HG	COMEX	$9,315	$6,900
Gold	GC	COMEX	$3,375	$2,500
Silver	SI	COMEX	$6,210	$4,600
Cocoa	CC	NYBOT	$1,120	$800
Coffee	KC	NYBOT	$2,772	$1,980
Cotton	CT	NYBOT	$1,260	$900

Margin Requirements (continued)				
Name	Symbol	Exchange	Initial Margin	Maintenance
Orange Juice	OJ	NYBOT	$2,520	$1,800
Sugar	SB	NYBOT	$1,330	$950
U.S. Dollar Index	DX	NYBOT	$1,330	$1,000
Crude Oil	CL	NYMEX	$3,881	$2,875
Gasoline	RB	NYMEX	$6,075	$4,500
Heating Oil	HO	NYMEX	$6,210	$4,600
Natural Gas	NG	NYMEX	$12,420	$9,200
Palladium	PA	NYMEX	$2,700	$2,000
Propane Gas	PN	NYMEX	$2,025	$1,500

Note: Margin requirements often change. Check with your broker for the most recent margin requirements.

Strategy Reviews

Long Futures

Strategy: Buy futures contract(s).
Market Outlook: Bullish or positive on underlying commodity.
Profit Point: Any futures price above the entry price for the underlying contract.
Risk: High. Limited only to price of futures contract falling to zero.
Breakeven: The entry price for the initial position.
Margin Required: Yes.

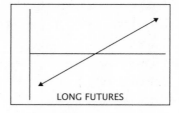

Figure A.1 Long futures risk graph.

Short Futures

Strategy: Sell futures contract(s).
Market Outlook: Bearish or negative on underlying commodity.
Profit Point: Any futures price below the entry price for the underlying contract.
Risk: Unlimited.
Breakeven: The entry price for the initial position.
Margin Required: Yes.

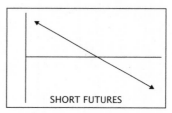

Figure A.2 Short futures risk graph.

Long Call

Strategy: Buy call option contract(s).
Market Outlook: Bullish on the underlying commodity.
Credit/Debit: Debit = the premium paid for the trade.
Profit Potential: Unlimited.
Profit Point at Expiration: When the futures price rises above the strike price of the option + the premium for the call option.
Risk: Limited to the premium paid or debit.
Breakeven: Strike price + call premium.
Margin Required: No. Call paid in full.

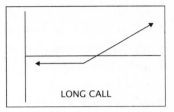

Figure A.3 Long call risk graph.

Long Put

Strategy: Buy put option contract(s).
Market Outlook: Bearish or negative on the underlying commodity.
Credit/Debit: Debit = the premium paid for the trade.
Profit Potential at Expiration: High. Limited to the price of the underlying asset falling to zero.
Profit Point: When the futures price falls below the strike price of the option – the premium for the put option.
Risk: Limited to the premium paid or debit.
Breakeven: Strike price – put premium.
Margin Required: No. Put paid for in full.

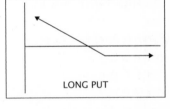

Figure A.4 Long put risk graph.

Short Call

Strategy: Sell call option contract(s).
Market Outlook: Neutral or bearish on the underlying commodity.
Credit/Debit: Credit = the premium received for the trade.
Profit Potential: Limited to premium.
Profit Point at Expiration: Any price below the strike price + the premium received.
Risk: Unlimited.
Breakeven: Strike price + premium received.
Margin Required: Yes.

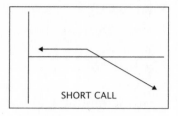

Figure A.5 Short call risk graph.

Short Put

Strategy: Sell put option contract(s).
Market Outlook: Bullish or neutral on the underlying commodity.
Credit/Debit: Credit = the premium received.
Profit Potential: Limited to the premium received.
Profit Point at Expiration: Any futures price above the strike price – the premium received.
Risk: High. Limited to the commodity falling to zero.
Breakeven: Strike price – premium received.
Margin Required: Yes.

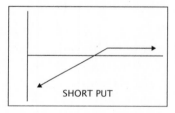

Figure A.6 Short put risk graph.

Bull Call Spread

Strategy: Buy call option(s) and sell an equal number of calls with a higher strike price with the same expiration months.

Market Outlook: Bullish on the underlying commodity.

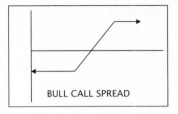

BULL CALL SPREAD

Figure A.7 Bull call spread risk graph.

Credit/Debit: Net debit = the price paid for the call – the price received for selling the call.

Profit Potential: Limited. Equal to the difference between the two strike prices – the debit.

Profit Point at Expiration: Any futures price above the lower strike price + the net debit.

Risk: Limited to the debit or cost of the trade.

Breakeven: Lower strike price + debit.

Margin Required: No. Strategist pays the debit in full.

Bear Put Spread

Strategy: Buy a put option contract(s) and sell an equal number of puts with a lower strike price.

Market Outlook: Bearish view on the underlying commodity.

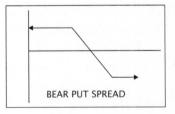

BEAR PUT SPREAD

Figure A.8 Bear put spread risk graph.

Credit/Debit: Net debit = the premium paid, or the cost of the higher strike price – the premium received for selling a put with a lower strike.

Profit Potential: Limited to the difference between the two strike prices – the debit.

Profit Point at Expiration: Any futures price below the higher strike price – net debit.

Risk: Limited to the net debit.

Breakeven: Higher strike price – net debit.

Margin Required: No. Spread or debit is paid for in full at the time of initiation.

Bear Call Spread

Strategy: Sell a call option contract(s) and buy the same number of higher strike call options with the same expiration months.

Market Outlook: Bearish or neutral on the underlying commodity.

Credit/Debit: Credit = the premium received for selling the call – the premium paid for buying a higher strike call.

Profit Potential: Limited to the premium received or net credit.

Profit Point at Expiration: Any futures price below the lower strike price + the net credit.

Risk: Limited to the difference between the two strikes – the credit.

Breakeven: Lower strike price + net credit.

Margin Required: Varies by brokerage firm.

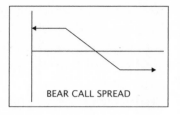

Figure A.9 Bear call spread risk graph.

Bull Put Spread

Strategy: Sell a put option contract(s) and buy the same number of lower strike put options with the same expiration months.

Market Outlook: Bullish or neutral on the underlying commodity.

Credit/Debit: Credit = the premium received for selling the put – the premium paid for buying a lower strike put.

Profit Potential: Limited to the premium received or net credit.

Profit Point at Expiration: Any futures price above the higher strike price – the net credit.

Risk: Limited to the difference between the two strikes – the credit.

Breakeven: Higher strike price – net credit.

Margin Required: Varies by brokerage firm.

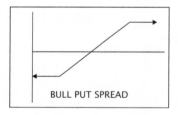

Figure A.10 Bull put spread risk graph.

Long Butterfly Spread

Strategy: Buy one call (or put), sell two calls (or puts) with a higher strike price, and buy one more call (or put) with a higher strike price.
Market Outlook: Neutral. Low volatility expected.
Credit/Debit: Debit = the cost of the out-of-the-money options – the premium from the in-the-money options.
Profit Potential: Limited to the difference between the two strikes – net debit.
Profit Point at Expiration: Any point between the two breakevens.
Risk: Limited to the net debit paid.
Breakeven: To the upside (higher strike price – net debit) and to the downside (lower strike price + net debit).
Margin Required: Varies by brokerage firm.

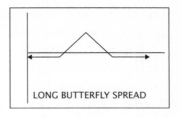

LONG BUTTERFLY SPREAD

Figure A.11 Long butterfly spread risk graph.

Long Straddle

Strategy: Buy put contract(s) and call contract(s) in the same numbers on the same underlying commodity, using the same strike price and expiration months.
Market Outlook: Price volatility expected.
Credit/Debit: Debit = the cost of the puts and the calls.
Profit Potential: Unlimited as the price of the underlying security moves higher; limited on the downside to the underlying asset falling to zero.
Profit Point at Expiration: Any price above the strike price + the premium or any price below the strike price – the premium.
Risk: Limited to the net debit.
Breakeven: On the upside, the breakeven = the strike price + the net debit. On the downside, it = the strike price – the debit.
Margin Required: No. Straddle paid for in full.

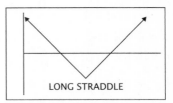

LONG STRADDLE

Figure A.12 Long straddle risk graph.

Long Strangle

Strategy: Buy put contract(s) and call contract(s) in the same numbers on the same underlying commodity, using the same expiration months but different strike prices. Both puts and calls are out-of-the-money.

Market Outlook: Price volatility expected.

Credit/Debit: Debit = the cost of the puts and the calls.

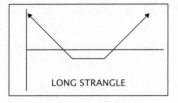

Figure A.13 Long strangle risk graph.

Profit Potential: Unlimited as the price of the underlying security moves higher; limited on the downside to the underlying asset falling to zero.

Profit Point at Expiration: Any price above the higher strike price + the premium or any price below the lower strike price − the premium.

Risk: Limited to the net debit.

Breakeven: On the upside, the breakeven = the higher (call) strike price + the net debit. On the downside, it = the lower (put) strike price − the debit.

Margin Required: No. Both puts and calls paid for in full at time trade is established.

Short Straddle

Strategy: Sell put contract(s) and call contract(s) in the same numbers on the same underlying commodity, using the same strike price and expiration months.

Market Outlook: Expect neutral or sideways trading.

Credit/Debit: Credit = the premium for sale of both puts and calls.

Profit Potential: Limited to the net premium received or credit.

Profit Point at Expiration: Any price between the strike price – the net credit and the strike price + the net credit.

Risk: Unlimited as the underlying asset price moves higher, limited to the price of the underlying asset falling to zero on the downside.

Breakeven: To the upside (strike price + net credit) and to the downside (strike price – net credit).

Margin Required: Yes.

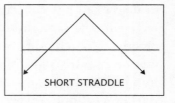

SHORT STRADDLE

Figure A.14 Short straddle risk graph.

Short Strangle

Strategy: Sell put contract(s) and call contract(s) in the same numbers on the same underlying commodity, using the same expiration months and different strike prices. Both puts and calls are out-of-the-money.

Market Outlook: Expect neutral or sideways trading.

Credit/Debit: Credit = the premium received for sale of both puts and calls.

Profit Potential: Limited to the net premium received or credit.

Profit Point at Expiration: Any price between the put strike price – the net credit and the call strike price + the net credit.

Risk: Unlimited as the underlying asset price moves higher, limited to the price of the underlying asset falling to zero on the downside.

Breakeven: To the upside (call strike price + net credit) and to the downside (put strike price – net credit).

Margin Required: Yes.

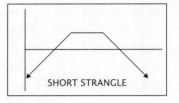

Figure A.15 Short strangle risk graph.

Long Shares (Stock or Exchange-Traded Fund)

Strategy: Buy shares of stock or ETF.

Market Outlook: Bullish on the stock or market.

Profit Potential: Unlimited.

Profit Point: The price of the shares (+ commissions).

Risk: Limited to the cost of the shares.

Breakeven: The price of the shares (+ commissions).

Margin Required: 50 percent of share price in margin account. 100 percent of stock in standard brokerage account.

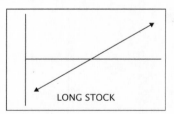

Figure A.16 Long stock risk graph.

Short Shares (Stock or Exchange-Traded Fund)

Strategy: Sell short shares of stock or ETF.
Market Outlook: Bearish on the stock or market.
Profit Potential: Limited to the share price falling to zero.
Profit Point: The price of the shares (– commissions).
Risk: Unlimited as stock price moves higher.
Breakeven: The price of the shares (– commissions).
Margin Required: Yes. 50 percent.

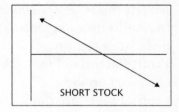

SHORT STOCK

Figure A.17 Short stock risk graph.

Protective Put

Strategy: Buy shares of stock or ETF and buy one put for every 100 shares purchased. (Can also be applied to futures.)
Market Outlook: Bullish on the stock or market, but looking for downside protection.
Profit Potential: Unlimited.
Profit Point: Any price above the cost of the shares + the debit for the put purchase.
Risk: Limited to the cost of the shares + the cost of the premium – the strike price.
Breakeven: Strike price + the premium paid for the put option.
Margin Required: 50 percent for stock and 100 percent cost of put option.

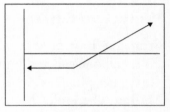

Figure A.18 Protective put risk graph.

Covered Call

Strategy: Buy shares of stock or ETF and sell one call for every 100 shares purchased.

Market Outlook: Moderately bullish on underlying security.

Profit Potential: Limited by the strike price of the call option.

Profit Point: Anything above the price of the shares – the premium received for the call sale.

Risk: Limited below the breakeven to the share price falling to zero.

Breakeven: Share price at initiation – call option premium.

Margin Required: 50 percent requirement on the underlying stock or ETF.

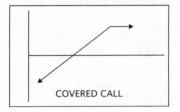

Figure A.19 Covered call risk graph.

Protective Collar

Strategy: Buy or own shares of stock or ETF. Sell one call and buy one put for every 100 shares purchased.

Market Outlook: Moderately bullish on underlying asset.

Profit Potential: Limited to the call option strike price – the stock price + the credit received from the sale of the call – the cost of the put option.

Profit Point: Above the breakeven.

Risk: Limited to the initial share price – the put option strike price (+ any debits or – any credits).

Breakeven: The price of the shares – the cost of the call option + the debit for the put purchase.

Margin Required: 50 percent requirement on the underlying stock or ETF.

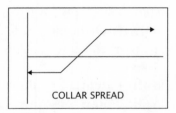

Figure A.20 Collar spread risk graph.

Additional Reading List

Alexander Elder, *Trading for a Living*, Wiley, 1993.

George Fontanills, *The Options Course: High Profit & Low Stress Trading Methods*, second edition, Wiley, 2005.

George Fontanills and Tom Gentile, *The Index Trading Course*, Wiley, 2006.

George Fontanills and Tom Gentile, *The Stock Market Course,* Wiley, 2001.

George Fontanills and Tom Gentile, *The Volatility Course,* Wiley, 2002.

George Kleinman, *Trading Commodities and Financial Futures: A Step-by-Step Guide to Mastering the Markets*, third edition, FT Press, 2004.

Larry McMillan, *Options as a Strategic Investment*, fourth edition, Prentice Hall, 2001.

John J. Murphy (New York Institute of Finance), *Technical Analysis of the Financial Markets: A Comprehensive Guide to Trading Methods and Applications*, second revised edition, Prentice Hall, 1999.

Jim Rogers, *Hot Commodities: How Anyone Can Invest Profitably in the World's Best Market*, Random House, 2004.

Jack Schwager, *Getting Started in Technical Analysis*, Wiley, 1999.

Jack Schwager, *Market Wizards: Interviews with Top Traders*, HarperCollins, 1993.

Jack Schwager, *The New Market Wizards: Conversations with America's Top Traders*, HarperCollins, 1992.

Glossary

account executive a salesperson employed by a stock exchange member broker/dealer, also known as a registered representative. The account executive gives advice on buying and selling securities, collecting a percentage of any commission income generated as compensation.

account sizing determining the appropriate amount of trading capital needed to trade a given group of markets using a given trading approach, without exceeding one's own risk tolerance level.

adjusted futures price the cash-price equivalent reflected in the current futures price. This is calculated by taking the futures price times the conversion factor for the particular financial instrument (e.g., bond or note) being delivered.

adjustment the process of buying or selling instruments to lock in profits or bring a position back to a desired risk level.

analysis paralysis when too much information is taken in, leaving an investor confused and unable to make any sort of investment decision.

annual return the simple rate of return earned by an investment for each year.

arbitrageurs (arbs) players who attempt to profit from price differences between two substantially equal assets. This might involve, for instance, buying a commodity on one exchange and simultaneously selling a similar commodity on another exchange in order to profit from the price differences of the two.

ascending base pattern the least common of the continuation pattern groupings. Angular wedging over a 9- to 16-week period with the deepest wave or trough being less than 20 percent in width is key. Three full waves need to develop, along with constructive volume characteristics during the base building, in order to qualify and before a breakout entry might be confirmed.

ask an indication by a trader or a dealer of a willingness to sell a security or a commodity; the price at which an investor can buy from a broker-dealer.

asset anything that an individual or a corporation owns or a balance sheet item expressing what a corporation owns.

asset allocation when money is divided among various types of investments, such as stocks, bonds, and short-term investments, you are allocating your assets.

assignment   the receipt of an exercise notice by an options writer that requires him or her to sell (in the case of a call) or purchase (in the case of a put) the underlying security at the specified strike price.

at-the-money   an option that has a strike price equal to the price of the underlying asset.

authorized participant   an investment firm that is recognized by an ETF sponsor as capable of creating and redeeming fund shares through the delivery of portfolio components (stocks or commodities). An ETF specialist is an example.

Average Directional Index (ADX)   a chart indicator designed to help traders measure trend intensity. Readings below 20 indicate a weak trend, while readings above 40 indicate a very strong trend.

average true range   essentially measures the average amount of day-to-day fluctuation in points and/or dollars for a given commodity contract. A handy tool for estimating relative risk between two commodities.

back-end load   a deferred sales charge, normally assessed when a fund investor redeems his or her shares.

back months   the futures or options on futures months being traded that are furthest from expiration.

backwardation   when the deferred-month prices on a futures contract are lower than those of the nearby months.

basis   the difference between the local spot price of a deliverable commodity and the price of a futures contract—usually the nearby—for the same commodity. One commercial user's/producer's basis may vary from another's owing to variations in local spot market prices.

basis point   a measure of a bond's yield, equal to .01 percent of yield. A bond whose yield increases from 5.0 percent to 5.5 percent is said to increase by 50 basis points.

bear market   a declining market usually lasting at least 6 months and normally not more than 18 months.

bearish divergence   occurs when an indicator starts moving to lower ground while price is rising or moving sideways.

bear call spread   a strategy that consists of buying a call and selling a call with a lower strike.

bear put spread   a strategy that consists of buying a put and selling a put with a lower strike price.

bear spread   a type of strategy that generates profits as the price of the underlying asset falls.

benchmarks   a gauge or barometer for the performance of an investment or investment portfolio.

bid   an indication that an investor or trader is willing to buy a security or commodity at a specific price. The current bid price is the price at which an investor can sell the security or commodity to another investor.

bid-ask spread   the difference between bid and offer prices.

binaries   a type of options contract with a "yes" or "no" feature. Bullish traders choose yes. Bearish traders choose no.

Black-Scholes model   an options model developed by Fischer Black and Myron Scholes in the early 1970s.

Bollinger bands   an indicator developed by John Bollinger to measure volatility and overbought/oversold markets by drawing standard deviation bands above and below an x-day moving average.

breakeven point   a point where a trade or position does not make any profits or suffer any losses.

breakout   a move above a resistance level or below support. A breakout accompanied by heavy volume is generally an indication that a market is ready to make a significant move higher or lower.

broker-assisted   when the trade is placed through a live broker, it is called a *broker-assisted* trade. Some online firms charge extra for the assistance of a broker.

brokers   in the trading pits, brokers are the people who bring in customer orders to traders.

bull call spread   a trade that involves the purchase of a call option and a sale of a call option with a higher strike price, both with identical expiration dates.

bullish divergence   occurs when an indicator starts moving to higher ground while price is declining or moving sideways.

bull market   a rising market over a prolonged period, usually lasting at least 6 months and normally not more than 18 months.

bull put spread   a strategy that consists of buying a put and selling a put with a higher strike.

bull spread   a type of trade that makes money when the price of the underlying security moves higher.

butterfly spread   an advanced options strategy that involves selling at-the-money options (the body) and buying out-of-the-money options (the wings).

call   a bullish type of option contract that gives the buyer the right, but not the obligation, to buy a specific asset at a specific price for a predetermined time.

capital gains   the profit from selling a security at a higher price.

capitulation   when investors, in disgust, throw in the towel on an investment. This is often followed by a reversal and rebound in the price of the security.

capped futures   a type of futures contract that is limited in price by a ceiling on the upside and a floor on the downside.

cash flow   the amount of net cash generated by an investment or business during a specific period of time. Also, the money received by a business minus the money that is paid out.

cash market   another term for the spot market. It is the current price of the commodity in the open market and differs from the futures market, which is based on expectations about future prices.

catalyst   an event that causes a reaction in the price of an asset. For example, an earnings report can be a catalyst for a big move higher or lower in a stock price.

clearing firm   an exchange member that is also a member of the clearinghouse. Clearing members deal directly with the clearinghouse to settle trades, deliveries, and margin. Nonclearing exchange members contract with clearing members to handle their back-office functions.

closed-end funds   a type of mutual fund with a fixed number of shares outstanding.

commission   a service charge or fee charged by a brokerage firm for arranging the purchase or sale of a security.

commodity   any bulk good traded on an exchange or in the cash market; examples include metals, grains, and meats.

Commodity Futures Trading Commission (CFTC)   the CFTC is an independent government agency that regulates the commodities market. See also www.cftc.gov.

commodity pool operator (CPO)   an individual or firm that operates one or more commodity pools. A commodity pool is a trust or syndicate that trades commodity futures or option contracts.

Commodity Research Bureau (CRB)   established in 1934, the CRB is a provider of market information for commodities and futures prices.

Commodity Research Bureau (CRB) index   first calculated in 1957, the CRB index is used to track the price changes in a basket of futures and commodities prices.

commodity trading advisor (CTA)   a licensed trading advisor who specializes in the trading of commodities.

consolidation   a pause that allows participants in a market to reevaluate the market and sets the stage for the next price move.

contango   when longer-term contracts carry higher values than short-term contracts. This is normal.

Continuous Commodity Index (CCI)   the original CRB index, before it was modified in 2005, is now known as the CCI.

contract   a unit of trading for a financial or commodity future. Also, an agreement between the parties (buyer and seller) of a futures or options on futures transaction as defined by an exchange.

contract month   the month in which futures contracts may be satisfied by making or accepting delivery.

correlation   a statistical measure of how two investments move in relation to one another. Correlation ranges between −1 and +1. Positive correlation denotes that the investment vehicles move in the same direction, while negative correlation characterizes an inverse relationship. A correlation of zero indicates that movements are completely random.

cost of carry the cost of owning and storing a commodity over a period of time. The cost of carry will influence the difference between the spot or cash price of the commodity and the price of the commodity in the futures market.

countertrend a move in the opposite direction during a significant advance or decline in the price of an investment.

countertrend indicator if an indicator declines to a low level, it signals oversold conditions, and traders look to buy. When it reaches a high level, the market is overbought, and traders look to sell.

crack spread the spread between crude oil and its products; heating oil and unleaded gasoline play a major role in the trading process.

creation unit a large block of exchange-traded fund shares that are created by a large institutional investor and made available for trading.

credit risk the risk of loss one assumes under a financial contract that a borrower or a counterparty to a derivatives contract may default or fail to perform its obligations.

crowd psychology a large group of people behaving in a similar manner or sharing the same (occasionally misguided) notion.

crush See **gross processing margin**.

cup-and-handle pattern a chart pattern that lasts from 7 to 65 weeks. The cup is in the shape of a "U" and the handle is usually more than one or two weeks in duration. The handle is a slight downward drift with low trading volume that develops within 15 percent of the cup highs and in the upper half of its weekly base.

day order an order to buy or sell a security that will expire if not filled by the end of the day.

day traders short-term speculators who buy and sell frequently throughout the trading day.

dealer agreement a contract between a brokerage firm and a mutual fund company that allows the brokerage to offer the company's shares and allows for the sharing of sales loads and other fees.

default a failure to live up to the terms of a contract or debt obligation.

delivery securities sellers must deliver the certificates on or before the third business day after the sale.

delivery date this is the third business day following a regular-way transaction of stocks or bonds, or the first day of the month in which delivery is to be made under a futures contract. Futures contract sales are made on a seller's option basis; therefore, delivery can be on any day of the month as long as proper notice is given.

delta a Greek that measures the change in the value of an option for every point change in the value of the underlying asset.

delta-hedged an options strategy that protects an option against small price changes in the option's underlying instrument.

delta-neutral strategy a calculated ratio of long and short positions so that the overall position is not sensitive to small changes in the price of the underlying instrument.

delta position   a measure of option price versus the underlying futures contract or stock price.

demand   the amount of a good or commodity currently used.

depletion   the consumption of natural resources that are part of a company's assets. Since oil, mining, and gas companies deal in products that cannot be replenished, depletion reduces the company's natural assets over time.

derivatives   investment securities that have values derived from the prices of other investments. Options and futures are examples of derivative securities.

discount brokers   brokerage firms that offer lower commission rates than investment dealers, but that, in contrast to full-service brokers, do not always offer advice, research, or portfolio planning.

divergence   when the move to a new high (or new low) in a market or security is not accompanied by a new high (or new low) in a technical indicator such as Relative Strength Index (RSI).

diversification   a risk management technique that mixes a wide variety of investments within a portfolio in order to minimize the impact of any one security on the overall portfolio.

dividends   the company profits that are paid out to shareholders.

double bottom buy   a type of chart pattern where a security reaches a low price, rallies up, drops to retest the previous low, and then reverses again to begin a major move higher.

double bottom pattern   price action of a security where it has declined two times to approximately the same level, indicating the existence of a support level and a possibility that the downward trend has ended. The double bottom is confirmed when the price of the security moves through its midpoint pivot, ideally with handle development in place.

Dow Jones Industrial Average (DJIA)   an average made up of 30 blue-chip stocks; 28 that trade daily on the New York Stock Exchange, and 2 stocks that trade on the NASDAQ.

downtrend   a prolonged move lower in the value of a security.

drawdown   losses in a trading account.

earnings growth   the rate of sequential profit improvement for a company or business.

earnings per share (EPS)   the amount of profits generated for each of the company's shares outstanding.

e-cbot   the electronic trading platform on the Chicago Board of Trade (CBOT) that offers trading in futures on various commodities and financials.

ego   in the market, ego is typically manifested as a desire to be right, even if the markets and your own trading approach suggest you are wrong.

elasticity   the degree to which consumers respond to price changes in a commodity. A measure of elasticity can be taken by dividing the percentage change in demand by the percentage change in price. A quotient over 1 indicates relatively high elasticity; inelastic demand is indicated by a quotient under 1.

Elliott Wave Analysis   named after Ralph Nelson Elliott, this form of technical analysis is based on the premise that markets can be predicted by observing and identifying repetitive patterns or waves. The three major aspects of wave analysis are pattern, time, and ratio.

EPS growth   the rate of sequential profit-per-share improvement for a company or business.

equilibrium price   a price level where supply meets demand. Buyers and sellers agree on price.

Excess Return contract   known as CERF, expiring in 2011, it is a nonoptionable futures contract that is smaller than the Total Return contract.

exchange   a place where an asset, option, future, stock, or derivative is bought and sold. The Chicago Mercantile Exchange (CME) and the Chicago Board of Trade (CBOT) are examples of futures exchanges.

exchange-traded fund (ETF)   an ETF is a pooled investment with shares listed for trading on the major stock exchanges.

exercise   the act of exercising the right of the option to buy (in the case of a call) or sell (in the case of a put) the underlying security. It is carrying out the terms of an option contract.

exercise settlement amount   the difference between the exercise price of the option and the exercise settlement value of the index on the day an exercise notice is tendered, multiplied by the index multiplier.

expense ratio   the amount of assets needed to pay annual operating costs and management fees of a mutual fund.

expiration date   the last day on which an option may be exercised.

exponential moving average (EMA)   a type of moving average that gives greater weight to the latest data. Some traders prefer exponential moving averages over simple moving averages because they offer better information regarding the most recent trends or prices.

fast market   a market may be designated as a *fast market* by the exchange it is traded on if it is presently experiencing high volatility and heavy trading. It may be difficult to get filled at a specific desired price during a fast market.

fear   in the markets, fear is manifested as a fear of losing money and/or as a fear of missing out on making money.

Fibonacci   a twelfth-century mathematician who identified certain ratios to be a common factor throughout the natural world, such as in DNA, music, architecture, and nature. In the financial markets, technicians use these ratios (for instance, 50 percent and 62 percent) in an attempt to locate key support or resistance levels that mark extremes in crowd behavior and price action.

Fibonacci numbers Leonardo Fibonacci discovered certain sequences of numbers whereby each successive number is the sum of the previous two. For example: 1-1-2-3-5-8-13-21-34-55-89-144, and so on. Similar ratios are believed to exist in financial markets.

fills "getting filled" is a term traders sometimes use when talking about the execution of an order. For example, if XYZ Futures were bought at 1,500, the trader was filled at 1,500. Traders want to get good fills on the orders because they want trades executed at the best prices possible.

filter a device or program that separates data or information in accordance with set criteria.

fixed supply a cap or limit on the amount of goods or products made available.

flat base pattern a type of chart pattern that occurs in the midst of an advance or decline when prices trend sideways for a period of time. It is considered a continuation pattern because it is a pause during an advance or decline.

float a stock's amount of shares available (the supply) to trade in the open market. The smaller the float, the easier it is for demand in the stock to lead to outsized gains.

floor broker an exchange member who is paid a fee for executing orders for clearing members or their customers. A floor broker executing orders must be licensed by the CFTC.

floor trader an exchange member or local who executes transactions from the floor of the exchange only for his or her own account.

forward contract an agreement between two parties to buy or sell a commodity at some time in the future. Similar to futures contracts, but not as easily transferred or canceled.

front-end load a type of mutual fund that charges a fee or commission when the money is initially invested.

front month the first expiration month in a series of months.

full carry the total costs associated with holding or maintaining a securities position. It is the full cost of carry, or carrying cost.

full-service broker a type of brokerage firm that provides not just stock quotes and trade execution, but also portfolio management, investment ideas, and research.

fundamental analysis the study of all factors that might impact the supply and demand of a commodity. Weather is an example of a fundamental analysis tool for agricultural commodities.

fungibility the ability to interchange assets of identical quality. Wheat stored in a grain elevator is fungible, as it is not specifically identified regarding its ownership.

futures contract an agreement to buy or sell a set number of shares of a specific security in a designated future month at a price agreed upon by the buyer and seller. The contracts themselves are often traded on the futures market. There are different types of futures contracts, including agricultural, financials, and metals.

gamma a Greek that measures the change in delta in relation to changes in the price of the underlying asset.

Gartley   a type of advanced pattern that attempts to find trend reversals using pivots and retracement levels.

Globex   an electronic exchange that offers trading in futures and options. Today, it is available almost 23 hours a day, five days a week.

good 'til canceled (GTC) order   a type of order to buy or sell stock that is good until it is canceled by the trader. Brokerages usually set a limit of 30 to 60 days, after which the GTC expires if not restated.

government subsidies   financial aid from the U.S. government.

grantor trusts   trusts used to hold assets or investment securities on behalf of investors.

greed   in the markets, greed manifests as a desire to make more money than is reasonably possible, given a trader's particular approach to trading.

the Greeks   statistical measures that help to explain the changes in options premiums.

gross processing margin   also known as crush, this is the amount of oil and/or meal that can be produced from soybeans.

growth rates   compound annual growth rate for the number of full fiscal years.

growth stock   shares of companies that are expected to show above-average increases in revenues and earnings in the future. In order to continue growing and expanding, these companies will retain most of their earnings in order to reinvest in operations.

head fake   a false breakout or reversal that is followed by a move in the previous direction.

hedge   a position that serves to mitigate the risk associated with holding another asset or investment.

hedger   an investor who uses the futures market to minimize the risk in his or her business. Hedgers may be manufacturers, portfolio managers, bankers, farmers, and so on. Hedging can help lock in existing profits and/or reduce the overall risk of loss due to fluctuating prices.

high implied volatility   implied volatility that is at relatively high levels compared to the underlying asset's historical volatility. Credit spreads—such as the bull put spread or the bear call spread—are best applied in markets with high volatility levels.

histogram   a method of plotting data at the bottom of charts that appears as a graph similar to a frequency distribution chart in statistics.

horizontal spread   sometimes called a time spread, the trade involves purchasing either call or put options and simultaneously selling the same type of option with the same strike price but a different expiration month.

human nature   traits that are innate to most human beings. Most important, in trading the markets, these traits can work against you.

implied volatility (IV)   a measure of volatility that is derived using an option pricing model. IV reflects expectations about an asset's future volatility.

index   a tool used to track price changes in a group or basket of investment securities.

index investing   a strategy that involves mimicking the performance of an index rather than making buy and sell decisions.

initial margin   the minimum amount of money that a trader must put up in order to enter into a trade in a given commodity, whether long or short.

initial public offering (IPO)   a company's initial sale of shares to the public.

in-kind exchange   certain transactions are deemed nontaxable under the Internal Revenue Code. An in-kind or like-kind exchange is the most common. In an ETF redemption or creation, ETF shares are exchanged for stock or futures. Each side to the exchange deals investment assets of the same value to the other (any balancing cash is deemed incidental and isn't recognized as income to the recipient).

institutional momentum   buying interest on the part of large players such as pension funds, mutual funds, and portfolio managers that can cause rapid upward movement in a stock price.

in-the-money   a call option with a strike price lower than the current price of the underlying asset or a put option with a strike price higher than the price of the underlying asset.

intrinsic value   the true value of a company or investment based upon factors such as net assets, dividends, earnings, and management quality, and the firm's competitive advantages and brand name. See **in-the-money**.

inverted markets   a term used to describe a situation where prices in the spot market are greater than in the futures market. Inverted markets can occur when there is strong present demand for a commodity.

iPath ETNs   debt instruments tied to one of the commodity indexes that trade on the exchanges just like exchange-traded funds.

lagging indicators   economic or financial variables that tend to follow economic activity or price moves in financial assets. A lagging economic indicator, for example, will reach a peak after a peak in economic activity.

large capitalization   publicly traded companies whose market values are in excess of $10 billion.

leading indicators   tools, data, or gauges that provide signals regarding future changes in the economy or security prices.

leverage   using small amounts of capital to control large amounts of a commodity or other asset. Margin is an example of using leverage.

limit move   the maximum daily price limit for an exchange-traded contract.

limit orders   orders to buy or sell investments at a specific price.

limit up, limit down   commodity exchange restrictions on the maximum upward or downward movements permitted in the price for a commodity during any trading session day.

liquidity   the ease with which an asset can be converted to cash. A large number of buyers and sellers and high volume of activity provide the best liquidity.

locals   traders in the pits who are not members of large organizations.

long call　the limited-risk strategy that involves the purchase of a call option to open a position.

long put　the limited-risk strategy that involves the purchase of a put option to open a position.

long straddle　a delta-neutral options strategy created by the simultaneous purchase of an at-the-money call and put with the same expiration date.

low implied volatility　implied volatility that is at relatively low levels compared to the underlying asset's historical volatility. Buying puts and calls is best applied in low implied volatility markets—such as the call spread.

maintenance margin　the minimum amount of money that a trader must maintain in his or her account in order to continue to hold a trade in a given commodity.

margin　a good faith deposit required to establish or maintain a commodity futures position. In the futures market, both sides to a trade—buyer and seller alike—post margin.

margin call　a brokerage firm's request for additional funds in a customer's trading account.

margin requirements　the amount of capital required by a brokerage firm to implement a trade or strategy.

margin-to-equity ratio　the amount of margin presently committed to commodity positions divided by the total amount of capital in your trading account.

marked to market　the process of repricing a commodity futures position against the current settlement price to reflect its current market value. Marking to market is done daily to determine account equity for margin purposes. Year-end marking to market, however, is required under the Internal Revenue Code to determine current tax liability. Each open Section 1256 position is *theoretically* closed out on the last business day of the year to arrive at a current gain or loss.

market capitalization　the total value of a company computed as the number of shares outstanding multiplied by the current stock price.

market orders　buying or selling securities at the price given at the time the order reached the market.

maximum drawdown　the greatest amount of capital loss that a trader is willing to withstand within his or her trading account.

mechanical trading system　a set of specific rules that govern buy and sell decisions with the intention of removing emotion from the decision-making process.

momentum　an indicator that alerts traders to overbought or oversold conditions using a formula that considers closing prices over a number of days. Momentum will oscillate above and below zero. When it falls to low levels, it indicates that the stock or index is oversold and due to bounce higher. However, when it rises to the high end of its range, the stock is overbought and likely to move lower.

momentum indicator　an indicator that uses price and volume for predicting the strength or weakness of a current market.

money management   the act of deploying trading capital in a manner that minimizes as much as possible the risks that you are exposed to, while simultaneously affording you maximum profit potential.

moving average   a measure of the average price for a given commodity over the past x number of days, typically used to define a market's trend.

moving average convergence/divergence (MACD) indicator   an indicator developed by Gerald Appel and calculated using three separate exponential moving averages. Typically used to track market trends, it can also be used to identify market turning points.

mutual funds   a type of investment where investors pool their money and then shares are issued to represent fractional ownership in the pool.

net asset value (NAV)   the value of an investment based on total assets minus liabilities divided by the number of shares. It's the amount shareholders should receive when redeeming mutual fund shares.

no-load fund   a type of mutual fund that doesn't charges a fee or commission to buy or sell shares.

nontrending   a market where prices have a tendency of moving in between two price points for a period of time. For example, if gold trades between $600 and $650 for a six-month period, it would be identified as a nontrending market or sideways-moving market.

offer   an indication by an investor or trader of willingness to sell a security or commodity. The offer, or asking price, is the price at which an investor can buy the security from another investor in the market.

off-floor trader   a trader who does not trade on the actual floor of an organized stock exchange.

one-standard-deviation move   a move in the price level of a security that is one standard deviation from the mean or average.

open interest   the number of options or futures contracts that have been opened and not yet closed out. Open interest gives a good indication of the contract's liquidity.

option   a trading instrument that enables the buyer to purchase (call) or sell (put) the underlying market at a specific strike price until a specific expiration date.

oscillator   a technical indicator used to identify overbought and oversold price regions.

out-of-the-money   an options contract that has no intrinsic value. A call option is out-of-the-money if its exercise or strike price is above the current market price of the underlying security. A put option is out-of-the-money if its exercise or strike price is below the current market price of the underlying security.

overbought   a term that describes a market in which more and stronger buying has occurred than the fundamentals justify. Prices have risen too far and are due to fall.

oversold   a technical analysis term for a market in which prices have fallen too far and are due to bounce higher.

passive management   an investing strategy that attempts to mirror, rather than out-perform, a market index. Despite the strategy's name, a commodity index portfolio manager must still buy and sell futures at times. Indexes may be reconstituted or rebalanced at times, requiring adjustments within the portfolio.

peak oil   an idea originally sparked by Shell Oil geologist M. King Hubbard back in 1956 that the world will reach a peak in the rate at which it can extract oil from the ground. Once this peak is reached, production rates will decline and will not be able to keep up with demand. When demand outpaces production, the world economy will no doubt receive a major shock. The ramifications of peak oil continue to be a hot topic of discussion, but unlike global warming, the forces underlying peak oil are generally not disputed.

%D   a secondary indicator used in computing stochastics. %D is computed by smoothing %K over a set period.

%K   the primary indicator value that is used to create or compute stochastics. %K is based on the high, low, and closing values of a stock or commodity.

portfolio volatility   the variability in the return or price performance of an investment portfolio.

postearnings drift   the fact that a positive earnings surprise can lead to an upward price tendency in the stock until the next report.

premium   the actual debit (cost) to buy an option; the amount you are credited as a result of selling an option.

price discovery   the process of finding the price that will match buyers and sellers.

price-earnings (PE) ratio   a PE ratio is computed by dividing the stock price by earnings per share.

price-earnings/growth (PEG) ratio   the PEG ratio compares a company's earnings growth rate to its PE ratio.

price gap   the difference between the opening price today for a given commodity and yesterday's closing price.

price-sales ratio   a ratio computed as the current stock price divided by sales per share.

production costs   the outlays associated with producing goods or services.

production-weighted   a type of index-weighting methodology whereby each commodity's weight is based on the amount of capital required to hold that asset.

ProfitSource   a sophisticated financial market analysis program designed to help traders identify winning trades by harnessing the power of Elliott Wave Theory as well as advanced scanning and searching functionalities (www.profitsource.com).

put   a bearish type of option contract that gives the buyer the right, but not the obligation, to sell a specific asset at a specific price for a predetermined period of time.

redemption unit   a large block of exchange-traded fund shares that is redeemed by a large institutional investor and no longer available for trading.

relative strength   a technical tool used to calculate the price difference between two securities over a certain period in an effort to determine weakness or inherent strength.

Relative Strength Index (RSI)   an oscillator calculated by using daily price changes over a specified day window, typically used to identify overbought or oversold situations, with high readings suggesting an overbought market and low readings an oversold market.

resistance   a price area where a security has a history of meeting selling pressure and moving lower.

retracements   a move counter to the prevailing trend. Technical analysts consider 33 percent, 50 percent, and 61.8 percent retracements to be significant.

return on equity (ROE)   an indicator of a company's profitability computed by dividing net income for the past 12 months by common stockholders' equity. The result is expressed as a percentage.

return on margin   the percentage of profit or loss based on the amount of margin used to enter the trade. If margin is $2,000 and the profit is $200, the return on margin is 10 percent.

revenue growth   the rate of sequential sales improvement for a company or business.

reversal   a change in the underlying trend of an investment.

risk   the potential financial loss inherent in an investment or strategy.

risk curve   a chart that shows the potential profit and loss from an option or an options strategy as it reacts to changes in the price of the underlying stock.

risk tolerance   the amount of risk that an individual trader is comfortable assuming.

rolling   the selling of futures contracts in the portfolio as they approach their expiration month and the buying of the same contracts in a deferred month.

rollover   reinvesting money from one maturing security to another one with a more distant expiration.

round-trip commission   the total commission costs associated with buying or opening a position and also selling and closing that same position. Normally, futures brokerage commissions are charged on a round-trip basis when a position is closed, either through a purchase, a sale, or a delivery. Commissions on futures options, however, are not charged on a round-trip basis; you pay a commission when you enter as well as when you exit the market.

seasonality   a consistent and predictable change in market activity that occurs during certain times of the year.

secondary market   the market where investors buy and sell existing securities.

secular   a market that trends for several years or more and goes beyond the length associated with normal cyclical markets.

settlement price   the official price at the end of the trading day that is based on a range of closing prices for a specific contract. It is used to determine margin requirements.

short call an unlimited-risk strategy that involves the sale of a call option to open a position.

short put a high-risk strategy that involves the sale of a put option to open a position.

signal an alert to enter or exit a position.

simple moving average the arithmetic mean or average of a series of prices over a period of time.

smoothing a mathematical technique that removes excess data unevenness.

specialist an exchange member that acts as the exclusive market maker for a stock or an ETF. Specialists hold inventories of shares from which they deal, continuously put up bid and offer prices, and manage the limit order book. Specialists are charged with maintaining a fair and orderly market and use their inventories to balance surges in supply and demand.

speculation the selection of investments with higher-than-average risk in order to profit from forecasted price movements.

speculator a trader who hopes to benefit from a directional move in the underlying instrument, attempts to anticipate price changes, and, through buying and selling futures contracts, aims to make a profit. The speculator does not use the futures market in connection with the production, processing, marketing, or handling of a product, and thus has no interest in making or taking delivery.

spot market same as the cash market. It is the immediate market where a commodity or other investment can be bought or sold.

spread a trading strategy that involves the simultaneous purchase of a futures or options contract with the sale of another.

spread order an order to buy one contract and simultaneously sell another.

standard deviation a statistical measure that tracks scattering from the mean.

stochastics an oscillator used to indicate overbought and oversold conditions for a security.

stop loss a risk management tool used to limit the losses from an open position. For example, a trader might place a stop loss 5 percent below the current price of a long position in order to limit the losses to only 5 percent.

stop-loss order an order placed to exit an open trade in an attempt to limit the risk on that particular trade to a given amount.

straddle the simultaneous purchase of a call and put option with the same at-the-money strike, expiration date, and underlying market.

streak a run of consecutive winning or losing trades. Traders must be prepared mentally to trade through losing streaks and must not become overconfident during a long winning streak.

strike price a market price at which the commodity (or stock) underlying a call or put option can be purchased (call) or sold (put).

structured notes debt instruments issued by investment banks whose returns are tied to the performance of an index.

supply the amount of a good or commodity that is available in the market.

support a price area where a security has a history of finding buyers and moving higher.

T-bills Treasury bills are short-term debt instruments issued by the U.S. government.

technical analysis the study of the price action of a security based on the theory that market prices display repetitive patterns that can be tracked and used to forecast future price movement. Technical analysis evaluates price movement by analyzing statistics generated by market activity—such as past prices and volume—to study market performance.

theoretical value the price of an option based on a mathematical model rather than the actual price in the market.

theta an option Greek that measures the impact of time on options premiums.

tick an increment of change in the price of a security. For example, if the S&P 500 futures contract rises from 1,300.00 to 1,300.25, it has increased one tick because it moves in .25 increments and each 25-point change is one tick.

time decay the fact that option premiums have a fixed life and lose value over time.

time value (extrinsic value) the amount that the current market price of a right, warrant, or option exceeds its intrinsic value.

top down approach a form of analysis or study that focuses on the big picture first and then narrows the study to specific details of the plan or investment.

Total Return contract a type of futures contract that accounts for three sources of return—futures, rolling of contracts, and collateral return.

tracking risk the risk that an index-tracking security, like an exchange-traded fund, will not move in the same manner as the index it is supposed to mimic, hence, the divergence between the return of a portfolio and that of the benchmark it attempts to track.

TRAKRs Total Return Asset Contracts are a type of futures contract that allows small investors to wager on a diverse set of investments, including commodities, without a futures account.

trading pits areas within the commodities exchanges where buy and sell orders are presented and matched.

trading plan a preset group of rules or guidelines (preferably put into writing) that serve as a road map to help you in making all trading-related decisions.

trailing stop a stop-loss order that moves along with the price of the commodity price. For example, a sell trailing stop order can be placed below the price of long position.

trending market   a market that is moving either up or down in an identifiable manner. For example, if oil prices rise from $50 to $70 a barrel, it's an uptrending market. If sugar prices fall from 16 cents to 10 cents a pound, this is an example of a downtrending market.

turning point indicator   an economic or financial variable that signals changes in economic activity or price changes in financial assets. For example, a turning point economic indicator might signal a bottom in economic activity and a potential rebound.

two-standard-deviation move   a move in the price level of a security that is two standard deviations from the mean or average.

underlying instrument   the trading instrument from which an options or futures contract derives its value. Soybeans are the underlying instrument for soybean futures.

uptrend   a prolonged move higher in the price of an underlying asset.

ValueGain   a stand-alone software program that makes use of a data feed to provide the most current financial metrics available. Also offers precomputed scans categorized by investment styles—growth, value, and income—based upon fundamental approaches used by leading analysts including Benjamin Graham, Warren Buffett, and Peter Lynch (www.valuegain.com).

value plays   investments based on specific valuation considerations such as book value or net assets.

value stocks   stocks that appear to be bargains because they are priced lower than their calculated worth.

vega   a Greek that measures the impact of changes in volatility on option premiums.

volatility   measure of the magnitude or speed of price moves over time.

volume   the amount of trading activity associated with a specific investment or market. Stock volume is measured in shares. Futures and options volume is based on number of contracts.

whipsaw market   a market that does not trend higher or lower, but makes frequent moves back and forth.

whipsaws   short-term trading signals without any follow-through. Instead, prices bounce higher and lower without developing a trend.

whipsaw signals   signals that lead to an entry into a position and are followed by an abrupt move in the opposite direction. Whipsaw signals can occur frequently in choppy markets and will cause traders to enter trades, only to exit them for a loss shortly thereafter.

widened   an increase in the difference between the spot price and futures price.

zero-sum game   a game where the winnings from one player are equal to the losses of another. The futures market is considered a zero-sum game because profits from one player are losses to another.

Index

A

A-class shares/B-class shares/C-class shares, 93
Action, in order placement, 43
Active management, 91, 115, 132, 136, 143, 146
Active trading, 12, 62, 64, 178, 312, 422
Adams Express Company, contact information, 102
Advancing market, 200–201
Adverse events, impact of, 312
Adverse price movement, 343–344
Adzuki beans, 122
AG Edwards, 435
Aggressive traders, 330–331, 353
Agricultural products, 8, 12, 427–428
AIM
  Energy (FSTEX), 96
  Gold & Precious Metals (FGLDX), 99
Airline industry, 6–9, 119
Alcan Inc. (AL), 75
Alcoa, Inc. (AA), 75, 80, 370
Alternate fuels, 78
Alternative energy/conservation solutions, 379, 390
Aluminum
  characteristics of, 122
  information resources, 155
  stocks, investment in, 71
  top producers of, 75–76
Aluminum Association, 155
Aluminum Corporation of China (ACH), 76
American Airlines, 9
American Century Global Gold (BGEIX), 98
American Century Investments, contact information, 100
American Depository Receipts (ADRs), 67
American Depository Shares (ADSs), 67
American Forest and Paper Association, 159
American Stock Exchange (AMEX), 67, 140
Analysis paralysis, 445

Anglo American plc (AAUCK), 71–72
AngloGold Ashanti Ltd (AU), 72
Annual returns
  index ETFs, 137
  index mutual funds, 131
  stock market investments, 96–99
Apex Silver Mines Limited (SIL), 73–74
Arbitrage, 104–105, 136
Arbitrageurs (arbs), 20–21, 136
Archer Daniels Midland (ADM), 86–87
Arrive contracts, 16
Ascending base patterns, 382–383, 397
Asking price, 2
Asset-based sales, 92
Asset classes, 116–117, 146
At the market orders/trades, 45, 300
At-the-money (ATM) options, 27, 234, 271
Authorized participant (AP), 105–106
Automated trading systems, 346, 358
Automatic investment program (AIP), 94
Average annual returns, 97
Average daily volume, 375–376, 397
Average Directional Index (ADX)
  characteristics of, 192–193, 208
  defined, 192
  trading applications, 193–195
Average price/earnings (P/E), 96, 98–99, 131
Average true range (ATR), 292–293, 295
Average volume, 67–68. *See also* Average daily volume
Aviation fuel, 77

B

Back-end load, 92
Backtesting, 308–309, 330
Backwardation, 126
Bank of Nova Scotia, 110
Bankruptcy, 76
Bar charts, 178, 184–186, 189, 196, 201, 249, 304, 306, 347, 406–407

Barclays Bank plc, 141–142
Barclays Global Investors, 110
Barley, 149
Barrick Gold Corporation (ABX), 72
Bartering, 106
Basis, 32–33, 63, 407
Bearish divergence, 205, 207
Bearish investors, 39
Bearish market, 277
Bearish trades, 229
Bearish trends, 175, 179, 182
Bear spreads
    call, 277, 458
    characteristics of, 28–30, 47
    put, 268–271, 277, 457
Beating the market, 115, 145, 360, 437
Benchmarks
    defined, 118
    growth stocks, 395, 397
    index investing, 125
    mining stocks, 70
    mutual funds, 91
    natural gas, 407
Berkshire Hathaway, 89–90
Best-case scenarios, 254
Bid(s)/bidding process, 2–4, 35
Bid-ask spread, 43, 93
Binaries, 61–62
Black, Fischer, 236
BlackRock Advisors Inc.
    contact information, 102
    GI Res (BACAX), 96
    Global Energy & Resources (BGR),
        101–102
Black-Scholes option pricing model, 236
Blended tax rate, 129
Bollinger, John, 195
Bollinger Bands
    calculation of, 195–196
    defined, 195
    development of, 195
    trading applications, 196–199, 208
Bond investing, 130
Bottoms
    double, 296, 387–388, 397
    double buy, 197
    signal of, 167
Bounce back markets, 200
BP plc (BP), 79–80
Breakeven, options trading, 249, 252–254,
    261. *See also specific types of options*

Breakout(s)
    defined, 202
    Elliott Wave trades, 230
    false, 202, 204, 206
    growth stocks, 379, 381–382, 386–390, 397
    implications of, 205
    pattern, 202
    source of, generally, 197, 200
    support and resistance, 202–203
    triggers, 230, 386
Broker(s), *see specific types of brokers*
    commissions, 36, 419–422, 434–435, 444
    dealer agreements, 97
    electronic trading, 421
    fees, 420, 444
    FCMs compared with, 430
    functions/roles of, 13, 35, 44, 106, 108,
        113, 143, 299–300
    initial contact, 421
    licensure requirements, 420, 422
    prospective, listing of, 434–435
    relationship with, 420, 421, 444
    selection, *see Broker selection*
    types of, 40
Brokerage/brokerage firms
    accounts, 141
    commissions, 100, 104, 116
    discount, 444
    ETFs, 106
    full-service, 423, 434, 444
    industry, history of, 444
    maintenance margin, 39
    margin calls, 164–165, 286
    online, 444
    short sales, 109
    web sites, 434–435
Broker-assisted trades, 421, 435
Broker selection
    electronic trading, 433, 436
    influential factors, 423, 435
    margin, 424–425, 435–436
    needs assessment, 421–423
    recommendations from friends, 420,
        434–435
Brown Brother Harriman & Co., 111
Buffett, Warren, 89–90
Bullion, 19, 59, 105, 109–111, 134, 144
Bullish divergence, 204–205, 207
Bullish flag pattern, 390
Bullish Gartley, 394
Bullish investors, 39

Bullish market, 262, 277
Bullish trends, 170, 175, 178, 181–182
Bull market, 160
Bull spreads
  calls, 265–268, 277, 457
  characteristics of, 29–30
  puts, 458
Bunge Limited (BC), 87
Butter, electronic trading, 431
Butterfly spreads, 271–277, 279, 459
Buy
  defined, 35
  limit orders, 45
  signals, 182–183, 185, 192, 197, 333, 361
  stop orders, 46
Buy and hold strategy, 219, 365
Buyer(s)
  price discovery process, 34
  roles of, 1–4
Buy low, sell high strategy, 109, 239

C

Calendar spread, 277
Call options
  breakeven points, 253
  buying strategies, 243
  characteristics of, 26–27, 231, 234,
    236–238, 278–279, 441
  covered, 464
  exit strategies, 243–244
  Greek examples, 240–242
  hedging, 256–257
  long/long position, 246, 265, 259–262,
    265, 277, 455
  short, 456
  speculation, 255
  spreads, 265–268
  writing guidelines, 245–247
Call ratio backspread, 277
Capital allocation, 333, 362
Capital gains, 90, 105–106, 109–110, 134, 136
Capital-intensive industry, 71
Capitalization, 139
Capital requirements, determination of, 311,
    317–324
Capitulation, 389, 395
Capped futures, 61–62
Card clockers, 36
Carnival, 9
Carrying costs, 20

Case studies
  Joy Global Inc., 387–390
  MEMC Electronic Materials, Inc., 383–387
  Ormat Technologies, Inc., 390–392
  World Fuel Services Corporation, 391–395
Cash, generally
  accounts, 106
  -based transactions, 108, 134
  burners, 377
  flow, 70, 377–379, 385, 396
  market, 16, 20, 31–33, 62
  -settled contracts, 61
Catalysts, seasonal patterns, 400–401, 404,
    417, 441
Catastrophic loss, 312, 359
Cattle, 12. *See also* Feeder livestock; Live
    cattle
Central Fund of Canada (CEF), 101–102
Central Group Alberta Ltd., contact
    information, 102
Chart/charting
  analysis of, 26
  benefits of, 180, 419
  patterns, *see* Chart patterns
  seasonal patterns, 399–406
Chart patterns
  ascending, 382–383, 397
  cup-and-handle, 384–386, 397
  double bottom, 197, 296, 387–388, 397
  double tops, 392
  flags, 390
  flat base, 380–381, 395
  Gartley, 394
  pennants, 382
  W, 390, 392, 394, 396–397
Cheese, electronic trading, 431
Chevron Companies (CVX), 80–81
Chicago Board of Trade (CBOT)
  e-cbot electronic platform, 128, 426–427, 444
  electronic trading, 426–427, 436
  functions of, generally, 13, 17, 27, 435
  going public, 37
  history of, 426
  index investing, 121
  margin requirements, 284–286, 450, 452
  options trading, 232–233
  order execution, 44
  pits/rings, 35
  popular commodity contracts, 51–54
  seasonal patterns, 409
  web site, 421, 426, 435

Chicago Board Options Exchange (CBOE)
  Futures Exchange (CFE), 60–61, 452
  Volatility Index, 452
Chicago Butter and Egg Board, 54
Chicago Mercantile Exchange (CME)
  electronic trading, 436
  functions of, 13
  Globex system, 143, 407, 429–432
  going public, 37
  history of, 426
  index investing, 121, 128, 138
  margin requirements, 450–452
  order execution, 44
  popular commodity contracts, 54–55
  TRAKRs, 144
  web site, 421, 429–430
China, economic growth in, 11, 66, 401
Choppy markets, 160
Class A/Class B/Class C shares, 92
Clearing firm, 36
Clearinghouses, 5, 36, 38, 48–49, 63, 158, 407
Closed-end funds (CEF)
  characteristics of, 100–101, 104
  information resources, 102–103
Closed-End Fund Association (CEFA), 102
Closing prices, 169, 202, 205, 290
Coal/nuclear, 380
Cocoa/cocoa contracts
  characteristics of, 23–24, 62, 64, 320
  14-day ADX, 194
  futures, 296–297
  index investing, 120, 124
  information resources, 157–158
  margin requirements, 286, 425, 452
  as noncomputerized commodity, 433
  popularity of, 56
  sample contract specifications, 451
Coffee/coffee contracts
  characteristics of, 2, 8, 12, 62, 64, 320
  gaps and, 294
  index investing, 120, 124
  information resources, 157–158
  margin requirements, 286, 291, 425, 452
  moving averages, 174
  as noncomputerized commodity, 433
  popularity of, 56
  sample contract specifications, 451
  Sugar and Cocoa Exchange, 55
  supply factors, 163
Collar
  protective, 464
  spread, 277, 464

Collateral, 119, 126, 128, 132, 138
Commission(s)
  characteristics of, 35, 40, 116, 444
  electronic trading, 421, 434–435
  index investing, 116
  trailing, 92
  types of, 42
Commodity/commodities, generally
  actively traded, 12, 62, 64, 422
  analysis, fundamental vs. technical, 25- 26
  characteristics of, 1–7, 11, 62–64, 438
  clearinghouses, 38, 63
  counter-cyclicality of, 116
  deliveries, 17, 21–22, 48–50, 63–64
  electronic trading, 36–37
  exchanges, 2, 4–5, 13, 34, 37, 63
  forward contracts, 16–17
  inverted, 22
  long-term investors, 9
  modern commodity trading, 17–19
  need for, 15–16
  open interest, 50–51, 64
  options spreads, 26–30
  orders/order placement, 43–48
  popular contracts, by exchange, 51–62
  speculators, 16–18, 23–25, 62–63
  spot market vs. futures contracts, 16,
    19–22, 62
  trading, historical perspective, 426
  trading pit, 34–36
  types of, 1–2
  volume, 22, 50–51, 64
Commodity brokerage representative,
    licensure requirements, 420, 422
Commodity contracts, see specific types of
    commodities
  futures contracts distinguished from, 6–8, 13
  index investing, 134
Commodity Futures Trading Commission
    (CFTC), 34, 430
Commodity markets
  bad days, 359–360
  dealing with, 358
  great days, 358–359
  how they work, 438–439
  nature of, 340–342
  quiet days, 358
  starting small, 360–361
Commodity pool operator (CPO), 317
Commodity producers, 67–68
Commodity-related areas, growth in,
    379–380

Commodity-related stocks
  commodity-backed open-end funds, 93,
    103–109
  cotton, 87–88
  energy, 77–83
  exchange-traded funds (ETFs), 109–113
  lumber, 83–84
  metals, 68–77
  mutual funds, 90–109
  soybean products, 86–87
  sugar, 85
  value of, 88–90
Commodity Research Bureau (CRB)
  CRB Commodity Yearbook, 153, 161, 399
  CRB Encyclopedia of Commodity and
    Financial Prices, 154
  contact information, 154
  functions of, 65, 128, 145
Commodity Research Bureau Index (CRBI),
  118–120, 123–125, 145
Commodity stocks
  cyclicality of, 89
  S&P 500 *vs.,* 89
Commodity trading advisor (CTA), 317
Computerized trading, 1, 4, 174, 436. *See
  also* Electronic trading; Online
  revolution
Concept factor, 377–378
Concept growth, 377–378
Condor spread, 277
Confidence, importance of, 354, 357
Confirmation, 197, 204–206, 381,
  392, 395
ConocoPhillips Company (COP), 79–80
Conservation, 379
Consolidation, 223, 385
Construction industry, 83
Consumer
  preferences, 152
  spending, 9
Consumption, demand *vs.,* 149–150, 160
Contango, 126
Contingences, in order placement, 43
Contingency plans, 336, 339, 346
Continuation patterns, 397
Continuous Commodity Index (CCI), 120,
  128, 157
Contract, generally
  specifications, 450–451
  sizes, standardized, 17
Contrarian investors, 135
Contratrends, 397

Copper/copper contracts
  characteristics of, 2, 69, 200, 320
  14-day ADX, 194–195
  14-day stochastics, 186
  information resources, 155
  margin requirements, 286, 425, 452
  popularity of, 57, 59
  sample contract specifications, 451
  stocks, 70
  top producers of, 74–75
Copper Development Association, 155
Corn/corn contracts
  characteristics of, 2, 36, 43, 313, 320
  e-cbot electronic platform, 427
  entry strategy, 329–332
  14-day relative strength indicator, 189
  14-day stochastics, 184–185
  gaps, 294
  index investing, 122
  information resources, 156
  margin requirements, 285, 291, 452
  options trading, 237–241
  popularity of, 51–52
  sample contract specifications, 450
  seasonal patterns, 413
  technical analysis example, 185
Corporate veil, 37
Corrective testing, 395
Correlation, 66
Cost basis, 110
Cotton/cotton contracts
  characteristics of, 62, 64, 320
  fundamental analysis example, 157
  gaps, 294
  index investing, 120, 124
  information resources, 159
  margin requirements, 286, 291, 425, 452
  popularity of, 56–57
  sample contract specifications, 451
  3-day relative strength indicator, 191
  top producers of, 87–88
  25-day relative strength indicator, 190–191
Cotton Incorporated, 159
Counterparties, 135
Countertrends
  impact of, 89, 393
  indicators, 188, 196
Crack spread, 58
CRB Commodity Yearbook, 153, 161, 399
Creation
  ETF index funds, 134–135
  unit, 104–105

Credit risk, 142

Credit Suisse Commodity Return Strategy
(CRSAX), 131–132

Crossovers, moving average, 170–171, 176–177

Crowd psychology, 336–337

Crude oil/crude oil contracts
characteristics of, 2, 4, 22, 35, 38, 46,
320, 442
electronic trading, 432
gaps, 294
index investing, 127
with MACD indicator, 180
margin requirements, 286, 291, 425, 453
options trading, 249–251, 253–254,
260–261
popularity of, 57
sample contract specifications, 451
seasonal patterns, 402, 405

Cruise industry, 9

Cup-and-handle patterns, 384–386, 389, 397

Currencies, types of, 320

Custody fee, 141

Cyclical businesses, 370

Cyclicality, 89, 383, 385

D

%D, 184–185

Daily momentum value, 205

Data Transmission Network (DTN), 128

Day orders, 44–45

Day traders, 176, 305, 440

Dealer agreement, 97

Debt instruments, 130

Declining market, 167, 200

Deer in the headlights syndrome, 312

Default, 17

Deferred deliveries, 20, 30, 32

Deferred option, 29

Deliveries, importance of, 17, 21–22, 48–50,
63–64

Delivery month, 43, 48–49

Delivery notices, 49

Delta Airlines, 9, 240–241

Delta and Pine Land Company (DLP), 88

Delta-neutral strategy, 251

Demand, 149–150, 160. *See also* Supply and
demand

Derivatives, 121, 127, 130, 231, 278

Deutsche Bank Liquid Commodity Index
(DBLCI), 118–119, 122–125, 127

Diesel fuel, 77

Direxion Commodity Bull 2X (DXCLX),
131–133

Discounts/discounting, 49, 100, 111, 410.
See also Brokerage, discount

Divergence, 204–207

Diversification
among markets, 312–315, 334
defined, 313
importance of, 117, 308, 353, 439
among trading methods, 315–317, 334

Dividends, 68, 90, 95, 112–113, 141, 281–282

Do-it-yourself investors, 423, 434

Dollar-cost averaging (DCA), 94

Dollar Index, 451

Domestic bond investors, 115

Double bottom
buy, 197
pattern, 296–297, 387, 397

Double top, 392

Dow Industrials, 320

Dow Jones
Index, 450, 452
U.S. Basic Materials Index, 133
U.S. Energy Index, 139
U.S. Oil & Gas Index, 133
U.S. Oil Equipment, Services, &
Distribution Index, 133
U.S. Precious Metals Index, 133

Dow Jones-AIG Commodity Index (DJ-AIG)
characteristics of, 118–119, 123, 125, 128
mutual funds, 132
Total Return, 121

Downside
breakeven, 252
risk, 257, 276

Downtrends, 191–192, 199, 222,
227–228, 258

Drawdowns, 309–311, 318, 321–323, 361

Dreyfus Premier NR (DNLAX), 96

Drought, economic impact of, 152, 163

Dual cyclicality, 386

Dual rebalancing policy, 122

DWS
AARP Gld (SGLDX), 99
Commodity Securities (SKNRX), 131–132
Global Commodities (GCS), 101, 103
Gold & Pr I (SGDAX), 99
Scudder (Deutsche Bank), contact
information, 103

DWS-Scudder's Commodity Securities Funds
(SKSRX), 121

Dynegy Inc. (DYN), 82

E

Earnings
    growth, 371–373
    information resources, 373
    report, impact of, 396, 440
    significance of, 112–113
Earnings per share (EPS)
    growth, 371, 375
    implications of, 69–70
Economic downturns, 89
Ego, 349–350, 352, 367
8-day simple moving average, 178–179
Elasticity, 78, 150, 160
Electricity futures, 407
Electronic trading
    benefits of, 36–37, 63, 295, 300–301,–432,
        444–445
    broker roles, 424
    at CME, Globex system, 429–431
    future directions for, 434
    at NYMEX, 430, 432
    order placement, 44
Elliott Wave analysis
    applications, generally, 230, 441
    defined, 209
    development of, 210
    Fibonacci numbers, 213–217
    Fibonacci time ratios, 217–218
    trend reversal trades, 224–229
    trends, trading with, 219–224
    Wave 5 buy/sell setup, 224–225, 230, 441
    Wave 4 buy/sell setup, 222–223, 230, 395
    Wave principles, 210–213, 230
Elliott Wave Theory, 26, 219, 393, 395, 397
Emotionally-driven trades, 339–340
Emotional response, control of, 441
Energies, types of commodities, 320
Energy, generally
    funds, 94–95, 130
    futures, 126
    information resources, 155
    markets, 22
    products, see Energy products
    stocks, see Energy stocks
Energy products
    characteristics of, 12, 62, 64
    electronic trading, 432
    index investing, 123
    margin requirements, 425
Energy stocks, characteristics of, 77–78,
        95–96. See also specific types of energies

Eni S.p.A. (E), 79–80
Enterprise Products Partners L.P. (EDP), 81–82
Entry
    signals, 166, 174, 176
    strategies, 196, 329–330
Equilibrium price, 151, 161
Equity
    curve, 414–416
    fluctuations, 313
    implications of, 40–41
    investors, 69
    margin and, 129
    mutual funds, 107–109
    swings, 322, 353
Ethanol/ethanol contracts
    e-cbot electronic platform, 428
    electronic trading, 431
    information resources, 156
    popularity of, 55
Evergreen Pr Mtl (EKWAX), 98
Excess Return contract (CERT), 128
Exchange-traded funds (ETFs)
    characteristics, 100, 113, 145
    cost basis, 110
    defined, 103–104
    electronic trades, 422
    growth stocks, 395
    index, see Exchange-traded index funds
    information resources, 112
    long shares, 462
    mutual funds distinguished from, 134–135
    mutual fund purchase/sale model, 135–136
    open-end, 121
    short shares, 463
    stock market trades, 104–112
Exchange-traded index funds, 122, 134–135,
        138–140, 145–146, 462–463
Exchange-traded notes (ETNs)
    index investing, 122, 141–143
    iPath, 143
Exchanges
    delivery rules, 48–49
    futures, 128
    going public, 37
    margin requirements, 40
    membership requirements, 37
    popular contracts, 51–62
    price limits, 44–45
    seat on, 37
    types of, 2, 4–5, 13, 34, 37, 63
    U.S., 34
    web sites, 421

Exit
signals, 166, 174
strategy, 196, 230, 306, 354–355, 405–406
Exotics, index investing, 122, 124
Expectations
importance of, 311–312, 388, 396, 413
realistic, 337–340, 354, 358, 360, 367
Expense ratio
index ETFs, 136–137
index mutual funds, 131
stock market investments, 91–92, 96, 98–99, 101, 111
Expiration date, 26, 232–234, 260, 441
Exploration companies, 68
Exponential moving average (EMA), 168, 172–173
Extrinsic value, 234
Exxon Mobil (XOM), 6–7, 9, 80–81, 112–113, 370

F

Fair value, 236, 278
Farmer's Almanac, as information resource, 165
Fast markets, 301, 334
Fear, 347–348, 352, 367, 417
Feeder cattle/feeder cattle contracts
characteristics of, 27
electronic trading, 431
information resources, 157
margin requirements, 286, 425, 452
popularity of, 54
sample contract specifications, 450
Fees, types of, 421–422, 440
Fibers, margin requirements, 425
Fibonacci
extensions, 230
historical perspective, 397
pattern analysis, 393–394
Fidelity Investments, *see*
contact information, 100
functions of, 113
funds, *see* Fidelity Select
Fidelity Select
Energy Service (FSENX), 95–97
Gold (FSAGX), 98
In Mt (FSDPX), 96
Natural Gas Fund (FSNGX), 94, 96
NR (FNARX), 96
P&FP (FSPFX), 96
Paper and Forest Products Fund (FSPFX), 94

50-day moving average
exponential, 177–178
impact of, 176, 377
simple, 178–179, 372, 397
55-day moving average, 176–177
Fills, 422, 435
Filters, types of, 175, 181–182, 184, 190
Financial advisors, functions of, 93
Financial growth stocks, 380
Financial statements, 386
First delivery day, 49
First Eagle Gold (SGGDX), 98
First notice day, 49
Fisher, Ken, 378
Fixed supply, 152–153
Flag patterns, 390
Flat base pattern, 380–382, 397
Flat traders, 18
Float, 376, 396
Floor broker, functions of, 45
Floor traders/trading, 128, 426
Foods, margin requirements, 425
14-day relative strength indicator, 189
Forecasting, 31–32, 63, 364
Foreign exchange products, 430. *See also* Exchange-traded funds (ETFs)
Forward contracts, 16–17, 51
Franklin Gold & Pr (FKRCX), 98
Freeport-McMoRan Copper & Gold Inc. (FCX), 74–75
Front-end load, commodity-based index mutual funds, 92, 95–96, 98–99, 131
Full carry, 30
Fundamental analysis
benefits of, 160, 440
characteristics of, 25–26, 90, 113, 445
data sources, 153–161
defined, 148
demand, 149–151, 160–161, 207, 440
equilibrium/equilibrium price, 151–153, 161
growth stocks, 395–396
supply, 147–149, 160–161, 207, 440
Fund sponsor, 134
Fungibility, 17–18
Futures commission merchant (FCM), 40, 42, 49, 127, 429–430
Futures contracts, *see specific types of futures*
call options, 243–244
characteristics of, 6–8, 13, 19–22, 62, 134
e-cbot electronic platform, 426

Futures market
  characteristics of, 117
  deliveries, 48
  hedging, 31–33
  leverage, 164

G

Gabelli Funds
  contact information, 103
  Global Gold Natural Resources (GCN), 101
Gains, tax liabilities, 129. *See also* Capital
  gains
Gambling, commodity trading compared
  with, 303–304
GAMCO Gold Van Eck International Gold
  (GOLDXINIX), 98
Gamma, 240–241
Gaps
  impact of, 392
  types of, 294–295, 297–299
Gartmore GI NR (GGNAX), 96
Gasoline/gasoline contracts, *see* Natural gas
  futures, electronic trading, 432
  margin requirements, 453
  popularity of, 57–58, 61
  sample contract specifications, 451
Geothermal power plants, 390
Global economic cycles, 9
Global economy, 9, 11
Global funds, 95
Global Natural Resources Fund (IGNAX),
  94, 96
Globex, defined, 444. *See also* Chicago
  Mercantile Exchange (CME), Globex
  system
Glossary, 467–483
Going long, 27
Gold/gold contracts
  with Bollinger bands, 197–198
  bull call spread, 266–267
  characteristics of, 2, 12, 19–21, 26, 43,
    62, 320
  e-cbot electronic platform, 429
  ETFs, 110
  futures, 220–221, 269–270
  gaps, 294
  hedging, 32–34
  information resources, 154
  losing trades, 336
  margin requirements, 286, 291, 425, 452

moving average trading applications,
  177–179
  options trading, 269–270
  popularity of, 57–59
  sample contract specifications, 450–451
  seasonal patterns, 401–402
  stock market, 70, 122
  support and resistance, 202
  top producers of, 71–72
  TRAKRs, 144
GoldCorp Inc. (GC), 72
Goldman Sachs Commodity Index (GSCI)
  characteristics of, 118–121, 123–125, 452
  Commodity-Indexed Trust (GSG), 121, 138
  Excess Return futures (CERFs), 138
  mutual funds, generally, 132
Gold Miners, ETFs, 140
Gold mines/mining, 69, 154
Good 'til canceled (GTC) orders, 44, 46–47
Google, as information resource, 373
Gorton, Gary, 65
Government subsidies, 149
Grain/grain contracts
  characteristics of, 17, 44, 62, 64,
    120–122, 128
  index investing, 123–124
  information resources, 156
  seasonal patterns, 416
  types of commodities, 320
Grantor trusts, 109–110
Graphs
  curve, 248–250, 252, 254, 257, 260–261,
    263–264
  histogram, 181
  risk curves, 266, 273–274
Greeks, 240–242, 252, 279, 348–349, 352, 367
Gross processing margin (GPM), 53–54
Growth-based companies, 377–378
Growth stocks
  breakouts, 381–382
  characteristics of, 370, 394–397
  dormant, 377
  earnings growth and, 371–373, 396
  examples of, 383–393
  expectations, 370
  growth, defined, 369–370
  growth factors, 370–371
  growth technicals, 380–382
  listing of, 379–380
  locating, 395
  timing factor, 443

Growth traders, 384
Guinness Atkinson
  Alternative Energy (GAAEX), 96–97
  Global Energy Fund (GAGEX), 95–96

H

Hand signals, 4, 35
Handle, defined, 385
Hard assets, 365
Hard red spring (HRS) wheat, 60, 128
Hard red winter (HRW) wheat, 52, 60, 128
Head fake, 202–204
Heating oil/heating oil contracts
  characteristics of, 2, 320
  electronic trading, 432
  margin requirements, 286, 425, 453
  popularity of, 57–58
  sample contract specifications, 451
  stock market, 77
Hecla Mining Company (HL), 73–74
Hedge funds, 375, 401
Hedgers, 7–8, 13, 62–63
HedgeStreet, 61–62
Hedging, 6, 21, 31–34, 62–63, 255–257,
  259, 392, 401–402, 405, 410
Henry Hub natural gas futures, 407, 432
High implied volatility, 238–239
Histogram, MACD, 181–182
Historical data, 153–154, 347, 402
Hoarding, 30
Hogs, 152. *See also* Lean hogs; Live hogs
Holding period, 129
Holding position, 40
Holdings, 96, 98–99, 131, 137
HOLDRs (Holding company depositary
  receipts), 140–141
Hot Commodities (Rogers), 66
HSBC Bank USA. 110
Human nature, 343, 346, 364, 367, 444
Hurricanes, economic impact of, 443
Hybrid traders, 440

I

ICON Energy (ICENX), 96
Imperial Sugar Company (IPSU), 85
Implied volatility
  defined, 238
  impact of, 272–273, 279
Inco Limited (N), 74–75

Index Trading Course, The
  (Fontanills/Gentile), 439
Index funds, 106
Index futures
  broad-based, 127–128
  narrow-based, 128–129, 146
Indexing/indexes
  active management, 115, 146
  benefits of, 116
  broad-based commodity indexes,
    118–119, 121
  characteristics of, 116, 145–146
  defined, 116
  Commodity Research Bureau Index
    (CRBI), 118–120, 123–125, 128, 145
  Deutsche Bank Liquid Commodity Index
    (DBLCI), 119, 122–125, 127
  Dow Jones-AIG Commodity Index
    (DJ-AIG), 118–119, 121, 123, 128, 132
  exchange-traded funds (ETFs), 122,
    134–135, 138–140, 145–146
  exchange-traded notes (ETNs), 122, 141–143
  futures, 122, 127–129, 146
  Goldman Sachs Commodity Index (GSCI),
    118–121, 123–125, 132
  HOLDRs, 140–141
  mutual funds, 122, 130–133, 135–137, 146
  performance, 125
  returns, 124, 126–127, 146
  risk management, 124–125
  Rogers International Commodity Index
    (RICI), 118–119, 122–124
  TRAKRs (Total Return Assets Contracts),
    118, 121–122, 143–144
  types of, 320
Index market, commodity trading in, 439
Index mutual funds, 145
Index-weighting, 118
India, economic impact of, 66, 401
Indicators, types of, 191–192
Individual investors, 281, 372
Individual retirement accounts (IRAs), 95
Industrial metals, 62, 64
Inflation, 66, 117, 342, 365
Information flow, 440
Information resources
  Index Trading Course, The
    (Fontanills/Gentile), 439
  Market Wizards (Schwager), 344–345, 437
  online, *see* Web sites
  Options Course, The (Fontanills), 442

reading list, 465
Stock Market Course, The (Fontanills), 442
Volatility Course, The (Fontanills), 442
Infrastructure, 380
ING
    Global Resources (IGRSX), 95–96
    Precious Metals (LEXMX), 99
Initial margin
    applications, 448–449
    defined, 284
    requirement (IMR), 40–42, 108, 119,
        289–290
    types of, 285–286
Initial public offerings (IPOs), 375, 390
Innovators, 395, 397
Institutional investors, 104, 134, 372,
    385–386, 396
Intellidexes, 139–140
Interactive Brokers, 434
Inter-commodity spread, 27
Interdelivery spread, 27
Interest rate, 237
Interest-related products, 430
Inter-exchange spread, 27–28
Intermarket spreads, 28
Internal Revenue Code, 19, 111, 129–130, 135
Internal Revenue Service, 130, 142
International Cocoa Organization, 158
International Coffee Organization, 158
International commerce, 122
International Paper, 113
International Sugar Organization, 158
Intracommodity spread, 27
Intrinsic value, 88–89, 234, 260
Introducing broker (IB), 40, 42, 423, 429–430
Inverted markets, 22
Investor emotion, impact of, 335–337
Investor psychology, *see* Mind-set;
    Psychological considerations
Investor's Business Daily (IBD), 373, 382, 392
iPath
    Dow Jones-AIG Commodity Return Index
        (DJP), 141
    ETNs, 141
    GSCI Excess Return Index, 143
    GSCI Total Return Index (GSP), 141
Iron butterfly spread, 277
Irrational exuberance, 89
iShares
    COMEX Gold Trust (IAU), 110–112
    Dow Jones Basic Materials (IYM), 137, 139

Dow Jones U.S. Energy (IYE), 137–138
Dow Jones U.S. Oil & Gas (IEO),
    137, 139
Goldman Sachs Natural Resources (IGE),
    137–138
GSCI Commodity Index (GSG),
    137–138
S&P Global Energy (IXC), 137, 138
Silver Trust (SLV), 110–112
Ivanhoe Mines Ltd. (IVN), 75

J

Joy Global Inc. (JOYG), 387–390
JPMorgan Chase Bank, 110

K

%K, 184–185
Kaiser Aluminum (KALU), 76
Kansas City Board of Trade (KCBOT), 52,
    59–60, 451
Kayne Andersen
    Capital Advisors, contact information, 102
    Energy (KYE), 101
    MLP (KYN), 101
KB Homes, 9

L

Lagging indicator, 165–167, 207
Large-capitalization stocks, 117, 370
Last trading day, 49
Leading indicators, 165–168, 207
Lean hogs/lean hog contracts
    characteristics of, 313, 320
    electronic trading, 431
    margin requirements, 425, 452
    popularity of, 54
    sample contract specifications, 450
Lehman Brothers Aggregate Bond Index, 115
Leverage, 23–24, 26, 63, 106, 130, 164, 255,
    281–283, 287–288, 290, 302, 332, 338,
    345, 365–366, 444
LIFFE CONNECT, 426
Like-kind exchanges, 135
Limit(s)
    down bid, 44
    order book, 104
    orders, 45, 47–48
    up bid, 44

Limited-risk
  position, 255–257, 276
  spreads, 397
  strategies, 443, 446–447
  trades, 260
Lind-Waldock, 434
Linear regression trend channel, 220, 222
Linn Energy, LLC, 82–83
Liquefied natural gas (LNG), 78
Liquefied petroleum gas (LPG), 77
Liquid contracts, advantages of, 51
Liquidity, 40, 50, 63–64, 67, 93, 104, 118,
    120, 433
Liquid market, 3–4
Live cattle/live cattle contracts
  with Bollinger bands, 197–199
  characteristics of, 27, 152, 197–198, 320
  electronic trading, 431
  gaps, 294
  information resources, 157
  long-term stochastics, 186–187
  margin requirements, 286, 291, 425, 452
  popularity of, 54–55
  sample contract specifications, 450
  seasonal patterns, 413–416
  short-term stochastics, 186–187
Live hogs/live hogs contracts
  with Bollinger bands, 198
  characteristics of, 27
  information resources, 157
  MACD indicator, 181–182
  margin requirements, 286
Livestock/livestock contracts, *see specific types
    of livestock*
  characteristics of, 12, 62, 64, 152
  index investing, 120–121, 123
  information resources, 156
  margin requirements, 425
Locals, 36
Long accounts, 40
Long call, 260, 455
Long futures, 454
Long position
  call options, 246, 260, 265, 455
  defined, 236
  determination of, 353
  implications of, 25, 27, 29, 48, 164, 196,
    284, 296–297, 308, 353
  moving averages and, 174–175
  options, generally, 233, 256–257
  put options, 231, 244, 455
  seasonal patterns and, 407, 414

Long premium, 236, 252
Long shares, 462
Long the spread, 30
Long tons, 69
Long trades, 175, 179
Long straddles, 277, 400, 459
Long strangle, 460
Losing streaks, 345–346
Losing trades
  exit strategy, 354–355
  hedging strategy and, 34
  leveraged, 23–24
  implications of, 109, 150, 302, 306,
    308–310, 313, 322, 330, 332
  psychological impact of, 174, 335–336,
    343–344, 367
Louisiana-Pacific Corporation (LPX), 84
Low implied volatility, 238–239
Low-probability trades, 229
Low-risk, generally
  buying opportunities, 206, 208
  high-reward option strategies, 437
  trades, 179, 443
Lumber/lumber contracts
  characteristics of, 2, 6, 12
  electronic trading, 431
  information resources, 159
  margin requirements, 425, 452
  popularity of, 54–55
  sample contract specifications, 450
  top producers of, 83–84

M

Macquarie Fund Advisors
  contact information, 103
  Macquarie Global Infrastructure (MGU), 101
Maintenance costs, 142
Maintenance margin (MM), 39–41, 106,
    285–286, 424–425, 448–449
Management fees, 91, 111, 141
Man Financial Retail Division, 434
Margin, *see specific types of options*
  account, 106–107
  calls, 119, 164–165, 286–287, 289, 424
  electronic trading and, 421
  index investing, 129
  maintenance, *see* Maintenance margin
  requirements, 25, 38–42, 63, 255,
    283–287, 318–319, 435–436
Margin-to-equity ratio, 324–325, 334
Marked to market, 19, 129

Market, generally
  capitalization, 67, 113, 118, 375
  corrections, 174, 392
  decline, 188
  equilibrium, 30
  makers, 4, 104, 135
  orders, 44–46, 299–300
  participants, 38
  pauses, 174
  price, 47, 105, 237, 278
  rallies, 178, 300–301, 417
  return, 101–111
  reversal, 300–301, 343
  risk, 117
  trends, 160, 340–343
  value, 107–109, 129
Market-if-touched (MIT) orders, 47
Market Vectors Gold Miners (GDX), 137, 140
Market Wizards (Schwager), 344–345, 437
Massisa S. A. (MYS), 84
Maximum drawdown, 310, 318, 321
Meats, types of commodities, 122, 320
Mechanical trading system, 305, 309–312
MEMC Electronic Materials (WFR), 383–387
Merrill Lynch
  functions of, 37, 143
  NR (MAGRX), 96
Metals, *see specific types of metals*
  characteristics of, 12, 62, 64
  electronic trading, 429
  growth stocks, 380
  index investing, 120, 122–123
  information resources, 154–155
  margin requirements, 425
  stocks, characteristics of, 68–71
  types of commodities, 320
Mexxam Inc. (MXM), 76
Midas (MIDSX), 99
Milk
  electronic trading, 431
  margin requirements, 452
  sample contract specifications, 451
Miller, Richard W., 372
Mind-set, significance of, 303, 342, 377
Mini contracts, 43
Minimum margin requirement, 284–288
Mining (NEM), 112–113
Mining companies/stocks, 68–71, 90
Minneapolis Grain Exchange (MGE), 27, 52, 60, 128
Mispricing, 136
Modern commodity trading, 17–19

Momentum
  growth-based, 371–372, 376
  indicator, 204–206
  institutional, 375–376
  measurement of, 182
  sources of, 220, 396–397
Money management
  buying decisions, 328–330
  capital investment, 289, 302–304, 334
  defined, 281, 333
  fast markets, 301
  gaps, 297–299
  importance of, 206, 288, 442, 447
  mechanical trading system, 309–312
  price gaps, 334
  profit maximization, 312–328, 333–334
  risk management, 289, 312–328, 333–334
  running the stops, 297, 299–300
  slippage, 297, 299–301, 334
  stops, 297–298, 330–333
  from top down, 302
  trading plan, 304–309
Money market instruments, 130
Month codes, 43
Morgan Stanley Commodity Related Index, 132, 252. *See also* MSCI
Morningstar, as information resource, 90, 136
Moving average convergence/divergence (MACD)
  characteristics of, 26, 179–181, 207
  default settings for, 180
  defined, 180
  histogram, 181
  as signal generator, 180, 182–183
  trading applications, 181–183
  as trend filter, 181–182
Moving averages
  calculation of, 168
  characteristics of, 168–169, 207
  convergence/divergence, *see* Moving average convergence/divergence (MACD)
  crossovers, 170–171, 176–177
  defined, 168
  exponential (EMA), 168, 172–173
  filter, 174
  growth stocks, 377
  intermediate-term, 171
  long-term, 168, 170–171
  price movement, impact of, 174–176
  short-term, 168, 170–171
  simple (SMA), 168–171, 179, 205, 372, 397

Moving averages *(Continued)*
  as support or resistance, 177–179, 205
  trading applications, 173–179
  whipsaws, 170, 174, 183
MSCI U.S. Investable Market
  Energy Index, 140
  Materials Index, 140
  World Materials Index, 132
Mutual funds
  actively traded, 136
  active management of, 91
  administrative costs, 92
  categories, 94
  characteristics of, 90–103, 113 , 134
  closed-end (CEF), 100–103
  commodity-backed open-end funds,
    103–109, 111
  defined, 90
  exchange-traded funds (ETFs),
    109–112, 145
  exchange-traded index funds, 134–140, 145
  expense ratio, 91
  growth stocks and, 375
  information resources, 90, 113
  minimum initial investments, 94
  Natural Resource funds, 94–97, 113
  purchase of, 283

N

NASDAQ, 67
Nasdaq 100, 320
National Cattleman's Beef Association, 157
National Corn Growers Association, 156
National Corn Index futures, 128
National Futures Association (NFA),
    34, 143
National Mining Association, 154–155
National Pork Producers Council, 157
National Soybean Index futures, 129
National Wheat Growers Association, 156
Natural gas/natural gas contracts
  characteristics of, generally, 2, 320
  electronic trading, 432
  index investing, 120–121
  information resources, 155
  margin requirements, 286, 425, 453
  sample contract specifications, 451
  seasonal patterns, 402–403, 406–409,
    415–417, 443
  stock investments, 78
  top producers of, 80–81

Natural Resource mutual funds, 94–97, 113
Net asset value (NAV), 93, 95, 97, 105, 283
Net assets, 96, 98–99, 101, 111, 131, 137
Neutral butterfly spread, 272
Neutral range-bound market, 277, 279
Neutral trading strategies, options, 255,
    258–259
Newmont Mining Corporation (NEM), 72,
    119, 370
New/novice traders, 68, 178–179, 353
New York Board of Trade (NYBOT)
  characteristics of, 88, 120, 123
  popular commodity contracts, 55–57
  margin requirements, 451–453
New York Cotton Exchange, 55
New York Mercantile Exchange (NYMEX)
  characteristics of, 2, 4, 6, 13, 37–38
  clearinghouse, 407
  ClearPort trading platform, 407
  COMEX division, 19–20, 43, 451–452
  electronic trading, 406, 430, 432, 436
  ETNs, 143
  Europe Products, 432
  natural gas, 406, 408
  popular commodity contracts, 57–59
  rings, 35
New York Stock Exchange (NYSE), 67
Next-day profit-and-loss statements, 5
Nickel, 69
9-day moving average, 176, 180–181
No-load funds, 93, 95
Nominees, for exchange membership, 37
Noncommodity-based products, 430
Noncomputerized commodities, future
    directions for, 433–434
Nonfat dry milk, electronic trading, 431
Nonseasonal patterns, identification of, 400
Nontrending markets, 404–405
Norsk Hydro ASA, 67
North American Palladium (PAL), 77
Notice-register, 143–144

O

Oats/oat contracts
  e-cbot electronic platform, 428
  margin requirements, 452
  sample contract specifications, 450
O'Brien, R.J., 435
Obstacle to success, types of, 347–350, 367
OCM Gold (OCMGX), 99
Offer/offering, 2, 4, 9, 35

Oil/oil contracts
  by-products, 9
  characteristics of, 2, 6, 10–12
  ETFs, 111–112
  prices, 9, 11
  refining, 78
  seasonal patterns, 403
  top producers/exporters/consumers/
    importers, 10, 79–80
Oilseed contracts, 62, 64, 123–124, 128
Oil Services HOLDR (OIH), 137, 141
One market at a time method, 322
One-standard-deviation move, 322
Online trading revolution, 425–429, 440.
    See also Electronic trading
On the spot delivery, 19
OPEC, 22
Open
  -ended portfolios, 134
  -end funds, 93, 103–111
  interest, 50–51, 63–64
  markets, 2, 376
  orders, 44
  outcry auction, 4, 34, 63
  positions, 48
Operating
  cash flow, 377–378
  expenses, 71
Oppenheimer's
  Gold (OPGSX), 98
  Real Asset Fund (QRAAX), 121, 130–132
Opportunity cost, 323
Optimistic expectations, 338–340
Option, *see* Options trading
  buyer, defined, 234
  writer, *see* Writer, options
Optionetics/Optionetics.com, 422, 441–442
Options trading
  basics of, 26–30, 63, 233–236, 276
  breakeven points, 249, 252–254, 276, 275
  buyers(rights, 242–245
  defined, 231
  e-cbot electronic platform, 428–429
  exercising options, 244–245, 441
  expiration date, 231–233, 260, 441
  Greeks, 240–242, 252, 279
  implied volatility, 237–241, 272–273, 279
  information resources, 234, 238
  position profit/loss, 250–251
  premium, 232, 238–239, 247, 252, 260,
    262, 441
  pricing models, 236–238

profit maximization, 246–249, 253–254,
    265, 268, 275, 279
  risk curve, 248–250, 252, 254, 257,
    260–261, 263–264, 266, 269, 273–274
  risk maximization, 246–247, 249,
    253–254, 266, 269–270, 275
  sample, 246–247
  spreads, 236, 265–276
  strike price, 232–236, 245–247, 253, 261,
    264, 268, 276, 275, 278, 441
  theoretical value, 237–237
  time decay, 242, 249, 251–252, 260, 269,
    272, 277
  trading strategies, 259–277
  types of, 231–234, 236, 278, 441
  underlying price, 236, 245, 250–251
  uses of, 254–259, 276–277, 443
  volatility and, 237–238
  writers' rights, 245–248
Options Trading Course, The (Fontanills), 234,
    278, 442
Orange juice/orange juice contracts
  characteristics of, 62, 64
  fundamental analysis, 157
  index investing, 120, 124
  information resources, 159
  margin requirements, 286, 425, 453
  popularity of, 56
  sample contract specifications, 451
Order(s)
  placement of, *see* Order placement
  types of, 44–48
Order placement
  electronic, 44
  five elements of, 43
  oral, 44, 47–48
  written, 44
Ordinary income, 110, 129
Ormat Technologies, Inc. (ORA), 390–392
Oscillator(s)
  divergence, 225, 227, 230
  implications of, 192–193, 408
Out-of-the-money (OTM) options, 234,
    243–246, 262, 264, 266, 271, 278
Outperforming, 145
Overbought
  conditions, 160, 208
  indicator, 184–185, 187–189, 192–193
Over-leverage, 288
Overpriced securities
  futures, 21, 28
  options, 238

Oversold indicator, 184–185, 187–188, 192–193, 208
Over-the-counter commodity index derivatives, 127
Overvalued market, 237
Ownership, 49, 90, 282, 375, 396

P

Palladium
  futures, electronic trading, 432
  margin requirements, 425, 453
  sample contract specifications, 451
  stocks, 71
  top producers of, 76–77
Pan American Silver Corporation, 73
Paper assets, 365
Parabolic advance, 341–342
Passive investing/investments, 91, 106, 115–116, 136, 145–146
Passive management, 116
Pass-through investments, 134
Pattern analysis, 387, 392–394, 396
Peak oil, 11–12
Pennant patterns, 382
Pension funds, 375
Performance bonds, 18
PetroChina Company Limited (PTR), 79–890
Petroleo Brasileiro S.A. (PBR), 81
Petroleum
  information resources, 155
  products, 77–78, 89, 120–121
Petroleum & Resources (PEO), 101
Phelps Dodge (PD) Mining Company, 74–75
Physical commodities, 199–200, 407
Pick-and-shovel companies, 379, 386, 397
PIMCO
  CommodityRealReturn Strategy Fund (PCRAX), 121, 130–132
  CommodityRealReturn TRAKRs (PCT), 144
Pit trading, history of, 426
Platinum/platinum contracts
  characteristics of, 320
  futures, electronic trading, 432
  margin requirements, 425
  popularity of, 57, 59
  stocks, 71
Popular contracts, by exchange, 51–62
Pork bellies/pork bellies contracts
  characteristics of, 12
  electronic trading, 431
  information resources, 157

  margin requirements, 286, 425, 452
  popularity of, 54–55
  sample contract specifications, 451
Portfolio
  diversification, 63, 146, 276
  risk, 117
  volatility, 117
Postearnings drift, 372
Potomac Fund Management, 132
PowerShares
  Dyn Energy (PXE), 137
  Dyn Oil & Gas (PXJ), 137
  Energy Exploration & Production (PXE), 140
  Oil & Gas Services Intellidex, 139
Precious metals, *see specific types of precious metals*
  characterized, 62, 64
  ETFs, 109–111
  mutual funds, 91–92, 97–100, 130
Premium(s), 49, 111, 232, 238–239, 247, 260, 262, 437
Price, generally
  discovery, 34–35
  gaps, 294–295, 33
  limits, 44–45
  momentum, 397
  movement, 290–291
  risk, 63
  swings, 400
  volatility, 125
Price/cash flow (PCF) ratio, 70, 72–75
Price/earnings (P/E) ratio, 68, 77, 95, 113, 137, 377
Price/earnings growth (PEG) ratio, 373–374, 384, 397
Price/sales ratio, 377, 397
Pricing
  changes, 2
  consumption and, 149
  downward pressure, 105
  growth stocks, 395
  impact of, 2, 9, 13
  influential factors, 2, 9, 11, 13, 67, 300
  production and, 148
  supply and demand, 148, 152
Producer Price Index, 117
Production
  costs, 68–69
  cycles, 147
  -weighted indexes, 118, 125
Professional money management, 91

Profit(s)
  hedging, 33
  leveraged, 23–24
  maximization, 302, 331, 354–355
  objectives, 405, 443
  -taking, 354–355
Profitability, 166, 321, 325, 339
ProfitSource, 373, 395
ProFunds
  Short Oil & Gas (SNPIX), 131, 133
  Short Precious Metals (SPPIX), 131, 133
  UltraSector Basic Materials (BMPIX),
    131, 133
  UltraSector Oil & Gas (ENPIX), 131, 133
  UltraSector Oil Equipment (OEPIX),
    131, 133
  UltraSector Precious Metals (PMPIX),
    131, 133
Propane gas
  characteristics of, 78
  electronic trading, 432
  margin requirements, 453
  sample contract specifications, 451
  top producers of, 81–83
Proper depth, 395
Proprietary trading systems, 430
Proxies, 117
Psychology of trading
  crowd psychology, 336–337
  daily market fluctuations, dealing with,
    357–361
  discipline, 362–363
  ego, 349–350, 367
  expectations, 337–340, 366–367
  fear, 347–348, 367
  greed, 348–349, 367
  losing streaks, 345–346, 367
  losing trades, 335–336, 343–344
  risk management, 344–345
  trading account sizing, 361–362
  trading plan, 350–357, 366–367, 442–443
  trend-following, 340–343
  winning streaks, 345–346
Public offerings, 37. *See also* Initial public
  offerings (IPOs)
Pullbacks, 174, 177–178, 202, 220, 230, 372,
  382, 392
Putnam Global NR (ERERX), 96
Put options
  buying strategies, 244–245
  characteristics of, 27, 231–234, 236,
    278–279, 400, 446

defined, 231, 234
exit strategies, 245
hedging, 256, 276
long position, 262–265, 276–277, 455
protective, 463
short, 248, 456
speculation, 255
spreads, 268–276
writing guidelines, 247–248
Put ratio backspread, 277

Q

Quality control, 391
Quantity, in order placement, 43

R

Range-trending markets, 404
Rates, types of, 320
Rayonier Inc. (RYN), 83–84
Real estate-related products, 430
Rebalancing, 65–66, 120, 122
Recession, 89
Redemption, 100–101, 104–105, 134–135
Redemption unit, 104
Refineries, 58, 78–80
Regulatory agencies, 34
Relative strength index (RSI)
  characteristics of, 26, 188, 204, 206, 208
  defined, 188
  as short-term indicator, 191–192
  trading applications, 189
  as trend filter, 190
Relative value, 199
Repurchase agreements, 130
Resistance level, defined, 200.
    See also Support and resistance trading
Resting orders, 47
Retail investors, 127
Retendered delivery notices, 49
Retracements, 220, 348, 385, 394
Return on equity (ROE), 378–379, 397
Return on margin, 29
Returns, components of, 126
Reuters/Jeffries CRB (RJCRB) index, 120, 128
Revenue growth, 374, 395
Reversals, *see* Market, reversals
  defined, 202
  influential factors, 201–206
  patterns, 392–393, 397
  pivots, 396

Reward-risk analysis, 137, 405
Reward-to-risk profile, 253–254
Reward-to-risk ratio (RRRs)
  defined, 27, 29
  Elliott Wave trades, 222, 230
  index investing, 125, 136
  options trading, 270
Rice/rice contracts
  e-cbot electronic platform, 428
  margin requirements, 452
  sample contract specifications, 450
Ring trading, 35–36
Risk
  assessment, 334
  calculation, 298
  control, 339, 345, 349, 365
  curve, *see* Risk curves
  expectations, 311–312
  exposure, 233, 308–309, 325, 366
  graphs, 454–464
  management strategies, *see* Risk
    management
  maximization, *see specific types of options*
  minimization, 302, 333, 343–344
  tolerance, 164, 302, 330, 353, 355,
    360–361, 403, 412
  tracking, 142
Risk-averse traders, 353
Risk curves
  bear put spread, 269
  bull call spread, 266
  butterfly spreads, 273–274
  characteristics of, 248–250, 254
  long call options, 260–261
  long put options, 257, 263–264
  straddles, 250, 252
Risk-free rate, 237
Risk management
  diversification, 313–315
  importance of, 9, 26, 62–63, 206, 307,
    362, 438, 446–447
  index investing, 146
  money management and, 289–299
  options trading, 255–256
  seasonal patterns, 407
RiverSource Precious Metals (INPMX), 99
Rogers, Jim, 66
Rogers International Commodity (RCI)
  Index (RICI), 118–119, 122–125
  TRAKRs, 144
Roll/rolling process
  futures contracts, 122, 126–128
  index ETFs, 138

index investing, 136, 142
  orders, 47
Rollover, 23–24
Rosetta Resources Inc. (ROSE), 82
Rough markets, 160
Round-trip commission, 42
Rouwenhorst, K. Geert, 65
Royal Caribbean, 9
Royal Dutch Shell Class A (RDSA), 80–81
Rubber, 122
Runners, functions of, 146
Running the stops, 299–301
Rydex Investments
  contact information, 100
  Precious Metals (RYPMX), 97, 99

S

S&P Depositary Receipts (SPDRs)
  defined, 139
  SPDR Oil & Gas Equip & Svc (XES), 137,
    139
  SPDR Oil & Gas Expl & Pro (XOP), 137,
    139
  SPDR Select Energy (XLE), 137, 139
  SPDR Select Materials (XLB), 137, 139
  SPDR Metals & Mining (XME),
    137, 139
Scalping a market, 306
Scholes, Myron, 236
Seasonal commodity patterns
  defined, 400
  identification of, 400–403, 417, 443
  identifying opportunities, 404
  information resources, 154
  live cattle, 413–417
  natural gas, 401–403, 406–409,
    417, 443
  options, 441
  significance of, 399, 416–417
  soybeans, 401, 403, 409–413, 417
  strategy selection, 404–405
  trade management, 404–406
  trends, 400, 404, 406, 417, 441
  weather conditions, impact of, 399, 410,
    413–414, 417, 443
Seat on exchange, 37
Second-guessing, impact of, 354, 362
Secondary market, 101, 104, 106
Section 1256 exchanges, 19, 129, 142
Secular trends, 370
Securities and Exchange Commission
  (SEC), 34

Self-defeating behavior, 328
Sell
  defined, 35
  limit orders, 45–46
  signals, 182–183, 192, 333, 361
  stop order, 46
Seller(s)
  contracts, 17–18
  price discovery process, 34
  roles of, 1–4
Semiconductor sector (SMH), 383–384
Senior debt securities, 141
Settlement price, 42, 45, 63
Shareholders, 91–92
Short account, 40
Short call option, 456
Short futures, 454
Short position
  defined, 236
  determination of, 353
  implications of, 18, 24–25, 47, 175, 196,
    284, 308, 409, 412
  options trading, 232, 234, 245–246, 248
Short premium, 236, 252
Short put option, 456
Short sales/short selling, 48, 107–109, 118,
    178, 191, 199, 208, 256, 258, 298, 365
Short shares, 463
Short-term indicators, 188, 191–192
Short the basis, 33
Short the spread, 28
Short tons, 69
Short traders, 40
Short trades, 175, 179, 297–298
Side-by-side trading, 426
Sideways market, 193, 205, 277, 405
Signal, defined, 166. *See also* Buy, signals;
    Sell, signals
Silk, 122
Silver/silver contracts
  characteristics of, 12, 320
  e-cbot electronic platform, 429
  ETFs, 110–111
  gaps, 294
  margin requirements, 286, 291, 425, 452
  popularity of, 57, 59
  price movement, 341
  sample contract specifications, 450–451
  stocks, 70–71
  top producers of, 73–74
Silver mines/mining, 69, 154
Silver Standard Resources Inc. (SSRI), 73
Silver Wheaton Corp. (SLW), 73

Simple moving average (SMA), 168–171,
    195–196, 205, 372, 396
16-day moving average, 176
Slippage, 297, 299–301, 334
Small-capitalization companies, 374–375,
    377, 396
SmartMoney, 90
Smoothing, 181, 184
Soft commodities, 55–56, 62, 64, 120, 122,
    124, 157–159, 320, 425
Soft red winter (SRW) wheat, 52, 129
Source/product spread, 27
Southern Copper Corporation (PCU), 74–75
Southern Peru Copper, 370
Southwest Airlines (LUV), 6–9
Soybean crush, 53, 428
Soybeans/soybean futures contracts
  with Bollinger bands, 196
  characteristics of, 297–299
  downtrend, 228
  hedging strategies, 257
  margin requirements, 286
  options trading, 233, 243–248, 253, 263,
    272–274
  popularity of, 51–53
  stock trades compared with, 287–289
Soybean meal/soybean meal contracts
  characteristics of, 151, 313, 320
  demand for, 151
  e-cbot electronic platform, 427
  margin requirements, 286, 452
  popularity of, 51, 53
  sample contract specifications, 450
  support and resistance, 203–204
Soybean oil/soybean oil contracts
  characteristics of, 320
  e-cbot electronic platform, 427
  margin requirements, 286, 452
  popularity of, 51, 53–54
  sample contract specifications, 450
  support and resistance, 201–202, 205
  20-day moving average, 175–176
  25-day simple moving average, 177
  55-day simple moving average, 177
Soybeans/soybean contracts
  with Bollinger bands, 196
  characteristics of, 6, 35, 44, 314, 320
  e-cbot electronic platform, 427–428
  gaps, 294–295, 297–299
  information resources, 157
  margin requirements, 291, 452
  options trading, 233
  product stocks, 86

Soybeans/soybean contracts *(Continued)*
  sample contract specifications, 450
  seasonal patterns, 403, 409, 413
  supply factors, 163–165
  10-day moving average, 169, 171
  25-day exponential moving average,
    172–173
  top producers of, 86–87
  200-day moving average, 170–171
  Wave 5 sell, 227–229
Specialists, 104, 135. *See also* Specialization
Specialization, 5, 416, 447
Speculators/speculation, 7, 8, 13, 16–18,
  23–27, 39–40, 54, 62–63, 69, 255–256,
  259, 284, 287, 364
Spot
  contract, last trading day, 49
  market, 16, 19–22, 33, 62
  months, 21–22
  price, 144
Spread(s)
  butterfly, 459
  calls, 457–458
  defined, 236
  growth stocks and, 396
  implications of, 26–30
  margins, 30
  orders, 47–48
  put, 457–458
  unwinding, 48
Stakeholders, 72
Standard & Poor's 500 (S&P 500) Index, 28,
  66, 115, 117, 320, 328, 451–452
Standard deviation, 96, 125, 137, 195–196,
  321–322
Starbucks, 9
Statoil ASA (STO), 81
Stillwater Mining Company (SWC), 76–77
Stochastics
  characteristics of, 184, 208
  development of, 183
  trading applications, 26, 184–188
Stock(s), *see* Stock investments; Stock market
  accounts, 100
  appreciation, 91
  brokerage firms, 422
  commodity correlation with, 146
  exchange, 104
  indexes/index futures, 134, 430
Stockbrokers, *see* Brokers

Stock investments
  implications of, 63
  long shares, 459
  short shares, 460
Stock market
  commodity trading in, 439
  forecasting, 364
  history of, 50
  influential factors, 9
  trading, *see* Stock market trading
Stock Market Course, The (Fontanills), 442
Stock market trading
  commodity trading compared with, 281,
    283–288
  futures trading compared with, 287–289
  purchases, 283
Stock traders/trading, 9, 18
Stop-limit orders, 46–47, 382
Stop-loss
  Elliott Wave trading, 221, 230
  limit, 165
  orders, 46, 221, 230, 296–299, 326–328,
    334, 405
  triggers, 326
Stop orders, *see* Stop-loss
  implications of, 46–47,
  running the stops, 297–298, 326,
    330–33
Straddle(s)
  characteristics of, 26–27, 249–250,
    252–254
  long, 277, 400, 459
  short, 461
Strangle(s)
  defined, 277
  long, 460
  short, 462
Strategy reviews, 454–464
Streaks, defined, 345
streetTracks
  Gold Shares (GLD), 110–113
  SPDR Metals & Mining (XME), 137, 139
  SPDR Oil & Gas Expl & Pro (XOP),
    137, 139
  SPDR Oil & Gas Equip & Svc (XES),
    137, 139
Stress, sources of, 305
Strike price, 26–27, 232–238, 245–247, 268,
  271, 278
Strong trends, 192

Structured notes, 130
Success factors, types of, 326, 333–334
Successful traders, characteristics of, 12–13,
 179, 350, 353, 358, 362–363, 365–366,
 438, 442, 448
Successful trading
 identifying opportunities, 445–446
 trade management, 445, 447
 trade selection, 445–446
Sugar/sugar contracts
 characteristics of, 2, 8, 12, 27–29, 62, 64,
  299, 320
 gaps, 294
 index investing, 120, 124
 information resources, 157–158
 with MACD indicator, 182–183
 margin requirements, 286, 291,425, 453
 noncomputerized commodity, 433
 popularity of, 56
 sample contract specifications, 451
 top producers of, 85
Suppliers, 395
Supply and demand
 global, 156
 seasonal patterns, 406, 410, 417
 significance of, 104, 160–161, 199, 300,
  364–365, 410
Support and resistance
 characteristics of, 199–202, 208,
  326–328
 defined, 200
 Elliott Wave trades, 230
 moving average as, 177–179
 options trading, 271
 resistance, defined, 200
 support, defined, 199–200
 trading off of, 202–206
Swaps, 130
Systematic trading, importance of,
 438, 444

T

Taxation
 mutual funds, 91
 tax brackets, 129
 tax efficiency, 136, 145
 tax liabilities, 105, 109–110, 129, 134,
  136, 146
 tax rates, 129

Tax professional, advice from, 129
Technical analysis
 Average Directional Index (ADX),
  192–195, 208
 benefits of, 25–26, 163–165, 206–207,
  396, 440–441, 445
 Bollinger bands, 195–199, 208
 classic tools of, 168–208
 fundamental analysis distinguished from,
  163–164, 207, 440
 defined, 147, 163
 goals of, 164, 207, 440
 indicators, 165–168, 207
 moving averages, 168–183, 207
 relative strength index (RSI), 188–192, 208
 stochastics, 183–188, 208
 support and resistance trading, 199–206, 208
10-day moving average, 169, 171
Terminology, *see* Glossary
TheIntercontinentalExchange, Inc. (ICE), 37
Theoretical value, 237
Theta, 240, 242, 252
13-day exponential moving average, 180–181
30-day moving average, 377
Tick
 implications of, 28–29, 446–447
 sizes, 44
Ticker(s), listing of, 43
Timber Hill, 37
Time
 decay, 242, 249, 251–252, 260, 269,
  272, 277
 frame, implications of, 186, 207, 416, 446
 premium, 234
 time, price, or execution contingency, 43
Timeline, peak oil, 12
To arrive contracts, 426
Tocqueville Gold (TGLDX), 98
Tops, signal of, 167
Total Return contract, 128
Total S.A. (TOT), 79–80
Tradable signals, 175
Trade execution, 35
Trade reporters, 36
Traders, *see specific types of investors*
Trading account
 debits to, 49
 equity in, 40–41, 363
 futures, sample, 41
 large, 323

Trading account *(Continued)*
  maintenance margin, 287
  opening, 39, 339, 422, 435
  size determination, 311, 317, 323–324,
    334, 361–362
  small, 323
  types of, 424
Trading capital, 164, 298–299, 302–304,
    307, 309, 323, 334, 352–353
Trading decisions, influential factors, 182, 386
Trading jackets, 36
Trading pit, 1, 4, 34–36, 299–301
Trading plan
  abandonment of, 349, 363
  capital investment, 367
  components of, 304–309
  defined, 350
  development of, 351–352
  importance of, 340, 350–351
  key elements of, 352–355
  revisiting/revising, 356–357, 366
  tenets of, 356
Trading process
  hand signals, 4, 35
  open outcry auctions, 4, 34–35, 63
  overview of transaction, 2, 4
  real-world example, 3
Trading range, 193, 258, 271, 273, 279,
    382, 404
Trading system, 308
Trailing stops, 355
TRAKRs (Total Return Assets Contracts),
    118, 121–122, 143–144
Transaction costs, 122, 142
Transport, 380
Transportadora Gas (TGS), 82
Treasury bills (T-bills), 42, 127, 130, 138, 304
Treasury bonds (T-bonds), 320, 450, 452
Treasury Inflation-Protected Securities
    (TIPS), 132
Treasury notes (T-notes), 138, 320, 450, 452
Treasury securities, 127. *See also specific types
    of Treasuries*
Trend(s)
  filter, 190
  indicators, 183
  reversal, *see* Trade reversal trades
  trading with, 219–221
Trend-following
  indicators, 166–168, 188, 207, 340–343
  seasonal, 402, 404, 409, 414
Trending markets, 404

Trend reversal trades
  indicators of, 207
  Wave 5 buy, 224–227
  Wave 5 sell, 227–229
Turning point indicator, 165–168, 184–185,
    207–208
Turnover, impact of, 136
12b-1 fees, 92
20-day moving average, 172, 175–176,
    181, 195
28-day moving average, 205–206
25-day exponential moving average,
    172–173, 177
26-day exponential moving average, 180–181
200-day moving average, 169–171
Two-sigma event, 346
Two-standard-deviation move, 322

U

Uncertainty, 16
Underlying
  assets, 104, 109, 134, 240, 242
  defined, 234
  instruments, 261
  market, 27
  securities, 205
  stock, 233
Underpriced
  futures, 21, 28
  options, 238
Undervalued
  growth, 386
  market, 237
United Soybean Board, 156
U.S. Department of Agriculture (USDA),
    156, 158–159
U.S. Department of Energy, Energy
    Information Administration, 155
U.S. Department of the Interior, 154
U.S. Dollar Index, margin requirements, 453
U.S. Geological Survey, 154
United States Oil Fund (USO), 111–113
U.S. Steel, 370
Universal Forest Products, Inc. (UFPI), 84
Unleaded gas contracts, 286, 320, 425
Unwinding spreads, 48
Upside breakeven, 252, 257
Uptrends, 179, 186, 191, 199, 227, 258,
    383, 402
Urea, electronic trading, 431
USAA Pr Mtl (USAGX), 98

US Global Inv
Gld (USERX), 99
W Pr (UNWPX), 98

V

ValueGain, 373
Value investors, 68, 89
Value plays, 88
Value stocks, 370
Value traps, 396
Van Eck
Global HA (GHAAX), 96
Global Hard Assets Fund (GHACX), 95
Vanguard
contact information, 97
Energy (VDE), 137
ETFs, 140
Materials (VAW), 137
Pr Mtl (VGPMX), 98
Vega, 240–242
Volatile market, 18, 277
Volatility
impact of, 31, 119, 117, 125, 160, 197,
237–238, 241, 281–282, 372, 405, 443
influential factors, 151, 208
information resources, 238
Volatility Course, The (Fontanills/Gentile),
238, 442
Volume, implications of, 22, 26, 50–51,
64–63, 101, 111, 202, 371, 375,
389–390, 395–397

W

Wall Street Journal, The, 373
Warehouse receipt, 49
Wave 5 support level, 224–230, 441
Wave 4 support level, 222–223, 227, 230, 395
W base, 386–388
Weak trends, 192
Weather conditions, economic impact of, 148,
152, 163, 364, 399, 410, 417
Web sites, as information resource, 2, 5, 90,
97, 100, 102–103, 132, 138–140,
143–144, 154–160, 373, 406, 426, 430,
434–435

Wedge patterns, 382
West Texas Intermediate crude oil futures
contracts, 143
Weyerhaeuser Company (WY), 83–84, 112
Wheat/wheat contracts
characteristics of, 2, 6, 12, 27, 31–32,
122, 320
demand for, 150
e-cbot electronic platform, 428
gaps, 294
margin requirements, 284–287, 291, 452
popularity of, 51–52, 60
price movements, 290–291
sample contract specifications, 450–451
sample trade, 327–328
supply and demand, 147–149, 152
Whipsaw(s)
implications of, 170, 174–175, 183, 362
market, 258
signals, 190
Widened basis, 32–33
Windfall profits, 359
Wings, bullish Gartley, 394
Winning streaks, 345–346
Winning trades, 160, 307, 309–310, 338,
344, 354–355
Wool/wool contracts, 122
World Agricultural Outlook Board, 156
World-class traders, 344
World Fuel Services Corporation (INT),
391–395
Worst-case scenario, 254, 311, 330, 362
W pattern, 390, 392, 396–397
Writers, options
defined, 232, 234
rights of, 245–248

Y

Yahoo Finance, 373
Yield, implications of, 95–96, 98–99, 101,
131, 137

Z

Zachs.com, 373
Zero-sum game, 40

FREE TRADING PACKAGE
(a $100 value)

From George A. Fontanills and Tom Gentile

Request your FREE Trading Package and learn more about high-profit, low-risk, low-stress trading strategies *that really work!*

The Trading Package is full of practical tips and useful information to guide you down the path toward successful trading. The trading fundamentals presented are based on the same proven techniques taught by Optionetics (www.optionetics.com), which was founded by George in 1993 to show individual investors how to profit in all market conditions. Since that time, Optionetics has become a leading provider of investment education services, portfolio management techniques, market analysis, and online trading tools to over 250,000 people from more than 50 countries worldwide.

To receive your FREE Trading Package, simply complete and mail (or fax) the form below to:

Optionetics
255 Shoreline Drive, Suite 100
Redwood City, CA 94065
Fax: 650-802-0900

You may also call 888-366-8264 (or 650-802-0700 outside of the United States), or email customerservice@optionetics.com

----

FREE Trading Package

☑ Yes! I would like to learn more about high-profit, low-risk, low-stress trading strategies. Please send me my FREE Trading Package today.

Name:_____

Address: _____

City, State:_____ **Zip Code:** _____

Telephone: _____

Fax: _____ **Email:** _____

I purchased this book from: _____